The Structure of Canadian History

J. L. Finlay/D. N. Sprague
University of Manitoba

Prentice-Hall of Canada, Ltd.,
Scarborough, Ontario

Canadian Cataloguing in Publication Data

Finlay, John L., 1939-
  The structure of Canadian history

Includes index.
ISBN 0-13-854331-3

1. Canada–History.   I. Sprague, Douglas N.,
1944   II. Title.

FC164.F55   971   C79-094086-8
F1026.F55

Prentice-Hall, Inc., Englewood Cliffs, New Jersey
Prentice-Hall International, Inc., London
Prentice-Hall of Australia, Pty., Ltd., Sydney
Prentice-Hall of India, Pvt., Ltd., New Delhi
Prentice-Hall of Japan, Inc., Tokyo
Prentice-Hall of Southeast Asia (Pte.) Ltd., Singapore

Production Editors: Joan McCracken and Jenifer Ludbrook
Design: Gail Ferreira

ISBN 0-13-854331-3

   2   3   4   5   W   83   82   81   80   79

Printed and bound in Canada

Contents

Acknowledgements

The authors wish to thank Professors Lovell Clark, Brian McKillop, and Gordon Rothney for their kindness in reading this work in draft form and for their helpful comments.

For Mary and
For Lawrence and David

The Invention
of the New World

I. The Old World Background to New World History

The background to Canadian history does not lie in voyages of discovery, in those, say, of Jacques Cartier. For that matter, the wider background to New World history is not to be sought in the voyages of Columbus or even in those of his predecessors. Discovery is but a first step, a prerequisite, and it is salutary for those living in the Americas today to realize how uninterested, in fact, fifteenth- and sixteenth-century Europe was in what its seamen had stumbled across. For instance, there were seven reprintings of a world geography reference book in France between 1539 and 1558 (a time which spans France's own early interest in the New World and Cartier's voyages) and in not one of these was any mention made of the New World. The real background, then, to Canadian and New World history after 1492 must be sought in the *invention* of the Americas; that is, in the recognition that something could be made out of mere discovery; something so attractive that Europeans would undertake the costly and dangerous task of crossing the Atlantic Ocean and conquering new territory. The nature of the invention may be understood from an examination of late medieval European society in the fifteenth century. At the same time, that examination will indicate why, initially at least, the Americas were so small a part of the European consciousness.

The fifteenth century was a time both of contraction and expansion in Europe—or, more precisely, of contraction in the East and expansion in the West. This pattern was to be seen, for instance, in the fortunes of that age-old Christian imperative to go forth and convert the heathen. In the

3

earlier Middle Ages, in the twelfth and thirteenth centuries, Christendom had expanded into the Middle East successfully taking Jerusalem and the Holy Land. Since then, however, the Islamic enemy had counterattacked, and with their thrusts, especially into the area of present-day Turkey, Christendom had been forced onto the defensive. A singular setback occurred when Constantinople, the headquarters of Orthodox Christianity, fell to Islam in 1453. Such developments contributed significantly to the diminution of missionary activity in the East. However, the impulse was not completely dead, and it found its outlet in the west in the Iberian peninsula. There the work of centuries was coming to fruition; the Christian reconquest of that area was capped in 1492 when Granada, the last stronghold of the Islamic Moors in Spain, was captured. The period and movement known in Spanish history as the *Reconquista* was now complete.

This pattern of withdrawal in the east and expansion in the west had mundane yet important consequences. Long-established trade routes in the Far East, especially for the all-important spices which made the foul, stinking living conditions and the food of the wealthy slightly more tolerable than they would otherwise have been, were disrupted by these new developments in the Middle East. Western Europeans began to seek to outflank these obstacles; and throughout the fifteenth century the Portuguese in particular were at the forefront of voyages of discovery aimed at finding an all-water route to the wealth of Asia. It was a venture which finally succeeded in 1486 when Bartholemew Diaz sailed beyond the Cape of Good Hope into the Indian Ocean, and in 1498 when Vasco da Gama reached India itself.

Accompanying this Western European search for new trade routes was a further development, a psychological one, which intensified that search and gave to the discovery and exploitation of new wealth a cutting edge never before known. The earlier Middle Ages had known wealthy individuals, of course. There is, for example, record of one William of Duvenwoorde (1290-1353) who was said to have enjoyed an annual income of some 70 000 *livres*, perhaps the equivalent of $1 million today. But William and others like him were not esteemed for their wealth. Indeed, they were distrusted. Wealth was something to be wary of, the occasion for sin in the getting and in the spending. Predictably, the watchdog of society's morals, the Church, was outspoken in its condemnation of the lust for gain as leading to "damnable avarice, sensuality and pride." In particular, the lending of money with a charge for interest, the very basis of a sophisticated, capitalist economy, was denounced by the Church in the harshest terms. But increasingly in the fifteenth century such attitudes were changing, and the old prohibitions were losing their force. The idea that economics was at most a branch of theology was breaking down, and faintly the more modern idea that economics was an autonomous discipline with methods and ends of its own was taking its place. The pursuit of wealth was more and more to be untrammeled by any other-worldly or countervailing considerations. And while the common people might never dream of becoming as wealthy as kings or princes, they began in an unprecedented way to see themselves as worthy of riches.

This intensified interest in trading for wealth, and the search for new routes to that wealth, were directed to Asia. When Columbus sailed due west from Spain in 1492 it was with the determination of avoiding the Portuguese sphere of influence and finding a shorter route to the Spice Islands, China, and Japan. The Americas were not thought to exist; and, to this day, the name of the islands where he made his first landfalls, the West *Indies*, serves to underline the fact that Columbus and Europe had made a gigantic miscalculation and had hit upon an unexpected world that was truly new.

The miscalculation, of course, did not remain a liability for long. It became apparent that this New World might yield immense wealth of all kinds, so that it became a legitimate alternative to Asia in this respect. At the same time, there were millions of souls to be saved through a new expansion of Christian missionary activity. Here, then, were two vital inventions of America. But a third kind of invention took place, and it is to this crucial development that this account must now turn.

Fifteenth-century Europe was changing not only physically and psychologically, but intellectually, too. Just as early economists had broken free from medieval constraints in order to direct men's minds to the question of *how* to acquire wealth, so, too, the students of political science had broken free from earlier approaches to statecraft. In place of theologically-structured discussions of the rights and duties of rulers and the ruled, intellectuals increasingly went back to history and sought to show *how* certain societies had managed to guard against the threat of chaos, *how* certain rulers had conducted themselves so as to make their power effective. At a time when Europe was plagued by a general breakdown of law and order (in England this was the time of the Wars of the Roses, in France the aftermath of the Hundred Years War and a situation where the French crown controlled only about a quarter of the kingdom) the appeal of political writers such as Machiavelli was enormous. *The Prince*, which he published early in the sixteenth century, is a superb example of a "how to" book. Any medieval discussion of the Christian duty owed by the Prince to his subjects is completely absent; everywhere is advice on how to gain and hold on to power.

The rulers of the late fifteenth and early sixteenth centuries showed themselves to be outstanding Machiavellians. Ruthless, scheming and despotic, they centralized their power and strengthened the royal courts and procedures. Their concentration of power was helped by the technological developments of weapons because the key to victory in battle was now the possession of artillery and professional infantry. Both were costly investments which only kings and princes could afford. These two developments helped spell the end of the feudal lord on horseback, who could, with his armed retainers defy the ruler and defend himself in his castle. In this new period the feudal noble was transformed into a courtier and the castle gave way to the country house or chateau.

There were those among the nobility who made the transition to the new order of things, who made their peace with the king and were rewarded with courtly hand-outs. They concentrated upon a methodical exploitation of their lands and ceased to see them as the means of supporting potential troops. But there were many who could not make the adjustment. For them, the newly emerging Europe, increasingly dominated by absolutist kings and merchant princes, was anathema. Their ideals, their glorification of military skills, courage, and honor, all built upon a servile base of obedient peasants, had no place in Europe. It became necessary to invent a new world where they could be accommodated.

Spain was the country best placed to invent this new world. There the missionary drive was most vital. There the far western search for new trade routes was strongly marked. There the new psychology of wealth was well developed, with Spain a leader in the production of wool and metal wares. And, finally, there the appeal of the feudal *hidalgo*, the knight on horseback, was most deeply entrenched. The *Reconquista* had kept these values to the fore, and the triumphant conclusion of that Holy War had seemed to confirm them.

But could the centralizing kings of Spain tolerate the *hidalgo*? Was there room in a country suddenly at peace for the soldier of fortune? Just at the moment when the reconquest was completed, the doors to the New World opened in the minds of those who identified with the life of the fighting nobleman and who imagined enoblement as legitimate even if it came by conquest of exotic people in a strange new world. If he remained in Europe, the soldier of fortune might be nothing more than a superfluous anachronism; but in the Indies this man—any man—might become a lord of land, of Indians, and of gold. So, the first invention of the New World was not by merchants or kings. The first invention was by Spaniards who envisioned the Indies as a place for advancing themselves by exporting feudalism after it had begun to decline in Europe.

II. The Spanish Model of Colonization by Conquest

The islands of the Caribbean did not provide the Spaniards with an ideal setting for enacting their invention of America, however. It was only a generation later, in 1519, that they undertook the conquest of Mexico and in so doing established the prototype of New World conquest. Later other Spaniards would apply it to Peru and the English and French would attempt the same project farther north. Everyone came to accept this first invention of the New World as the most plausible. The salient features of the Spanish subjugation of Mexico are therefore important to Canadian history because it is the Spanish precedent which makes intelligible Jacques Cartier's apparently foolish quest for the Kingdom of the Saguenay twenty years later. Cartier and the others were not fools, they were only unoriginal. They attempted no more than the Spaniards. They came away with less because in the north there was less to take.

The great attraction of Mexico was that it was organized as an advanced civilization under Aztec rule in such a way as to satisfy the three needs of European expansion. The need for missionary work was pointed up by the nature of the Aztec religion, which required the sacrifice of thousands each year to the gods. Then there was Aztec wealth. These people might have lacked metal tools; they might have lacked domesticated animals larger than turkeys. But they did have horticulture, and farming was a technological advance which made others possible. Their capital, Tenochtitlan, on the site of present-day Mexico City, was a large city containing over a quarter of a million inhabitants (contemporary London had some 50 000). Not only was it impressive in scale, it was also built of stone. The dominant structure was a huge pyramid at city centre, crowned with a sacrificial altar. There was every sign of wealth; gold and silver seemed plentiful too. And finally, here was a formed society, a sophisticated ordering of peoples, one which could be taken over in its existing form. All the Spaniards had to do was take the place of the Aztec overlords. The *hidalgo* would have his peasantry ready-made.

What increased the attractiveness of Mexico was the fact that this appetizing prize was sufficiently flawed internally that its ability to withstand external aggression was small. The technological deficiencies hinted at above also meant that the Spaniards enjoyed immense military advantages. The invaders possessed artillery and horses, which together gave them a mobility and a power infinitely superior to their enemy's. Also, the Aztec civilization had been imperialistic, and there were subject tribes eager to rally to the Spaniards as a means of gaining revenge. Above all, Aztec society was psychologically unprepared to confront invasion.

The collapse of the Aztec Empire had its roots in the society itself.

Aspects of the Aztec religion had become self-defeating. Human sacrifice had been practised on such a massive scale (the coronation of a new emperor might be marked by as many as 80 000 sacrifices) that the population could not have been expected to defend the regime spontaneously. More important, perhaps, was the fact that the population had been conditioned to be extraordinarily obedient and passive, since one principle of selection for sacrifice was criminality, often of a minor kind. For such a people the substitution of one ruling class for another would be largely a matter of indifference. Then, too, Aztec society had been filled with self-doubt. There had been three successive crop failures between 1505 and 1507 and in this frightening setting rumors of doom circulated widely. Prophecy had foretold that the world would end one day; now all the signs pointed to an imminent fulfillment. In 1511 a comet confirmed the worst fears of many. By 1515 garbled tales of the sighting of strange, bearded men with fair skins began to filter through to Tenochtitlan. In that year a trunk was washed ashore and provided confirmation for the rumors. When the Emperor Montezuma opened it he found, in addition to unusual jewelry and trinkets, clothing abnormally large and a frightening weapon. This last was clearly a sword, but it was not carved out of wood and set with obsidian chips; instead it was entirely of an unknown substance. This mood of doubt and vague apprehension served to rejuvenate the myth of Quetzacoatl, the god who would come in the fullness of time to slay the emperor and forbid human sacrifice. The prophecy foretold that "when the world is become oppressed, when it is the end of the world, at the time of its ending, he will come to bring it to an end."

Given these various factors, the march of the Spaniards from the coast to Tenochtitlan was easily accomplished in less than six months under their leader, Cortés. Montezuma, the emperor, was convinced that Cortés was Quetzacoatl, and when the invading force reached the capital he abdicated and surrendered his empire. Even when the Aztec nobility repudiated Montezuma's act and attacked the Spanish, the new order was not seriously imperiled. Cortés and a small remnant of his original force escaped to the territory of Indians hostile to the Aztecs. In the following year, thanks to clever tactical maneuvering, superior weaponry, and the backing of his Indian allies, Cortés successfully defeated the nobles' rebellion.

By 1521, in a mere two years, a force of some six hundred men had defeated and entirely subdued an empire of over one million people. After subjugation came serfdom and baptism. Individual Spaniards received lordship over villages of Indians; they became *encomenderos*. Cortés himself became a feudal lord with supreme authority over his vassals and their serfs. The conquest had succeeded brilliantly. These invaders, the *conquistadores*, were enriched and ennobled. The New World had proved worthwhile; in particular, a handful of Europeans had invented it as their opportunity to revitalize a way of life which was slipping away in Europe. Soon others would attempt the same further north.

III. A French Imitation of the Spanish Model

Not surprisingly, the conquerors of Mexico published their exploits, and found eager readers in Europe. In time their works were translated into other languages (two Englishmen, Richard Hakluyt and Robert Eden, were leading translators). In this way a wider audience learned of the fabulous wealth and opportunities of the New World, which was portrayed as a paradise densely populated with guileless and loving people who lived on the produce of a bountiful nature. Since they were no match for artillery and muskets, Europeans had nothing to do but to move to America, master the people, and enjoy sumptuous leisure by putting their Indian serfs to work.

So Englishmen, Frenchmen, and others began to imitate the Spanish example in those parts of the New World not yet effectively occupied. There had been scouting ventures before this; for instance, Henry VII of England had sent John Cabot to Newfoundland in 1497 and Francis I of France had sent Verrazano to explore the North Atlantic coast of America in 1524; but more ambitious undertakings began only after the additional incentive of more Spanish conquests in the manner of Cortés. After news of Pizarro's conquest of Peru, the French decided it was time they broke Spain's monopoly. Pizarro had defeated the Incas in 1530 with only two hundred men under his command, which was taken as proof that Cortés' feat had not been simply a lucky accident. In 1534 Francis I commissioned a decayed squire from Brittany, Jacques Cartier, to "discover . . . countries where it is said that he should find great quantity of gold and other valuable things." It should be added that Cartier also believed he might find a northwest passage to Asia and the Spice Islands.

The first French expedition reached North America too late in the summer to do more than stake a claim to the territory. North of what is now called Anticosti Island, Cartier encountered a tremendous current which led him to believe that this channel to the west might be a river running out of northern Asia. He also made contact with the native people, enough to dismiss them as "the sorriest folk there can be in the world." Unlike the people Cortés and Pizarro had plundered, these northerners "had not anything above the value of five sous, their canoes and fishing nets excepted." Since the season was turning cold and provisions were running low, Cartier decided to return to France with two native people, train them as interpreters, and persuade his patron to support a second voyage. Columbus had used these means to gain further support from his patrons when he came home from his first voyage. It worked for Columbus; Cartier gambled that this would be sufficient to maintain the interest of his king as well.

Jacques Cartier returned from his first voyage with nothing more than two unhappy Indians and the unsolved mystery of what lay beyond the Gulf of St. Lawrence. This was enough. Francis I agreed to support another expedition with sufficient provisions to stay over the winter the following year. On this second voyage, Cartier commanded three ships rather than the two of his first and he arrived in the gulf early enough in 1535 to have ample time for exploration. At the spot where the gulf narrowed to what was evidently the mouth of a river he found a village, Stadacona (the site of the later Quebec). This was the home of the two Indians, now interpreters. All were welcomed. Then, with roughly one third of his men, he continued up river to the head of navigation. Here, stopped by rapids, he found himself at a town site called Hochelaga. Like Stadacona, this village was no more than a collection of bark longhouses surrounded by corn fields. The appearance of the place—and the people—was hardly encouraging. But Cartier climbed a rise above Hochelaga, a promontory he named Mount Royal (or Montreal); and, from this vantage point, the explorer beheld a panorama which was awe-inspiring in comparison with the village below or with the rocky coast of Labrador which he had described as "the land God gave Cain" on his previous visit. From Mount Royal, Cartier said that he could see "for more than thirty leagues round about." Between the Laurentian and the northern Adirondack mountains he saw "the finest land it is possible to see." The valley before him looked "arable, level and flat." And in the midst was the river, "large, wide and broad." He was disappointed that it was not navigable any farther; still, he found himself imagining the St. Lawrence Valley as a land hospitable to farming, and he saw the site of Hochelaga as the location of an entrepôt for the whole continent. Here at Mount Royal he was already about a thousand miles from the Atlantic coast and, according to his guides, this water highway could take a traveler another thousand miles inland. What of the interior though? Then, with gestures and signs, his guides from Hochelaga gave information for which Cartier had almost abandoned hope after the rocks of Labrador and the bark homes of Stadacona and Hochelaga. "Without our asking any questions or making any sign, they seized the chain of the Captain's whistle and a dagger-handle of yellow copper-gilt like gold ... and gave us to understand that both come from up that river." The waterway to which they pointed was the Ottawa River. But they could not venture further. It was too late in the summer and, without benefit of a ship, the travelling would have been doubly difficult. So Cartier went back down the St. Lawrence and rejoined the rest of his company encamped near Stadacona.

Over the long winter the French learnt more about the interior. They learned it was well populated and the people were wealthy. The chieftain in Stadacona, Donnacona, was eager to please the French by telling them what they wanted to hear. Cartier determined to return to France to win command of an adequate expeditionary force to take this kingdom. As soon as the ice was out of the river he set sail for home, having kidnapped Donnaconna and others with him.

The old chief realized that if he wanted to return to his people he would have to give a convincing performance for Francis I. Learning of the European desire for spices, he added to his tales of gold and jewels stories about the cinnamon, cloves, and oranges which grew in the fabulous Kingdom of the Saguenay. In time these stories would have their effect, and a little later a Spanish spy at the French court reported to his king that "the King of France says the Indian king told him there is a large city called Sagana, where there are many mines of gold and silver in great abundance, and men who dress and wear shoes as we do; and that there is abundance of cloves, nutmeg, and pepper." But more than five years passed before Francis I could bring himself round to financing another expedition. By this time Donnacona had despaired, sickened, and died of smallpox.

Still, in 1541 an expedition was funded. It was modelled on the Spanish plan, and was about the same size as the body of men Cortés had used to conquer the Aztecs. There was support staff including stonemasons, carpenters, plowmen, and even women, but fighting men predominated. There were seven hundred soldiers and sailors to operate from twenty small boats complete with artillery. The plan called for the French to establish a stronghold near the mouth of the entrance to the Gulf of St. Lawrence, then move inland to the interior, find the kingdom of the Saguenay and subdue it by playing off one Indian population against another. After the conquest, the conquerors were to divide the spoils and the people in accordance with the system used to subdue the Aztecs. "In order to encourage . . . those who will undertake the expedition" the King promised a division of the booty (one third for himself, one third for the commander and one third for the men). He also promised baronial social status to these soldiers of fortune: "We grant to our Lieutenant full power and authority in the lands . . . to grant in fief and seigniory . . . . " The native people were to be looted and then made into Christian serfs. Their conquerors, some of whom were nobodies in France, would become nobility by virtue of their migration to this part of the New World and by their conquest of it.

The expedition was to be under dual leadership. The King's lieutenant,

Jean-François de la Rocque, sieur de Roberval, a nobleman and a soldier, was to have the supreme command on land and, at sea, immediate command over five ships, half of the force which was assembled. Jacques Cartier, the man with precedence by virtue of his experience, was the junior commander by virtue of his lack of military experience and inferior social position. Perhaps he would rise in social status by conquest. For this reason he may have been the more anxious to embark. Impatient with delays, Cartier set out first with his five ships with Roberval's permission; the sieur was to follow as soon as he assembled his artillery.

When Cartier arrived in the Gulf of St. Lawrence in late summer of 1541, he promptly set to work constructing his base in accordance with the plan. From this time onward everything went badly. The Indians were angered by Cartier's failure to return Donnacona. They were not soothed when the French captain informed them that the Indians Cartier had taken in 1535 were great lords in France and refused to return. So, over the winter, friction increased. Roberval did not arrive in the early spring, and Cartier began to suspect the Kingdom of the Saguenay was a myth. In the meantime, the soldiers under his command were acting as if they had no need to go further in search of treasure. They occupied themselves by gathering "precious stones" that lay conveniently all about. If Cartier suspected that these jewels were less than they seemed, this did not prevent him from allowing his men to barrel them up and load this cargo on board ship. With nearly a dozen barrels of this treasure, he set sail for France.

Before Cartier reached the open sea, however, he happened to encounter Roberval with the other half of the expedition. But Cartier had no intention of lingering any longer in this land God gave Cain. Disobeying orders from Roberval to return to the St. Lawrence, he slipped into a fog bank and sailed to France. Roberval was left to see for himself the poverty of the native people, the harshness of the climate, and the barrenness of the land. This French aristocrat and his five ships went up river to explore the country and complete their mission. At Cap Rouge they spent the winter, five months of incredible misery. Then they, too, returned to France as quickly as they could. Roberval had found nothing of value, and the barrels of treasure Cartier had carried home proved to be nothing more than quartz crystals. The only prize from the expedition was enrichment of the language. Henceforth, anyone wanting to convey the idea of worthlessness in an object had only to call it a Canadian diamond: *"Voilà un diamant de Canada."*

IV.   An English Attempt to Imitate the Spanish Model

The Cartier-Roberval expedition of 1541-43 confirmed that the territory around the Gulf of St. Lawrence was not fit for conquest on the Mexican pattern. Sixty years later the English proved that the New World as far south as Chesapeake Bay was similarly unfit.

English interest in a conquest of America had been discouraged in the sixteenth century, mainly because Queen Elizabeth had tended to oppose those who would openly challenge the Spanish monopoly; even after the defeat of the Spanish Armada in 1588 she continued this policy. But in 1603 the Queen died, and with her passing went the old policies in this regard. The new monarch, James VI of Scotland, James I of England, was willing to give his blessing to Britons taking their share of that "world of ground ... unconquered." It is important to grasp, however, that although James approved such undertakings, he would not support them financially. Approval without support was the policy of the English monarchs. Where the rulers of Spain and France had both appropriated men and materials for conquest, the expedition soon to leave England was blessed by the Crown but supported privately by members of the Virginia Company of London.

Nevertheless, the Virginia Company aimed for the same goal as earlier ventures. It did not intend to promote colonization in the sense of settlement. Rather, whatever colonization there was would serve merely as a first step to conquest and exploitation. Those hired by the Company and sent out were soldiers with orders to subdue the Indians, and any artisans with them were intended to teach the defeated natives to become New-World perfumers, goldsmiths, glassblowers, and the like.

According to plan, some 100 employees of the Virginia Company boarded three ships in December 1606 and sailed for the New World. They arrived in Chesapeake Bay at the end of April and explored the territory for an appropriate site for launching their mission. The spot selected for building the base of operations was a low-lying peninsula forty miles from the mouth of a river they named the James. It seemed to make good military sense to start from here because, on the river side, the water was deep enough to serve as an anchorage, and, on the land side, the area was defensible against the Indians. But the natives proved far more difficult to subdue than was expected. In this vicinity, the native people were under a government more powerful and unified than any other on the Atlantic coast. Their leader, Powhatan, did have his enemies. They were the Monacans to the west. But Powhatan felt entirely competent to deal with them using his own resources. The Monacans, for their part, were too far inland to serve as alternate allies for the Company. Worse, while the invaders were kept at a distance by Powhatan, they were attacked and weakened by malaria. The English invasion languished in the swamp they named James-town.

But the Company back in England had invested too much to give up after one year. In the following spring, despite the attrition of their force in Virginia from 120 people to just 40, the survivors were re-supplied, rein-forced, and given more time to fulfill their mission. But by the spring of 1609 there was still no improvement. It was becoming difficult to recruit capital and personnel for this do-nothing expedition. Still, too much had been committed to make complete withdrawal easy. Therefore, the men in America were ordered to hold their ground, and even to cultivate it, as the Indians were reluctant to supply them with food any longer. As an econ-omy measure and rather than admitting defeat, they were ordered to remain and to produce their own food. Normally, soldiers were expected to fight and to die, to go hungry and perhaps even to starve, but military men—especially of noble or gentle birth—would never be expected to do the work of plain farmers. Imagine Cortés or Roberval working with a spade instead of a sword. But this is precisely what the Company ordered its men to do. Understandably, the directors of the firm had to subject their employees to a discipline harsher than standard military practice to get them to perform this new demeaning work. The managers sought and found a disciplinarian equal to the task. Sir Thomas Dale was recruited in the Netherlands to go to Virginia and make the party self-supporting. He imposed the death penalty for idleness as well as insubordination, for swearing as well as for failure to attend church. By 1612, Virginia's "starv-ing time" was ending.

The Virginia Company could whip its employees into growing their own food, but survival did not spell profit. The expedition was able to feed itself after 1612, but, it should not be overlooked that it had failed in its original mission. The region of Chesapeake Bay had been proved to be no more fit for conquest than the area around the Gulf of St. Lawrence. It seemed only a matter of time before the stockholders would recognize this fact and abandon Virginia entirely.

Yet abandonment did not occur. Between 1612 and 1614, John Rolfe began growing tobacco and, by using a better curing process, was able to produce a superior "sotweed" than that which was imported to Europe by Spain. As nearly everyone began to grow tobacco, Virginia took on a new meaning and value, especially to the Company. Jamestown became the first North American boom town. This new invention of America was pro-claimed in 1614 by one Ralph Homar writing from Virginia itself. He debunked the stories of fabled wealth easily obtained by conquest. But he did not fall into cynicism or disillusionment about the New World. "I will not . . . speak more than is true," he promised, reporting that there was no gold nor native population able to enrich the invaders, "nor will the deer come when they are called." Homar admitted the soil was less than perfect and heavily forested, but "if any man doubt the goodness of the ground, let him comfort himself with the cheapness of it." The lure of cheap land and large profits from producing tobacco for the Virginia Company revitalized the New World for Englishmen.

The Virginia tobacco bonanza, which began after 1614, could not be expanded into every region of North America, however. The coast of Labrador was a rocky desolation, and the St. Lawrence area—so icebound in winter—seemed hardly more inviting for agriculture in summer. Thus, the English did not imagine any extension of their agricultural invention north, nor did the French at that time. Since 1543 they had decided that the area was not suitable for conquest; and, because they were not then interested in overseas farms, it remained forgotten by almost all save fishermen. The northern areas of the New World were left virtually undisturbed by Europeans, left as a homeland for people whose primary achievement was survival and whose pride was sheer endurance in a rugged landscape and an impossible climate. Yet even while the Virginia Company was willy nilly inventing commercial cash cropping in America, the French in the far north were on the point of making yet another invention. This was the beginning of a new chapter in the history of European expansion, and the first in Canadian history proper.

PART ONE

France in North America

CHAPTER ONE

The Canadian Fur Rush

I. Retreat to Fishing; Advance to Fur Trade

The original invention of America, that of a transplanted and rejuvenated feudalism, had been abandoned by the French in failure and disillusionment in 1543. After the Kingdom of the Saguenay had proved illusory, there was no incentive to return to the region of the St. Lawrence on a permanent basis. The use of North America by Frenchmen, therefore, reverted to an earlier one, a form of exploitation which predated Cartier. This was the cod fishery.

The formal discovery of the fishing potential of the "new-found land" may be dated in 1497, the year John Cabot sailed there. He reported on his return to his employer, Henry VII of England, that there was no gold, nor silver, nor northwest passage in that part of the world. Cabot was able to confirm what other European sailors may have known for some time, namely, that the sea was "swarming with fish which can be taken not only with the net, but in buckets let down with a stone." By the early years of the sixteenth century a flourishing cod fishery had developed on the Newfoundland Banks. But although the fish resources were incentive enough to draw fishermen across the Atlantic, they were not sufficient to make them go to Canada to live. For these Breton, Basque, English, and Portuguese fishermen, the Banks were inviting as a resource base, but home was in Europe. To their homelands they always returned.

No matter how casual the contacts of these fishing expeditions with the territory of the New World, they did provide European mariners with a growing body of knowledge about the water approaches to the strange

19

lands. Cartier had been no exception. Long before he made his first voyage as a potential conqueror, he had been to America as a commercial fisherman. Even as Europeans were getting to know the land and its people through the cod fishery, so too the native peoples were becoming acquainted with the Europeans. If the Indians cheered Cartier's arrival in 1534 and "made frequent signs to us to come on shore", as Cartier reported, it was because trading had been taking place for decades before this date.

At first, no doubt, only curios were exchanged. But very quickly it became clear that the Indians had particular cravings. As Cartier reported, the "savages showed a marvellously great pleasure in possessing and obtaining... iron wares . . . . ." Here, although European metals made better knives than stone, iron and copper kettles were the special marvel. Until European trading contact, the Indians had been obliged to cook by the clumsy and time-consuming method of heating stones and then dropping them into wooden bowls, thus boiling their contents. But unlike wooden bowls, the new vessels could be placed directly over a flame; there was no comparison between a European's metallic kettle and an Indian's wooden bowl.

For their part, the Europeans were happy to accept furs. In signalling to Cartier in 1534, the Indians had "held up . . . some furs on sticks." Furs were one of the few commodities that the Indians possessed which were valued in Europe. Cartier's men quickly acquired whatever pelts they could, so much so that after trading the Indians "went back naked without any skins on them." The scene of laughing, naked Indians with arm loads of kettles may have amused the Europeans, but to the Indians it was a happy exchange. They knew what they wanted, and since the apearance of the strangers was still so unpredictable, the Indians knew they should acquire as many as possible whenever they could.

By the mid-sixteenth century the occasional ship completely laden with trade goods would sail to the St. Lawrence for the express purpose of trading for furs. This was a small-scale business, however, because the furs sought were the luxury pelts of ermin and marten. These were used as trim on the robes of superior state officials, higher ecclesiastics, and others of the very loftiest positions in European society. The demand for such furs was not great enough to call into existence anything more than casual trading. But about the end of the sixteenth century a change in men's fashions led to a mass demand for a kind of fur that was abundant, and consequently cheap, in North America but nearly extinct, and therefore expensive, in Europe. It suddenly became *de rigueur* for gentlemen to sport a broad-brimmed felt hat. Given the tendency of rabbit-and woolen-felt to droop, a more suitable fiber for the hats was needed, and this was the soft undercoat of the beaver. Scandinavian and Russian supplies were soon exhausted, but in America there seemed to be an umlimited supply. On this basis it was possible to transform a fur *trade* into a fur *rush*.

Great profits were to be made. For one iron kettle a trader could buy an Indian's robe consisting of between five and eight beaver skins. The more worn the robes the better they were for felting. As the garments were worn with the fur side next to the wearer, the beaver guard hairs would fall away after a year or so; the remaining pelt would become soft and greasy, and what was left was the undercoat, ready to be removed from the skin and matted into felt. The Indian would gladly trade what to him was a worn-out robe for a new kettle. The trader, in turn, sold the garment as better than new since it was ready for felting. In Paris, one "greasy beaver" robe—yielding sufficient felt for six to eight hats—could be sold, at times, for enough money to buy more than one hundred kettles. The costs of venturing out to the Gulf of St. Lawrence would be high, of course, but even so, very handsome prices yielded equally handsome profits. Here was an incentive to make the French think seriously once again of permanent settlement in the St. Lawrence area.

II. A Fur-Trade Outpost

In 1588, the French king, Henry III, gave the valuable monopoly of fur trading in Canada to two nephews of Jacques Cartier, as a form of compensation for the expenditures which the Cartier family had made in exploring that part of the New World earlier. But it soon proved impossible for them to keep interlopers out of their area. By 1600, the necessity of establishing someone on the spot as a permanent policing agency was inescapably obvious.

The person now responsible for this undertaking was Pierre Du Gua, sieur de Monts. It was he who held the monopoly in 1603. It was therefore de Monts who took the initiative to plant a permanent settlement in Canada. The site he chose for this outpost was on the Bay of Fundy because this location seemed close enough to the open Atlantic to maintain contact with the fisheries and France, yet close enough to fur sources as a base for this operation. The location failed, however, in the primary requirement of serving as a strategic obstacle to interlopers trading near the mouth of the St. Lawrence. Accordingly, the base was moved from Port Royal to a more suitable spot on the recommendation of the company's cartographer and soon-to-be-manager, Samuel de Champlain. The site selected was at the head of the Gulf of St. Lawrence, Quebec. In 1608, Champlain and some twenty employees established the Quebec *Habitation*.

From this center of operations the company was able to patrol its monopoly. At the same time it was able to establish and expand trading relations with the Indians. This was the critical undertaking, for it was on the native people that success or failure of the venture depended. It was they who found and killed the beaver; and they who wore the beaver skin robes, preparing the pelt for sale to the traders. Without Indian goodwill there could be no fur rush, not even a fur trade.

The nation which soon became the primary source of fur was the Huron. They had the largest population and were the most technologically advanced of any of the Indians north of the Great Lakes. These people were the northernmost farmers of America; on the basis of their agricultural surplus they had established a far-flung trading empire. With the arrival of the French, it seemed that their opportunity to trade over an even greater territory was at hand. This mutually profitable relationship between Indian and European was sealed when Champlain agreed to accompany Huron warriors into the territory of their inveterate enemies, the Iroquois, in 1609. Champlain won the undying friendship of the Huron by participating in a season of blood sport, made successful for the Huron by the use of French firearms.

Still, the colony did not grow. In this first generation the French established neither a conquest culture, a new society modelled after the Spanish subjugation of Mexico, nor a commercial agricultural frontier, the invention the English were then making in Virginia. The French fur frontier required a few farmers to provide food for the clerks and warehousemen, and there was little urgency even for this since yearly ships from France permitted a constant flow of supplies. Consequently, as late as 1627 there was only one farmer at Quebec *Habitation.* What was established was a trading presence, with the metropolis of Paris making good use of a distant hinterland. In this way, even though the French enjoyed hegemony over almost the entire area of present-day Quebec and Ontario through their Indian allies, the colonial foundation in 1627 was just 100 traders and one farmer. With this modest establishment, the monopolists were content. The government of France, however, was coming to a more grandiose conception of overseas expansion.

III.   Fur-Trade Outpost to Overseas Settlement

The seventeenth century was a crucial period in the development of the modern French state. The preceding century had been a time of chaos, with the country violently divided between Catholic and Protestant (Huguenot) armies. In addition, the Spanish-Austrian house of Hapsburg was taking advantage of the internal weakness of France to strengthen its own position. But the slide into anarchy was arrested at the very end of the sixteenth century, and the turning of the tide was symbolized by the accession to the throne of a new dynasty, the Bourbon, founded by Henry IV, who became king in 1589. It was under the Bourbons that the monarchy became the principal agent for unification, overcoming the country's divisions by a centralizing administration. In the 1620s and 1630s this Bourbon policy was fostered by the leading minister of the day, Cardinal Richelieu.

Two elements in his policy were of special relevance to the French presence in North America. Richelieu observed that the increasingly powerful countries of Europe, England, and Holland, were building up their strength by paying attention to overseas trade and the acquisition of colonies. Openly basing his plans on those of England and Holland, Richelieu tried to initiate vast schemes for the organization of trading companies in which private initiative would be encouraged by state backing and investment. North America had its place in this scheme of empire. Implementing the first element of his policy, Richelieu revoked all previous monopolies and launched the Company of One Hundred Associates in 1627. In return for the monopoly of the fur trade, the Associates had to support the migration to Canada of 200 colonists per year. Twenty years of expanding fur trade had established the claim to wide territory but had not secured it by effective occupation. Settling a large population would consolidate the claim. A growing population in Canada would be the insurance against embarrassment by invasion and overseas defeat.

The second element was Richelieu's determination to make Canada an exclusively Roman Catholic colony. Internal division was to be avoided by insisting upon religious uniformity—there would be no Protestants. This total exclusion of Huguenots was consistent with a general repression of Protestantism which Richelieu saw as a necessary precondition for bringing political peace to France. Much of the trouble of his century he could attribute to the experiment in religious toleration established by Henry IV in 1598 through the Edict of Nantes. But since then the Huguenots had been in retreat and, one by one, the Protestant enclaves which had flourished previously were reduced. By 1627, only one Protestant stronghold remained and this place was under siege. In fact, it was before the very walls of La Rochelle, the last Huguenot stronghold, that the charter for New France with its Protestant exclusion was sealed between the French government and the One Hundred Associates. Richelieu wanted to avoid exporting the conflicts to the new land where a peaceful and prosperous New France was expected.

From the start, the company found it easier to make promises than fulfil the bargain. The organizers ran into problem after problem even though the company did make a great effort to keep its part of the contract. In 1628 alone, no less than four ships with 400 settlers set sail for the St. Lawrence. However, the entire expedition fell prey to British privateers, the Kirke brothers. The next year the Kirkes returned to the gulf, sacked Quebec *Habitation*, and took possession of the area for Charles I. It is true that by the peace treaty of St. Germain-en-Laye, 1632, the territory was returned to France, but the Company of One Hundred Associates had been hit so heavily that the promotion of settlement was now regarded as an expendable frill. After 1633, when there were profits, they were diverted to recoup old losses. The population, which was intended to number about two thousand by 1633, was but a few hundred. By 1635, France was on the point of committing herself fully to involvement in the Thirty Years War between 1618-48. In this struggle for survival in a European-wide war little energy could be spared for such luxuries as the French presence in the New World.

However, the vacuum which this created was more than filled from a source very different from company or state. Where the fur rush had pioneered and the state had briefly followed, the Catholic Church now moved in to reap the harvest—but of souls rather than empire or profit.

IV.   Overseas Settlement as Missionary Ordeal

The first half of the seventeenth century was a vibrant period in the life of the Catholic Church, especially in France. The drive of the Counter-Reformation, the Church's response to the challenges of Luther, Calvin, and others in the preceding century, was coming to a climax. There was an extraordinary vitality in Catholicism. Inevitably, French involvement in the New World would draw in this deeply-felt religious dimension sooner if not later.

An important aspect of this French religiosity was a harsh streak which in many ways was similar to the puritanism that was struggling for control of the English church at the same time. It was to be seen, for instance, in the various religious societies formed to cater to the narrow piety of the *dévots* who felt that the mainstream of the Church had become much too lax. The most extreme of these societies was the powerful *Compagnie du Saint Sacrement*, a secret association that had been founded in 1627 and included highly placed state officials. Its outlook and influence may be judged by the widespread assumption that it was behind a highly organized and effective crusade against the playwright Molière, whose only crime was satirizing overzealous Catholics. This same puritanism was to be seen in another tendency, Jansenism, which burst out openly about 1640. It stressed the limited, sinful nature of man, his total dependence upon God, and insisted upon predestination. Jansenism was eventually condemned by the Church, but Jansenist tendencies were prominent throughout the seventeenth century.

A very different form for French Catholic loyalties was provided by the Jesuits. This order had been founded in the mid-sixteenth century by an ex-soldier. Immediately, it became the leading example of Counter-Reformation zeal. By the 1620s it had also become extremely influential, known particularly for its educational and missionary work in which the order displayed a suave flexibility in dogma and methods. Indeed, it was resentment against this flexibility which had given the narrow Jansenists such a following, and these two bodies were always in conflict. But in an odd way, Jansenist and Jesuit converged. From their military origin, the Jesuits had developed a fanatical conception of duty and self-sacrifice, just as the Jansenists had developed a sense of moral superiority, if not invulnerability, out of their narrow puritanism. In the New World setting, the bickering between these two styles of Catholicism continued; but, as will soon be apparent, in their zeal they had something important in common.

The puritanical fanaticism of the Jesuits was revealed in their *Relations*, annual reports between 1632 and 1673, in which the order's missionaries in North America reported to their superiors. They, in turn, edited and published these accounts for wide circulation among pious members of the French gentry and aristocracy. One of the aims of the *Relations* was to attract financial support, and so accounts of the terrible suffering and ghoulish martyrdoms were included. But at the same time, the *Relations* were published with a view to attracting additional recruits to the missionary field, and so there is some basis for interpreting their gruesome detail as an indication of a subliminal longing for such treatment. It is worth comparing this aspect of North American experience with that of, say, Mexico where the main missionary activity was carried on, not by Jesuits, but by the pre-Reformation Franciscans. There, martyrdom was viewed merely as a remote possibility; in Canada, it was actually sought, and frequently found.

The initial Jesuit experience of suffering in Canada was gained among the migratory tribes along the Gulf of St. Lawrence. Nomadic hunters and gatherers, the Indians lacked villages and surplus food. Hunting continually, they wandered in pursuit of game, feasting some days and starving on others. The cold and snows of winter were simply endured, for shelter was minimal. Bringing Christianity to these nomads was an incredible ordeal. In his first week among the Montagnais, Father Le Jeune found himself overcome by a violent fever. "Being cured, I tried to follow them during the winter, and I was ill the greater part of the time." Le Jeune concluded in 1634 that "not much ought to be hoped for from the savages as long as they are wanderers; you will instruct them today, tomorrow hunger snatches your hearers away, forcing them to go and seek their food in the rivers and woods."

The futility of the project on the gulf led the missionaries to conclude that the Huron made better prospective converts. These people were farmers and sedentary. As Father Garnier put it in 1636, "the country of the Hurons is the *sancta sanctorum*. It is of all the country where we are, the field where our fathers hope to establish the most beautiful mission because they are a stable nation and not vagabonds like most of the others." And there was an additional reason, perhaps, for concentrating in Huronia, the area between Lake Simcoe and Georgian Bay on Lake Huron. The Huron were the middle men in the trade between the French Regime and the Indians north of the Great Lakes. The fur rush had made them so dependent upon French fur traders, that they could hardly refuse to accept French missionaries.

It was not long before Huronia was the area of greatest Jesuit concentration. Missions were established in four of the largest Huron villages. At a spot near today's Midland they built a fifth mission which they called Ste-Marie. It was intended to serve as a missionary capital, the nerve centre for the whole project. Here was a white settlement that would act as a bridge between two cultures.

Still, conversion took place only slowly. In part it was the difficulty of communication, translating Catholic theology from French to Huron in ways that would compel belief as well as comprehension. But equally obstructive was a contradiction which the Huron spotted in European culture itself. On one side, the Jesuits were attempting to impose self-denial and chastity, while on the other, their trader compatriots pursued profits and human appetites in much the same way as the Huron men and women themselves.

Then, between 1635 and 1640 a series of devastating smallpox epidemics struck. It is possible that as many as 70 percent of the Huron died, for they had no resistance to this imported disease. However, as the Indians lay dying, the Jesuits baptised them and received them into the Church; under the circumstances, little chance of apostasy existed. In an age which believed that life was but a vale of tears—a preparation for the glory to come—such conversion was as successful and as wonderful as any other. In this light, the epidemics were—to borrow a phrase often applied to a later period in Canadian history—a fortunate calamity. To the Huron, however, death by smallpox was unspeakably vile. It was a plague and the Jesuits were the cause. In 1640 an old Huron woman, with reference to the missionaries, asserted that "if we do not put them to death promptly they will ruin the whole country. They came to a village where everyone was well; as soon as they were established everyone except three or four died. They moved and the same thing happened . . . . They visited the cabins of other villages and only those into which they did not enter have been exempted from illness or death." Had it not been for the need to maintain peace with the French to continue the trading connection, it is highly likely that the Huron would have granted the Jesuits the martydom they seemed so fervently to desire. But the epidemics did not kill everyone, and since the fur trade had become the mainstay of the economy, there were simply fewer people to receive limited goods. Those seventeenth-century Europeans who were inclined to romanticize the native people of the New World as "noble savages" would have done well to ponder this decision of the Huron elite. Technologically they were less advanced, but in social priorities the Huron were as sophisticated as businessmen anywhere.

The fur rush was continued and the Jesuits maintained their presence accordingly. By 1647 there were eighteen priests and twenty-four laymen in the missions to the Huron, whose own population had shrunk from about 30 000 to less than 10 000. The marvel of what was happening in Huronia encouraged other religious groups to enter this earthly purgatory which was Canada. In 1639, two women's orders arrived, the Ursulines and the *Hospitalières de la Miséricorde de Jésus de l'ordre de Saint Augustin.* But an even more significant reinforcement was the contingent sent by the *Compagnie du Saint Sacrement.* Under the command of Paul de Chomedey, sieur de Maisonneuve, forty zealots arrived at Quebec with the intention of establishing a mission near the hostile Iroquois, whose tortures were recounted in the Jesuit *Relations.* Consider this example: "It is only a neat trick with them to make a cut around the thumb of a captive near the first joint; and then, twisting it, to pull it off by main strength, together with the sinew, which usually breaks towards the elbow or near the shoulder, so great is the violence employed." The Iroquois had acquired a reputation as devils incarnate. But now in 1642 Maisonneuve and his company of men and women were going to establish a settlement at the gates of hell itself. Far upriver from Quebec, far to the south and east of Huronia, on the island with the promontory Cartier had called Montreal, they would establish a mission to convert the pagans by good example. The Iroquois failed completely to anticipate this daring maneuver. Montreal spent its first year in complete peace. Maisonneuve and company attributed their survival to divine intervention.

This initial good luck, and the determination of the settlers, eased Montreal over the year of its greatest vulnerability. Before the Iroquois discovered the settlement it was well fortified. And, in time, the strategic value of the site ensured that it would not be abandoned. Montreal, at the confluence of the Ottawa and St. Lawrence, was ideally situated to become the headquarters of the fur trade. Eventually it would be profits, not piety, which determined Montreal's growth and significance. But this was still in the future. In this period of company and government neglect, from the 1630s through the 1650s, it was evangelism which mattered for Canada as for Montreal. Thus, during this generation, the evangelical conception of America overrode the commercial. In the St. Lawrence region, the most active agency of colonization was the Church. Although the original extremism of intentional martyrdom was eventually softened, it did not disappear. The new zeal, which can be dated in 1659 with the appearance of Bishop Laval, was the determination to build a truly religious society, a theocracy, in French North America.

V.   The Danger of Inter-Imperial Rivalry

Meanwhile the Company of One Hundred Associates was struggling to meet its obligations. As has been indicated, the setbacks of the early years meant that trading profits could not be spared for settlement. The business of bringing over colonists and establishing them on the land was expensive and undesirable. It was also unnecessary. Commerce could expand over large territories through Indian alliances. The land did not have to be occupied by Frenchmen to realize large profits from the fur rush. And yet the legal obligations could not be completely ignored.

The Company tried the expedient of making seigneurial grants, and large blocks of territory along the banks of the St. Lawrence River were granted to individuals as fiefs. These seigneurs promised to promote settlement in return for the privileges of nobility they might exercise over the people they recruited from France to be their peasants in Canada. Predictably, it was easier to obtain would-be barons than would-be serfs. Consequently, although nearly seventy such fiefs were conceded by 1660 (twenty went to the Church), such concessions resulted in little settlement. Nevertheless it would be a mistake to call this means of recruitment a complete failure. Between 1642 and 1663 population increased from under 300 persons to more than 3 000. Since deaths nearly equalled births in this period, the population had grown more by immigration than by natural increase. Furthermore, since the clerical population in 1663 was only 5 percent of the total, the growing numbers of people cannot be attributed to missionary activity alone. But compared to other colonies in North America, the population of New France was insignificant—less than one third of the

Dutch, and less than one-twentieth the number of the English colonists at the same time.

The most important obstacle to population growth was the menace of the Iroquois Confederacy. Ever since the time of Champlain there had been enmity with them, and with the Mohawk tribe in particular. Beginning in 1640, at the time Maisonneuve was on the point of establishing Montreal, this enmity was creating greater violence. The Iroquois had been trading with France's great rival, the Dutch, who since 1624 had been established at Fort Orange, later to be renamed Albany. The Iroquois had quickly exhausted the supply of beaver within their own territory, and had been obliged to seek supplies from northern tribes by making peace with the Huron. The French had very naturally moved to prevent such a development; in 1624 and again in 1633 they had effectively blocked Iroquois bids for division of the trade. The French and Huron preferred monopoly even though it meant collapse of the Iroquois economy. In desperation, supported by the Dutch, the Mohawk Indians planned a war of unprecedented aggression against the French and Huron. The limited blood sport of an earlier period gave way in 1641 to unlimited war, and in the next ten years (to judge by what happened at Trois Rivières) of any forty colonists only ten were likely to survive. The wrath of the Iroquois fell with tremendous fury.

For Huronia the climax came in 1649. In March, in the snows of late winter without the cover of trees in full leaf, about 1 000 Iroquois warriors fell upon Huronia and killed everyone they could find. They captured the Jesuit Fathers Brébeuf and Lalement, led them to their camp, and tortured them to death. The remnant of the Huron was completely demoralized. Father Ragueneau attempted to lead them to Manitoulin Island which was defensible and bountiful. But the Huron insisted upon taking more immediate refuge at nearby Christian Island. Throughout the winter they starved. Some who did not succumb joined other Indian tribes and were assimilated. The remainder—barely five hundred in number —limped into Quebec to tell the story of the destruction of Huronia. This fragment, hundreds of miles from home, was all that remained of a once powerful nation. Between 1635 and 40, they were weakened by smallpox; in 1649 they were decimated by war, in 1650 they starved. Epidemics, war, and starvation was a sequence that would recur again and again as Europeans traded, invaded, allied, and oversaw the destruction of the Indians. The Huron were the first in Canada to experience it fully.

The Iroquois had assumed that once the Huron had been removed they would be able to take over their trading empire. But quite unexpectedly the elimination of the Huron proved to be the opportunity for the Ottawa Indians who traded with the French at Montreal. The Iroquois had concluded that the French themselves would have to be driven out. The

Huron had been destroyed as a people even though only a quarter had actually been killed in battle; no doubt the same kind of terrifying, lightning attacks would have a similar effect on the French, demoralizing them totally and making them lose the will to persist.

Such fierce onslaughts naturally had their effect. Years later an Iroquois chief bragged that his tactics were so effective, that his 500 warriors were able to keep an equal force of French so close to their fortifications "that they were not able to go over a door to pisse." There were more deaths than births. Old settlers were giving up and returning home. Newcomers were diminishing. This was not all. Even the steely Jesuits were beginning to rethink their position. The earlier zeal for martyrdom was giving way to a greater sense of realism; and, increasingly, the Jesuits were appealing to France for military protection. The mystical age was passing away and was being succeeded by that of bureaucracy. In 1658 François de Laval was made bishop and Vicar Apostolic of New France—though as yet Quebec was not made a bishopric. No sooner was Laval established in his new office than he began to press for assistance from the mother country. In this plea, the ecclesiastical authorities were joined by the civil. Iroquois attacks were disrupting the fur trade, so much so that traders along with disillusioned settlers were abandoning Canada. Officials were wondering whether to follow. In 1661 it seemed that the French presence in North America was coming to an end. New France, like Huronia, was moving toward extinction. It had been an invention that had failed.

CHAPTER TWO

Trading Post to Planned Society

I. A Small and Vulnerable Colony

Richelieu's attempt to transform the fur rush into a venture in colonization had begun as an enticing dream, but within a generation it had turned into a nightmare. Admittedly, there was a sizeable French presence in North America; by 1660, over 700 families had settled between Quebec and Montreal and about 100 others had located at Port Royal and other places around the Bay of Fundy. The Church was active, with 150 people in seven different religious orders still pursuing their mission to the surviving remnant of Huronia east of Quebec on the Ile d'Orléans. Then, too, there were other Indians to be converted. There was, on paper, a compact structure of civil administration. Interest in the fur trade continued, even though Iroquois interruptions had made it unpredictable and caused it to develop along new lines, with merchants now employing French *coureurs de bois* as middlemen between themselves and the Indian trappers to replace the Huron and the terror-stricken Ottawa. The fur trade still continued as the mainstay of an economy that was occasionally rewarding. But this state of affairs was well short of what had been intended. A fur trade that functioned intermittently was not an adequate base for long-term growth. The destruction of Huronia was an irreparable setback to the missionaries. In the 1650s, more missionaries departed than arrived. But above all, the population was small, just one tenth of what Richelieu had expected in 1627. This was crucial. Richelieu had always envisioned the colony as nothing without a large and growing population. He invented New France as an outpost of empire to play a part in the worldwide expansion of French trade. More particularly, a sizeable French population would help deny the St. Lawrence region to France's great rivals, the English and the Dutch. Thus, having failed to settle sufficient people, Richelieu may be said to have failed in his invention.

But there was a French presence. In 1660 it was approaching a total of 3 000 people (2 500 in the St. Lawrence Valley and about 500 in Acadia). Some were fur traders, some were missionaries, but many were farmers. On this basis it might have been possible to invent, inadvertently so to speak, yet another America. Even if the fur trade had withered and the missionaries had lost heart—even if the English managed to keep Acadia (the most recent conquest had been in 1655)—a scattering of French-Catholic farmers between Quebec and Montreal might still have continued. Under these circumstances it would have had about the same prospects as Plymouth Plantation on Cape Cod Bay in 1626, the year that tiny colony of English Protestants separated themselves from the promoters who had underwritten their migration in the *Mayflower* in 1620. From this comparison it is evident that large population is not necessarily a prerequisite for the prosperity even of an agricultural colony. In 1626 Plymouth Plantation was six years old and had fewer than 400 people, yet the leader of the settlement, William Bradford, was guardedly optimistic about future prospects. Bradford said "they know not well how to . . . supply the yearly wants of the Plantation. . . . yet they undertook it. . . . . " They were sobered at the prospect of independence but not demoralized. Of his own generation he said the succeeding ones should sing this praise: "Our fathers were Englishmen who came over this great ocean and were ready to perish in this wilderness; but they cried unto the Lord, and He heard their voice and looked on their adversity." The colony survived even though all other settlements grew more rapidly. By 1660 Plymouth Plantation had just 2 000 people—less than New France at the same time. More important than the number of people was their attitude toward their prospects. The success of separatist colonization depended largely on the perception that that society had of its situation. In the face of their difficulties, would the colonists feel they might somehow survive, or would they consider the abandonment of their venture more reasonable than holding on?

In the case of New France, the second possibility seemed more probable than the first. This tiny colony was losing its will to withstand further attacks from the Iroquois. But it was not because New France was outnumbered by the Indians. By 1660, about the time that the colonists were awaiting renewed onslaught from their inveterate foes, at least 1 000 of the nearly 3 000 population of the colony were able-bodied men who—had they still been in France—would have been liable for conscription into the army. To be sure, the Iroquois Confederacy could mobilize some 2 300 warriors against them, if all fought together. But no such army was harassing the French. It was but one Iroquois nation, the Mohawk, with about 500 warriors, that was the main and longstanding threat. On the score of manpower, then, New France had no reason to despair.

More significant than numbers was the nature of the attacks. The Mohawk war against the settlements between Montreal and Quebec was a guerilla war. The French had superior weapons and numbers, but the Iroquois had more patience and style in the art of ambush. One of the first historians of New France, Dollier De Casson, described it as a war of nerves. The following incident was characteristic. A group of settlers working in a field had posted one of their number as a sentry atop a large stump, the better to view the field. An Indian hid in the shadow of another stump. By stages, the attacker drew closer to the guard without being seen by him or the workmen. "Finally the fox got so near to the badly perched bird that he leaped up all at once on to him, seized him . . . and dashed off with his load much as a thief would carry off a sheep." The victim and the workmen alike were too shocked to do anything more than cry out shouts of surprise and anger. The sentinel found his death in an Iroquois bonfire; the others found a more prolonged anguish in the terror of the example.

This demoralization was intensified by the apparent inability of New France to organize effective militia units for their own defense. The social structure was organized about the seigneurs, a nobility which historically had taken the lead in military matters in France. But in the colony the seigneurs had never acquired this function. Instead, they were merely settlement agents responsible for recruiting peasants and establishing them on the land. In this they had been reasonably successful; sixty-nine (of whom seven were from religious orders) had made 708 concessions of land between Quebec and Montreal to individual settlers, mainly between 1650 and 1655. By this means the distinctive pattern of a linear village of riverfront farms emerged. These peasants, who were mainly town-bred artisans back in France (and therefore considered inferior material for the armies and for fighting) were given no military leadership by their seigneurs. When governors attempted to exercise this role under *their* authority, the settlers, in large part, seem to have ignored the effort. They preferred unorganized self-defense to an organized colonial militia, and defense from France to that supplied from resources on the spot.

Official inertia was not restricted to military matters; there was a general paralysis in the direction of the affairs of the colony. A council composed of the three governors (the Governor General of Quebec and the governors of Montreal and Trois Rivières), the Superior of the Jesuits, and several other notables, met regularly, but bickered constantly. They argued especially over the question of the use of brandy in the fur trade. Kettles had long since lost their place as the most coveted European trading commodity. The Indians craved brandy so much that the Jesuits saw no alternative to a total ban. The secular arm insisted, however, that some liquor would have to be traded or the furs would go to the Dutch and English, who had no such scruples. Each side asserted its position with equal certainty; each claimed the authority to prevail. This impasse pointed to a fatal flaw in the colony Richelieu had invented under company auspices in 1627. In matters of Church and State there was no clear supremacy of one side over the other.

But even while the fatal shortcomings of the colony were becoming apparent, developments in the mother country were reaching a conclusion which would highlight what was needed in New France, and therefore indicate the lines on which that change could be brought about.

II.   A Modernizing Mother Country

The overhaul of the French state by the Bourbon monarchs was described in the last chapter simply as a program of centralization. For purposes of more detailed analysis, that centralization may be divided into two main components. The first was an innovation in government known as absolutism. This term draws attention to the fact that the key to the modernization process was the lead provided and the part played by the Crown, which was to rule absolutely over all sections of society. The basis for this development was the doctrine of divine right, the notion that the king had been chosen and instituted by God. The central authority of the Crown was to be insisted upon; to this end, any rival power center was to be undermined. Thus, for instance, the ostensibly very Catholic Louis XIV did not hesitate to quarrel with the Pope, even to the point of instigating street fighting in Rome, in order to uphold what he saw as *his*—or French—*national* rights as opposed to those of the international church. It is for this reason that Bourbon policy in ecclesiastical matters is referred to as *Gallican* in contrast to the Papal alternative, known as *Ultramontanism*.

Just as the Church was subordinated, so also the judiciary was made to realize that its function was not to act apart from the Crown, but to facilitate the royal will, not to review or to check it. To prevent competition from a legislative branch the French parliament, the Estates General of France, was simply not summoned. For one hundred and seventy-five years after 1614 France did without any national representative institution at all, a condition which was changed only by the shock of the French Revolution. This placing of the Estates General in suspension is the clearest indicator of the successful taming of the nobility. But it did not happen without a struggle. As Bourbon centralism became ever more effective the feudal nobles staged a last-ditch stand; from 1648-53 France—and especially Paris—was convulsed by the *Fronde*. But these unsuccessful risings of the nobility merely exposed the weakness of the feudal regime and intensified the Bourbons in their determination to humble the mighty. Louis XIV dealt the nobility a death blow when he built Versailles, making it into the cultural capital not only of France but of Europe as well. Anyone hoping for recognition or power had to be there in full-time residence. In this way, the nobility was cut off from its local roots, robbed of its independence, and reduced to courtier status as servants of the king. As a class they had been emasculated.

With the nobility tamed, the way was open for the Crown to extend its bureaucratic control over the country. The civil service was expanded, and its personnel was organized. Increasingly the claims by those of noble birth to positions of power were being challenged and overruled by claims of talent. Indeed the late seventeenth century was a golden age for the meritocracy. Within the Church, the army, the navy, and the civil service generally middle-class functionaries rose to prominence as never before. In this modernization process a key official was the *intendant*, a high-ranking bureaucrat, recruited and appointed on the basis of merit, who was sent as the king's personal representative to oversee administration in the provinces, and report directly to the king. Under such coordination, the business of the kingdom was conducted with unprecedented efficiency.

The second component in centralization was the central planning of the economy in accordance with a doctrine known as mercantilism. The basis of this idea was the belief that the amount of wealth in the world was limited; thus for any state to increase its prosperity, and hence power, another state would have to lose that much. It was possible to increase one's wealth by war, of course, and although nations showed themselves increasingly ready to do so, this was regarded as distinctly old-fashioned. Empire by trade was coming to be regarded as more desirable than empire by conquest. But trading empires would not arise without state encouragement. By means of government bounties, producers were encouraged to export goods abroad, and so acquire the money of competitor countries. At the same time, tariffs for exclusion of certain imports were regarded as essential because purchases abroad involved a loss of specie to competitor nations. Thus, state intervention in otherwise free markets was one requirement. Yet another mercantilist necessity was the acquisition of diverse sources of supply to obtain from overseas colonies materials which could not be procured at home. It was precisely this kind of thinking that lay behind Richelieu's reorganization of New France in 1627. The St. Lawrence Valley would provide France with furs and naval supplies, thus eliminating her reliance upon Scandinavia and the outflow of bullion to that part of the world. At the same time, French possessions in North America would deprive the British of access to these staples in Canada. The same logic applied to sugar and the French presence in the West Indies.

And yet it is important to note that French pursuit of mercantilist ends was vitiated by a flaw in French society. In her mode of modernization, France had not managed to break sufficiently with the older ways. This can be seen in the affairs of the king, the modernizing agent himself. The nobility might have been tamed, but an aristocratic ethos persisted to impede the full working-out of meritocratic bureaucracy. Versailles domesticated the nobility, but at an enormous expense. Furthermore, the intendant was never completely supreme in the provinces, for the aristocratic governor was not abolished, merely pushed somewhat aside by the new creation. The old order had not been eliminated, and so modernization was only partly successful. This was especially the case in trade. The whole business of merchandising was regarded as work for inferiors, so much so, in fact, that no aristocrat could take part in retail trade without losing status, that is, without derogation and becoming a commoner. Louis XIV was so eager for economic development that he wanted to break this old prejudice, but he went no further than to make exceptions of certain key trades to which *dérogeance* would not apply.

The fact was that a business outlook was foreign to the vast majority in French society. The repugnance of trade was reinforced further by venality, a practice which permitted many of the bureaucratic positions, including judgeships, to be treated as personal property and bought and sold much like real estate. Since these offices carried noble status, and since nobility was so highly valued, the practice for successful bourgeois was to buy offices, thus buying themselves out of trade and commerce and into the aristocracy. Consequently, in France, capital did not accumulate in private hands and economic development depended upon the king, who was usually at war, and a gap opened between the French and their competitors, the Dutch and the English. There were few nobles in Holland; it was a nation of bourgeois. In England, although there was a hereditary aristocracy, *dérogeance* had never been an inhibiting factor. Participation by the nobility in trade and commerce had long been a marked feature of its economy. English lords of the manor had become landlords by taking a personal interest in their holdings and sinking large amounts of capital in the hope of boosting yields. Many turned to the commercial production of wool. Their French counterparts preferred exploitation of the feudal rights and dues to augment their income. At a time when feudalism seemed fated to die a death of obsolescence, the old nobility, *noblesse d'épée*, assisted by an army of aspiring pettifogging lawyers, who were would-be entrants to the *noblesse de robe*, revived feudal customs for their cash value to the aristocracy.

These impediments to change can be exaggerated, however, because the mid-seventeenth century was still the early stage of modernization in France, and the shortcomings of the French pattern were not to show up fully until the eighteenth century. In fact, in 1661, the time was ideal for Richelieu's failed invention of New France to be resurrected and implemented again, this time with success, thanks to the intervention of a modernizing mother country.

III.   Colbert's New France

One way of summing up absolutism and of explaining its initial superiority over the system it replaced is to draw attention to its creation of a controlling center. Where feudalism had been decentralized and diffused, absolutism was centralized and concentrated. New France was not a feudal society but authority was dangerously diffuse. The colony was suffering from the glaring need for a controlling center. Was the colony a trading outpost, a missionary frontier, or an agricultural settlement? Was the civil government sovereign, or did it share power with the Church? What liberty did the individual settler enjoy? Was he free to decline the government's order that he enroll in militia companies? What was the status of the colony itself? Was it to be closely tied to France, or self-reliant and therefore granted a good deal of autonomy? Operational answers to all these questions were lacking in the colony. In the mother country, the answers were ready for export.

Given the problem of defense, civil and church authorities both invited any action from the metropolis which would guarantee security; and, in 1661, there was a change in France that gave them reason to think the mother country would be unusually receptive to their appeals for help. Louis XIV, who had come to the throne in 1643 as a child, came of age, and on the death of Richelieu's successor, Cardinal Mazarin, took over the personal direction of state affairs in 1661. He was eager to capitalize on the advances made by his Bourbon predecessors and by the dominant position in Europe that France had won through the Thirty Years' War. In this ascendancy he was aided by his leading minister, Jean-Baptiste Colbert. This forty-four-year-old former businessman was the ideal bureaucrat under whose direction the caliber of the civil service was improving daily. Together, monarch and minister turned to New France and were delighted to discover the very formlessness of the colony. It meant that they could treat it as a laboratory in which to experiment, and build the ideal community which stubborn tradition prevented them from doing in France itself.

Thus, the appeal for aid carried by Pierre Boucher in 1661 came at just the right moment. Had an urgent request for assistance come earlier the government might have been too preoccupied with foreign wars to spend time and trouble upon the tiny settlement, and the disheartened settlers would have abandoned the St. Lawrence. If it had come later, France would once again have been involved in European affairs, and indeed after 1672 interest in New France did decline dramatically. The 1660s, however, was the perfect decade, free from pressing concerns in Europe, a time when the bureaucracy was approaching its creative zenith. In that brief interval New France was transformed.

In 1663 the Company rule was abolished. The colony became, in effect, another province of the motherland, essentially no different from Normandy or Saintonge. But there were some differences, and these are significant in showing the goals of absolutism freed from tradition. Thus the Sovereign Council of New France was set up as the counterpart to a *Parlement* in a region of France; but in the colony the individuals who filled its positions served at the pleasure of the king; they were not people who bought title to governmental posts with cash. This is not to say social *status* was never sold in New France, only that *control* of the colony was never for sale. In a *Parlement* of France, by contrast, one could, for example, buy judgeships; this venality was not exported to the colony. Then, too, the legal profession was excluded from New France. No shadow of representative government was permitted. The absolutism—that is, the control—was intended to be perfect.

But even more significant than making New France a province was the drive and organization that this decision implied. The mood in 1661 had been one of defeat, indeed demoralization; the new royal initiative convinced the settlers that the resources of the metropolis would be put behind them, that it was worth continuing. In this sense, initially, it was a morale boost that Louis XIV provided. As the developments of the period between 1661 and 1672 are considered, it becomes clear that nearly as much already existed materially in New France as was contributed afresh. The qualification is true even of the psychological boost, since the royal initiative was slow to manifest itself. In 1661 Colbert was still consolidating his authority over his department. Consequently he had to move cautiously with his actions in New France, for he had enemies who would seize any indication of incompetence. The king himself, remembering the Fronde, had similar fears. The delay between the decision to plan a New France and its implementation seems unnecessarily drawn out unless these facts are kept in mind. Although civil and clerical authorities were assured in 1661 that the new monarch would take an unprecedented interest in protecting and promoting the colony, it was not until 1663 that the Company rule was formally suspended. A military campaign against the Iroquois did not come until 1666. And economic development did not receive much attention until after 1667. Then, in 1672, European war diverted the attention of the French government away from Canada and it was never to be redirected to the colony with quite the same intensity as in the nine years following royal assumption of formal responsibility in 1663. Therefore, if New France is described as a planned society, this must refer to the colony primarily between 1663 and 72 and to the activities of one planner, Jean-Baptiste Colbert.

Colbert's first move was to rationalize authority, to declare who was sovereign and by what agency. He accomplished this by creating a Sovereign Council consisting of a figurehead governor, a circumscribed bishop and an intendant of justice, finance and administration. In other words, his first move was to invest sovereignty in an official, the Governor, in charge of practically everything, to accompany him by the majesty of the royal symbol, and aid him by a bureaucrat in charge of religious affairs. He did this in 1663, but without filling the office of intendant. It took Colbert two years to find the appropriate candidate for this all-important office. When the search was only half completed he despaired that all who seemed qualified "lack the mettle" and those who were willing to undertake the long voyage and rude conditions "lack the intelligence, integrity and ability needed to be of some use there." His solution was to create a kind of caretaker government for the interim. But to boost morale of the settlers in the meantime, he did send some soldiers with the promise of more to follow.

It was not until February of 1665 that Colbert found his man to fill the office of intendant. This person was Jean Talon. He had intelligence and equal amounts of courage and integrity. In the summer of 1665, Talon departed for New France. He had agreed to serve two years, although he stayed until 1672, the end of the dynamic formative years. Talon's arrival at Quebec coincided with that of Alexandre de Prouville, sieur de Tracy, commander of the long-awaited regiment to fight the Iroquois. Tracy had been ordered to New France by way of the French possessions in the West Indies. Now, with his one thousand soldiers, and the Sovereign Council with its intendant, the new regime was launched with all the pomp and excitement of people in small communities who hope they are on the threshold of greater things to come.

But it was not until 1666 that Tracy and his men engaged the Iroquois in their own territory. Then it was anti-climactic. Colbert had anticipated pitched battles between French soldiers and the Iroquois warriors. For this reason, the men who were ordered to bring the war to the Iroquois were veterans of the Carignan-Salières regiment. But the fighting that was anticipated never occurred, even though in one of three campaigns the regiment was marched into the very heartland of the Mohawks. The Iroquois fled from the advancing enemy, and the French destroyed the Indians' food supply in the autumn of 1666. Then they returned to Quebec and called it victory. In the following year, having suffered more by starvation than war, the Mohawks negotiated a truce in this long war that had raged intermittently from 1609 and that would flare up again in the future. In the interim, there were nearly twenty years of peace.

By 1667, therefore, the military survival of New France seemed secured. The administration of the colony had already been established on lines of centralized efficiency. Now it was possible to implement more comprehensive plans of social and economic development. In the next five years, steps were taken to augment the population, integrate the central administration with local institutions, and promote self-sufficiency and diversity in the economy—but all the emphasis was placed on the St. Lawrence area. Apparently Colbert and Louis XIV were content simply to maintain a claim on Acadia for no more than its strategic value. No significant attempt was made to foster the growth of Acadia's economy or augment the population of the small groups of fishermen and farmers scattered around the half-dozen settlements on the south shore of the Bay of Fundy. They had their own governor, but as a result of neglect and isolation the population, which barely exceeded 500 in 1660, totaled no more than 1 000 a half-century later.

In the St. Lawrence region, by contrast, the growth of population was encouraged by a variety of means. But even here, natural increase was recognized as the most important source of colonists. Incentives were therefore fixed to encourage large families. Parents of ten children or more were awarded handsome annuities. People marrying young (under 20 for males, 16 for females) received royal wedding dowries. Conversely, fathers whose children moved beyond these thresholds without marrying were fined each year that youth extended into celibacy. Since the population of New France doubled every twenty years, it might be concluded that these cash incentives were successful, but since the same tendency occurred in the British colonies *without* this system of bounties and taxes a better conclusion would be the suggestion that the program was simply another reinforcement for a distinctive system of social values. In other words, while it is true that these bonuses were *intended* to make the population increase rapidly, they were dispensible. The population was going to grow at an explosive rate anyway. But they certainly did not impede the tendency. In 1663, the population of the colony was nearly three thousand; in 1676 it was almost ten thousand.

Of course not all of the growing population could be accounted for by natural increase. More than four thousand were immigrants, recruits whose passage to Canada had been paid for by the government of France. More than one third were soldiers. Four hundred of the nearly 1 000 soldiers of the Carignan-Salières regiment were persuaded to remain as settlers, when the others returned to France in 1668. Similarly, in 1669, six army captains arrived in Canada and became seigneurs. With them were companies of about fifty men each, their former soldiers, now colonists. Since this tended to unbalance the ratio of men to women, the government found it necessary to import marriageable women at the same time that it promoted the migration of men. The women were not prostitutes, nor even anyone who happened to volunteer. They were carefully screened candidates selected from orphanages; hence they were named *filles du roi,* not *filles de joie.* They, and the others who were transported at government expense, were carefully chosen. In Colbert's words, "in the establishment of a country it is important to sow good seed." In his view, the quality was more important than the quantity. Thus, between 1663 and 1672, only about 4 500 people were transported to New France as the "seed" population. The colony was never used as a dumping ground for people who were considered superfluous or undesirable at home.

Since the government was now the agency for recruiting settlers and transporting them to Canada, it also assumed responsibility for their orderly settlement upon the land. To this end the seigneurial system, established by the Company, was continued. In its extension, however, it was even more clear that it would operate by enjoying all the formalities and none of the functions of feudalism. That is, the seigneur, after 1663 as before, was a high status landlord but not a commander. The lord of the manor might demand respect and nominal rents, but the peasants owed service to no one but the state. This was made perfectly clear when all the able-bodied men in the colony were organized into militia companies in 1669. The colonial militia had its captains, but they were not seigneurs. The *capitaines de milice* were appointed by the governor from the population of ordinary citizens, and the individuals chosen seemed to be known and respected in their particular localities. These men had apparent leadership qualities which the government was willing to recognize to a limited extent for a limited period. Consequently, the *capitaine de milice* was the local commander and intermediary between the individual citizens, the *habitants,* and the government. By this agency, central administration was brought to the population at large without creating a nobility, a military aristocracy such as still persisted in France as an obstacle to modernization. Thus, by commoner-militia captains it was possible to organize military defense without enhancing the power of the seigneurs. The function of the seigneurs was to subdivide their fiefs, usually into eighty-acre concessions, as rapidly as they could find the peasants, the *censitaires,* to take them. The system was predicated on a reward system of status rather than money or power. The more tenants a landlord had, the richer he was in esteem.

These were the foundations for Colbert's economic program: the Sovereign Council had been defined as the controlling center. The Carignan-Salières had secured a truce in the war with the Iroquois. The government was recruiting and transporting settlers. Orderly settlement without weakening centralized authority was achieved by perpetuating a somewhat remodeled version of the seigneurial system. Coincidental with the arrival of the intendant, Jean Talon, was the launching of the program of economic development itself. Here there were two strategic objectives. One was simply subsistence, that is, self-sufficiency in the production of food, clothing, and shelter. To further this goal, the major prerequisite was elimination of the terror of the Iroquois. Progress here was therefore immediately noticeable after the truce in 1667. But the other goal, economic diversity, required more than willing hands clearing hardwood forests. Mining and manufacturing required skilled labor, capital investment, and managerial talent. Between 1667 and 1672 all were provided abundantly but with little effect. Jean Talon was the skilled manager. There was no stinginess in the money invested. Skilled workers were recruited in France. But the shipbuilding industry, for instance, did not take off immediately because, despite the readily available wood, there was no locally-made iron and rope. Consequently, it continued to be cheaper to build ships in France. Similarly, the colonists were encouraged to fish and produce an exportable agricultural surplus, so that New France might fill the role for the French West Indies that was played by New England for the British "sugar" islands. But this failed too. When the St. Lawrence River was open for safe navigation the Caribbean was dangerous because of the hurricane season there. Consequently, the Dutch and the British, already providing the French sugar producers with their slaves, enjoyed a continuation of the opportunity to provide everything else as well.

There were two economic activities beyond subsistence agriculture that enjoyed better fortunes. One was the brewery business; a brewery established by Talon outlasted his tanneries. The other activity that enjoyed a long history was the fur trade. Colbert had intended that this original invention of New France would wither. Indicative of that attitude was his early decision to rent it to a company for a sum equal to the annual cost of the civil administration, or about one fifth the amount annually invested to develop such industries as shipbuilding.

The lure of the fur trade was primary, however. A few good seasons in the hinterland could yield phenomenal returns. But individuals who accumulated fortunes in this manner did not invest their money in shipbuilding or tanneries, enterprises with mercantilist legitimacy; they spent what they made as fast as they earned it, or invested their fortunes like Frenchmen in France. They bought status. They accumulated *gloire* rather than wealth or power. This had absolutist legitimacy and this was certainly at least half of the plan for New France which Colbert set down after 1663, but it spelled defeat for his economic program. The plan for diversification was a failure. Yet the colony did not collapse. It doubled in population every twenty years, and its fur trade expanded south to the Gulf of Mexico, north to Hudson Bay and west as far as the Rocky Mountains. Half of the plan, the economic side, was a partial failure. But the other half, the plan pertaining to social organization and control, found enough material support from the trade in the pelt of a rodent "the bigness of a water spaniel" that a New France did in fact arise on the banks of the St. Lawrence. Thus, the colony proved the irrelevance of economic development to social happiness, as an examination of relations between individuals and the state as they persisted down to 1760 will make apparent.

CHAPTER THREE

State and Individual in New France

I. The Long-term Consequences of Authoritarian Government

In one decisively important regard, the colony of New France deviated very little from the social and institutional model invented by Colbert. For nearly one hundred years, the colonists lived quite contentedly under authoritarian government. From 1663 to 1760 there was no demand for significant departure from this pattern. Its very stability tended to confirm the outsider's opinion that the government was despotic. There was not even any potential challenge to despotism. There were no newspapers, and therefore no effective forums for public opinion. There was no parliament, and therefore no body to represent the views of the common people or even belief that government should be based on the consent of the governed. There was no toleration of dissent, and therefore no religious pluralism or legitimate political factions. And since there was no freehold land tenure, and therefore no truly private property, the possibility of an effectively independent landed interest in opposition to the Crown was minimal. What had been planted and perpetuated, in the eighteenth-century English view of it, was a "perfect system of French despotism."

In addition to being authoritarian, however, the government of New France was paternalistic. In other words, the king governed in New France through agents by the same kind of legitimacy that justified his rule in France and, until very recently, used to justify a father in the governing of his family. The head of a family who only disciplined its members was a despot or a tyrant; the good father was a good provider as well as a stern disciplinarian. It was precisely thus in matters of State. The good king was a father to his subjects, a provider as well as a law giver. Accordingly, Louis XIV expressed his intent to "pay heed to all the inhabitants' complaints and their needs, and attend to them as much as he possibly can...."

In large part, the promise was fulfilled at home. But this was especially so in the case of his subjects in New France. There was no freehold land tenure, but there were no landless poor. Every man was assured a minimum of about eighty acres for himself and his heirs, conditional upon the payment of nothing more than allegiance and an annual token-offering to him who held the land in the king's name. Similarly, there was no representation, but neither were there direct taxes. And, although there was no toleration of religious or political dissent, there was little indication of a sense of deprivation on this account. That is, laws were obeyed remarkably well without compulsion. Finally, although there was no vehicle such as voting or a newspaper for articulating public opinion, the means for collecting individual opinions were diverse and constantly in operation. It was Colbert's preference that no person assume to speak with any authority greater than his own voice. He said, it is "a good thing that each man speak for himself and that no one speaks for all." His intention was to prevent anything that would "give a corporate form to the inhabitants of Canada," but this did not mean an individual might not register requests or grievances which the appropriate agent ought to consider seriously. Thus, the authoritarian government of New France was benevolent because it was paternalistic. A more succinct way of making the same general point is simply to report that in the eighteenth century the government of France usually spent about six times more in the colony than it derived in revenue from indirect taxation upon imports and exports. There is another effective clue to the well-being of the colony in the surprised comment by a new intendant that more children had died in the preceding year by drowning than from any other cause. He did not mean that drownings were unusually high, but that the tremendous infant mortality of old France and of Europe in general was unknown on the St. Lawrence.

Returning to the perspective of the eighteenth-century Englishman, however, the benevolence of a despotism made it no less despicable. It only made the "yoke of tyranny" seem less burdensome. Paternalism can make authoritarianism seem humanitarian, but this was unacceptable because it encouraged lethargy and stagnation. In the 18th and 19th centuries, many Englishmen and Americans were quite smug in their general agreement that starvation was nature's way of teaching self-reliance and individual initiative. English critics who denounced New France as despotic would, upon learning of its paternalism, simply change the target of the denunciation. Thus it was with Francis Parkman, a Victorian American, the first writer in English to be fully acquainted with the history of New France. Referring to the benevolence of Louis XIV, Parkman wrote: "Not only did he give money to support parish priests, build churches, and aid the seminary, the Ursulines, the missions, and the hospitals; but he established a fund destined, among other objects, to relieve indigent persons . . . . " This was a terrible mistake in Parkman's view because the state "subsidized nearly every branch of trade and industry, and . . . did for the colonists what they would far better have learned to do for themselves." Under these circumstances, the colonists had no school for learning the virtues of self-reliance, thrift and industry. Population doubled every twenty years, but economic development lagged far behind New England's. Here, for Parkman, was the ultimate proof of the superiority of Anglo-Saxon social values, government, and institutions.

More accurately, of course, this was simply the confirmation of the fundamental differences between New France and New England, or old France and early modern Britain. In the English world, by the last quarter of the 18th century, it was assumed generally that the good of society was served best by leaving each individual as free as possible to pursue his own self-interest. The heavy hand of government, restraining and regulating mankind, was to be removed. "The sovereign is completely discharged" and it is the "invisible hand" of nature that governs details of wages, prices, the pace and direction of development. According to this view, government had only three functions, three simple operations that it pursued with the consent of the governed in a frugal self-denying way. The first was military defense, that is, protection of the society from invasion. The second was justice, protecting innocent individuals from oppression by other individuals. The third was "creating and maintaining certain public works and certain public institutions which," in the words of Adam Smith, whose championing of this viewpoint appeared as *The Wealth of Nations* in 1776, "it can never be for the interest of any individual, or small number of individuals, to erect and maintain, because the profit could never repay the expense . . . . " In other words, a government, for example, might create a fire department if businessmen were not motivated to pool their capital to provide a service to extinguish fires, and if it was demonstrated that such an institution was indispensable to the public good.

In France and New France, by contrast, it was far more common for individuals to assume that government should be active, not passive, because individuals, far from being free and equal, were recipients by birth of positions in an organic community of structured inequality. Consequently, a good king, like a good father, had to intervene continually, in the minutest details, not only to maintain order but even to guarantee a minimum level of prosperity. In other words, absolutism found its justification in its ability to administer a pattern of social relationships based on status, whereas the English alternative, the "system of natural liberty," found its justification in its ability to promote progress in the sense of economic development.

Which goal is more desirable? Those who prefer size-growth of an economy will be forever troubled by the comparatively unimpressive economic development of New France. They will have to say absolutism rather than climate or geography failed, because New England, which was nearly as impossible by climate and geography, was a libertarian success-story. Those who prefer human values to property rights, on the other hand, will forever defend the statism of New France and denounce the New Englanders because, although they were more successful in economic development, they will argue that Yankees were greedy materialists, obsessive-compulsive in attitudes toward work, and extraordinarily litigious toward one another; in all, a society that had lost its soul in gearing everything to the mad pursuit of wealth. Those who prefer human development to material progress will point forever to New France for the availability of its justice, the balance of its authorities, the *joie de vivre* of its citizenry and the adventure of its clandestine economy, all of which will now be discussed. Thus, the problem is not determining whether New France was paternalistic or comparatively stunted in economic development. The problem is assessing the significance of these facts.

II. The Administration of Justice

Perhaps nothing illustrates better the day-to-day significance of paternalism in Colbert's planned society than the administration of justice. In England and colonial America, justice, like fire extinguishing, was dispensed in accordance with principles of the free market rather than according to notions of *noblesse oblige*. Under the Anglo-Saxon adversary system, competing lawyers were hired to tell a story in an open court and a panel of jurors decided which agent performed more credibly. Justice therefore depended upon three variables: money as competent lawyers who knew their law and had the rhetorical skills to do good service with that knowledge were expensive; the competence of the jurors as this panel decided between the conflicting accounts presented; and the judge, who controlled the presentation of evidence and summed up the conflicting stories. Under this model, justice could be painfully slow and even more painfully expensive. But in New France, justice depended upon one variable only; the competence of the judges charged with dispensing it.

Under the inquisitional system of New France, there were no lawyers and no juries, and the accused man was considered guilty until he proved himself innocent. To facilitate the story-telling, torture was permitted but this was unusual. In fact, there were less than twenty such instances of this "extraordinary questioning" in the whole history of New France. Furthermore, torture did not always spell conviction, because nearly one third of the accused persons questioned under duress established their innocence. But this was up to the judges to decide. It was they who heard the accused man's testimony and that of his accusers or defenders. They heard them all individually and in private. Consequently, no one contributing evidence for or against was exactly sure of the other witnesses' testimony. When the judges thought they had heard enough to come to a decision, they rendered the verdict and sentenced at once. The penalties were arbitrary, that is, at the judge's discretion. If conviction meant execution, this was carried out quickly, frequently on the same day as the verdict. Sometimes, in accordance with the custom in Europe and to create an especially strong example the condemned person would suffer the severance of his right hand just before hanging. After the sentence was carried out, again for the assumed deterrent value, a victim's head and hands might be displayed in public as a reminder of the fate of convicted robbers, rapists, and murderers.

Since the inquisitional system depended so much upon the discretion of individual judges it could be regarded as government of men rather than the rule of law. Clearly, the system was vulnerable on this account—it was only as good as the officials who made it work. But judgeships were not for sale as in France itself. Furthermore, the judicial system was subject to the continual scrutiny of the intendant, who in all instances save one, Bigot, the last, were competent civil servants who filled their positions with intelligence and integrity. Then, too, there was a liberal right of appeal. There was a hierarchy of officials through whom a case might be appealed, even to the intendant himself.

From the ghoulish cruelty of the punishments imposed by inquisitional justice, the system could be open to criticism from the standpoint of its brutality. Accused persons who were tortured or condemned persons who had their hands severed just prior to their execution by hanging would certainly have agreed that the judicial system dispensed retribution, that is revenge, rather than relief for victims and rehabilitation for offenders. Yet this criticism applied to any system in which punishment was regarded as the most appropriate response to social deviancy. Thus, in eighteenth-century England, for instance, theft was a problem and hanging or transportation, which in many cases was equivalent to the death sentence, was the solution.

What was unusual about the administration of justice in New France was how swiftly and impartially it seems to have been dispensed. Despite the lack of lawyers and trial by jury what was lost was primarily the expensive court costs and lawyers' fees. What was gained was swift, inexpensive justice for all. The evidence for this alleged superiority of the inquisitional system over the adversary system employed at the same time in England and the British colonies is varied. Close examination of the record of a small but random assortment of criminal cases tends to substantiate the claim of swiftness and impartiality. The low rate of capital convictions (only sixty-seven executions for the whole period of one-hundred years) might confirm a low incidence of the capital offenses, robbery, rape and murder, rather than the superiority of the system; but since busy judicial officers were not ordinarily busy condemning felons, the inference which follows most easily is that they were vastly more occupied in the dispensation of distributive rather than retributive justice.

Still, it might be argued that less than one person per year was executed in New France because officials were simply so lax in enforcing obedience. Nothing could be further from the case. Obedience to authority, complete and consistent, was always expected and demanded. The government of human affairs extended into the minutest details, even to the hours during which one was permitted to allow one's dogs to roam free, to the standards of quality and prices of merchandise, and to the regulation of children's playing in the streets of Quebec. This was absolutist administration. But it might also be said that the removal of barking dogs in the evening assured a better night's sleep. Regulations covering quality and prices protected consumers. The ban of snowballing in the streets prevented injury to children and pedestrians alike. In short, it might also be said that this close regulation was simply good government.

III.   Competing Authorities in Administration

Vigorous government might have weighed more heavily upon the shoulders of individual citizens had the power of civil administration not been divided by competition between individual administrators, or had the vigorous church authority not operated as an even more tangible competing authority. In the secular realm, the competition was between governor and intendant, ostensibly cooperators, not rivals. But the governor general was invariably chosen from the old military nobility, the *noblesse d'épée*, and the intendant was always an official selected from the new nobility of the civil service, the *noblesse de robe*. There was inherent competition in this dichotomy of social positions; the governor's status was superior to the intendant's, but the inferior noble was the official whose class was on the rise; conflict arising from status anxiety was therefore inevitable. The structure of the administration served to accentuate the tendency. Nominally, the governor was superior to the intendant in authority as well as social rank; he was, after all, the personification of the monarchy. But the intendant exercised more power in his day-to-day management of finance, justice, police and civil administration. He did more than the governor and therefore counted for more. Louis de Buade, Comte de Frontenac, governor of New France from the year of the departure of the first and, perhaps, best intendant, Jean Talon, tried to amend this. From the moment of his arrival, Frontenac attempted to inflate his office with the regal majesty befitting a king's representative. His court became the focal point of the colonial status hierarchy, but this did not alter the fact that the power center was the office of intendant. In a showdown, the governor was supposed to be supreme, but he could not override his intendant's judgements in the areas of his responsibility without showing good cause. This was usually difficult. Therefore the two officials wrangled constantly, with each tattling on the other in reports home to the minister, who replied—just as monotonously—that they ought to learn harmony and good will.

The Crown had not intended to create a system of checks and balances at the pinnacle of colonial society; but this, very nearly, is how the separate offices of governor and intendant related to one another. The problem was that the governor seemed to have status more than power, and the intendant to have more power than majesty. Their relative economic positions were even more anomalous since the richer in money might be the poorer in status. Wealth, power and status are normally congruent, however. In most societies, the wealthiest individuals are also the most powerful and therefore the ones who enjoy the most prestige as well. But in New France, the social pyramid came to an apex at two locations. The governor, as the king's viceroy, enjoyed a higher status than anyone in the colony. This alone was enough for him to command the highest respect of the seigneurial class. Thus, when the governor made his annual progress from Quebec to Montreal it was a matter of high honor among the seigneurs to have him stay on their particular seigneuries, to afford him the ceremony due to his office. But when the *habitants* of that place were instructed to leave whatever they were doing and appear at the manor house in their best clothes, hats in hand, they appeared, but they did so without enthusiasm. In their view, the intendant was the most powerful person in the colony, and such obeisance to the governor was a ceremony that seemed superfluous to say the least.

At the same time, it should be noted that the seigneur-governor and habitant-intendant identifications were neither very clear nor fixed. Both classes and all individuals in the colony could take advantage of the fact that authority was not monolithic in order to appeal, or more effectively to threaten to appeal, to the rival hierarchy whenever the other appeared to act harshly. They could be certain that each hierarchy would be only too happy to take up a complaint, forwarding it if necessary to the common superior, the Minister of the Navy in Paris.

This same principle of competing authority applied to relations between individuals and the church. Here the fate of the tithe sought by Bishop Laval is the clearest illustration of the colonists' winning the freedom they wanted by playing one authority against another. Laval attempted to obtain a tithe for the support of the secular clergy, the parish priests. The original proposal was, as in France, for one thirteenth of the value of the produce of the land. When the colonists objected to the civil authorities that this was outrageously high, the bishop was persuaded to reduce his demand to one twentieth. The colonists objected again. Finally, Bishop Laval had to settle for half his original demand. But the colonists interpreted this tithe as one twenty-sixth of the wheat only rather than of the entire produce of the land. The civil administration sustained them in this interpretation.

This fact of competing authority created degrees of freedom in practice that were never recognized in theory. It was simply what happened in the course of establishing authoritarian government while consciously avoiding the imposition of tyranny. It was merely the fruit of the common-sense recognition that "the Canadians are difficult to govern" and in their governance, finesse was preferable to force. Authoritarian government was thus diluted in the competition. So also was the authoritarian church made less able to pursue its every whim. In New France the Church was privileged and established, of course, but it was not free to establish the theocracy Bishop Laval had intended. It was subsidized by the civil administration and well attended by the colonists, but not recognized as having any coercive power of its own. When it became fashionable for women to wear blouses with plunging necklines the bishop denounced these "scandalous nudities" and ordered the women to change their fashion. They ignored him. When the bishop ordered the priests to withhold the sacraments from all such women until they covered their charms more completely, they appealed to the intendant and the governor to intervene in their behalf. The State responded and the women were saved their fashions. But when the men attempted to launch the customs of bringing their dogs inside the church for Sunday Mass and of getting up and going out for a smoke during the sermon, the State intervened to uphold decorum.

Such disputes were so frequent in the eighteenth century that they draw attention to the clarity of the dynamics of competing authority. As much as this, they also point to the importance of another theme: the unusually keen status consciousness in New France.

IV.   Status Consciousness

Traditional societies were, by modern North-American standards, very status conscious; that is, their people—even those low in the social hierarchy—were concerned with their individual prestige in ways that seem far more intense than their economic circumstances could justify. This is because the connection between wealth and status today is so direct: no money means no status. But before the age of mass conspicuous consumption, individual prestige was not so closely related to wealth. In traditional society, social position was free in the sense that it was supposed to be inherited. If a person survived, he belonged—but at the station of his father. In one sense people were more secure, but, in another sense, near equality within strata meant keen competition for fine gradations of prestige within that rank. Then, too, there was the stimulus of the exceptional case of social mobility. There were those individuals who, most frequently by distinction in war or marriage, gained promotion from one large stratum to the next. With modernization, this social mobility accelerated but the means shifted to ascent by acquisition. Now wealth was more important. In France, as has been shown, the system of inherited status was overlaid by another system of achieved status. At the top of the hierarchy there were two nobilities, the old *noblesse d'épée* and the new *noblesse de robe*. In New France, this tendency was even more pronounced. The new tendency to display whatever status material prosperity made possible extended even to the peasantry.

Legally and technically, the *habitants* of New France were just peasants, mere concession holders, only *censitaires*. But the relatively greater abundance of resources in Canada made them more worthy in practice than they were in law. Consider the circumstances of two farmers, one an *habitant* of New France and the other a French peasant. The Canadien, Jean C., was a typical *habitant* in the sense that he held a concession of average size—it was the usual farm about 150 yards wide and 2,500 yards long. About one quarter of this holding was tillable soil, so the land he farmed was just over twenty acres. He had some livestock, implements, a house, a barn and stables. This farm cost him two bushels of wheat, a live capon and—in 1968 Canadian dollars—about twenty cents per year in rent to his seigneur. Pierre B. a French farmer in Normandy, with roughly the same amount of land, livestock, and building accommodations paid annual rents equal to about six-hundred 1968 Canadian dollars. Furthermore, Pierre B. in France had taxes to pay. Jean C. and his Canadian neighbors were exempt from all direct taxes, except the tithe of one twenty-sixth of the wheat produced, but a person could evade this too by simply not growing any. Relative to their cousins in France, the farmers in the colony lived like privileged gentry.

But in New France status-seeking went further than this greater margin of spending power would suggest. In the colony there was a remarkable tendency to act as though that margin was much more than it actually was. Thus, it was so important for the *habitant* to have the esteem of his neighbors that he would go so far as to run into debt in order to spend freely and make his mark. Because of this additional factor, then, status-seeking in New France went to the modern-day extreme of conspicuous consumption. Thus, one man might button his coat with shell, while another would purchase buttons of sterling silver, cutting back on necessities in order to gain this little increment in prestige. Such spending was a source of continual consternation to officers of the government. The people had a remarkable tendency to feed and house themselves only if their "provision leaves enough to be well clothed; if not, one cuts down on the table in order to be well dressed." Or farmers might have more horses than cattle. These were not usually draft animals. Oxen pulled the plow. More commonly, horsepower was used to pull the calèche or sleigh for social occasions, or carry individuals riding for pleasure. Apparently nearly every young man had his own horse for racing or calling on the unwed beauties of his neighbourhood. Officials could hardly bear the contrast between their social-conscious *bons vivants* on the St. Lawrence and the thrifty protestants of New England. "The English colonist amasses means and makes no superfluous expense; the French," Father Charlevoix complained, "enjoys what he has and often parades what he has not."

Other officials put their complaint even more bluntly. Champigny, an intendant, complained that "The men are all strong and vigorous but have no liking for work; the women love display and are excessively lazy, those of the country districts just as much as the towns' people." Poor but pretentious is the version of the *habitant* that comes through in the testimony of observers who were in a position to report accurately what they saw. The problem is not whether their moral judgement fits, for value judgements are irrelevant. The difficulty is explaining a highly developed status consciousness among people who, by modern standards, were economically in no position to afford it. Relatively comfortable with that little they had, the *habitants* preferred to enjoy their status quo rather than discipline themselves to underconsumption on the expectation of developing a larger estate in the future. The reasons for this preference are varied but not complicated. In the first place, if it is recognized that satisfaction with economic attainment, the decision that *this is enough*, is a function of expectations as much as—perhaps more than—a function of actual income, then it becomes clear that the *habitant*, free of the burden of heavy rent and exempt from taxation, was in fact more like a French *noble* than *paysan*. Here was the social basis for an ethic of consumption rather than production, even though economic realities dictated that this aristocratic ethos would be gratified by simple pleasures. Continual idleness was not possible, but there were five months of winter during which time the *habitant* was relieved from much of the humdrum work of farming and more free to enjoy celebration. This line of analysis only accounts for the origins of status consciousness, however.

The relatively greater abundance of New France does not explain why the colony failed to go beyond status consciousness and passive consumption into career consciousness and active production. That is, in New France, the population remained generally *un*commercial. In New England, on the other hand, the colonists started out like the *habitants* in the sense that they were soon aware that they were materially better off than their cousins in England, but they, despite climate and geography, felt compelled to improve this marginal difference and develop a commercial culture. Perhaps the religious difference accounts for this different motivational response. Maybe there was something about the aloneness of the Protestant individual (the person who was saved by faith alone) that made him into such a compulsive striver. In this view, profit was only the carrot, anxiety was the mighty stick. Each person had to pursue a calling with all his strength because it was only this way, desperately, that one proved oneself worthy for the wrathful, vengeful Judge waiting at the end. Perhaps Catholicism with its curative intermediary, the priest, militated against the discharge of this productive energy for the simple reason that one did not feel so despised and rejected. To feel in touch with salvation, a Catholic had simply to maintain communication through the holy sacraments. Thus, it was worthiness in the sight of man that was troublesome; hence the excruciating status consciousness. This is highly speculative, of course. But the fact remains that surprisingly few colonists in New France seemed to have been motivated to a production work-ethic.

Then, too, there were factors in the structure of the situation that tended to discourage the exceptional few who did try to become the commercial producers Colbert expected as the model French-Canadian. The Jean C. who decided to sell his herd of horses and replace them with cattle, to produce beef for cash, and build up his eighty-acre concession into an expanding cash-crop operation, faced three obstacles to his success. One was the lack of attractive and accessible markets. Ship captains who brought cargoes of manufactured goods from France were not interested in hauling agricultural produce back with them. Anything grown in New France, even before shipping charges, was more expensive in the colony than in the mother country. Sometimes French merchants accepted grain as payment for debts, but the price was always about half of what the Canadian farmer believed it was worth. Sometimes, especially in the later years, ship captains would sail in ballast to the Caribbean islands for sugar as their return cargo to France. It might seem that these vessels would have been a usable transportation link between the St. Lawrence region and a market for their agricultural surplus. But the ships going between the St. Lawrence and the Caribbean were too few and the voyage too hazardous, owing to the hurricane season in the tropics during the months the St. Lawrence was open for navigation. Also, the items most in demand in the West Indies were "refuse" fish as food for the slaves, and white oak as material for making sugar barrels, and the New Englanders provided both at prices that were difficult to beat. Thus, as a market for agricultural produce, the islands of French West Indies were hardly any more attractive or accessible than the markets of the mother country.

Still, the colonists might have gained entry to the home market by doing as the Virginians had done, that is, by producing a staple commodity such as tobacco, which was of high value relative to bulk and therefore able to sustain the high costs of trans-ocean shipping. If not tobacco then perhaps some other staple, such as hemp, could have been the commodity to solve the problem of the market. But then there was another obstacle, another impediment to commercial agriculture that would have frustrated the would-be capitalist farmer. This was the immobility of land, that is, the extreme difficulty of buying and selling holdings in order to consolidate small farms into large commercial operations. The *Coutume de Paris*, the system of precedents and traditions in which the colony was instructed to find its legal moorings, placed a number of brakes upon real estate deals. It imposed a tax, known as a *quint,* that amounted to one fifth of the sum that a person received as his compensation for rights to a seigneury or a concession. (It will be remembered that there was no private property, as such, so it was the title that was sold, not the land itself). Customary law also defined a *retrait lignager* by which any relative of the seller could buy the land back within one year by refunding the sale price. Or, similarly, there was *légitime* by which sales were voided if a lawful heir appeared who claimed the holding as his legitimate inheritance. Clearly these safeguards operated to stabilize land tenure and prevent land speculation. In most of the English colonies there were no such safeguards, although some observed the custom of primogeniture, which functioned vaguely like *légitime*. More characteristic of the English pattern was the province of Connecticut. Here land titles circulated on a great carousel of speculation. Any given piece of land was likely to change hands at least four times in any twenty-year period. In New France, by contrast, there were concessions that did not change hands at all in the sense that they stayed in the same family for generations. If what happened in the parish of St. Famille on the île d'Orléans is any indication of the general pattern in French America, one fourth of the concessions were subdivided for the purpose of accommodating the succeeding generations within the same family. In a sample of more than seventy farms, only ten were absorbed by other concessions between 1670 and 1725. Since consolidation is an indicator of developing commercial agriculture, this is a hint of the small scale on which it occurred and therefore a hint to the relevance of the *quint, retrait lignager,* and *légitime* as obstacles to prevent its occurrence.

Still, a determined producer of a cash crop eager to take his profits and "increase his estate," as the English called the game, could do so, but he would have to be patient. There was also the social stigma of production for its own sake, the apparent meaning of the production work-ethic. Benjamin Franklin in mid-eighteenth century America might rationalize the virtues of thrift and industry as leading to health and wisdom. Certainly, from his autobiographical account, cheerful striving after wealth bought leisure and influence. But in New France, it always seemed more sensible to enjoy today on the chance there might not even be a tomorrow. People worked, of course, but the work ethic in New France was geared to production for consumption, for living "nobly," rather than frugally. Thrift and business were regarded as degrading.

Even if Jean C. ignored his neighbors' whispers behind his back for his plunge into commerce; even if he overcame the marketing difficulties, or the frustrations of consolidating his holdings for economy of scale; even if he were to double his capital every ten years, as certain planters in South Carolina did in the eighteenth century, what would he gain that he did not already have? Here we return to the structure of authority in New France, because here, unlike the English pattern in which status followed power and that came after wealth, power was the monopoly of the king. To be sure, there were small groups of colonists who gathered about the governor for social and economic favors, but there was no assembly, no system for recognizing and rewarding colonial bigwigs by bestowing upon these wealthy entrepreneurs the rights of running the colony because they had demonstrated their ability at gaining economic success. Consequently, no myth of success developed as a dynamic of early French-Canadian society. Comfortable with quite little, and satisfied with what they could appear to be, the *habitants* of New France developed status consciousness rather than capitalism.

V.   Easy Money

French-Canadian status consciousness sustained the anomaly of great ostentation and small wealth. This was true even of the top echelon of society, the seigneurial class. They held the highest rank and displayed the greatest ostentation, but as seigneurs, they were quite poor. The revenues from tenants were far too low to support them in elite style. How, then, did they maintain that style which led one military officer newly arrived in the colony around 1750 to exclaim that "Quebec is more full of pageantry than is the court of France"? The answer is the fur trade. It was by their connections with the governor that they gained licenses to trade at the western posts. But this is not to suggest that they controlled this economy, only that they received the furs, and sold them to merchants based in La Rochelle or Bordeaux. The prices paid were usually enough to maintain local notables, but only if they spent their cash as fast as they received it, and even this practice was sometimes not enough. Aubert de la Chesnaye, for example, was active in the fur trade and accumulated more seigneuries than anyone in Canada ever did. But when he died, he was so heavily in debt that his holdings were divided among creditors, merchants in France.

In New France the fur trade expanded, maintaining its primacy in the economy. In 1739 at the high point of state-subsidized economic diversification (fisheries, shipbuilding, iron production and naval stores), the value of fur was still 70 percent of the total exports. But the fur-economy did not develop. The size of the hinterland increased enormously but the hinterland-metropolitan relationship did not change. The trade continued to be dominated by families of merchants with their base in La Rochelle and Bordeaux. In the colony itself there was no indigenous commercial class. When the exceptional Canadian appeared to gain entry to this monopoly he found his enterprise was usually shortlived. As he lacked connections and experience, he tended to fall victim to the tendency in his society toward excessive consumption of working capital.

The use of the fur trade, the mainstay of the economy in New France, as a provider of status rather than of capitalist accumulation was not restricted to the seigneurs or would-be merchants. For if there were no *bougeois gentils-hommes* in New France, there were no *bourgeois paysans* either. Just as the seigneurial elite participated in the fur trade for the *gloire* it sustained, so also did the *habitant*. The main sequence in the life of the ordinary colonist may have been to establish himself on a concession, find a wife, and start his family. For the next few years he would clear more land and then, with his first children old enough to run the farm and feed the stock, he and a friend, perhaps unmarried and still in his teens, would acquire a canoe load of trade goods. Together they would venture out to the area of the Great Lakes, thus participating clandestinely in the fur trade as *coureurs de bois*. Then, tired of adventure, both could return home again once more to farm, the younger man beginning his family. Both would have gained a little money and the esteem of having been to places beyond the rapids. Thus, the lure of the fur trade was more than economic, more than the attractions of the Indian way of life, and more than a desire to escape the tedium of regulated existence in the settlements on the St. Lawrence. Here, too, the reward was primarily status, the prestige one gained as a person who had ventured west, despite the dangers and rules against trading without a license.

Thus, French Canada before the conquest was a world of broad horizons. Its economy was a scene of constantly expanding adventure in the fur trade rather than the pursuit of profits. And, although there was no legislative assembly or trial by jury, social justice was guaranteed by a plethora of competing authorities. Its history was not impressive for its economic development, but this land of harsh climate, this Siberia of the New World, sustained a tolerably good life for its colonists, and the social existence was even better. New France was not the economic success story of the New World, but for the merchants in La Rochelle to whom it was a base for the fur trade, the land was no less precious than was New England for the New Englanders. By 1750, there had been invented in North America two cultures; each was a new nation in its own right. Yet both were provinces of empires and quite content to continue as such for the indefinite future. But for both, a conflict of empires was soon to bring changes neither expected nor desired.

PART TWO

Britain in
Place of France

CHAPTER FOUR

Imperial Adjustments and Colonial Reactions

I. Conflict of Empires

Two inventions had inspired the migration of Frenchmen to North America. One, the fur rush, was economic. The other, the vision of a New France, was a social and religious ideal. The first entailed a kind of frontier that was far flung and ever expanding as it followed new sources of supply always further west and north. The second invention called for a mode of settlement that was less a moving frontier and more a recreation of the metropolis itself within the limits defined by the arable land along the St. Lawrence River and to some extent on the Bay of Fundy in Acadia. In this way, the history of the French presence in North America to 1760 was divided: the quest for fur led to claims of continental proportions; the advance of settlement was confined primarily to one river valley.

Division entailed a fatal weakness that Colbert had foreseen as early as the 1660s. He appreciated that the economics of the fur trade dictated continual expansion, but he foresaw a time when France would be claiming the heart of the continent by virtue of the alliances between a few fur traders and the Indian nations. But while the fur frontier could claim the territory, it would not be able to maintain that claim as only settlement could. In Colbert's opinion, it was wiser to restrict the colony to effectively occupied territory than to embrace indefensible claims to the whole continent. In his words, if "too vast an area" were claimed, "one would perhaps one day be obliged to abandon a part with some reduction of the prestige of His Majesty and state."

Perceiving the dual character of, if not the conflict between, the fur trade and settlement, Colbert preferred to reduce the fur rush and develop the settlement on the St. Lawrence by diversifying its economy. He preferred a compact colony with an economic future in agriculture, lumbering, ship-building, and the fisheries to a settlement that was a mere adjunct of the beaver bonanza and certain to lead France into future embarrassment by expanding into far more territory than French numbers could effectively defend.

From the first, however, Colbert's compact colony policy was frustrated. Although he instituted a system of limited licenses, every year more trad-ers ventured out without them. Furthermore, these *coureurs de bois* were encouraged by the officials in the colony, sometimes even by the governor and intendant themselves. By 1700, the result was communication with an enormous hinterland, an empire built on fur rather than by settlement. Its influence extended as far north as Hudson Bay, west to the Saskatchewan River, and south through the Mississippi Valley all the way to the Gulf of Mexico. This was an imperial presence through control of the Indians by trading alliance, not occupation by Frenchmen tilling the soil. Even the food for the handful of persons at the few posts in the hinterland was usu-ally brought in from the St. Lawrence region rather than produced on the spot.

Officially, the metropolis opposed this expansion; but the lure of profits and imaginative interpretation of the regulations sustained it nevertheless. Then, after 1700, there arose a new motive to claim the continent, a reason not only to establish ever-widening trading alliances with the native peo-ples, but to fortify their land at strategic points with Frenchmen as well. The king of Spain died in 1700 and left his empire to the grandson of Louis XIV. The potential power that this conferred upon the Bourbons was frightening to Europe, especially to a maritime power like Britain, which feared the colonial and trading challenge of a combined French-Spanish empire. Accordingly, in 1702, Britain joined the war against Louis XIV to maintain the balance of power. And the French king, in his turn, decided to fortify his holdings bordering on the British in North America. Thus, if Louis XIV emerged the victor, he would dominate all of Europe and most of the Western Hemisphere. Should the war go badly, North American holdings could be used as sacrificial pawns to divert the enemy from more valuable holdings in Europe or the Caribbean. Eleven years later, sacrifice was demanded. Defeated in the Old World and the New (Acadia, for instance, had been seized by the British in 1710), the French negotiated a settlement. By the Treaty of Utrecht, 1713, France made sweeping conces-sions to the British. For the first time Louis XIV promised to recognize the legitimacy of the Protestant succession in England. More important, French territory was also conceded, virtually all of it in North America. Louis XIV gave up Hudson Bay, Acadia, Newfoundland, and the fur lands south of the Great Lakes.

The year 1713 thus marked a turning point in the history of New France. The effect of the Treaty of Utrecht was to pose limits on French expansion that were more real and binding than any previous royal edict. Henceforth, the growth of New France seemed bounded by two long river corridors, the St. Lawrence and the Mississippi. The French traders were deprived, apparently, of the rich fur reserve draining into Hudson Bay, and the *habitants* lost the security of the approaches to the St. Lawrence by British occupation of Newfoundland and Acadia.

From 1713 on, the history of the colony focused on resistance as officials concentrated their efforts to nullify the effects of the Treaty of Utrecht. They built a chain of posts from the western shores of Lake Superior through the Lake of the Woods and Lake Winnipeg to the Saskatchewan River in order to intercept the trade in furs that was supplying the British trading posts on Hudson Bay. Similarly, a chain of posts was built in the upper Mississippi region to protect the commercial flank in the southwest; and, to compensate for the loss of Acadia and Newfoundland, Cape Breton Island was fortified by the building of Louisbourg. In the St. Lawrence Valley itself, the intendant, Gilles Hocquart, resurrected the old economic program of state-sponsored immigration and diversification of the economy. Almost 2000 settlers (most of them soldiers) were recruited for service and subsequent retirement in the colonies. New industries, in particular shipyards and ironworks, were established in Quebec and at Trois Rivières. In short, from 1713, New France prepared for war with the British, a war to decide whether the future of the northern half of the continent would be merged with that of the British colonies or continue on a separate course.

Nearly thirty years of preparation seemed justified when war resumed between the two mother countries in 1741. Although none of the fighting touched the St. Lawrence Valley, Louisbourg, the fortress on Cape Breton Island, was taken in 1745 by an expedition of New Englanders under the command of the governor of Massachusetts. By the Treaty of Aix-la-Chapelle in 1748, the stronghold was returned to France. But this peace could not be final. The British had not tested the new defenses at Quebec and Montreal, and until they had done so, they would never accept the fact of a French presence in the north. Every year after 1748, war seemed ready to resume. In 1755, the British deported more than 5000 Acadians, French settlers in what was now Nova Scotia, because they thought they posed a potential threat in the war that was now beginning afresh.

The mood in New France was not hopeless. Although the population of the St. Lawrence area was only about 60 000 people in 1750, far less than one tenth of the British non-slave population to the south, there was a basis for a measure of self-assurance on the French side. They had a well-organized militia and, more important, regular troops from the mother country were stationed at strategic points. The command was unified and ties with the allied native peoples were close. In the British colonies, by contrast, the militia was poorly organized, and there were few British regulars in America or manned fortifications on the frontiers. Command was divided colony by colony and working alliances with the Indians were almost non-existent. Thus, a better accounting of numbers on the two sides would be the population of any one British colony against the whole of New France rather than that of all British colonies together. Division was so rife on the British side that the colonists could not even agree in principle on a common plan for defense. The one conference convened by the mother country to discuss the problem in 1754 ended at Albany in bickering and recrimination.

In the meantime, open conflict had developed in the Ohio Valley to determine whether the territory was a French fur reserve or land open to British land speculators and farmers. As the war expanded, it was the might of British seapower rather than the numerical superiority of the Anglo-Americans that was the key to eventual conquest. In fact, in the early years of fighting, from 1754 to 1756, the Americans were told to defend themselves and everything went in favor of the French. Defeat followed humiliating defeat, and these fortunes did not begin to turn until the war came under energetic coordination of the British prime minister, William Pitt the Elder, after 1757. British regulars were now sent to North America, and the navy was used to bottle up the French fleet in home ports. By this strategy of blockade, Louisbourg fell in 1758, and Quebec fell to Wolfe's seaborne force the following year. The conquest of the remainder of the region took another twelve months; even then, the American phase of this, the Seven Years War (1756-1763), ended three years before the fighting elsewhere. It was not until 1763 that the conquest was recognized by the Peace of Paris, in which the French used North American holdings once again, as in 1713, as a sacrificial pawn. But in this round of concession they sacrificed the whole region of the St. Lawrence without regret. In fact, the leading French intellectual of the day, Voltaire, was rather pleased with the outcome. It seemed to him that the war had gone so badly for his country that the French might have been expected to give up something more valuable, such as the sugar islands in the Caribbean. But in negotiation all they lost, in his phrase, were a "few acres of snow." Still, with this loss, Colbert's dream of a New France in America also vanished, forever.

II.   Consequences of Conquest

The British acquisition of New France was something of an accident in the fortunes of war and the diplomacy of peace. But the change itself was monumental in the legal sense that the people of a whole colony ceased to be French and were reduced at once merely to *canadiens*—just residents of a place known as Canada, which the British insisted upon renaming Quebec. Still, the change of names and monarchs was relatively easy for most people to adjust to, and only about three percent of the population preferred to leave the colony rather than swear allegiance to the new king. Thus, the soon-to-be Bishop Briand was not fighting a contrary current of opinion when he told his countrymen that the British were "our masters" and ought to receive "what we owed the French when they ruled." But the succession of monarchies and change of names were the easy changes; there were others in the shift of mother countries that had much broader social and institutional implications. After all, conquest implied subjugation and social reorganization. But did either tendency follow in fact? These issues, more than two centuries later, are still far from resolved. The only report that can be made here is to suggest a range of possibilities confined to two levels: one is on the level of individual reorientation and the other is the official, more political changes that were intended or foiled.

Obviously, on the individual level, social consequences are the more difficult to study as well as more controversial to interpret. For instance, it may be that the Conquest marked a turning point in the history of the people due to the emigration "home" of the "Canadians of the upper class who refused to submit." This would be particularly important if the 97 percent of the people who were left behind were forced into a pattern of a child-like "subordination" as Michel Brunet, the leading spokesman for this "social decapitation" hypothesis has asserted. But, at another extreme, Jean Hamelin has denied that any such decapitation occurred with the emigrations between 1760 and 1764. He has argued that this out-migration was "merely the repetition of a recurrent phenomenon" since opportunists had always been coming into the colony "to enrich themselves and return . . . . The evil existed from the beginning . . . . " In Hamelin's view, the *canadien* elite had always been transient rather than closely integrated into the larger society of New France.

One fundamental assumption both points of view reflect, however, is the apparent agreement that there is an important link between social character and leadership; and, if that is broken by the loss of a society's *natural* leaders, the society as a whole loses impetus and pride. Or, to make the point another way, the followers of Brunet or Hamelin both seem to assume that the leaders of any society are important psychological projections of the people as a social organism. Their primary disagreement is over who, if anyone, filled that need in New France before 1760. Brunet imagined that there was a French-Canadian commercial class who were the "natural leaders" and "would have grown and would have played a more important role" in the history of the *canadien* nation had they not been displaced by the British; Hamelin asserted that the pre-Conquest elite was not *canadien* nor were there any other leaders who expressed the ethos of their society better. New France itself was locked into an "anemic collective survival."

But since there are many indicators that the traditional character of New France was aristocratic, consumption oriented and status conscious at all levels of social hierarchy, it is perhaps a mistake to place too much importance on those colonists or transients who did business in the colony. It is possible that future research will establish that the local militia captains were far more important as the "natural leaders." Interestingly, Michel Brunet himself has observed that "the militia captains continued to exercise their former functions . . . . " Here was a point of continuity, for good or ill, that may have been far more significant than the loss of the three percent of the people who emigrated. Still the debate continues.

The significance of the transition from French to British rule at the official and institutional level is more clear, and thus less controversial. There is general agreement among historians that the military governors—Haldimand, Murray, and Carleton—were relatively humane in their supervision of the transition from French to British rule. Not the least of their accomplishments in this regard was a pragmatic attitude toward the imperial plan for Quebec's place in the empire. The first instinct of the policy makers was to assimilate the *canadiens*. The Royal Proclamation of 1763 made it plain that such a program was intended in religion and law. Also, the seigneurial system of land distribution was to be discouraged by offering freehold, thus making the way open for an influx of English settlers. To make this development the more sure, British soldiers who retired in America were invited to immigrate and take up free land for agriculture. As soon as enough of these freeholders arrived to warrant their due importance, the governor was to call a general assembly of their representatives "to make, constitute, and ordain Laws . . . agreeable to the laws of England." Thus by stages, Quebec, along with Spanish Florida and the other recent acquisitions, would truly become a British colony. Eventually the *canadiens* were supposed to become English colonists in their own right—even their Catholic Church would be incorporated into the Church of England.

Such a design never materialized. In this failure, another policy, that of the continuation of absolutism, emerged by default. The shift from institutional transformation to a continuation of the existing system is explained by the failure of private soldiers and officers to come north to claim their land in sufficient numbers. Since the English part of the population did not increase according to plan, James Murray, the governor at the time, did not call an assembly. Instead he governed with the assistance of an appointed council consisting primarily of seigneurs and Catholic clergy. Here was absolutism rather than freehold democracy. Murray even gave his backing to the establishment of Jean Briand as a Roman Catholic bishop, a position to which Briand was consecrated in 1766. Thus, under Murray, the administration of Quebec was even more absolutist than in the years of the French regime. The supreme authority then had been shared by at least two officials, the intendant and the governor.

The irony of a continuing absolutism did not end with the departure of Murray in 1765. His successor, Guy Carleton, went further in preserving Quebec as Murray had left it. Carleton soon came to know the province as a colony that was accustomed to government from the top. More particularly, he saw the *habitants* as peasants who were naturally deferential toward their superiors, the seigneurs and the clergy. Here was "perfect subordination" too valuable to throw away. In 1769, Carleton therefore recommended statutory recognition of Quebec's institutional and social life as he imagined it had always been. The clergy and the *canadien* squire-archy of the province cooperated in this project of institutionalizing the seigneurial system since they saw their opportunity to gain more influence than they had exercised previously. At first, British officials balked at the proposal. But then came the threat of open rebellion in the colonies to the south. In 1774, by the Quebec Act, the seigneurial system was confirmed, the Church regained its tithe, French civil law was recognized, and authoritarian government was endorsed by dropping any reference to representative institutions for the present or the future. Naturally, the ascendant clergy and seigneurs were pleased.

Criticism of the Quebec Act in Canada came from another source. There was a small but significant group in the province that felt the retreat from anglicization was a betrayal of promises made between 1760 and 1763. This was the English-speaking mercantile community of Montreal, which had begun to replace the French traders with the change of mother countries. Since 1760 these opportunists had been arriving in Quebec to enter into trade or speculate in land. But from the first, their influence was disproportionately higher than their numbers. They were not farmers or frontiersmen, but profiteers with connections in London who arrived to draw the promise of the northern economy into their own pockets. As a social group these merchants were self-assertive and purposeful; soon they were the most outspoken of any segment of the population of the province. By 1770 they numbered about one hundred and fifty, but their behavior betrayed an expectation that government and society existed to serve their private ends.

From the beginning of British rule, they showed themselves critical of it. Their animosity in these early years was not against the French. Indeed, they established close relations with the French, whose cooperation they needed in the fur trade, especially their skills as *voyageurs*. The elite of the fur trade sealed this working arrangement not only in the *camaraderie* of the Beaver Club but also by taking French-Canadian wives—as did McTavish, McGill, and Frobisher. For the moment, their animosity was directed against British policy and British governors.

To begin with, they opposed the provisions of the Royal Proclamation, which discouraged the fur trade; more particularly, they objected to the licensing system and to the stipulation that trading could only occur at designated posts. They criticized Murray for not relaxing these rules. Since he had used discretionary power to avoid calling an assembly, why could he not use discretionary authority in this case? For two years the affairs of the colony were frozen in a power struggle between the governor, allied with the clergy and the squirearchy, on the one side, and the merchants, unassisted, on the other. The traders emerged victorious. They appealed to the mother country on the twin grounds of constitutionalism and mercantilism. They had a right, they claimed, to an assembly, and London had an interest in expanding trade. Governor Murray was recalled.

The new governor in 1766 at first seemed the true champion of the merchants' cause. Carleton vigorously supported their wish to see the trade restrictions relaxed. In 1768 control of the fur trade was transferred to the colony. The handicaps that previously had given an advantage to traders operating out of Albany, New York, or Hudson Bay, were now removed, and the competitive edge was, as in the days before the Conquest, with Montreal. Soon merchants in New York were conceding as much by moving to Quebec; it was a movement that increased as the American Rebellion came closer, and those merchants who wanted to retain their metropolitan connections looked to their future.

For reasons of trade, the merchant interest in Quebec also found a basis to tolerate the Quebec Act, despite its provisions for authoritarian government. The statute that recognized Murray and Carleton's absolutism by decreeing that government was to be appointed by council rather than by elected representatives also formally restored the pre-Proclamation boundaries. But like greedy children, the businessmen wanted everything their own way. They still found much to criticize in Carleton and in the regime he personified, since he allied himself more closely with the seigneurs and the clergy than with them. Above all, he continually refused the merchants an assembly, which they expected to dominate (since they alone had experience with representative government), and they alone, as the Protestants in an empire that denied the vote to Catholics, would have the vote. But these were reasons for discontent, not rebellion. It was otherwise with other English colonists to the south.

III. Consequences of Reform

The rationale for Britain's empire, as for that of France, was the same mercantilism that has already been described in connection with Richelieu's reorganization of New France in 1627. Mercantilism, a system of closed commerce with mother country and colonies bound together by a tight network of navigation laws to keep trade out of the hands of foreigners, used tariffs as a major mechanism of control. Thus, in the eighteenth century, New England distillers of rum were allowed to import their raw product, molasses, duty free from the British West Indies; but if they chose to import from the French West Indies a tariff of sixpence a gallon, considered prohibitively high, had to be paid. But if tariffs were useful in shaping trading patterns, they were also useful in raising revenue. After 1763, when Britain was pinched economically due to the burden of war debt, it seemed reasonable to expect that the yields of the North American customs should pay the cost for administration of the mercantilist bureaucracy. But here the expectations of British politicians were dashed.

By and large, the colonists in North America had accepted the mercantilist framework and acquiesced in their allotted place in the system. That is, the acts of trade were obeyed tolerably well without compulsion because, usually, it was in the colonists' economic self-interest to sell their raw materials and buy their manufactures in accordance with the law. By 1760 the British empire was very much in fact what it was supposed to be in theory. The colonists enriched the mother country, and the rate of return to themselves was high enough that, in material terms, the ordinary people were better off in America than their counterparts in England.

But to this general pattern there were exceptions. The colonists jibed when it came to paying the taxes on molasses and tea, and they smuggled both with impunity. Earlier governments had been able to ignore these evasions, preferring to let sleeping dogs lie. But by 1763 the government of George Grenville could not afford to be so lax. In 1764 he confronted Parliament with the astonishing fact that over the years the average cost of maintaining the American custom service was £8 000. The average annual collection was £2 000. To remedy this state of affairs Grenville brought in the Sugar Act, by which the tax on molasses was halved and its enforcement made much more strict. However reasonable this measure seemed to Grenville and Parliament it caused resentment in America, for, as it was pointed out in Britain itself, "to execute [the laws] afresh made them have the appearance of new laws."

Within a year, resentment increased to a frenzy of opposition as Americans protested Grenville's next reform, a suggestion that the colonial assemblies provide revenue to pay for an army that was now needed to police the frontier separating the old colonies from the *canadiens* and Indians. With the acquisition of Quebec, British North America had become a mixture of diverse—and antagonistic—ethnic groups. In addition to the Protestant-Catholic tension exacerbated by the inclusion of the people in the St. Lawrence region, the inclusion of the fur-trading frontier sharpened the antagonism between farmer-settlers and those who wished to keep the west as a fur reserve. This conflict widened into one between Indians and whites in 1763, when native peoples south of the Great Lakes united in Pontiac's Conspiracy to halt the threat of advancing settlement from the east. The difficulty and expense of suppressing this rebellion dramatized the need for keeping the three populations of North America separate, and for arming the boundary between them at strategic points. It was the cost of stationing British regulars that became Grenville's first concern. Now, the North American deficit could be expected to rise to about £300 000 per year.

Grenville warned that if the Americans failed to devise acceptable means for "defraying the expenses of defending, protecting and securing" the expanded empire on their own, he would impose a form of colonial sales tax after one year. When the colonists failed to comply, Grenville brought in the Stamp Act of 1765. After November 1, all licenses, land titles, private contracts, bills of lading, almanacs, and newspapers were required to carry a revenue stamp. This tax would not generate a large revenue, only about £60 000 a year, but it would establish the principle that the cost of colonial administration was a responsibility of the colonists themselves rather than of the mother country. At the time, the million-and-a-half inhabitants of North America were virtually free of tax, whereas the eight million people of Britain were laboring under huge national debt, so huge that merely to service it cost almost one hundred times the yield of the proposed Stamp Act each year. It seemed, therefore, a reasonable beginning; as Charles Townshend, soon to be chancellor of the Exchequer, asked, "Will they grudge to contribute their mite to relieve us from the heavy weight of that burden which we lie under?" It seemed especially sensible to anyone who paused to consider that a large amount of the debt had been incurred by fighting a war in which the Americans were the chief beneficiaries.

IV. Rebellion

Events immediately showed, however, that to the colonists such a scheme was not so reasonable. From the first, in all the colonies from New Hampshire to Georgia, the tax was a nullity. Riots and organized opposition prevented the law's implementation from Boston, Massachusetts, to Charleston, South Carolina. The Stamp Act was nullified for the very simple reason that no one was permitted to fill the office of stamp master. Without stamps, there was no tax. This was not all. The colonists demanded repeal, enforcing their demand with vigilante groups to coerce merchants into cancelling orders of goods from Britain until Parliament changed its mind about taxing the self-governing colonies of British America. Finally they succeeded. In the spring of 1766 the hated tax was repealed. However, at the same time that it was admitted to be inexpedient in practice, the law was affirmed to be fully legitimate in theory by another measure, the Declaratory Act, passed right after the Stamp Act's demise.

Here the American question might have remained—for generations, perhaps. But the new chancellor of the Exchequer, Charles Townshend, reopened it one year later with a scheme the colonists had to accept. He pointed out that they objected to the Stamp Act because they claimed it was beyond the jurisdiction of the British Parliament. The colonists maintained that only the legislatures to which they elected representatives had the power to tax them, and they reconciled this view of the constitution with continued membership in the empire by drawing a distinction between internal and external taxation. An internal tax was a levy upon property by a local legislature elected by the taxpayers to defray the cost of government in its limited business of providing security for liberty and property. External taxes were tariffs that generated a revenue incidentally, but were imposed by the imperial legislature primarily to regulate trade in the imperial interest. Townshend regarded the distinction as utterly false since it seemed to him that Parliament's power extended, in the words of the Declaratory Act, to all areas whatsoever. Still, to demonstrate his leadership, as well as to establish the supremacy of Great Britain over the colonies, he proposed some external taxes, import duties, for the purpose of generating American revenue. In May of 1767 taxes were imposed on tea, paper, glass and paint pigments. Once again the colonists from New Hampshire to Georgia complained bitterly. Once again they organized a boycott.

With the death of Charles Townshend in 1767 and after several other changes of government, the new ministry of Lord North decided to repeal the Townshend program in the spring of 1770. By then it was clearly no more than a continuing source of discontent in the relations between the colonies and mother country. Lord North preferred to drop the American question and get on with more important matters in the nation's business. Therefore, on April 12, 1770, Parliament repealed the hated Townshend duties, all but the small tax on tea, which was retained to save something of the principle of parliamentary supremacy. The important point was North's obvious acceptance of the probability that colonial administration was always going to be run at a deficit. Never again would Parliament attempt anything like a Stamp Act or the Townshend duties. Great Britain would continue to be satisfied with the mercantilist advantages derived from an overseas empire. There would be no attempt to generate imperial tribute, particularly if the colonists denounced it as such.

Ironically, this concession was a disappointment to many of the colonists who had grown accustomed to expecting the worst from British ministries since 1764. The escalation of this resentment, an almost paranoid pessimism, is the major significance of the American Revolution as it pertains to Canada because the colonists who were most afraid were the ones who called themselves Patriots. It was they who distinctively affirmed that the British constitution was safe only in America because at home, in England, public virtue had been corrupted by private greed and false principles. Effeminacy, luxury, and sin were rampant there, especially in the circles of government where wicked men pursued public business for private gain. In Great Britain, the constitution was out of balance. The king, lords, and commons were not independent of one another and so were no longer in a position to check one another's tendency to tyranny; they were increasingly united in one vast conspiracy for personal aggrandizement, with the arch-conspirators going under the name of *king's ministers*. Now Lord North, the king's first minister, had withdrawn the Townshend scheme, and the True Patriots were not pleased. Their disappointment was two-sided. On the one hand, the ministry's retreat was interpreted as a strategic withdrawal to plot subtler means of subverting American liberty. On the other, the retreat had a more personal significance. In all the leading urban areas of America, in Boston, New York, Philadelphia and in Charleston, obscure political hacks, such as Sam Adams of Boston, had achieved public renown and personal success for the first time in their lives by denouncing, from the moment of the Stamp Act, the threat of British tyranny. No new dish of outrage from Britain meant lean days. As the months passed into years, the stature of politicians whose popularity depended upon British tyranny diminished progressively. They knew there was a ministerial plot to subvert American liberty. They despaired for their colonies and themselves. Their influence faded inexorably.

Then in 1773 Parliament passed a law with American implications. In the course of regulating the affairs of the East India Company, the House of Commons legislated some provisions that would make legitimately-imported British tea cheaper, and therefore competitive with that smuggled into the colonies from Holland. Ardent Patriots like Sam Adams interpreted cheap tea as the means of seducing the Sons of Liberty into paying the tea-tax remnant of the Townshend scheme. Thus, the ministry had paused for three years "not to repent their evil deeds, but rather to collect themselves, and devise some measures more effectual. For so far from giving over the execrable design, the plan of oppression is renewed." Adams and the others decided to "venture upon a desperate remedy" to prevent the tea from being landed. On December 16, 1773, one hundred and fifty Sons of Liberty, disguised as Indians, boarded three ships in Boston harbor and "in a very little time," according to Sam Adams, "every one of the teas ... was immersed in the bay, without the least injury to private property."

Of course the East India Company regarded their tea as of some value; in fact, by their accounting, £10 000 of private property had been destroyed wantonly and in public view. In the weeks that followed, tea parties occurred elsewhere. There was even a second one in Boston and the ministry decided to make an example of Massachusetts. A bill to close the port until Boston's town meeting voted restitution to the Company passed the British House of Commons without division on March 25, 1774. Although the innocent as well as the guilty would suffer thereby, the innocent shared responsibility, in North's view, because they failed to act on their own to punish vandals acting under the guise of patriotism. This was not all. Three other bills were passed to ensure that the first would not be nullified. The Port Bill shut down Boston's commerce, and the other measures suspended the constitution and brought the province of Massachusetts under martial law, until order was restored.

The rest of the thirteen colonies that had spawned protest movements since 1764 viewed Lord North's program of coercion as the Intolerable Acts. To them the Quebec Act, which passed Parliament at the same time as the "Coercive Acts" was widely regarded as the model of government intended eventually for every colony. Consequently, the twelve protesting colonies except Georgia sent delegates to Philadelphia in September, 1774. There they agreed to make common cause. The delegates drafted a Bill of Rights in which George Grenville, Charles Townshend, and Lord North were characterized as vultures picking over the carcass of a dying empire, rather than as administrators who intended no ill but found themselves in a difficult constitutional situation nonetheless. Finally, the Congress approved yet another boycott upon British imports until Parliament relented. Then they agreed to meet again in May, 1775, "unless the redress of grievances, which we have desired, be obtained before that time." When they reconvened, it was to plan war. By April, skirmishing occurred between colonists and British regular troops just outside Boston. Thus the rebellion began, more than a year before the colonies declared their independence. The fighting lasted nearly a decade. Then, weary of the contest and divided at home, Great Britain agreed in 1783 to recognize the united colonies as independent states.

V.   Loyalism—Situational and Personal

Of course, not everyone, perhaps not even a majority of the colonists in America, welcomed independence. Nor was it a majority of the colonies that seceded from the British empire. By 1763 there were nearly thirty distinct provinces that together made up the English possessions in the Western Hemisphere. They varied from the sugar islands of the West Indies to the fur-trading territories on Hudson Bay. Only thirteen joined the rebellion. The others remained aloof, either passively neutral, unreceptive to American requests to join, or else actively hostile to the rebels' attempts to force acquiescence. Then, too, there were many persons resident in the rebellious provinces who actively opposed separatism, even though they were hopelessly outnumbered. In Virginia, for instance, the Loyalists were probably less than ten percent of the population. Still, here and there in the other twelve rebellious colonies there were partisans who were well aware of the Patriots' justification for rebellion but who refused to foreswear their allegiance to the British king. Thus, there were two kinds of loyalism. One phenomenon was the loyalism of whole provinces; the other was the loyalty of individuals resident in colonies that did rebel. The first loyalism was quiet and situational; the other was tumultuous, painfully personal, and frequently ended in persecution or exile.

Consider particular cases. There was no independence movement in the British West Indies, for instance. Here is the most conspicuous example of situational loyalty. The islands produced but one product, sugar, and it was produced by slave labor. Soil exhaustion determined that the cost of West Indian sugar exceeded the world price. As a matter of course, the owners of the land and slaves had requested and received a protected market in the British empire. Thus mercantilism, metropolitan economic policy, guaranteed their profits. The plantation owners were more than deferential to the mother country, and most of them actually lived there. They, the West India lobby, were one of the most powerful interest groups pressuring Parliament. They were more influential than the North American interest; they were nearly equal to the East India lobby. Abolition of slavery would have occurred to them sooner than rebellion against the authority of Great Britain.

The newly arrived businessmen in Quebec were loyal for much the same reason. They were interested in realizing maximum profits from the northern fur trade. Thus, economic interest isolated them from the Thirteen Colonies as much as similar motives made an independence movement unthinkable in the West Indies. As for the *canadiens*, it has already been shown that the clergy and squirearchy had more to gain from British than American affiliation, since the Patriots expressed real hostility to any idea of established religion and hereditary aristocracy. The British did not. But this contrast should have operated as a powerful incentive to make the *habitants* join the American army that invaded Quebec over the winter of 1775-1776. In some areas, such as the upper Richelieu River Valley—where profiteers had moved in as seigneurs and had begun to exploit feudal dues with unprecedented ruthlessness—they did. But elsewhere the overwhelming majority knew the Americans as enemies rather than as liberators, and remained aloof accordingly. They did not rally to the Americans or to the British, but were neutral.

The same combination of situational factors led to neutrality in Nova Scotia, St. John's—later renamed Prince Edward—Island and Newfoundland. In the last example, the colony was a fishing station; in fact, the bulk of Newfoundlanders maintained permanent residences in Great Britain since settlement on the island was prohibited. The prohibition notwithstanding, there were more than 10 000 permanent residents on the eastern tip of the island between Trinity and Placentia bays. Their orientation was completely eastward to Britain. It never occurred to them to join the rebellion.

Similarly, on St. John's Island, the population was small, only numbering about one thousand in 1776. It was recently arrived from the British Isles as settlement had not begun until 1765; therefore, the orientation was still completely toward the metropolis. These recent immigrants had no desire to jeopardize their stake to the rich soil on which they had just settled. Even if the issues of the dispute reached these settlers, the people had a greater desire to build on their dream of security and prosperity in the New World than to choose ephemeral political issues agitated in other colonies by persons none of them knew.

Similar isolation operated in Nova Scotia, but this case was complicated by the fact that half of the population had recently arrived from New England. Some definitely leaned in the direction of their rebellious cousins, but since so much of the rest of the population was British-born, and since nearly everyone had settled within one generation, society and politics had not yet crystallized. To the extent that this conflict was a source of anxiety, the psychological energy generated was discharged in religious revival fostered by Henry Alline rather than in political slogan shouting. Then, too, it might be mentioned that, then as now, Halifax was a naval base, and besides the economic hold this had upon the hinterland, the daily presence of British warships most certainly served as a sober reinforcement of the already firm British orientation of these early Nova Scotians.

Loyalty in these areas was therefore a function of the configuration of circumstances. These provinces were Loyalist because any other position was simply unthinkable. The loyalism in the colonies from New Hampshire to Georgia was different. Following the tide there meant joining the Revolution, reluctantly perhaps, but still this was the best way to safeguard one's life and property from the mob.

From New Hampshire to Georgia loyalism was a risky option. From the outbreak of fighting in 1775, but especially after Britain's recognition of American independence in 1783, Loyalists found themselves expelled from their homes. The wealthy ones could afford to move to Great Britain; but the vast majority were of the "middle sort," and these had to find their refuge in what remained of British North America. The great bulk of them sailed from New York to the Atlantic region of British North America. A few went to Newfoundland, a few to St. John's Island, but most—about 25 000—moved to Nova Scotia. There they settled for the most part in the western portion, and existed quite apart from the Nova Scotians, whom they looked down upon for their having been but lukewarm in support of Britain in the late war. Not surprisingly, the Loyalist newcomers on the western shore of the Bay of Fundy were accomodated in the establishment of a new province, New Brunswick. The imperial authorities were happy to go along with this wish for independent organization, for they believed that small separate colonies were preferable to single large ones; a policy of divide and rule might prevent another war of independence. It was this policy that accounted for the fact that barely populated Cape Breton was raised to the dignity of a separate colony at this time, a status that it kept until 1820, when the island was reunited with Nova Scotia.

But in one case the settlement of the Loyalists was not simple at all. Some 10 000 chose to go to Quebec, where they expected to find the kind of environment that they had known in their previous homes; that is, freehold land tenure, English laws, a Protestant establishment, and representative government. All were lacking in Quebec. Here was a potential clash of cultures that obliged the British legislators to amend the Quebec Act, which they did by the Constitutional Act of 1791. At the same time, Quebec was divided into two distinct provinces; an upriver portion west of Montreal known as Upper Canada, and the downriver part to the east, the old Quebec, now called Lower Canada.

The western portion had received the greater part of the Loyalist newcomers because it was relatively empty. There were no seigneuries, only mile after mile of unoccupied waterfront on Lake Ontario inviting newcomers to carve out farms. After 1791, they made the transition to provincial status with the same relative ease as the Loyalists in New Brunswick. An elected assembly was set up; English civil and criminal law was to be used; the established religion was to be the Anglican. Perhaps most important to the Loyalist mind, land was to be freehold, so that it could be bought and sold easily and surely.

The eastern portion of Quebec presented a much more difficult problem. Even after the Loyalist in-migration the population was still overwhelmingly *canadien*. Nevertheless, the British colonial form of government was granted for the benefit of the newcomers. In addition, land lying outside the seigneuries was to be held as freehold but the existing seigneurial system was retained. Civil law continued to be French. The Catholic Church maintained its privileged position. Thus, although there were some important changes designed to accomodate the English-speaking newcomers, in several ways the distinctive French character of the province was maintained. In other words, the Constitutional Act of 1791 provided a legal framework for two societies in one state. But since it soon became clear that *canadiens* were at a disadvantage in using the foreigners' mode of government, representative government was at first only the instrument of subordinating the majority. Here was the basis for conquest culture, for the coexistence of superior and inferior ways of life.

In the first years after the fall of Quebec in 1760, the mass of the population could have felt but slight humiliation. To the ordinary inhabitants who retained their possessions, continued to make their customary living, spoke their familiar language, obeyed the old laws, and maintained the traditional religion, the slight British presence before 1783 can have been no more unsettling than an abrupt change of administration. Common people did not feel conquered until their way of life was submerged under a set of parallel institutions established for the benefit of the incoming minority. This is what happened after 1783. The British, crucially strengthened in numbers and attitude, felt themselves to be in possession of everything substantial. The French were left with everything the British regarded as ephemeral. Now, clearly, there was a dualism of superior-inferior.

It is more difficult to assess the significance of Loyalist migrations to other colonies, to the areas on the Bay of Fundy, and west of the Ottawa River. Here the Loyalists could set up the kind of society they knew, almost by themselves. What kind of provinces were these? The problem has been finding an appropriate synonym for loyalism. *Loyalist* is not sufficient, by itself; it only denotes the position chosen, not the reasons for taking it. Nor have the labels from the right-left political continuum been particularly instructive, since there is so little evidence that Loyalist migrants were significantly less *liberal* or notably more *conservative* than the relatives they left behind in the republic. Liberalism and conservatism were not even current concepts then. It may be that the opposing sides are more comprehensible from the perspective of temperament rather than from the standpoint of ideology. Individuals had to decide whether Parliament was behaving stupidly or tyrannically. To be a Patriot, in the American sense, one had to be ready to believe that there was a plot to enslave the colonies. Then it was only "common sense" to deduce at the time of the Intolerable Acts, with Josiah Quincy, that "Britons are our oppressors: WE ARE SLAVES." But anyone who had been unable to see intentional tyranny in the Stamp Act would be likely to regard the Patriots' deduction as "enthusiastic." The Loyalist was inclined to see himself as an isolated sceptic in a world gone mad. Thus, Peter Oliver thought that if the leaders of the revolt had "told their deluded Followers that an Army of 30 000 Men were crossing the Atlantic in Egg shells, with a Design to roast the Inhabitants alive and eat them afterwards, the People would have first stared, and swallowed down the tale, whole."

It was "enthusiasm," the crazy willingness to believe anything, especially if it was conspiratorial, that the Loyalists denounced. They were the sceptics of the revolution. They did not believe Parliament aimed to enslave America. They did not have faith in American pretensions—rampant after 1775—that the United States, on a republican course, would be a better, freer England. This scepticism is what made the Loyalists un-American, the opinion that led to their expulsion.

There was nothing in this viewpoint that was incompatible with the attitudes of the English-speaking colonists already in Canada; the immediate and perhaps long-term impact of their arrival outside the settled portions of Quebec was simply to reinforce the British hold on the regions to which they fled. But in the case of Quebec their migration had the more profound significance that has already been mentioned: after 1783 the *canadiens* continued to be the numerically superior group, but with the establishment of parallel British institutions the majority of the population began to be treated as exceptional and minor. Here was the Conquest that was more tangible than the military occupation, and a change in the affairs of the *canadiens* that was more revolutionary than the American Revolution had been for either the Americans or the Loyalists.

CHAPTER FIVE

Expansion

I. Old Staples

At the conclusion of the American Revolution, the British peace negotiators might have been expected to insist upon a border between their possessions and those of the United States that would reflect the existing limit of effective American occupation: the Appalachian Mountains. But at the negotiations, the diplomats representing Great Britain showed themselves to be more interested in appeasing the late enemy than in defending the claim that made the most historical and legal sense. American settlement had not yet penetrated the Ohio and Mississippi valleys, and, by the treaty negotiations ending the Seven Years War, the British had fallen heir to the French claim to the area. But the other interest prevailed and the United States boundary was drawn through the Great Lakes. Thus, the old Canadian southwest was lost.

Montreal fur traders adjusted by expanding their operations into the region north and west of Lake Superior. To faciliate the enormously long lines of supply that this required, an association of Montreal partners was formed, calling itself the North West Company. Through the employment of technological innovations such as the steel trap, and organizational novelty such as the idea of the wintering partner (employees in the hinterland who received rapid promotion and a large share of the profits), these "Montreal Pedlars" built a successful transcontinental trading system. By 1800 the North West Company was garnering more than four times the amount of fur collected by the Hudson's Bay Company and all other Canadian rivals combined.

At the same time, farmers in the Canadas enjoyed a large measure of prosperity from the export of grain to the British market, a fact that was particularly important in Lower Canada. Here, rather than spending their profits in the approved American manner of expanding their base of production, the *canadiens* spent their income as consumers. One taste that was indulged with nearly unbridled enthusiasm was education. Prospering fathers sent their sons to college, thus financing the family's entrance into one of the learned professions of medicine or law.

Here were economic and social tendencies that deepened the lines of conquest culture. Not only were there dual institutions: representative government, freehold land tenure, Protestant religion for the English; political quiescence, seigneurial system, and Catholicism for the French. There was also a duality of life expectations: commercial agriculture, trade and dominance for the English; consumer farming, the professions, and acquiescence for the French. Yet, this pattern of duality was not initially denounced.

Along with prosperity, there was a second factor that sustained *canadien* quiescence. The other reinforcement was the French Revolution. By 1792, the upheaval in France had given rise to a regime that was militantly exporting republicanism and anticlericalism, to the horror of the clergy and seigneurs of New France. Both groups responded by transferring allegiance from a France that was rapidly disappearing to the British institutions that were just then arriving. The Church and the French-Canadian squirearchy heaped mountains of praise upon Great Britain for the leadership that country provided in the counterrevolution. As England emerged as the refuge and the fortress of European conservatism, a wave of Anglomania broke out in Lower Canada, with the Catholic clergy in particular assuming responsibility for maintaining a sort of permanent witch hunt to eradicate what few signs of sympathy there were for the French Revolution among the *canadiens*.

Given the enjoyment of prosperity and revulsion at the French Revolution, there was more cause for indifference than for activism among the mass of the citizenry during the first years of representative government in Lower Canada. This, and the other reason of simple unfamiliarity with the new institutions, enabled the English minority to dominate public affairs without an outcry of protest. They had only sixteen of the fifty seats in the Assembly, but they were the one self-conscious group whose private interests could be articulated easily in terms to suggest a public purpose. Thus, representative government worked to the advantage of the English despite their minority position. *Canadiens* did not challenge their predominance in the control of provincial affairs for another decade.

After 1800, the province began to experience a period of profound economic dislocation. One reason was declining agriculture. In part this was due to methods that resulted in the soil being mined rather than worked. It was common practice, for instance, for the farmers to pile the winter's accumulation of manure on the ice of the St. Lawrence River rather than spreading it over the fields each spring. Also, the agricultural depression was attributable to the pressure of increasing population, which meant the already diminishing surplus would be more in demand for local consumption. But another factor in the dislocation of the economy was a dwindling participation of the *canadiens* in the fur trade, since the exploitable fur was becoming relatively more accessible to traders from Hudson Bay, to the detriment of the North West Company.

Of course, these changes affected the Montreal English-speaking elite as much as the *canadiens*. The major alternatives to the fur trade now had to be developed and this meant increasing emphasis was placed upon land speculation and forwarding Upper-Canadian and American grain to Britain. Land speculation was especially attractive. In fact, this enterprise had been moderately promising since the arrival of the Loyalists, because the newcomers were farmers in large part and they wanted land in freehold. This meant that the brisk market in acreage, which had been such a conspicuous aspect of the English colonies from the beginning of their settlement, now began in Canada as well. But the land the merchants bought first was purely speculative because the Crown was the primary land-settlement promoter between 1783 and 1792. The people to be settled in these years were displaced persons, the refugees from the American Revolution, rewarded by a grateful mother country. Every Loyalist was provided with land free of charge. Everyone received the implements necessary for farming; and each was guaranteed subsistance for up to three years from his arrival. But these extraordinary gifts were not continued for long.

After 1791, the Americans who emigrated to Canada, swore loyalty to the king and received only land, were less likely to be motivated to leave the United States by political reasons. It was also hoped by land speculators such as John Richardson that they would be less likely to take what the Crown offered free, and instead purchase retail the land such as he and his friends acquired wholesale. They would not charge a great deal for the privilege of settling on land more strategically located than were the Crown reserves. But then how much did one need to ask for land which was acquired for less than one penny an acre?

Here it might be wondered how the Crown could be a land settlement agency, dealing directly with immigrants for "wasteland" and indirectly through speculators in the more desirable acreage. The answer is that no such pattern was ever intended. Technically, land speculation was illegal. No individual could purchase more acreage than he was likely to use, no one could buy land for the sole purpose of selling it in the future. No individual could claim more than 1 200 acres of crown land for his own freehold. Speculators such as Richardson evaded the law, however, by promoting deals through a system of so-called leaders and associates. The leader, that is the speculator, would obtain a vast tract of land for the payment of survey and registration fees, ostensibly because he represented a group of settlers, the associates, who were either non-existent or individuals giving their names for a price and too poor to care how the land was used. The real associates were recruited, one by one, as they became purchasers of the land the Richardsons of Canada had received virtually free.

The relationship of leader and associate did not end with the cash transfer when the settler bought his farm. Since the big speculators were also the established merchants, they found it expedient to plant branch stores wherever settlement proceeded. Having sold pioneers their land, they now provided them with the calicoes, broadaxes, and other necessities of pioneering. The terms of credit were fairly generous and longstanding. The merchants awaited the farmer's first cash crop, potash from the ashes of the settlers' felled trees. In time, the other marketable crops of grain, saltbeef, and pork would follow. The mercantile firms centered in Montreal and branching out into the expanding agricultural frontier were the farmers' access to the markets of the world. The settlers, in turn, were the consumers of imported goods shipped into the hinterland by those same businessmen.

To facilitate this commerce, the English-speaking elite proposed a program of modernization and internal improvements. They aimed to make Lower Canada more commercial and to link it more closely with the relatively more dynamic economic development of Upper Canada and the United States. More particularly, they sought the dissolution of the seigneurial system as a first step toward the development of capitalist agriculture in Lower Canada. They wanted roads and canals linking the lower St. Lawrence with the American and British Great Lakes region. The merchants also wanted financial institutions as well as the public purse to provide support to advance their scheme of development. But the businessmen's program also involved social change, changes as radical as abolition of the seigneuries. They wanted to shift the burden of taxation, for instance, from commerce to agriculture, that is, from excise taxes to land taxes, and they wanted modernization of legal procedures as well as land tenures.

The merchants' program of modernization could also be interpreted as a plan to move Lower Canada from a conquest culture to a monoculture, to eradicate all the many dualisms and make everything uniformly British. The British saw nothing sinister about assimilation. In their view, the reward for giving up the traditional culture would be greater opportunity, the full participation in the enterprise of social ascent by economic acquisition. How could anyone oppose this?

Young *canadien* professionals, mostly lawyers, had increased in numbers due to the prosperity of the 1790s. But now in the distorted and less prosperous economy of the new century, there were more *canadien* lawyers than the population or circumstances could support in the manner that the newcomers expected. Consequently, the young lawyers constituted a kind of intellectual proletariat, and just as they began to sour in the disappointment of their interrupted expectations, the English-speaking elite of the province launched their program. It was the young *canadien* lawyers who rose as spokesmen for the majority to oppose it.

The opposition had a different definition of the problem. While conceding that conquest culture was not appropriate for the future, the new spokesmen for "the people" believed that the commercialism advocated by the "transient" English merchants was not for the general good, but to advance a few private interests. The real impediment to social happiness was a failure to recognize the culture of the majority as the one that ought to determine the shape of administration. The problem as they saw it was the governor's failure to heed the true spokesmen for the people. The British continued to govern Lower Canada as if the majority did not count and as if they deserved no better fate than subordination.

Between 1805 and 1810 the English and *canadien* parties wrangled over this question, the issue of the future destiny of Lower Canada: was the province to be commercial and British, or traditionally—yet democratically—*canadien*? The year 1805 marked the beginning of the open conflict when the Assembly approved a bill to build jails at Quebec and Montreal, but refused to shift the cost away from commerce by imposing a land tax to pay for them. The same Assembly also refused to enact legislation for the gradual abolition of the seigneurial system. The business elite, which dominated the legislative and executive councils, took these actions as an open assault upon commerce and progress. They urged the governor to exercise his veto. When they failed in this, they took their case to the imperial authorities and failed there as well.

Meanwhile, the British party thundered denunciations of the French Canadians publicly and in private. At a dinner to honor the valiant English minority in the Assembly, a toast was offered "To Our Representatives in the Provincial Parliament who proposed a Constitutional and proper mode of Taxation for the building of Goals and who opposed a Tax on Commerce for that purpose as contrary to the sound practice of the Parent State." Then came another toast more like a prayer: "May the Commercial Interest of this Province have its due influence in the administration of its Government." After these proceedings were reported with emotional embellishment in the English press, the French-Canadian-dominated Assembly called the editors to the house to apologize for the libels they had printed, and the battle was on.

Ultimately after this, and later episodes of conflict along the same lines, the outcome was on the side of the English party; by 1854 they had won nearly everything they had demanded in the way of banks, canals, and institutional changes such as universal freehold land tenure. Thus, they achieved their added security for profits from land, grain and imports. But even in the long-term, these were not as great as the money that had been made in the fur trade. Nor were the new lines of enterprise as profitable as the "gambling trade" in timber, the staple that almost immediately dwarfed fur and everything else in its importance. It is to the meteoric rise of this trade that the rest of this chapter must turn.

II. The Timber Rush

The reason the timber industry rose so quickly and on such an enormous scale was war. In 1807 Napoleon blocked Britain's access to the timber in northern Europe. Naturally, the British government looked to Canada as an alternate supplier, and found the stock more than ample. In 1800, importations of wood from the colonies had been negligible. In 1808 they were impressive. By 1810 they were large enough to be regarded as the chief determinant of prosperity in the two Canadas and New Brunswick. For the next thirty years, wood, by itself, consistently accounted for more than half the total value of all exports from British North America.

The crisis of 1807 was the immediate cause for the beginning of this new industry, but the long-term factor that sustained the Canadian timber trade was a heavy tariff imposed upon the Baltic product, a tax that was occasioned by the Napoleonic wars but continued long after they were over. In part, the duty was simply to gain more revenue, but it was also to encourage British merchants to obtain their wood in Canada. The tax on foreign wood was increased by stages to more than 100 percent by 1815, but colonial timber was never taxed. So long as the tax on Baltic timber amounted to more than its whole value, conditions were exceedingly favorable for Canada to maintain itself as Great Britain's woodyard. The colonial commodity could bear the higher cost of transportation and return a handsome profit. To be sure, this made timber about twice as expensive in England as it would have been otherwise. Still, the shippers and dealers wanted their excessive profits to continue, and this led them to exert every pressure imaginable on Parliament in order to maintain the tariff long after it had served its purpose of meeting the crisis brought on by Napoleon.

Perhaps because of the remarkable profits to be made, the trade itself made great headway soon after the first tariff increases were imposed. The naval contractors who were accustomed to buying wholesale in the Baltic sent agents to Quebec City and Saint John, New Brunswick, to set up branch offices there. Originally they simply purchased whatever timber the local people provided. Within three years, however, they underwrote the cutting operations themselves to guarantee the supply they predicted they could sell in England. In this way, the British buyers were assured cheap and continuing sources.

Canadian businessmen never moved into this middleman role of the lumbering business to any large extent. They preferred to sink their capital into investments that would always return something; freehold land, for instance, never vanished. But timber, usually carried on the oldest, least seaworthy vessels, failed to reach its destination so frequently that it was an uninsurable cargo. But, even if wood had been transported in more reliable vessels, unlikely from an economic standpoint since timber was of so little value relative to bulk, there was still the difficulty of predicting the market. The metropolitan market seemed as unpredictable as the Atlantic Ocean. Thus Canadian businessmen regarded the timber trade as suitable for no one but a merchant with great backing, capable of absorbing heavy losses. They described timber as essentially a "gambling" trade, difficult for people to enter unless they were terribly foolhardy or very lucky. It was not until the 1830s that any colonial firms appeared. Then, of necessity, there would be a branch office in Liverpool or Glasgow. In time, the branch would grow into the main trunk of the operation and another metropolitan business would emerge. Only the origins of the relatively new company would differentiate it from the other, older firms.

The risks of timber marketing that dampened Canadian enthusiasm to enter the business were real, but too frequently they were exaggerated. While timber dealing was inherently speculative it was a very stable kind of speculation. The stability of the roll of firms engaged in the trade attests to this fact. Some two dozen firms were among the first. These same companies continued to operate until the timber was "done", or until economics attracted them elsewhere—back to the Baltic area, for instance, once the imperial preference dried up between 1840 and 1860. The greatest real barrier to Canadian entry was psychological, a handicap of nerve. Given the choice of investments they believed to be secure, although small in return, and those they feared as reckless, with illusory large profits, they preferred the security of transatlantic marketing of staples with which they were already familiar. Thus, they speculated in land, or marketed grain or fur; and the fortunes made by timber middlemen were usually acquired by Englishmen and spent in England. This is the important point to which it will be necessary to return later: although timber dwarfed every other aspect of the Canadian economy, the entrepreneurial role was played usually by foreigners, not Canadians. In this staple trade, and throughout the period of its dominance from 1810 to 1840, the Canadians were quite literally the hewers of wood and the drawers of water.

III.   Lumbering as a Primitive Technology

The lumber the English merchants would buy were either hand-hewn timbers or precisely-cut planks no thinner than three inches. Since the sawn product required precise milling and was still vulnerable to warping in transit, the dominant export was square timber. Canadians could produce marketable timbers in the woods with hand tools, and no matter what this wood went over or through on its course to Quebec or Saint John it would still be as salable as when it was squared where it fell.

In the period between 1800 and 1840 the proportion of planks exported continually declined. Square timber increased every year. This predominance of the squared log as the unit of production meant that the logging that occurred was incredibly wasteful. In the forests of New Brunswick and the Ottawa River Valley only about one tenth of the trees were good for square timber, but nearly everything else was ravaged in the process of felling and squaring these largest of the red and white pines.

An outline of the actual cutting and squaring operations will make clear why this was so. The smaller trees in the path of the large pines had themselves to be felled, and arranged so as to provide a bed for the falling giants. And then, once the selected pine had been brought down, it had to be examined for any sign of rot that had previously escaped notice; the slightest discoloration of the heartwood would disqualify any tree that seemed otherwise superior. Rejects were abandoned where they fell. The sound at heart were squared prior to removal. First they were topped and limbed, and then a workman called a *liner* whisked the bark from two sides and drew lines to indicate the size of the finished timber. Another worker, the *scorer*, would then use his axe to cut a row of notches to the line about every three feet. The first squaring began when he split away the slabs of wood between notches, working as close as possible to the line. Finally came the *hewer* with his broadaxe, hewing right to the line and no further. A skilled workman could swing the twelve-inch blade of his broadaxe with the deftness of an artist and make a side so square and smooth it would appear to have been worked with a plane. When he finished his last stroke of the second side, the half-completed timber would be rolled ninety degrees and the same sequence of lining, scoring and hewing would be repeated to finish the stick of wood perhaps one or two feet thick on each side.

Some idea can now be gained of the waste involved in the timber trade. A gang of six men working through the winter could produce nearly six hundred timbers. But to obtain this amount of exportable lumber they had to lay waste a forest. To make matters worse, the dead trees, and the slabs and chips produced in squaring, provided tinder for forest fires; in the summer, when the loggers had left the woods, the lightning storms would spark fires among the slash littering the ground, and destruction would be complete.

In the meantime, the lumbermen would have rafted their exportable timber to market. With the coming of spring, and high water in the rivers, they turned their attention to the construction of rafts, monumental works of axemanship. The idea was to join the whole winter's work into one body to be rowed and sailed to market. An average size St. Lawrence timber raft actually covered about the same area as a modern football field. In fact three-hundred feet was a mediocre length. Obviously rafts of this size were far too unwieldy to run the small rivers draining the areas where timber was cut. In the first miles of their transit to market, the logs might be borne by streams so narrow that rafting was impossible, and then the lumber would have to be floated down as individual sticks. But as soon as water volume permitted, the timbers were gathered into *cribs* or *drams*. It was these units that made up the rafts, even the very largest, so they had to be built with ingenuity and craftsmanship, otherwise the raft would disintegrate in the first rapids and a winter's work would scatter in the great river like so many snowflakes.

A St. Lawrence dram was a frame of timbers defining a rectangle about ten yards wide and thirty long. The frame went over a layer of side-by-side timbers covering the area defined by the frame. A second layer of timber rode on top. In part, it was simply the weight of the top layer and the buoyancy of the bottom that held it all together. Of course the frame was pegged. But protection against the rapids was guaranteed by lashing the whole assembly together with *withes*, a kind of cable made from twisting saplings the thickness of a man's thumb. Ten of these drams, each containing about four hundred timbers and lashed to the end of another, made a St. Lawrence raft. They were one of the most common sights of early nineteenth-century Canada, whether the observer was looking at the Saint John, Ottawa, or St. Lawrence rivers. They were also the largest manmade structures of the day. As remarkable as their size and bulk was the incredible fact was that they were entirely without metal components. As these enormous craft heaved and groaned through the rapids of Canada's largest rivers, the half-dozen men at the oars and sails had great reason for pride in what they had accomplished themselves—by hand.

It may be that the timber trade provided "an occupation which was picturesque and romantic," but for the most part the timber trade was simply back-breaking manual labor of the most primitive kind. The organization of the timber trade, at least in its North American aspect of procuring the actual timbers, was wasteful, short-sighted and, quite simply, primitive. Nineteenth-century lumbering was more like an ancient mining operation than modern manufacturing. The evidence for this has already been shown in the description of the cutting; it is also evident in a description of the lumbermen when they were not wrecking the forests. The season of hard isolation ended when they tied up their rafts in the coves of the timber merchants in Saint John or Quebec. They stepped on shore as men who had lived months in the bush without amenities or the company of women. Ordinarily they worked in the woods from September through June and usually when they were paid they received their year's wages in one lump payment. July and August were months of unbelievable roistering wherever the raftsmen gathered. It was during these weeks that the raftsmen spent their pay in a whirl of drinking and wenching. "Anything short of murder may be committed with impunity; and even murder has been allowed to pass comparatively unnoticed . . ." This is how one newspaper editor described the woodsmen after their release from spartan celibacy with ten-months' pay in gold to spend, and spend it they usually did. When they were penniless and exhausted, the lumbermen would then return to the bush, with only some gaudy new clothes, including perhaps a top hat and umbrella, to show for their previous year's labor. Of course there were some lumbermen who "made timber" as a means of acquiring the cash to buy themselves farms or starts in business, but they were the exceptions. Normally, the lumbermen were men without property or future. Their impact on society then, according to critics of the trade, was to reinforce a feckless, easy-come-easy-go outlook. They were kind of proletariat, exploiting themselves as much as the forests they ravaged.

IV.   The Timber Staple and Industrialization

The suggestion that workers in the timber trade normally labored ten months for nothing more than a two-month spree implies that they worked hard without advancement. This point applies even more broadly, beyond the individuals who worked in the woods, to British North America as a whole. In fact, it is not unreasonable to suggest that the trade in hand-hewn square timber, the dominent staple between 1810 and 1840, was an economic bonanza but no mode of development. In a colony such as New Brunswick, seventeen out of every twenty residents may have been directly dependent upon trade by 1810, but in New Brunswick and elsewhere the timber trade was not a staple trade organized or pursued in a way to encourage economic growth and change.

In one respect, this was an unvarying dynamic of modern colonization. All the new societies launched by Europeans migrating to new lands began by producing exportable staples. Under the condition of initial settlement the newcomers invariably exploited some commodity—gold, tobacco, fur, timber—that was readily available in their new land and in heavy demand at home. A marketable staple insured the growth of the colony, and colonies became nations as they invested the profits from their staple trades in the development of intricate industrial structures. But in the colonies of the nineteenth century, which grew into the underdeveloped countries of the twentieth, development did not take place since the profits from the staple were siphoned away from the hinterland, or invested to increase the production of the raw material rather than to industrialize. All European colonies began as nothing more than supply bases. Some still are.

To the extent that the timber trade dominated the economy of British North America, so also did it retard industrialization. The evidence is fairly clear that the bulk of the profits went to British shippers and timber importers, such firms as Pollock, Gilmour and Company based in Glasgow. To be sure, there were colonists who managed the gangs of laborers who did the actual cutting and rafting of the wood. They amassed considerable personal fortunes, but relative to the amount of money that was generated in the overall wrecking of the pineries of the Canadas and New Brunswick, these were merely the crumbs of a harvest feast.

Not only did comparatively few of the profits fall to Canadian producers, but those Canadians who made their money in the production of square timber were disinclined to invest their capital in anything other than more of the same. They might have invested in sawmills and exported sawn lumber, but their market connections were entirely British before 1840, and to these agents lumber was not wood if it was not hand-hewn timber. Colonists learned this lesson early and bitterly. In 1806 Philemon Wright, for example, experimented with a scheme for sawing logs into inchboards and scantlings to sell for export. That year Wright spent over a month rafting a winter's work of sawn lumber from Ottawa to Quebec, but when he arrived at his destination he could not find a buyer. He returned to producing square timbers and to the task of making their supply more cheap and efficient, building slides around waterfalls for instance. Thus, the dynamics of the timber trade militated against the rise of Canadian industries using logs as a raw material in manufacturing for export. Like the fur trade, the new staple held its predominance but did not develop the economy. To repeat the earlier analogy, it was a kind of mining operation, recklessly depleting the natural bounty and leaving only a desert behind. Occasionally a contemporary witness took note of this tendency. One such observer was Peter Fisher, the first historian of New Brunswick. He published a scathing critique of the wastefulness of the timber trade in 1825. The point of his writing was to warn his fellow colonists that the trade which generated "great riches" was not yielding any improvement of the colony. On the contrary:

"The persons principally engaged in shipping the timber have been strangers who have taken no interest in the welfare of the country; but have merely occupied a spot to make what they could in the shortest possible time. Some have done well, and others have had to quit the trade; but whether they won or lost, the capital of the country has been wasted, and no improvement of any consequence made to compensate for it, or to secure a source of trade when the lumber shall fail. Instead of seeing towns built, farms improved and the country cleared and stocked with the reasonable returns of so great a trade; the forests are stripped and nothing left in prospect, but the gloomy apprehension when the timber is gone, of sinking into insignificance and poverty."

Fisher was a contemporary critic who said the timber trade was even inimical to agriculture. This was a point usually missed by his contemporaries and frequently even by later historians. Occasionally the myth is still perpetuated in the suggestion that the timber cutters "opened frontiers" for settlement by accomplishing some of the drudgery of pioneering by clearing trees in advance of the settlers' arrival. Actually this rarely happened. Most of the pineries were on land that was poorly suited to farming, either because the soil was too rocky or too sandy. But if the timber cutters did happen to work through potentially fertile farmland, what they left was an enormous amount of inflammable litter, not half-cleared land that invited conversion into family farms. In this sense, the timber cutters ruined arable land as well as the rest. But the adverse effects of lumbering upon agriculture did not end here. The apparently insatiable demand of timber cutters for labor and the good wages for winter work drew countless thousands of young men from the farms every autumn, but did not release them in time for planting the following spring. Still, the wages of timber making were more attractive than farming. Lumbering expanded, commercial agriculture went into relative decline.

The growth of the timber trade at the expense of agricultural development might have been a harmless, even beneficial, trade-off if the industry had been organized in other hands. But the sad fact was that by concentrating the profits in the firms of foreigners, Canada was capital poor throughout the period that timber making was the predominent enterprise. Consequently, population grew, the volume and value of exports increased, but the pace of overall development was slow, frustrated at every turn by a lack of investment capital available in Canada. Nothing illustrated this better than the difficulties involved in launching Canada's transportation revolution. Since the 1790s there was an awareness of a need to make the St. Lawrence navigable by ship to the Great Lakes. This meant canals around a half-dozen cataracts in the St. Lawrence and around the falls on the Niagara, but there was always too little money; thus, the capital had to be recruited in England. The system the Canadians needed was eventually built, but the capital that had to be imported to build those canals later was not available in Canada earlier because it had been exported in the form of hand-hewn timbers. The profits, according to one official who should have known, went to "partners in English or Scotch houses who generally returned home to enjoy the fruits of their labor."

It is probably too much to say categorically that the timber trade was an unmitigated disaster in the development of British North America. But it is reasonable to suggest its benefits were more ephemeral than tangible. The historian who wishes to celebrate the timber trade, will sum it up as "picturesque and romantic in itself," and useful because lumbering "gave to this country a technique of broadaxe and raft that has permanently enriched its cultural heritage." In this way, A. R. M. Lower and Michael Cross have seen lumbering as "one of the fountainheads of Canadian civilization." Perhaps the *joie de vivre* it engendered overbalances the waste that attended the enterprise from 1810 to 1840. But when the industry was launched in 1807, no one debated its pros or cons. In that early year, the new trade developing by leaps seemed unambiguously good. Not the least of its benefits was the production of a vital commodity for the British market, then in death struggle with Napoleon. Canadians received good wages. They helped Great Britain in a distant but desperate war. Soon that war would embroil British North America as well. In this context, sober reflection upon the long-term developmental implications of the timber trade was unthinkable, let alone debatable.

CHAPTER SIX

War Returns to British North America

I. Mr. Madison's War

As the last two chapters have shown, the wars in which Britain had been engaged since 1793 had had their impact upon British North America, but that impact had been indirect and of such a kind that the colonists, other than newspaper editors, could look upon the conflicts with detachment. They were protected by the greatest naval power in the world, and the British in North America also enjoyed privileged access to a seller's market in the metropolis. The timber boom, in the short term, provided ready money and attractive wages. Thus, the hardship of war seemed even more remote. But now, in the first decade of the nineteenth century, British North America itself suffered a war. Now it seemed that complacency was no longer possible.

The first hint that this was so occurred in 1807. For the last four years British warships had been stopping and boarding merchant vessels of the United States to recover deserters from the Royal Navy. Since 1793 the British navy had lost four thousand to five thousand seamen a year in desertions alone, and many of the fugitives found their way to the United States where they enjoyed peacetime sailing and better pay. Since the British denied that a man could shed his citizenship as easily as his shirt, they paid little heed to the certificates deserters received from American magistrates to make them citizens of the United States. In 1803 British ships at sea started boarding American vessels and restoring British seamen to their rightful service. The trouble in 1807 occurred when the *Chesapeake,* an American naval ship, refused to recognize the signal of the *Leopard,* a British frigate. The English ship fired on the American and twenty-one Americans were killed in the chase. Finally the *Chesapeake* was boarded and four of her crew were taken into custody. Naturally, the United States reacted to this "Chesapeake affair" as a cause for war. "War Hawks" in Congress demanded an immediate invasion of Canada. Expecting attack, Britain reinforced her colonies. But the American president, Thomas Jefferson, preferred what he called "peaceful coercion" instead.

Jefferson's action was to impose an embargo on all American shipping. After December, 1807, it was illegal for any vessel of the United States to venture into transatlantic commerce. This would solve the problem of impressment by avoiding it. The embargo would also eliminate the other source of conflict with the British, their refusal to recognize American vessels as neutrals, free to trade with either side in the war. Jefferson considered his embargo coercive in that it meant withholding American staples from both sides so long as neither permitted the United States freedom of the seas. In practice, however, the coercion affected American shippers far more than it distressed either Great Britain or France.

Nevertheless, a form of embargo continued beyond the presidency of Thomas Jefferson. His successor, James Madison, persuaded Congress to continue the "peaceful coercion" by continuing the boycott in a somewhat less rigorous form. Still, both belligerents continued to act as if the United States were of no importance. The French seized vessels in Europe if they had stopped first to trade with the English. The British seized American vessels that did business with Napoleon. Finally, in the summer of 1812 Madison addressed Congress to announce that economic sanctions had failed. He said both belligerents refused to treat the United States with the respect due to a sovereign nation. Madison asked for war. Since the belligerent that had insulted the national honor more was Great Britain, the enemy in what he and other Americans now declared to be a second war of independence would have to be the former mother country.

New Englanders were horrified; they preferred running the embargo and taking their chances with impressment or confiscation to a total interruption of trade, particularly by declaring war on the world's foremost sea power. But Westerners were pleased with the prospects for success in "Mr. Madison's war." Andrew Jackson, the future president and then a general, announced with pride and confidence that "We are going to fight for the re-establishment of our national character, misunderstood and vilified at home and abroad . . . . to seek some indemnity for past injuries . . . by the conquest of all the British dominions upon the continent of North America." Surely this would follow even without the enthusiasm of the New England states. There were seven million Americans and only 700 000 residents of the "British dominions." How could the people of six disunited colonies resist invasion when they were outnumbered ten-to-one by the invader, and when the forces of their mother country were totally engaged elsewhere?

II. Lower Canada:
The Crisis of War Resolves Crises in Politics

Ironically, in Lower Canada, the threat of American invasion had a unifying effect, and interrupted a conflict that had begun as a contest between agrarian and commercial interests in 1806. That year, the most pro-agrarian opponents of the mercantile clique established a newspaper, *Le Canadien.* Here they exalted the traditional laws, customs, religion and education of the colony. They strove consciously to cultivate national feelings around these cultural artifacts. Then they developed the notion that the matter at issue was far more important than this or that narrow economic interest. The matter at issue was the future of the *nation canadienne.* The only way for this precious entity to survive and prosper would be through the active involvement of the majority of the citizens, and the functioning of the assembly as the power center of *canadien* nationality.

Naturally, this escalation of the controversy brought the writers for *Le Canadien* into open conflict with the seigneurs as well as with the British business elite. The landowners allied to thwart the twin threats of democracy and commercialism. They founded their own paper, *Le Courier de Quebec,* later renamed *Le Vrai-Canadien,* to warn of the evils of commercialism and majority rule. They pined nostalgically for the reincarnation of the *ancien régime* under their leadership. But the seigneurs constituted a class in deep decline. The more important opponents of the young *canadien* professionals were the merchants and, after 1807, the governor, Sir James Craig.

Governor Craig was a military man of considerable experience, who arrived in the colony when the mother country was engaged to the fullest extent against Napoleon, and just as the United States was beginning to make threats because of the violations of their rights as neutrals. At first, Craig attempted to remain aloof from the factional wrangling in the colony. But his Protestant respect for middle-class ideals of enterprise impelled him into an alliance with the "most respectable" merchants. Then, after a setback in the election of 1808, his contempt for *canadien* aspirations for majority rule only increased. He dissolved the House in 1809. After the reelection of a similar group he dissolved the Assembly yet another time, less than one year from the time of its election.

The second dissolution precipitated such a crisis and such vituperation in the press, that Craig felt justified in taking emergency measures. In the midst of the third election campaign since his arrival just three years before, he rounded up the editors and chief contributors of *Le Canadien*. In all, more than twenty of the most ardent young nationalists were in jail on charges of seditious libel. In the election that followed, their side, the *Parti Canadien*, came back stronger than ever.

The crisis demonstrated to the British party that the institutions of representative government were unworkable in Lower Canada so long as the colony was not "unfrenchified." The Chief Justice, Jonathan Sewell, recommended assimilation by encouraging a large immigration from the United States and by uniting the two Canadas, thus drowning French nationalism by making the *canadiens* a minority without a hope until they changed "their habits, religion and laws." But this would take time. Craig preferred a remedy that could be immediate though no less effective. His preference was for revocation of the Constitutional Act of 1791, thus suspending representative government altogether.

Authorities in London, involved in the final, most desperate, phase of the struggle against Napoleon, wanted no trouble in Canada, and trouble there would surely be with suspension of the Constitutional Act. In 1811, therefore, Sir James Craig was recalled and his program of repression was repudiated. The new governor was Sir George Prevost, and his mandate was for moderation. He disassociated himself from extremists and promoted the moderates of the two leading parties. Just as this program of moderation was beginning to have a visible effect, the external threat appeared and temporarily united the province completely.

If the *canadiens* disliked the merchants for their commercialism, their religion, and their smug arrogance, they could see all these qualities in the Americans to an even greater extent. In fact, since 1807, the *canadiens* had learned to denounce the English as no more than "Yenkés." But now, in 1812, the British party appeared as eager to drub the invaders as any of the others. Thus, mutual hostility was displaced in the face of a common enemy and the *canadiens*, whom Craig had recently denounced as "traitorous demagogues," proved themselves to be thoroughly loyal, and the Assembly—so recently denounced for its incipient republicanism—voted more financial support for the war than any other in British North America. One crisis negated another.

III.   Upper Canada:
The Crisis of Civil War Threatens Civil War and Subjugation

The same could not be said of Upper Canada. Here, the settlers between the Niagara Peninsula and Detroit were notable for their *lack* of enthusiasm and for their increasing division as the war crisis came upon them. If Canada was to be invaded from the United States, it was their farms that would be the most likely battlegrounds. The Atlantic colonies were more than adequately protected by British sea power, and Lower Canada was relatively well protected by natural barriers. But Upper Canada was little more than an extension of the State of New York from one side and Michigan Territory from the other.

Moreover, Upper Canada could be looked upon as an extension of the United States in more than the geographical sense. Since 1792 Americans had been pouring into this part of British North America along with that tide of settlers that rolled westward in search of free land. When these northerly settlers left the United States, none of them had foreseen a second war with Britain, nor was there anything political in their migration. American officials therefore expected them to welcome an invasion as a liberation from monarchy and a reunion with republicanism. Thus, ironically, their origins only made them vulnerable to attack by their fellow Americans.

The settlers recognized that fighting in defense of British North America would embroil them with their relatives to the south, but they also knew that taking the American side would jeopardize their new homes in Canada. Neutrality, therefore, seemed the natural release from the double bind that was not of their own making. Their solution was the source of a tremendous problem for Governor Isaac Brock. He alternated between cool depression and angry desperation as he worked unsuccessfully to mobilize Upper Canada for war. Brock called out the militia; some elements refused to muster; others mustered but suffered too many desertions to be dependable in battle. The assembly of the province was hardly more cooperative. When Brock asked for war measures the legislature refused. Thus, Upper Canada prepared for conquest; the militia was at half strength, individuals openly encouraged surrender before the fighting began, and the lawmakers refused any action which would compromise the citizens' full enjoyment of peacetime civil liberties. General Brock had 1600 British regulars with which to defend the province. He reported his situation as "critical."

Fortunately for Canada the Americans had gone to war for the sake of national honor. Had they sought more, surely nothing could have prevented the fulfillment of Henry Clay's bellicose boast to his fellow senators that "the militia of Kentucky are alone competent to place Montreal and Upper Canada at your feet." But as it turned out, the militia of Kentucky did not even leave the state, nor did that of any other (New York's militia intended to conquer Lower Canada but thought better of it after the initial skirmish). For most Americans, just declaring the war had been enough.

Thus the initial American plan of a triple invasion failed from the start. A mixed force of militia and regulars under General Hull did cross into British territory, but the amateur soldiers proved incompetent in face of a joint British-Indian threat, and they withdrew to Detroit where an invading Brock compelled them to surrender. Shortly thereafter, a second force performed less disgracefully in the east by crossing the Niagara River. The battle that followed at Queenston Heights went badly for the British regulars and colonial militia, and Brock himself was slain. But eventually British reinforcements turned the tide, and when the New York militia refused to leave their state by crossing the river, the battle became a British triumph. The third force, a militia attack upon Montreal, likewise fizzled out when the troops proved reluctant to leave their base. Thus, at the end of the first year of the war, all three attempts of the United States to conquer British North America had failed. In fact, the British held American territory.

In 1813 the Americans aimed to recover by water what they had lost on land. A naval victory on Lake Erie isolated the British in Detroit, and when the British attempted a retreat they were almost completely destroyed at Moraviantown. Another American naval force moving across Lake Ontario landed at the capital of Upper Canada. York, later renamed Toronto, was looted and then burned. But these successes on the lakes were not followed by successful invasions over land. Thus, once again, the Americans made bold strokes that looked better in dispatches than in fact. After two years of war, British North America was still neither defeated nor occupied.

In the third year of the affair, selective use of British sea power humiliated the United States. A force entered Chesapeake Bay and proceeded up the Potomac River to the capital, whose defenses were commanded by none other than the president himself. More humiliation followed when British forces dealt Washington, D.C. the same treatment American forces had given York the year before. Mr. Madison's own residence was scorched, and the War Hawks' enthusiasm for continuing the war declined. Peace negotiations between representatives of Great Britain and the United States began late in the summer.

In negotiating a settlement, Great Britain held the best cards. It was American, not British territory that was occupied by invading troops. Napoleon had just abdicated, and, while the English were certainly war weary in Europe, they were anything but weak. In fact, at the very moment negotiations began, veteran forces of British regulars were on their way to America. But the American spokesmen affirmed with great clarity that their country would continue the war forever rather than sacrifice a single square inch of the ground so recently hallowed by their generation of patriots. This bluff carried the game. The British negotiators withdrew their demands for territorial concessions. The Treaty of Ghent emerged simply as the instrument for ending the fighting and returning to the status quo before the war.

Businessmen in Montreal had seen the resumption of war with the United Stated as a good opportunity to amend the blunder of the boundary settlement of 1783; and, therefore, they had hoped to recover the land south of the Great Lakes between the Ohio and the Mississippi rivers. Naturally, they were disappointed when the British negotiators proved no more forthright in 1814 than in the earlier negotiations. But for the British the War of 1812 had been an unpleasant distraction from which they wanted nothing more than escape. Their last interest was the dream of a few traders for a commercial empire of the St. Lawrence. It mattered little to the diplomats that the war was a three-year waste. The important objective was simply ending it. The treaty did just that. Appropriate to this end was the battle of New Orleans, a needless encounter that occurred two weeks after the peace treaty was signed because there was no way to notify the players sooner that the game was over.

IV.   Consequences of War and the Return to Peace

In many ways, then, the War of 1812 had been a fiasco. But its impact was nonetheless real. First, it had been shown that no one power could dominate the entire St. Lawrence. On their side, the Americans saw that British sea power would prevent their attempts to conquer her colonies. On the other, the Montreal merchants finally realized that their dreams of recovering the old north west were delusions. In other words, the war established a balance of power that led to a boundary which would be permanent. This realization was cemented more firmly in 1818, when the two nations agreed that the latitude 49 degrees north from the Lake of the Woods to the Rocky Mountains would be the boundary in the West. In the east, the Americans were compelled to accept permanent exclusion from the inshore fisheries of New Brunswick and Nova Scotia.

Furthermore, the balance of power led to the notion of an "undefended" border. By the Rush-Bagot agreement of 1817 Great Britain and the United

States agreed to limit their armed naval vessels on the Great Lakes. This was not the end of war scares between Britain and the United States over British North America, but it was a crucial step in the emergence of the undefended border.

A second way in which the war had significant impact was in its effect upon the self-image of British North Americans. While the Montreal merchants were disappointed by the frustration of their territorial aspirations, they were a tiny minority. More typical were the colonists who wallowed in self-congratulation over the idea that they, with only a little help from British regulars, had held the numerically superior Americans at bay. Particularly caught up in this mood of elation were those Upper Canadians who felt their loyalty had never wavered. Thus, anti-Americanism, which was strong after the American Rebellion, emerged even stronger after the War of 1812.

This intensified loyalism could be seen in the changed attitude to the border. Previously the Upper Canadian authorities had been keen to attract Americans as potential settlers. Farmers were needed to fill up the vast expanses, and Americans who knew how to clear land and bear the privations of pioneer farming were to be preferred to British immigrants, for whom the axe was simply an unfamiliar tool. But now, after 1816, new laws aimed at discouraging American immigration went into force to prevent subversive republican and democratic notions from entering the province. The purity of the stock became more important than the pace of development. One postwar governor said as much himself when he declared that "the speedy settlement of the Colony, however desirable, is a secondary object compared to its settlement in such as a manner as shall best secure its attachment to British Laws and Government."

This comment also draws attention to another lesson of the war. The Americans had been beaten back, it is true, but few could fail to recognize that had they been more purposeful in their invasions they could not have failed. Therefore, if British North America were to remain British, it was especially important for inland Upper Canada, not defensible by the Royal Navy, to have a population who would not hesitate to fight off the Americans should they invade again.

Entirely in keeping with this new policy of increasing the population from loyal stock were the steps taken by authorities to encourage British soldiers to settle in Upper Canada close to the American border. Also, assisted passages were provided for immigrants from Britain, and settlements of Scots appeared. But as it happened, the authorities did not have to persist for long with such schemes; the tide of immigration was soon running so fully that official encouragement became unnecessary. British North America loomed as a promised land on a scale that was without precedent.

New World prosperity exerted an extraordinary pull because Old World famine, industrial squalor, and political unrest began to push Europeans out as never before. During the twenty years of the Napoleonic wars there was no manpower to spare for colonization, but after 1815 Britons appeared superfluous by the thousands. Now emigration was viewed as the safest, most expedient means of coping with the potentially explosive problem of useless numbers. Between 1815 and 1850 nearly three million people were pushed out of the British Isles and were drawn to North America. About two million landed to participate in the industrialization of the United States. The British colonies, one tenth as large, and not yet industrialized, received one third of the flow of this great migration.

One reason British North America received so many emigrants was because Quebec was the cheapest New World destination, owing to the number and kind of ships that engaged in the timber trade. By 1815 nearly 600 ships a year called at Quebec alone. These were the oldest, least seaworthy vessels of the British merchant marine. They leaked far too badly to carry outbound cargo of any value; coal, perhaps, but nothing more. But with the installation of a few bunks and some crude provision for cooking, the holds easily converted into areas for hauling passengers. Thus, the timber ship emerged as the most inexpensive means for an impoverished Scot or Irishman to get to America.

The immigrants who volunteered as the paying ballast to the shipowners were treated little differently than the cargoes of coal or cobblestones they replaced. The ships were so crowded that there were usually more passengers than sleeping quarters. There was no comfort or privacy under these conditions. They usually ran low on food and sometimes even on water. But there was never a shortage of vermin and disease. In one year, about one third of the season's migration died within five months of their arrival. Of those immigrants who survived, three fourths moved from Quebec to the northeastern United States after recovering from the ordeal of the crossing. Three times the British Parliament passed legislation to ameliorate conditions for passengers, but on every occasion the shipowners simply found new ways of evading the laws pertaining to such basic matters as crowding and provisions. According to A.R.M. Lower, until steam replaced sail, conditions on the passenger-carrying timber ships were more abominable than upon the slave ships of the previous century: "Every slave thrown overboard meant so much money lost; every emigrant less decreased the ship's liability to have to feed him, and more room for those that were left."

Of course there were better ships for those who immigrated with a little money. For this "better class" of immigrant, usually English, perhaps Scots but almost never Irish, there was plenty of land available in Upper Canada. Taking advantage of their arrival was a group of speculators who perfected the leader-and-associate system of land speculation. In 1823 they formed the Canada Land Company, purchased one million acres of crown land, and proceeded to sell over half their total acreage over the next ten years. The farmers who bought their subdivisions, in their turn, produced cash crops such as wheat. But the merchants who anticipated great profits from exporting grain abroad were disappointed. In fact, in 1830 they exported less wheat than in 1800. Thus, immigration after the war was enormously significant, but more clearly for social than economic reasons. It served to impress the British stamp more firmly, especially upon Upper Canada. But the economy after the War of 1812 simply expanded along the old lines of the old staples rather than industrializing on the strength of an agricultural surplus. Of this there was little. So much was devoured by the timbermakers working their way north and west up the Ottawa River Valley.

V.   Post-War Expansion and Conflict in Rupert's Land

So far as British North America was concerned, the impact of war was felt most significantly in the more settled areas. But there was also a part of the British empire in North America that was not yet colonized, but which did experience the effects of war, and, if at the time the impact seemed slight in comparison to what has just been described, the later consequences would loom large indeed. For this peripheral area of the empire was Rupert's Land, the land held by the Hudson's Bay Company, the crossroads of the continent, and in the opening years of the nineteenth century the last haven of the fur trade.

At this time the fur trade was in deep decline. Long-term trends in that direction had been accelerated by the war and the closing of the continent of Europe. In reaction, the Montreal traders reorganized the North West Company in 1805 with some effect. The less-flexible Hudson's Bay Company fell behind to a distant second place. The British firm handled only 15 per cent of the fur trade; 80 per cent was in the hands of the Montreal rivals. Indeed, in 1806, it seemed for a while that the Canadians might buy out the English competition.

But toward the end of the Napoleonic wars a dramatic change took place in the fortunes of the Hudson's Bay Company. A major factor in its rejuvenation was the entry into the Company's direction of a group of men headed by the Earl of Selkirk. This Scottish peer was appalled at the destitution of so many Britons, especially the Scots-Irish. He decided that assisted emigration was the key to improving their condition. After trying without success to establish a settlement in Upper Canada, he chose to concentrate upon that uncolonized part of the New World that was accessible from Hudson Bay by way of the Nelson River and Lake Winnipeg. This is why he decided to buy into the Company, and why Selkirk and his associates worked for a preponderant voice in the Company's affairs.

Selkirk's colonization scheme could be seen as incompatible with the fur trade. Insofar as the "Montreal peddlars" perceived it as such, it meant certain conflict, perhaps even war between the two firms. From the first, the North West Company took this view because, as they had expanded operations west to the Pacific, the Montrealers had used the area Selkirk intended to colonize as their base of supply. Since the 1790s their wintering partners had been provisioned by the Métis, a mixed race born of voyageur fathers and Indian women, in the Red River region as buffalo hunters. Twice annually hundreds of the bison were hunted down and butchered. The women cut the meat into large thin slabs, dried it in the sun, and then tied the meat in bales. The final processing involved pounding the large, dried pieces, mixing them in a kettle of fat with berries, and pouring the mixture of grease, meat, and fruit into buffalo-hide bags. This was pemmican. One pound was the equivalent of four pounds of fresh meat. It was not altogether unappetizing and pemmican, properly cured and cared for, would keep for years. Pemmican fed the wintering partners. Without it, Montreal could not have been the springboard of a transcontinental fur trade. For this reason, the Montreal traders took great offense at the Hudson's Bay Company's attempt to launch an agricultural settlement for impoverished Scots, retired employees of the Bay, and British migrants precisely in the center of their pemmican supply area. The survival of their fur trade depended upon the failure of the settlement scheme.

But Hudson's Bay Company officials resented the competition of North West Company traders. It tended to drive up the cost in trade goods that had to be paid to the Indians. In this sense, philanthropy made good economic sense; and, therefore, they proceeded with their settlement scheme in exactly the same fashion that colonies were launched by other British trading firms in the seventeenth century. By virtue of royal charter the Company claimed sovereignty over the land and its people. Thus, the person named to be governor was an employee of the firm. Each colonist, in his own turn, was also signed on as a company servant. But there was one important distinguishing characteristic between this venture and that of, say, the Virginia Company. Unlike the merchants who attempted to colonize Virginia, those who backed settlement south of Lake Winnipeg were intending to plant a colony where another commercial company was already active. Consequently, conflict to the point of war between the two firms, one British and the other Canadian, was inevitable.

The Nor'westers reacted immediately. As soon as they learned of the

Hudson's Bay Company's intentions they began a newspaper campaign in Scotland to frustrate the recruitment of settlers there. The Indians and climate were depicted in terms to arouse terror and discouragement. Thus, Simon McGillivray under the name of "Highlander" wrote in the *Inverness Journal* that "Even if [the immigrants] escape the scalping knife ... they will find it impossible to exist in the country."

Lord Selkirk's agents were able to recruit only 105 servants to embark on the colonizing adventure. They left Scotland in 1811 too late to reach Lake Winnipeg before freeze-up. In the following spring their journey up the Nelson River and across Lake Winnipeg was arduous indeed. This avenue to the heartland of North America had advantages for fur traders, since it was so much shorter than the route over the Great Lakes, but the trek of Governor Miles Macdonell and the Selkirk settlers proved that the Nelson River was inappropriate for settlers. It was nearly impossible for colonists to arrive at the destination inland during the same summer as their arrival on the Bay. Nevertheless, Macdonell and his group arrived in 1812 and were succeeded by a second company of settlers, who set out in 1813. Neither natural obstacles nor North West Company hostility had killed the project. A showdown was likely.

The occasion for confrontation was an edict proclaimed by Governor Macdonell in January of 1814 that forbade exportation of any provisions produced by anyone within the territory of his jurisdiction. The Pemmican Proclamation seemed necessary because by 1814 there were nearly two hundred settlers established near the site of present-day Winnipeg. They were farmers—in fact they were expressly forbidden to take any part in the fur trade—but to date no crops had succeeded. Food was in such short supply that without the North West Company's pemmican, Macdonell feared that the settlement would surely starve.

The Métis, anxious about the security of their hold on the land from the moment it was renamed "Assiniboia" (on the map the colony encompassed a huge territory, including the southern part of the present-day province of Manitoba and parts of the states of North Dakota and Minnesota), now became resentful when Macdonell assumed the authority of restricting their commerce with North West Company traders. When the first brigades came down Lake Winnipeg from the western posts, they expected to be resupplied and the Métis middlemen obliged. Macdonell agreed to a compromise and a clash was avoided for the moment.

The directors of the North West Company were insulted at the very idea of compromise, however. When they heard of the proceedings at Red River they sent a commander of their own, Duncan Cameron, to organize the Métis and disperse the Hudson's Bay Company settlers. When Cameron arrived on the site of present-day Winnipeg, Macdonell was out of the colony, recovering his health at York Factory. This gave Cameron the opportunity to rule with all the imperiousness so recently displayed by Macdonell. He proclaimed that better land and more clement weather awaited the settlers in Upper Canada. In June, 1815, with the recently returned Miles Macdonell, a healthy but discouraged governor, over 150 of the colonists were transported by North West Company canoe to this promised land in the east. About sixty settlers remained. They were harassed all summer by North West Company Métis; then they were reinforced in November by more Hudson's Bay Company settlers who accompanied the new governor, Robert Semple.

Governor Semple, like Macdonell, believed himself to be the supreme authority in Assiniboia. Like his predecessor, he did not have the allegiance of the Métis. The harassment of the previous year grew more serious in 1816. Semple aimed to impose order and respect for the authority of the Hudson's Bay Company. Accordingly, when a group of about thirty-five armed Métis approached his headquarters, he rode out to meet them with twenty-six volunteers. Semple approached the group like a father about to discipline a gang of unruly children. In the course of his speech he reached for someone's gun, there was one shot, and shooting became general. All the casualties were on the side of the whites, Governor Semple and twenty-one of his fellows being killed. Perhaps for this reason the episode is remembered as an atrocity rather than a military engagement. This affair of June 19, 1816, is remembered as the Seven Oaks massacre, not the battle of Seven Oaks.

Whether its opening action was a battle or a massacre, the contest between companies was a war nonetheless. Before it ended in 1821, Lord Selkirk himself had came from Scotland to command Swiss and German mercenaries in the fight to beat the Métis and Canadians who presumed to act as if Rupert's Land belonged to them rather than to the Hudson's Bay Company. But the British firm had the legality of a royal charter and the resources of a growing number of stockholders in their favor. In 1821, the two companies merged into one. Thus, the Montreal peddlars settled for stockholder status themselves and Montreal ceased to be the springboard to the prairies. Henceforth, the supplies for the Hudson's Bay Company fur trade would move by ship to Hudson Bay, then by York boat up the rivers that fed into the Bay. The time of the *voyageur* was gone, forever.

CHAPTER SEVEN

Political Wrangles

I. The Transatlantic Interest in Reform

With the end of a war so widespread that it had repercussions as far away as Rupert's Land, people at all levels now enjoyed release from the hardships war conditions had imposed. In individual terms, peacetime meant an open invitation for everyone to indulge rising expectations. For the governing classes in Britain, this meant preserving their monopoly of political power in order to increase their economic advantage by such devices as mercantilist privilege. But for the British middle and lower classes these were precisely the obstacles they hoped to have removed. Similarly, in the United States in the same post war period, the general scramble encouraged by prosperity was also the occasion for great political wrangling and demands for reform. The precise issues in America were different, of course, but the underlying thrust was identical: in both countries there was a remarkable turning in the direction of questioning oligarchic exclusiveness.

For a variety of local reasons, British North America was not immune from polarization either. Even if there had been no influence exercised from Britain and the United States, there would have been controversy along the lines that divided the expectant colonists from those already privileged. But there were influences from immigration. Even though it was actively discouraged, there was continued immigration of Americans who brought populist slogans demanding government by the "real people" rather than by the "money power." The Britons, far more significant both in numbers and in the strength of their influence after 1816, contributed that outlook conveniently summarized by the slogan that the one legitimate object of government was providing for "the greatest happiness of the greatest number."

But even without utilitarian radicalism from Britain or republican influences from the United States, oligarchy throughout British North America was vulnerable to attack, because here the tendency toward oligarchic dominance was especially pronounced. The existence of oligarchies in the first place had not emerged by accident. Oligarchy was the deliberate aim of the imperial authorities in their reorganization of the colonies after 1783. It was commonly agreed that the thirteen rebellious colonies had strayed because in their earlier history they had upset the traditional balance between monarchical, aristocratic and democratic elements by giving far too much voice to the "democratical." There was too much democracy, too little monarchy, no true aristocracy, and no established church at all. There were no nobles and bishops in a colonial equivalent of the House of Lords governing by hereditary right. To be sure, there had been governors' councils and upper chambers of the legislatures in America, but these bodies had been filled by wealthy colonists for short terms, in some colonies for no more than one year, and they had been elected by the members of the lower house rather than appointed by the Crown. Other royal prerogatives, such as appointing the judiciary and assenting to legislation, were compromised in practice by governors who strove to avoid arousing popular indignation. Thus, the effective pivot of every British colony before the American Revolution was the popular will. Since it was considered axiomatic in 1783 that democracy was the prelude to anarchy, eighteenth-century Englishmen interpreted the American Revolution accordingly.

The remedy for the British colonies after 1790 was to strengthen the aristocratic and monarchical elements of the constitution. Ordinary freeholders would elect whomever they chose for the Legislative Assembly, but the governor would determine the membership of the upper house, the Legislative Council. Also, he would have complete freedom in choosing his circle of ministers and advisors, the Executive Council. Since councillors, whether legislative or executive, would always come from the upper class with its "more refinements, more elegance and fashion," and since appointments ordinarily would run for life, the colonial aristocracy would thus emerge with a stronger voice than had been the case in the British colonies that rebelled and seceded in 1776.

The essential element in this second empire was to be the freedom of the executive, that is, the governor and his council, to govern with minimal checks from the people. So long as the costs of government were low, and so long as the imperial authorities were prepared to support the civil administration by revenues other than those generated by local taxes (and therefore beyond the control of a local legislature), the prospects for continuing oligarchy remained bright. Thus, a major provision of the Constitutional Act of 1791 was the Crown reserves. Just as the Anglican Church was to be supported by Clergy Reserves of one seventh of the land of Upper Canada, so too was the governor to be supported by Crown reserves of equal size. The income from these lands, as they were sold off over the years, was to defray in large part the salaries of the whole civil service, and in this way maintain the oligarchy's freedom from legislative control exercised through their power or the purse. In time, this scheme tended to break down, however, because the costs of government went up but the yields from the Crown Reserves and other executive-controlled revenue failed to keep pace. Consequently, legislative grants began to play a larger role in provincial finance; the first grant by the legislature of Upper Canada, for instance, was made in the heady years immediately after the end of the War of 1812. But even so, the executive, thanks to various payments from sources beyond the control of the Assembly, enjoyed a good measure of independence.

Such executives were extremely powerful, and it was soon realized that the enjoyment of economic opportunity depended upon allegiance to them. Thus, in New Brunswick, leading lumber interests allied with the governor and his henchmen, and in this way secured access to Crown reserves of timber land. In Upper Canada, promoters eager to charter banks or build canals adhered to the government. There soon developed in British North America an association between office and economic privilege, and, for others, a feeling that privileges flowed more readily to those already privileged. As reform developed, therefore, it focused its attacks increasingly upon the oligarchy's main strength, its lack of accountability to the people.

II. The Reform Impulse in the Maritimes

This reform impulse was to be experienced throughout British North America, or rather, it should be said, throughout settled British North America; clearly, in those areas where population was sparsely established the problems just alluded to did not, and could not, arise. Thus, the Red River colony was not yet affected by such developments; nor was Newfoundland, for this island was still an anomaly within the empire.

Newfoundland had played an important part in imperial thinking from a very early period; it had been claimed for England as early as 1583 by Sir Humphrey Gilbert and a settlement charter had been granted as early as 1610. Although this early venture was virtually a failure, settlement on the island slowly increased, and by the end of the eighteenth century had reached about 20 000. But such growth was offset by the peculiar perception of the place that persisted in the minds of authorities in the metropolis. Imperial interest lay in the cod fishery, and the island was seen as nothing but a vast platform on which the catch could be dried and repairs to equipment carried out. Newfoundland had no official or legal population at all, and what elementary law and government existed was dispensed by the naval commanders of the fleet in the area. In this way, for almost two centuries, a society unfolded without any of the normal accompaniments of British colonial tradition. By 1820 there was still no common law nor were any political institutions established, representative or otherwise.

It was only in 1825 that London began to move Newfoundland closer to the norm. In that year the island finally moved up to colonial status. But even then, with a population approaching 60 000, there was no willingness to grant representative government. That concession was not made until 1832. Furthermore, as London conferred the *forms* on Newfoundland, the colony did not at once acquire the mind to make them work. The long education in passive acceptance was difficult to break, and the fact that the 1830s was a decade of economic disaster further retarded advancement. In this regard, the school system in particular lagged far behind those in other colonies. The result was that political life in Newfoundland was marred by extraordinary violence, with political divisions drawn along lines of religion, that is, Catholics versus Protestants. In this way, the change that brought Newfoundland representative government also brought election days so riotous that the constitution was changed again to make nearly half the seats in the Assembly appointive rather than elective. In this colony, reform meant more oligarchy not less.

But it is important to bear in mind that Newfoundland was an anomaly, for her three Maritime neighbors all became less oligarchic in the same period. In one way this was surprising, since Prince Edward Island, Nova Scotia, and New Brunswick all had oligarchies that had been particularly powerful and were, as yet, unchallenged. In all three colonies the Executive Council and the Legislative Council were one body, unlike the situation in the two Canadas. In financial matters, the executive could be even more independent as they held lucrative timber limits—even on Prince Edward Island. Yet despite the compactness of executive authority and the oligarchies' independence in finance, changes occurred that tended to make administration more open and responsible to the electorate. Furthermore, they occurred relatively easily and without that acrimony characteristic of the political life of Newfoundland and the Canadas at that time.

It was New Brunswick that pioneered in reform, and the reason for this lead was the colony's booming timber trade. So avid were the timber dealers for access to crown land that the executive was able to sell large areas, thereby building up a vast treasury beyond the control of the Assembly. So vast did these sums become that the interest alone threatened to keep the executive in funds for all time. Still, the executive's control of the timber lands antagonized those who were outside the charmed inner circle, and these disappointed outsiders began to agitate through the Assembly for limitations upon the executive. Eventually in 1837 a deputation to the Colonial Office in London produced a scheme whereby the Assembly was given control of all revenue, including that produced from the sale of crown lands, in return for the granting of a civil list to the executive from which judges and civil servants were to be paid, automatically and without appropriation.

At the same time the imperial authorities instructed the governor to integrate government more closely with popular demand by bringing members of the Assembly into his Executive Council. Subsequently, the new head of the Executive Council was Charles Simonds, who had led the opposition forces in the Assembly in their fight for control of the revenue. Such a move was a key development in weakening executive independence and oligarchic influence by granting increased authority to the voice of the popular party.

Much the same process unfolded in Nova Scotia. There the popular party's champion was Joseph Howe. First he made a reputation as a newspaper editor. Then he entered the Assembly in 1836 fresh from a triumphant acquittal on a charge of having libelled the colonial oligarchy. Under Howe's leadership the House passed Twelve Resolutions in 1837, claiming sweeping powers for the Assembly against the executive, and even going so far as to call for the election of the members of the Executive Council by the Assembly. This seemed excessive, but London was prepared to compromise with instructions that the New Brunswick pattern be imposed on Nova Scotia. Subsequently, members of the Assembly did join the Executive Council, and, for a time, this was enough even for Joseph Howe since he too accepted a seat on the Council on these terms.

Soon the New Brunswick formula of trading a civil list for greater control of the executive extended to Prince Edward Island as well. There, the oligarchy consisted of a narrow clique of absentee landlords who controlled gigantic estates. The tenant-settlers, for their part, argued that they could not pay rents, and that their landlords should be dispossessed. The reform forces began to make headway in the late 1830s, and like Howe, who was open to more American notions, began to agitate for an elected Legislative Council as a means of giving the popular forces more power. But here as well as elsewhere, the Colonial Office refused. Instead they imposed the New Brunswick and Nova Scotian experiments, and were able to stifle this agitation. In 1839 the council was split into legislative and executive sections, and two assemblymen were taken into the Executive

Council. For the moment, this was enough. Prince Edward Island joined Nova Scotia and New Brunswick in reducing the political power of the local oligarchy without much strife or rancor.

The basic explanation would seem to lie in the fact that in each Maritime colony, except Newfoundland, society was extremely homogeneous. Despite recent immigration the society which mattered was still overwhelmingly that of the Loyalists; thus Howe himself, one of the more outspoken of reformers, fitted this type. A similar tendency existed elsewhere. The result was that it was very difficult to accuse the reformers of disloyalty, either to the imperial connection or to the dominant ethos of colonial society. But it is clear that, in settings of heterogeneity and pluralism rather than homogeneity and monoculture, it would be much more difficult to keep disagreement within bounds, as a family quarrel, so to speak. Rather, the disagreement would intensify, acquire cosmic proportions, and end in allegations of disloyalty both to empire and to colony. This is precisely what happened in the two Canadas.

III.   Reform as Majoritarianism in Lower Canada

It has already been shown that in Lower Canada conflict between an aroused electorate and an entrenched oligarchy involved French-English hostility and had simmered since 1807. The temporary unity and calm that marked Lower Canada during the War of 1812 and the conciliatory gestures of Governor Prevost have also been noted. But in 1820 Prevost's successor, the Earl of Dalhousie, arrived fresh from governing Nova Scotia, and quickly found himself embroiled in a bitter power struggle with the Speaker of the Assembly, Louis Joseph Papineau.

Dalhousie's contempt for Papineau, and his tendency to regard this man as typical of his countrymen, led the governor to ally himself almost immediately with the merchant group that shared his prejudices. In 1822, for instance, Dalhousie followed their advice in recommending that the mother country unite the two Canadas, which would give the obvious commercial and political advantages that would follow to the British. Union would restore the economic unity of the St. Lawrence region, and thus facilitate such projects as canal construction between Montreal and the lakes. Papineau and his majority in the Assembly of Lower Canada consistently opposed public support for canals as too costly, even though the consequence was to retard the transportation revolution and thus the development of both Canadas. Clearly this opposition merely underscored

the political attraction of union to the British of Lower Canada, since uniting with colonists of the same ethnicity and social character in the upper
province appeared to promise easy subordination of the "unenterprising"
French in Lower Canada. Papineau appreciated this as well, and therefore
went in person to London to lobby against the proposal on the grounds
that union was inspired by nothing more than extravagance and bigotry.
When he was successful, the hatred between him and Dalhousie increased
proportionately.

In 1827 the governor dissolved the Assembly and plunged the province
into a bitter election contest for the express purpose of ridding himself and
his friends of Papineau. But the new House was still loyal to Papineau's
volatile leadership, and reelected him as Speaker accordingly. Dalhousie
responded by proroguing the Assembly and quitting the province in a
fury.

What Lower Canada needed at this point was a new governor to serve as
conciliator between the embittered *canadiens* in the Assembly and the
English entrenched in the legislative and executive councils. The Colonial
Office obligingly provided such a mediator in Sir James Kempt. His brief
tenure as governor demonstrated the importance of his office in the working of the anomalous constitution of early nineteenth-century Canada.
Kempt was conciliatory to the French without infuriating the English.
Thus, democracy and oligarchy came to a truce by 1830 when the governor
retired.

Still, the conflict in Lower Canada that was moving the province to legislative deadlock was more general and fundamental than the periodic
intransigence of its governors or the hotheadedness of leaders in the
Assembly. Kempt's replacement, Lord Aylmer, was not nearly as bigoted
as Dalhousie, yet he found his administration even more deadlocked than
Dalhousie's in 1827—and Aylmer accomplished this in two rather than in
eight years. By 1832 the government of Lower Canada was at a complete
impasse, and the general population was far more aroused than ever
before. Since the objects of denunciation were the cholera imported by the
timber ships carrying immigrants out from the British Isles and the favoritism that meant most government offices of honor and profit went to
English rather than to *canadiens*, the proposed remedies sounded like democratic reforms. Popular spokesmen demanded close regulation if not a
total ban on immigration and complete control of Crown patronage. On
the level of appearances these propositions could be seen as signaling a
developing reform movement, except that the aroused rural population
was more profoundly interested in scapegoats than in democracy.

The people were already suffering from the effects of repeated crop failures. Crops failed because of soil exhaustion and outmoded agricultural
practices. Rather than popularize the need for technical improvements, the

politicans informed uneducated farmers that their crisis would be less severe if there were no more immigrants coming into the province by the thousands, bringing disease, competing for the vacant land, and threatening the purity of French Canadian customs and institutions by their unfamiliar ways. Furthermore, the politicians continued, if the seigneurs were not rack-renters and if all the good offices did not go the *Anglais*, the government and authority would be closer to the people, and thus more interested in helping them restore prosperity by promoting traditional agrarianism rather than by fostering a commercialism that only served to erode further the character of the French-Canadian nation.

As Papineau's followers gained more support from the people but failed to win concessions from the government, they became increasingly radical, that is, nationalist. Soon this nationalism was running in a republican course.

In February, 1834, the Legislative Assembly went so far as to petition the British Colonial Office, in a list of grievances that was no less than *Ninety-two Resolutions* by name and content, for a republican constitution. The existing Legislative Council was denounced as "the most active principle of evil and discontent in this province" because the Council consistently opposed the will of the elected Assembly. The upper house was therefore "the servile tool of the authority which creates, composes and decomposes it." The cure was to make the Council an elective body like the Assembly. Only then would it "conform to the wishes, manners and social state of the Inhabitants of this continent." By the same stroke this would end the "scandalous favoritism of the governors" who preferred to appoint English over French. In Resolution 75 it was pointed out that of the total population of the province, "those of French origin are about 525 000, and those of British or other origin 75 000," but nearly 80 percent of the 204 government appointments were distributed to people "apparently of British or Foreign origin." There were only 47 government appointees who were "apparently natives of the Country, of French origin." Then, for the second year running, the Assembly refused to vote supplies to the government they cursed in such sweeping terms.

Governor Aylmer responded by dissolving the House and hoping for improvement after the election. But the electorate returned a legislature even more thoroughly republican than its predecessor. Twenty-four members had previously refused to assent to the Ninety-two Resolutions. All but three were defeated in their bids for reelection. Now the colony seemed at a critical point, with the possibility of an American-style rebellion in the foreseeable future. Great Britain moved to prevent this. In the spring of 1835, Aylmer was recalled and a Commission of Inquiry under his successor, Lord Gosford, was instructed to investigate the whole range of grievances that were apparently bringing not only Lower Canada but also other provinces, even havens of loyalism, to advocate open republicanism.

IV. Reform as Sectarian Conflict in Upper Canada

By 1834 it seemed that Upper Canada was nearly as close to rebellion as the lower province. In December, republicanism appeared to be rampant there as the Assembly adopted the Seventh Report on Grievances, a critique of the status quo every bit as scathing as the Ninety-two Resolutions and just as dogmatic in its advocation of the "elective principle" as a cure-all. Less than fifty years after its founding, the province of Upper Canada seemed to have forsaken its Loyalist destiny.

Previous chapters have pointed out the various steps taken by the authorities, both in Britain and in the colony, to maintain Upper Canada as a British society, carefully preserved from the taint of American republicanism. Such institutional safeguards as the Clergy Reserves for the Anglican Church, or such legislative enactments as the 1816 ban on American immigration, did much toward this end, but there was one deviant phenomenon that the Family Compact, the province's British-oriented Anglican oligarchy, seemed incapable of eradicating. This was the extraordinary demand for "enthusiastic" religion.

The early immigrants had been overwhelmingly evangelical; Presbyterians and Baptists, together with their near relations, the Methodists, had flooded Upper Canada, and later waves of Anglicans from Britain had not been able to stem this tide. Nor was this surprising. Evangelical religion fostered by itinerant preachers was the primary, perhaps the only possible and effective, social cement in such a vast and thinly settled territory where there were few neighbors, hardly any villages, and not even the rudiments for Anglican parish organization. West of York, later Toronto, Upper Canada was only a geographical expression, but the preacher, the meeting house, and the emotional exhortation were tangible evidence of people drawing together occasionally and for these moments feeling slightly less alone than they actually were. If there were officials at York who denounced this as "noxious," then they were simply showing the depth of their misunderstanding. The sectarians did not see themselves as particularly American or British. Their one clear identification was with their particular Protestant sect.

It was inevitable that social conflict would eventually develop between these two models, the Family Compact's pro-British elite and the sectari-

ans with their backwoods evangelicalism. But it was not until 1820 that it
flared openly. Even then the struggle opened rather inadvertently, after
one Robert Gourlay, a newcomer from Scotland, circulated a questionnaire
among the pioneer population. His object was to collect information for a
book to be published in Great Britain promoting emigration. But some of
his questions aimed toward evaluation more than description. Thus he
asked, "What, in your opinion, retards the improvement of your township
in particular, or the province in general; and what would most contribute
to the same?" A storm of controversy soon developed over Gourlay's
findings. In addition to poor roads, and a general lack of internal improvements, his respondents believed that the extreme dispersal of settlers arose
from the large tracts of land, held back from settlement by speculators and
the government in the form of Clergy and Crown Reserves. Gourlay called
for a commission of inquiry. The government ignored his demand. Then
Gourlay called for basic reform, particularly of the governor's power to
dispense patronage, namely "to give away land at pleasure . . . to grant
licences, pardons and I know not what . . . . " Now the government acted.
Robert Gourlay was arrested and prosecuted for writing "scurrilous and
seditious libels" and ultimately he was expelled from the province.

In the 1820 election, protesters calling themselves "Gourlayites" were
elected to the Assembly for the express purpose of opposing the government. They, no less than Gourlay himself, were dismissed as republicans
and denounced as traitors. Polarizing opinion seized upon the question of
nationality as a means of highlighting this initial split. The oligarchy
tended to claim that post-1792 immigrants from the United States were
not to be treated as British, and that accordingly their citizenship rights
were forfeited. This "alien question," which centered about the Bidwells,
father and son and prominent Reformers, continued to dominate the
1820s.

The alien question was accompanied by a host of other contentious
issues such as the validity of the Reserves, the question of the links
between Church and State, patronage, and the argument over open or
secret balloting. In each case the tendency was to couch the debate in
terms of British or American alternatives. Since Upper Canada was a British community, the preferred alternative was plain at every point. These
people opposed the notion accepted by Americans that the State was
purely secular. In their view, "there should be in every Christian country
an established religion, otherwise it is not a Christian but an Infidel country." Similarly, they opposed American notions of democracy on the
grounds that "something like an aristocracy" was "essential to the happiness and good government of any people." But what the leading spokesmen for this point of view—John Strachan, John Beverley Robinson, and
Christopher Hagerman—failed to take sufficiently into account was that

their opponents could advocate separation of Church and State or curtail-ment of aristocratic power without being particularly "Yankee."

The people of Upper Canada, especially in the western part of the prov-ince, did have many attitudes and patterns of speech in common with the Americans on the other side of the lakes. In fact, European travellers who toured the United States as well as Upper Canada remarked often that on the British side of the line the feeling was "totally Yankee." Furthermore, to a degree, the critics of the government *were* consciously imitating Ameri-can patterns. This was certainly true of the government's most outspoken critic, William Lyon Mackenzie, editor of the wildly scurrilous newspaper, *The Colonial Advocate.* But Egerton Ryerson, equally critical of the idea of an established church, was no less Loyalist than his father, the "Yankee" who brought his family to Canada after the American Revolution.

The Ryersons were far more typical than the Mackenzies. The only unvarying constant of the highly-charged and changeable political climate in Upper Canada after 1824 was opposition to established religion. Some-times opposition would run toward other objectives, frankly republican, such as the proposal to change the face of the Legislative Council by the "elective principle." But in the decade after 1824, the voters constantly vacillated from one position to another. The province had not made up its mind on many matters other than the Clergy Reserves, but within the Assembly, in the Seventh Report on Grievances, the representatives then sitting did formally adopt the republican model as the means to defeat the governor and the "corruptionists" who gathered around him for his favors.

V.   The Failure of Rebellion in Lower Canada

The adoption of the Seventh Report of Grievances in Upper Canada and the Ninety-two Resolutions in Lower Canada created the impression at the Colonial office that both Canadas were on the brink of rebellion. Although the British authorities responded in 1835 by appointing the Gosford Com-mission to look into the affairs of both provinces more closely, the Com-mission's presence was felt more directly in Lower Canada because there Gosford also had immediate responsibility for governance.

Initially Gosford's manner was conciliatory, but within one year he found himself as deadlocked with the Assembly as had any of his prede-cessors. The reason was that his instructions from the colonial secretary made it clear that Gosford was not empowered to recommend any basic changes in the constitution. The Assembly responded by withholding supply. The Gosford Commission retaliated by reporting that conciliation would avail nothing. The governor, as commissioner, recommended that a show of force was needed.

The imperial government, in which Lord John Russell was a dominant figure obliged by putting Gosford's recommendation before Parliament early in the spring of 1837, presenting it as the Ten Resolutions. Two points were primary: there would be no structural change in the constitutions of the colonies agitating for change and, in the event that legislatures fought governors on this point by withholding supply, governors were now authorized to remove funds from provincial treasuries without legislative appropriation.

As far as the *Patriotes* of Lower Canada were concerned, this was the end. On April 14, 1837, in *Vindicator*, one of their most outspoken newspapers, they warned their readers that

> "the die is cast; the British ministry have resolved to set the seal of degradation and slavery on this Province, and to render it actually, what it was only in repute—the 'Ireland' of North America . . . . One duty alone now remains for the people of Lower Canada. Let them study the history of the American Revolution . . . ."

Now the drive for constitutional change developed into an independence movement. In May, a public meeting of delegates convened to denounce British "lying" and "oppression." All the bonds with Great Britain were said to be those of force rather than of friendship. It was said that their "true friends and natural allies were on the other side of the 45th parallel." Louis Papineau was proclaimed national leader, and steps were taken to repeat what the Americans had done between 1774 and 1776. An association to end trade with Great Britain, reminiscent of the American Association of 1774, emerged. After this meeting, an extralegal government—the Assembly of Six Counties—appeared to administer the affairs of the province, despite the continued existence of the legally constituted administration under the British.

The English party, and some French Canadians holding appointments to various public offices, counterattacked. They launched a newspaper campaign that was extraordinary for its verbal abuse. The Montreal *Gazette*, for instance, denounced Russell's Ten Resolutions as far too mild to meet "the thraldom of a Frenchified revolutionary faction" and demanded military action to break up "the treasonable designs" of "Papineau and his faction."

The *Patriotes* moved against the dissident minority with a program of harassment very similar to the American Patriots' treatment of Loyalists in the American Revolution. The idea was to discourage and terrorize the opposition so completely that they would either abandon their stand or quit the province altogether. *Fils de la Liberté*, the Sons of Liberty, shaved the manes and tails of Englishmen's horses. Groups of young *Patriotes* stamped through the streets of English neighborhoods at all hours shouting threats and singing bawdy songs.

While loyalists and patriots prepared for civil war, Lord Gosford attempted to restore respect for regular government. To conciliate those who wanted to see strong measures taken against the radicals, he purged the militia and judiciary of anyone who took any part in the attempt to set up the extralegal institutions. To conciliate those who wanted to see the establishment of majority government, he called a session of the Assembly. But less than a week after they began to sit, the members of the legislature once again began wrangling against the government. A purge of the civil service, in any case staffed primarily with British, did not affect the radicals, whom the British party wanted to see gibbeted. The governor and his authority became irrelevant as the crisis was taken to the streets of Montreal in clashes between gangs of loyalists organized as the Doric Club and the other side, the *Fils de la Liberté*.

At this point the hierarchy of the Catholic Church swung behind the governor to stem the drift toward rebellion and civil war. The bishops were in full sympathy with the cause of *survivance*—in this sense they were nationalists—but they had not a particle of enthusiasm for supporting a war of independence—to them this was only rebellion. Early in November, the bishop of Montreal, Monseigneur Lartigue, issued an order unequivocally condemning the French Canadian leaders who were seeking to destroy duly constituted authority and bring the province to the edge of war. They, for their part, disclaimed any intention of launching rebellion. The *Patriote* leaders said they merely wanted to bring about the disintegration of arbitrary government. At the same time, a few of them denounced the church authority as a force for tyranny as bad as the British insofar as it did not share their objective of justice for all.

This quarrel between clerical and lay leaders flared at a critical moment. On November 6, a street fight between political gangs resulted in property damage, and Lord Gosford gave in to the demands to restore law and order. He called out the British garrison to patrol the streets and prevent public meetings. The governor also ordered the arrest of leading *Patriotes*, whom he now intended to hold responsible for recent events.

On November 22, Charles Perrault, Jean Chenier, and Louis-Joseph Papineau withdrew from Montreal to the security of nearby towns. The government assumed that they were retreating to mobilize the *canadiens* in open rebellion and pursued them in force accordingly. The *Patriote* leaders were not yet ready for war. At St. Denis and, most notably, at Saint Eustache there was fighting that resulted in a rout by British troops. Perrault

and Chenier were fairly effective commanders of rather unprepared fol-
lowings. But Papineau had no intention of fighting a rebellion or of being
captured and hanged as a rebel. Disguised in women's clothing he fled for
security to the United States. Thus ended the first rebellion of 1837.

VI.   The Failure of Rebellion in Upper Canada

Even more than military unpreparedness or incompetence, it was ambivalence that was the most probable reason for the failure of the independence movement in Lower Canada after it reached the point of armed
struggle; that is, the mass of the people were probably confused by the
conflict that broke out between the clergy and lay leaders just at the time
the fighting with the British reached its critical point. The Church said it
was everyone's duty to obey. The radicals urged everyone to resist. Yet
both kinds of leaders were nationalist in their own way. What divided
them from one another was means more than ends. Thus, the ambivalence
of the mass of the people could only have been the stronger.

A similar kind of ambivalence worked against the radicals in Upper
Canada. In this province the division among reformers had occurred earlier, and the confusion therefore had more time for resolution. Unfortunately for the rebels, the decision was made for loyalty to Britain.

As early as 1834 there was a division among the leaders for reform. One
group around William Lyon Mackenzie was concerned with rights and
wrongs. They were dogmatic republicans, very much like those Patriots in
the old empire who were so wrapped up in protest that they seemed to be
more concerned with the principles of government than with its processes.
The other faction, centered upon Egerton Ryerson outside the Assembly
and Robert Baldwin within, was only slightly less critical of the Family
Compact than Mackenzie and his friends, but it was quite unlike the
radicals. This group was more interested in the practice of government
and its results than in moral purity for its own sake.

It is not difficult to see how this division among leaders blunted their
effectiveness as an instrument for revolution. But what is even more
important is to appreciate how this same conflict dulled the "enthusiasm"
of individual voters. It has already been mentioned that the electorate continually shifted its support between opposition and support for the governor and his friends. Even the politicians were confused. The electorate as a
political body was truly an unformed mass as far as attitudes toward basic
reform were concerned. But then in 1836 they reached what might be
regarded as a point of decision.

In some respects the election of 1836 in Upper Canada was a sordid, drunken, violent spree that is best forgotten. But in another respect the election of 1836 is uniquely important, as the outcome of the confrontation between politicians, people, and issues determined the course of political development for decades to come. The factor that added special color to this contest was the province's new governor, Sir Francis Bond Head, and his decision to involve himself directly with the electorate, face to face, in the campaigning.

Head had been governor of Upper Canada since 1835—his coming was the result of the Assembly's adoption of the Seventh Report on Grievances. Somewhat predictably, from the moment of his arrival, Sir Francis was convinced that "a good feeling pervaded a majority of the people" since he believed that the "strong republican principles" of the Assembly were unrepresentative of true public opinion. Nevertheless, his first impulse was to be conciliatory to the Assembly by promoting moderate reformers to his Council. When it seemed a year later that nothing short of republican reform would satisfy the Assembly he dissolved the House. Thus began his two months of electioneering in May of 1836.

Just two years before, a general meeting in Toronto established an organization called the Canadian Alliance to "enter into close alliance with any similar association that may be formed in Lower Canada or the other colonies, having for its object 'the greatest happiness of the greatest number'." By the summer of 1836 this happiness meant concrete projects rather than rhetorical moralism. A similar meeting of like-minded people now wanted their legislature to direct its attention "to the improvement of the land we live in, rather than to the consideration of abstract questions of Government." This Sir Francis promised to deliver. In a tour of speechmaking he constantly returned to the same basic point: "Can you do as much for yourselves as I can do for you? If you choose to dispute with me, and live on bad terms with the mother country, you will, to use a homely phrase, only quarrel with your own bread and butter." Then, too, he played on Loyalist sympathy and anti-American sentiment. With liberal quantities of liquor and bullies at the polls, reformers were routed.

After the election it was the opinion of Mackenzie and his friends that the result was not a true expression of public opinion. Yet how wrong he was in his judgement is illustrated best by the failure of his rebellion, the revolution that was called and in which few participated—not even Loyalists took part to give their rebel enemies a good beating. In its one battle, the march down Yonge Street on December 5, 1837, just one person was killed.

The failure of the rebellion was no occasion for reformers to become cynical about reform. The significance of this failure was not that the people could not be relied upon. In simplest terms, their failure to rebel American-style meant only that these colonists preferred to interpret the "great-est happiness for the greatest number" in concrete terms rather than as moral abstractions. There was self-discovery in this too, as Upper Canada was little tempted to follow Mackenzie-type reformers again in the future. Thus, the political style that called on voters to project their personal frus-trations as public problems—a style that was then and continued to be such a conspicuous feature of the American political tradition and which the Loyalists rejected in the eighteenth century—was rejected by the 'late' Loyalists in their turn. By 1838 there was no sign that anyone in Upper Canada regretted having failed to launch a "manly resistance" against the "poor deluded miserable ductile dupes of the dirty tools of arbitrary pow-er," as Mackenzie had invited the year before. But people were talking a great deal about vast, new internal improvement schemes the government would underwrite. They also began to talk again about reform, and while the new scheme was not republican, it still promised to promote "the greatest happiness for the greatest number."

CHAPTER EIGHT

The Durham Solution

I.   British Radicalism Discovers Canadian Majoritarianism

The news of rebellions in both Canadas shocked the mother country. The government of Lord Melbourne, not a particularly strong one at this date, was assailed by the opposition, the charges against the government being couched in the traditional liberal form that had been used to explain the earlier revolt of the Thirteen Colonies: administrative neglect and petty tyrannies of long standing had been responsible. So successful was this assault that by the beginning of 1838 the fall of Melbourne, a latter-day Lord North, was being widely predicted.

But what was to be done? The rebellions were over almost before they had begun. In this sense there was not even a crisis to face. Still, support for the rebels in Lower Canada was strong. And at least an appearance of action was necessary against what had taken place in the other Canada. Melbourne's first response therefore was to act by striking a commission to investigate the origins of the turmoil and recommend changes for the future. Melbourne succeeded in recruiting the undisputed champion of the cause of liberal reform in England to take the post of High Commissioner, visit British North America, and establish the truth on the spot.

The darling of British "radicalism", the cause that championed voting by secret ballot, extending the franchise to all male taxpayers, and legislative reappointment among other measures, was John "Radical Jack" Lambton, the first Earl of Durham and "King of the Coal Country". Durham's appointment delighted radicals because they believed Radical Jack's heart was with the real people; thus, he would not hesitate to name the nabobs who brought disorder to the colonies. But this prospect did not distress the ministry. Melbourne was pleased by Durham's acceptance since it instantly quieted the opposition trouble-makers who rallied to the Canadian question to embarrass the government.

True to his reputation, Lord Durham prepared himself for his duties weeks before his departure. He talked to merchants who conducted their business in the colonies. He read documents including such items as the Ninety-two Resolutions and Seventh Report on Grievances. In this way, Durham gained a preview and preconception of what awaited him in the two Canadas. He set out to fulfill his mission early in the spring of 1838 with his retinue, which included two especially trusted associates, Charles Buller and Edward Gibbon Wakefield.

The emissaries of inquiry arrived in Quebec on a beautiful spring day in May, and since Durham's reputation as a reformer had preceded him, people welcomed him like warm sunshine after a long winter. Recently there had been two political executions in Upper Canada. More were expected in the lower province. The jails of both Canadas were filled with hundreds of accused rebels awaiting trial and possible execution. The constitution of Lower Canada was suspended—in fact, the colony was under a martial law more stringent than in the years immediately after the conquest. Upper Canada was less under a lid of repression but the people were no less desperate—for economic reasons. The loyalist Assembly elected in 1836 had enacted a series of internal improvement schemes in keeping with their promise to promote economic development rather than dispute abstract principles of government. But one of those recurring "panics" that periodically interrupted the rapid growth of the United States and Great Britain in the nineteenth century hit in 1837. As a consequence, Upper Canada was severely shaken and the public treasury nearly bankrupt.

Since Durham was to fill the position of governor general of all of British North America at the same time that he was the High Commissioner to investigate the disturbances in the Canadas, and since he was given extraordinary powers to cope with the emergency situation, it was expected generally that he would deal with these matters boldly. He put his associates, Wakefield and Buller, to work heading committees set up to examine land questions, particularly how the Clergy and Crown Reserves affected economic development in Upper Canada. Durham himself dealt with the investigation of the causes of the rebellions, seeking long-term remedies and a way out of the immediate problem of the disposition of accused rebels. First he pronounced banishment upon those already in exile. Then he banished eight of the most serious offenders already in custody, sending them to Bermuda. The rest he pardoned.

Durham then began to hold private audiences to deal with the major question of appropriate reforms to prevent the recurrence of such disturbances. He talked to delegations from the maritime colonies, for instance, to determine their reaction to the federation of all the provinces of British North America in one legislative union, a pet solution that had occurred to him even before he left England. From the perspective he had acquired before leaving Britain, this seemed an attractive solution since it would create a structure too large for the local oligarchy of any one colony to dominate. Equally important, a federal unit would have a revenue base large enough to handle internal improvement schemes on a much greater scale than any one province could undertake by itself. The one thing wrong with this idea, Durham discovered to his surprise, was that no one wanted it. The Maritimers were especially adamant. In the summer of 1838, their representatives told him they would suffer almost any fate before they would willingly allow themselves to be dragged into a union—federal or otherwise—with the obstreperous Canadians.

Thus, the High Commissioner abandoned his idea of confederation. But other schemes attracted him in its place. During an eleven-day visit to Upper Canada he had occasion to talk to William and Robert Baldwin, who proposed a reform acceptable to the people of the maritime delegations but less all-embracing in its scope than confederation. The Baldwins suggested that the most useful reform would be recognition of the principle that a colonial governor should choose his closest advisors, the members of his Executive Council, *entirely* from the leadership of the majority group of the Assembly. Furthermore, the representative of the Crown should be governed by their advice in all matters that could be construed as "domestic concerns." Here was the means for avoiding the deadlock between levels of government as effectively as by the "elective principle" without, in fact, transforming the colonies into "republics." Here, also, was the means for making "a permanent connection between the colonies and the Mother Country" since no administration responsible to an Assembly would be vulnerable to charges by demagogues that it was a government acting in the interests of a foreigner or an unpopular oligarchy.

The logic of the Baldwins' proposal attracted Durham instantly. He was prepared to recommend its concession to every colony in British North America, except Lower Canada. The canadiens, as a "race", were an enormous disappointment to Lord Durham. His preconception had been that they were led by visionaries contending for free government against a "petty, corrupt, insolent Tory clique." In reality, however, he found that the *canadiens* were defenders of tradition. This was unforgivable, especially since the French Canadian majority in the Assembly obstructed "the progressive intrusion of the English race." Durham discovered that the Tories of Lower Canada were actually the proponents of material progress; it was the popular majority that was "backward." To concede self-government to such traditionalists as these was out of the question. Yet the constitution of Lower Canada, no less than the others, needed reform. Thus Durham faced a real dilemma.

It was in the midst of pondering these large questions of reform that the governor was interrupted early in the autumn. The Melbourne ministry informed Lord Durham that his banishment of the political prisoners was illegal, because the jurisdiction of his commission did not extend as far as Bermuda. He might have banished the worst of the rebels to Newfoundland or Cape Breton Island—territories that were part of British *North America*—but not to Bermuda, an island beyond his jurisdiction. Durham was furious. This action belied the promises of firm support that the government had extended when Durham was given his commission. It also came as a vote of no-confidence. Durham resigned and quit the province after less than six months in office.

On Durham's departure, Sir John Colborne resumed his military command of the civil administration. This move, made nearly a year since the first rebellion, meant a sudden interruption of French Canadians' hopes that reform would be accomplished without their waging a war of independence. In response, the *patriotes* rose a second time. This second rebellion, early in November of 1838, was suppressed with far greater force than the first, and martial law was imposed even more stringently. In the wake of the recriminations that followed, twelve persons were executed and fifty-eight were exiled. These exiles, to Australia rather than to nearby Bermuda, were sanctioned by the imperial authorities.

II. The Durham Report

At the time the *patriotes* staged the second rebellion, Durham was on his way to England. Shortly after he arrived home he heard of the renewed "troubles." Durham, along with his assistants, set to work writing the report that would reveal for all what they supposed was the significance of the recent history of the two Canadas. The highly controversial recommendations, which appeared early in 1839, made the *Report on Canada* immensely readable then and nearly as interesting now. The influential London *Times* promptly identified its author as the "Lord High Seditioner."

Far from sedition—or even radicalism—the controlling assumption of the report was that the "British possessions in North America" existed as a "New World" for the "suffering classes of the mother country." These territories were seen by Durham as places to which impoverished Britons might migrate for a better life without the need to abandon their British manners or citizenship. But two factors in the Canadas impeded the fulfillment of this role. One was a system of land distribution that, in Durham's opinion, aided "land jobbers" more than "emigrants." He therefore recommended reform of the system of land distribution involving abolition of the Clergy Reserves and land speculation. Only then would there be a "sound system of colonization." The other flaw that Durham identified was a constitutional arrangement that impeded the provision of "good government." The primary recommendation here was that "the colonial Governor . . . be instructed to secure the co-operation of the Assembly in his policy by entrusting its administration to such men as could command a majority . . . . " So simple was his proposal that Durham thought that the "change might be effected by a single dispatch containing such instructions . . . . " But his proposal would only apply to limited areas of domestic concern. There would have to be limits to the autonomy of the colonies, since they would still continue to be "colonial possessions." Thus the Lord High Commissioner proposed that the responsibility of the governors to the assemblies would not extend to matters that concerned relations with the mother country or economic development. Four such areas were enumerated: "the constitution of the form of government, the regulation of foreign relations and trade . . . and the disposal of the public lands." Since these matters covered about three-quarters of the areas to which colonial legislation even then pertained, the autonomy Lord Durham proposed was very limited indeed. But this would satisfy reformers in the "British possessions."

Lower Canada was a special case. The limited autonomy Durham proposed for English-speaking colonists did not extend to "the French in Lower Canada." It has already been mentioned that he was disappointed with what he thought he had learned of the struggle there. In his words, "I expected to find a contest between a government and a people: I found two nations warring in the bosom of a single state: I found a struggle, not of principles, but of races . . . . " (Durham's conception of *race* assumed a person could change his race by altering his habits; in other words, he believed the *canadians* were "mild and kindly . . . honest, very sociable, cheerful and hospitable" because they were "without education," not because these behavioral modes were genetically inherited; in this sense, Durham was not a racist.) That there should be *two* races in one state was astonishing, and the earl was enough of an ethnocentric English aristocrat and radical modernizer to assume that the world was civilized only to the extent that it was anglicized and industrialized. Since the conflict in Lower Canada was between a "race" of "progressive English" and the "stationary French race," the progress of the colony depended upon the triumph of the British party. It was for this reason that self-government could never be entrusted to the "obviously inferior" French majority. The solution, in Durham's opinion, was the legislative union of the two Canadas, at the same time placing the *canadiens* in a minority position. Durham believed this would be the most expedient means of discouraging the cause of *"la nation canadienne,"* and hastening "the process of assimilation." Here was the "first object." "I repeat that the alteration of the character of the province ought to be immediately entered on, and firmly, though cautiously followed up; that in any plan . . . with this end in view, the ascendancy should never again be placed in any hands but those of an English population."

When *canadiens* learned of the Durham Report they realized that this was yet another dose of what they had been hearing from local sources more or less constantly since about 1807. To be shocked one must be surprised. The *canadiens* were not shocked as they read Durham's opinion that "there can hardly be conceived a nationality more destitute of all that can invigorate and elevate a people, than that which is exhibited by the descendants of the French in Lower Canada, owing to their retaining their peculiar language and manners." Nevertheless the Durham Report did interest those who read it in translation and by installments in Etienne Parent's newspaper, *Le Canadien*.

The people of the rest of British North America were no less interested. The Reformers of Upper Canada were especially enthusiastic about Durham's recommendation that a governor should be bound by the policy of advisors chosen only from among the leaders of the elected majority in the Assembly. The advocates of constitutional change were extremely vulnerable to accusations of disloyalty from the moment of Mackenzie's absurd rebellion. But now, with no less than a peer of the realm advocating Baldwin's alternative, "Durham Meetings" sprang up all over Upper Canada in the spring of 1839 to show support for the idea.

The elite of Upper Canada might join the London *Times* in denouncing Durham as the "Lord High Seditioner" for his advocacy of constitutional reform, but on one point they too supported his recommendation. This was the proposal to restore the economic unity of the Upper and Lower Canada, a pet idea of businessmen in Lower Canada since it was first proposed in 1822. Still, it was difficult for the elite of Upper Canada to be enthusiastic about the Report, given the scathing language with which Durham attacked them for their "monopoly of power." He dismissed them as power-hungry speculators who "acquired nearly the whole of the wastelands of the Province . . . [and] the chartered banks, and, till lately, shared among themselves almost exclusively all offices of trust and profit." Durham believed that by making the Executive Council "responsible to the people" the monopoly would be broken and the happiness of the colony, if not of the "Family Compact," would prevail.

But whether any of Durham's recommendations would go into effect depended upon the still shaky government of Lord Melbourne. In the spring of 1839, Melbourne found the idea of ministerial responsibility a "logical absurdity" for a colony. The other recommendations, the proposals pertaining to crown lands, the unification of the Canadas, and the planned assimilation of the French, were less repugnant in principle, but Melbourne was reluctant to act on any of them immediately. Thus, while the recommendations of the Durham Report were not officially adopted, the discussion that began from the moment of the Report's appearance set the terms in the debate that could not end until the British colonies were autonomous, and the special case either anglicized or recognized as a nationality unlike any other.

III. An Attempt to Implement the Cultural Dimension of the Durham Solution

Anglicization made good sense to the British colonies. Surprisingly, at first, the prospect of assimilation was tolerable even to Etienne Parent. If it was accompanied by responsible government, monoculture seemed a reasonable price to pay for the defeat of oligarchy. For Parent, in April of 1839, reform was more important than *survivance*. But the editor of *Le Canadien* changed his mind as soon as it became clear that subjection and subordination were the aims of the union's English spokesmen. Legislative union was not to be the means for reform so much as the way to punish the "French" for their rebellions of 1837 and 1838. The Montreal *Herald*, for instance, proposed that the representation in an eventually united province should be 103 seats to 25 in favor of the English. The *Gazette*, another Montreal paper, suggested that literacy in English, rather than property, ought to be the prerequisite for a man's right to vote. As bigotry became the most salient motive for the support by the English press for the union of the Canadas, only *vendus*, the name given to *canadiens* who had sold out for government salaries while eagerly claiming to serve the people, continued to support the idea of union.

Foremost among the union's opponents was Bishop Lartigue, the cleric who figured so prominently in the opposition to rebellion. The man who had so staunchly upheld the British government now opposed its plans because of the proposals for changing education patterns. Instead of Church-run schools and the traditional curriculum, the Report proposed universal education of a completely secular nature as part of the anglicization process. Lartigue judged that the *écoles neutres* would mean *décatholiciser*. He opposed that prospect with a vengeance, and thus he opposed the idea of uniting the two Canadas as well.

Confused by the many recent reversals in position of their clerical and lay leaders, the ordinary people of Lower Canada grew apathetic to the turns in the history of their province after 1837. Perhaps for this reason, as much as any other, it was possible to implement the union scheme to "swamp the French" despite all leaders, except *vendus*, protesting. The new governor general, Charles Poulett Thomson, whose middle name usually appeared in French with only one 't', was instructed by the Colonial Office "to obtain their co-operation by frank and unreserved personal intercourse." In fact he forced the union through. But there was no third rebellion.

Thomson assumed authority in October of 1839, and about one month later he summoned the tribunal that Colborne had used to maintain a semblance of civil administration in the context of martial law. Thomson outlined the probable terms of union: equal representation (there were then about 650 000 people in Lower Canada, now to be renamed Canada East, and only 450 000 in the Upper Province, now to be renamed Canada West); assumption of the debts of both as one (the public debt in Upper Canada was £1.2 million; Lower Canada owed a mere £95 000); and no responsibility of the provincial ministry to the Assembly. Then the tribunal was instructed to vote its assent without discussion. The union proposal carried.

Flattering himself that this exercise represented the "deliberate wishes" of the people of Lower Canada, Thomson took the proposal to Toronto. Here he had to meet an Assembly, since civil government had not been suspended after the one feeble rebellion in Upper Canada. To obtain approval, he could not resort to "despotism." But this required no genius on his part. The Assembly was already favorably disposed to union for its favorable economic implications. As for the constitutional terms, there were too few reformers in the Assembly to push for "independent responsible government" as one of the conditions for uniting the two provinces. The colonists of Upper Canada insisted on only two additional points: Kingston should be the capital of the United Province, and English should be the sole language of record.

Before the end of his third month in the Canadas, Thomson had an outline of a Union bill to send home to Westminster for formal drafting and legal enactment. In London the terms were modified yet further. There would be a civil list making the salaries of civil servants payable from the provincial treasury without special appropriation. To bring the province into line with the practice at Westminster, and to cut down the opportunity for members of the Assembly to vote supplies for extravagent schemes of local improvement, it was arranged that money bills were to be introduced by the executive only and not by private members.

One year later the legal existence of the United Province of Canada was proclaimed. There was no responsible government as Durham had recommended. In fact, the constitutional arrangement was even more "despotic" than before in view of the new powers formally assigned to the executive. The only other change was an alteration of political boundaries to hive off the "French" in a harmless ghetto. *Canadien* radicals predicted trouble; but there was none. There were no riots until 1841, when the first elections took place. Even so, riotous elections were perfectly normal in a time when people voted publicly by voice rather than in seclusion by secret ballot. In 1841 it appeared that anglicization and pacification would proceed without difficulty. The rebellions had more than failed. The rebels were routed.

IV. The Concession of Responsible Government

The failure of the rebellions and the adoption of only the anglicization recommendations of the Durham Report placed Canadian Toryism in a more privileged position than it had ever enjoyed before. The Loyalist refugees from the American Revolution were not nearly as privileged then as the Tory victors appeared in 1840. Yet the movement to reform the constitutions of all the provinces of British North America was so encouraged by the Durham Report that its resurgence outlasted the documents' official rejection. Before the rebellions it was easy and common to label all reformers as republican and disloyal for their advocacy of doctrines inimical to the British constitution. Indeed, the "elective principle" did conform to an American prototype. But after the rebellions, when reformers identified themselves with the Durham Report and "responsible government," it was impossible to stigmatize their proposal as a Yankee import. This is the irony of the Tory ascendancy after the rebellions: they had no ammunition to fight reform now that it aimed for nothing more than the adoption of the British constitution in its "latest form." In this sense, the so-called "struggle" for responsible government was no stuggle at all, because when the change was finally made, no group or principle was repudiated except perhaps the Americans and the American constitutional model.

In the half century or so from the time responsible government was first proposed in 1807, to the moment of its concession in 1846, the chief opponents of the idea were in Britain, at the Colonial office. It was they who had ignored the first request for the implementation of the principle of "ministerial responsibility" when *canadien* nationalists proposed the idea. They reacted similarly a generation later, in 1828, when Dr. W.W. Baldwin in Upper Canada wrote to the Colonial Office to suggest that they permit establishment of

"a provincial Ministry, if I may be allowed use of the term, responsible to the

Provincial Parliament, and removeable from office . . . when they lose the confidence of the people as expressed by the voice of their representatives in the Assembly . . . . "

Of course nothing came of the idea then, any more than in 1807. In fact, as late as 1840, the colonial secretary, Lord John Russell, still believed the idea was "absurd". To him, it was "impossible for a Governor to be responsible to his Sovereign and a local legislature both at the same time."

The logical inability of a colonial governor to follow the advice of a "provincial ministry" should it run counter to his instructions from the Colonial Office, was the sense in which Russell found the idea of responsible government "inadmissable" as well as "impossible." But it should be pointed out that responsible government in this sense, of governors choosing ministers capable of commanding parliamentary majorities, was ordered by the Colonial Office as it became increasingly clear that any other policy would lead to rebellion. Thus, in 1839 Lord John Russell informed the governor of New Brunswick that henceforward a new policy would govern the tenure of public office. Until that time, public officials had held office "during good behavior," that is, as long as they did not warrant dismissal by the executive for pernicious conduct. Now they were to hold office "during pleasure," that is, while the executive found it useful to retain them—in other words, while they continued to enjoy popular support as expressed by the Assembly. In the Canadas, too, Charles Thomson, who became Baron Sydenham after 1840, selected his staff for the Executive Council from among the politicians who led the Assembly. To be sure, Sydenham set policy, disposed of the patronage, and did what he could to manage the legislature. But since there were no true parties in the sense of disciplined organizations of politicians who divided over policies as well as over spoils, and since he did not push through policies repugnant to the majority of the members, Governor Sydenham did, in fact, head a responsible government in everything but its inadmissable sense. Or, as it has been put, after 1839 British North America enjoyed administrations "responsive, if not responsible, to popular control."

After Sydenham was killed by a fall from his horse in the autumn of 1841, he was succeeded by a governor who appreciated even more frankly that popularity with the legislature was a prerequisite for ministerial office. Although Governor Sir Charles Bagot supervised the dispensation of patronage and reviewed legislation, actual leadership in the legislature fell to colonists who commanded the confidence of the House. Bagot was governor, but Francis Hincks, Louis H. LaFontaine, and Robert Baldwin were the government's leaders. Although responsible government was still not conceded in principle—an objective Hincks, LaFontaine, and Baldwin all shared—in 1843 Bagot informed the colonial secretary that "whether the doctrine of responsible government is openly acknowledged, or is only tacitly acquiesced in, virtually it exists."

This was too frank for Lord Stanley, the new colonial secretary. Although expediency might dictate goodwill between a governor and a local legislature, the strength of empire, in Stanley's opinion, necessitated the rejection of responsible government as a doctrine. When Bagot resigned in 1843 to retire and succumb to terminal illness, Stanley chose a successor to hold the line where he meant it to be held. Stanley's choice was Sir Charles Metcalfe, a hardened veteran of thirty-seven years of military service in India and most recently the governor of Jamaica.

Predictably there was trouble between Metcalfe and the reform leaders almost from the moment of the governor's arrival. Since the reform leaders controlled the majority, they wanted control of the patronage, to set policy, and to operate independently of the governor's interference. But this was responsible government in its inadmissable sense. Metcalfe therefore refused the reformers' demands, dissolved the House, and plunged the province into an election very much like that of 1836, when Sir Francis Bond Head also campaigned for a cooperative majority. In this episode of 1844, Metcalfe won the nickname "Charles the Simple" from the reformers. But the governor's supporters out shouted his opponents at the polls, and Metcalfe won a majority as well. Subsequently he staffed the council with more compliant ministers. This might have led to trouble as serious as anything in 1837; but developments in Britain were leading to revisions in the old theory of empire.

In 1846 the British government repealed the most important of the mercantilist statutes—the pillars of the old empire. The Parliament of Great Britain embraced free trade, and thus, in effect, declared the whole world their empire, since the areas that were officially colonies were no longer the privileged suppliers of raw materials and buyers of manufactured goods. From an economic standpoint, there was no longer any sense in which responsible government was inadmissable.

In the new government that took office in 1846, Lord Grey, the Earl of Durham's brother-in-law, became colonial secretary; at the same time, Lord Elgin, Durham's son-in-law, became governor general of Canada. Dispatches made it plain that as soon as circumstances permitted, responsible government was to be established. In 1848 full responsible government came into effect first in Nova Scotia. When the legislature met early in that year it became clear that at the recent election the Liberal forces had defeated the Conservative following of the then government leader, James W. Johnston. Wthin a few days, Johnston submitted his government to a vote of confidence, and when he lost, resigned. The governor then invited the Liberals to form a government in which Joseph Howe was prominent. This was responsible administration; soon it followed in the

Canadas as well. After an election in December, 1847, once it became clear in January, 1848, that the incumbent government could not win a vote of confidence (the Reformers defeated it 54-20) the Executive Council resigned, and Elgin called upon the Reform majority, led by Robert Baldwin and Louis LaFontaine, to form the new council, dispense the patronage, and set policy.

The principle of responsible government was conceded in 1848, but it was years before the reality of the autonomy that was conceded in principle became fully established in practice. It was one matter for the mother country to hand over the patronage and the right to set policy. It was another for Great Britain to accept powerlessness in the face of statutes "repugnant to the laws of England." Here was the real test of colonial autonomy.

In 1849, the parliament of the United Province of Canada tested their autonomy further by passing a statute to compensate those who had suffered losses in the Lower Canadian rebellions of 1837 and 1838. Controversy arose because many of the people who were to receive compensation were, in fact, former rebels, and the opposition regarded the bill as a subsidy to treason. Elgin shared their displeasure with the law. The question was whether he would disallow its passage. He signed.

Of course the Rebellion Losses Bill was primarily of local significance. It did not directly contradict any established policy or statute of Great Britain. Responsible government was not fully tested until a provincial ministry chose to pursue a course directly contrary to that of the mother country. This precedent occurred in 1859. The government of the United Province of Canada imposed a 20% duty upon imports in order to generate revenue for public works projects. English industrialists feared that such a measure would encourage Canadian manufacturing at the expense of British, and they petitioned the Colonial Office to disallow the Canadian tariff on grounds that the law was directly contrary to Parliament's policy of free trade. The colonial secretary obliged the manufacturers by informing the colonial ministry of their grave concern. The government dangled the threat of disallowance should Canada not change her policy voluntarily. Politely, yet forthrightly, the ministry reminded the British that Canada was now in certain respects independent: "Self-government would be utterly annihilated," they said, "if the views of the Imperial Government were to be preferred to those of the people of Canada. It is therefore the duty of the present government distinctly to affirm the rights of the Canadian legislature to adjust taxation of the people in the way they deem best." The Colonial Office backed down.

...icance of Responsible Government

The establishment of Canadian autonomy without the repudiation of the imperial connection was a historical achievement that has inevitably bulked large in histories of Canada, sometimes in terms more mythical than real. It should be repeated that reference to a Canadian *struggle* for responsible government is somewhat misleading. To be sure, there were groups in British North America who actively pursued this goal, but the impetus for this change in the 1830s was in the Maritimes and came to this area from the metropolis. The metropolitan initiative in the form of the Durham Report was even more evident in the 1840s. Thus, the *concession* of responsible government would be a more accurate description; it was simply a happy coincidence that the mother country grew out of mercantilism at the same time that the pressure for greater independence reached critical proportions in the colonies. It was therefore possible for the Canadians to gain their autonomy without severing the imperial tie.

A second misapprehension about responsible government is that it was a reform movement that necessarily brought government closer to the people by giving their representatives control over the executive. Actually this change moved the politicians ever further from the people they were intended to serve, since it reinforced the drive for members of the legislatures to join with disciplined party organizations. Henceforth independent members, those who strove to serve constituencies above party, would be regarded by the other members of the legislature somewhat contemptuously, as simply "loose fish." Elgin observed as much, succinctly yet clearly, when he referred to responsible government as a procedure rather than a principle, "not a measure but a method." He meant that the majority grouping in the legislature had to act cohesively in order to maintain their grip on power and patronage. Thus, responsible government helped transform political factions into political parties. In theory, popular forces could control the parties, but in practice this operated only in the negative sense of voting the "ins" out of office at each general election every four or five years. Between elections, the only check on the majority was the opposition, and, as events were to show, this was usually but a feeble check indeed.

But in another sense the emergence of disciplined parties highlights what may be the major real significance of the achievement of responsible government: when Canadians opted for the British system of "responsible" rather than the American model of "republican" government, they were not only indicating a preference for British over American models, they were also affirming a distinction between themselves and the Americans that went back as far as the old regime in the case of the *canadiens* and the American Revolution in the case of the rest. ...., "the government which governs best governs leas...................... their consti- tution, legislative, executive, and judicial branches were separated and coe- qual in authority. In the American system, vigorous government was intended to be nearly impossible. But in the Canadian version of the Brit- ish constitution, power was concentrated in the Legislative Assembly. In British North America, wherever responsible government existed, the pro- vincial ministers were free to confront the needs of their developing com- munities, quickly and vigorously, unimpeded by competing levels, limited only by the will of their majority organized as a party in the legislature. They might choose to dig canals or build railways. A government might even choose to do nothing at all. There were vice-regal governors, but with no constitutional basis for interference. There were executive, legislative and judicial powers in operation, but no belief that these functions of gov- ernment should operate to "check and balance" one another as in the United States. After 1850, the legislatures of British North America were free to plot their own courses just as forthrightly or evasively as they chose.

CHAPTER NINE

The Price
of Autonomy

I.   Transportation, Tariffs, and Visions of Imperial Grandeur

More relevant to businessmen than constitutional changes in the 1840s
were the economic transformations. At first businessmen were optimistic,
especially about the profits inherent in the creation of the United Province
in 1841. Canadian businessmen, especially the mercantile clique in Montreal, were among those who were far more pleased than chagrined over
the terms of Union. In fact they had been active promoters of the idea
since 1822, the year a bill to unify the two Canadas had almost passed the
British House of Commons. Then, as now, the attraction was economic.

At the time of the Union's proclamation, it was also disclosed that a loan
of £1.5 million had been guaranteed by Britain to assist in paying off the
public debt of the United Province. Now it seemed that the transportation
improvements Montreal businessmen had demanded since the 1790s and
needed imperatively since the 1820s were at hand.

There was some question whether the time had already passed for Canadian canals, however. The Americans' Erie Canal, which had been in
operation since 1825, served roughly the same hinterland as the canals
proposed for the St. Lawrence. New York had already surpassed Boston,
Philadelphia, and New Orleans as the commercial center of the United
States. The gamble was whether Montreal, with an improved waterway on
the St. Lawrence, and trading advantages in the British imperial preference, might still catch up and so establish the Canadian city as the entre-
pot for North America. This had always been the dream behind the vision
of a commercial empire in Canada; in 1840 it finally seemed to have some
chance of realization.

By 1841 there were still major obstacles to overcome in the St. Lawrence River system because so little progress had been made toward developing its transportation potential earlier. At this date only one canal was operational on the St. Lawrence itself. This was the Lachine Canal, which gave access to the Ottawa River but left the rest of "the aorta of the north" unnavigable beyond Montreal. Thus, the five cataracts of the Long Sault were still impassable, and the only water connection with Lake Ontario was a roundabout course the British had built for strategic reasons. In the 1820s the British government had responded to the strident plea for internal improvements by agreeing to build a canal at its own expense, providing it was not on the St. Lawrence, as this was too near the American border. The canal to which British military engineers gave their assent would link Montreal with Lake Ontario by rivers and lakes between Kingston and Ottawa, then called Bytown. When this project, the Rideau Canal, was completed in 1832 schooners and steamers wishing to haul freight between Montreal and the Upper Lakes could do so, but only by sailing from Montreal to Bytown and then slowly down to Kingston. Bulky cargoes could not bear the cost of transportation. Consequently, even though the Welland Canal, started by William Hamilton Merritt and finished in 1829 with support from the province of Upper Canada, bypassed Niagara Falls, thus connecting Lakes Erie and Ontario, the city it served, even after completion of the Rideau Canal, was New York, not Montreal. It was cheaper to move bulky cargo across Lake Erie east to the Welland Canal, then over Lake Ontario to the Erie feeder at Oswego, rather than moving the whole distance of the Erie Canal from Buffalo. But in either case, it was the American rather than the Canadian city that was served.

Now in 1841, the merchants of Montreal looked forward to a change. Canals on the St. Lawrence, with locks one hundred feet long and nine feet deep, and the Welland Canal, improved to the same standard, would give the Canadian metropolis access to an inland water-transportation system at least 30 percent better than New York's. In 1848 it would cost fifteen dollars to move a ton of cargo to New York City from Lake Ontario, but over the Canadian waterway it would only cost ten dollars.

Even though shipping costs from New York to Europe were cheaper than from Montreal, the merchants counted on the advantages of imperial preference, the pattern of tariffs that defined the old colonial system as an economic trading community with preferred status for participating members. Before their secession, the Americans were included in this pattern, but immediately after, they were excluded completely. From 1815 they were granted limited access to the British trading community, but British North Americans enjoyed a distinct preference that persisted down to 1843 through a series of redefinitions. By the last of these mercantilist measures to be passed, the Corn Laws, Canadians gained their most privileged position ever. The Canada Corn Act of 1843 imposed a tariff of five shillings per bushel on all grain imported to Britain from foreign places such as the United States. The duty on Canadian wheat was nearly half that, just three shillings per bushel. Furthermore, American wheat milled into flour in Canada could enter Great Britain as Canadian flour. To the business class of Montreal this was ideal. The transportation revolution was under way and expected to be fully completed before the end of the decade. Now there was a reaffirmation of imperial preference just at the time the Canadians wanted it affirmed. In 1843, Canadian businessmen cheerfully predicted "We are destined to become a wealthy and powerful country at no remote period."

Then the bubble burst. The set of changes that gave victory to political reformers boded ill for Canadian businessmen. In 1846, Sir Robert Peel, who had been moving his party in the direction of free trade for some time, carried the repeal of the Corn Laws. In its wake the preference for Canadian timber came down, and with it the whole system of Navigation Acts that had been the old basis for empire. The colonies of British North America were now more free, but they were also left more alone. Especially so were the businessmen.

II. A New Strategy

By 1849, Montreal's vision of empire came crashing down. "In 1843 we triumphed," one investor remembered at the end of the decade, "so I commenced my Welland Mills and finished them about mid-summer last ... my mill has done nothing since it was finished." The problem was more than losing their privileged market and having to adjust to world competition, for the merchants found themselves facing the further humiliation of witnessing their oldest competitors thrive on the change. As Britain moved to free trade, the United States adjusted to take maximum advantage of the temporarily buoyant British market. They removed their duty on Canadian wheat for reexport, and the farmers of Canada West rushed to take advantage of the lower freight rates from New York. Canadian merchants despaired: "the glory is departed," one of them lamented.

Canadians had been mistaken to put such heavy reliance upon imperial preference in the first place. They were wrong to assume that a tariff in Great Britain could have the effect of funneling the produce of a continent to one warehousing point for transshipment to the world at large. Nevertheless, they had assigned omnipotence to their metropolitan connection, and planned everything accordingly.

Canadians had also been mistaken in assuming that British consumers would tolerate artifically expensive bread indefinitely for the sake of business interests overseas. To Canadians, though, imperial preference was only a small favor a grateful mother country should extend in return for the continued loyalty of the colonists. To Britons, on the other hand, preference was a subsidy that enriched shippers and merchants, and was the reason why bread and wood cost much more than they should. The Anti-Corn Law League, led by Richard Cobden, was more concerned with the price of bread than with empire. Mercantilism was Goliath. Cobden was David. When free trade slew the tariffs, virtue triumphed.

Canadian business declined precipitously. By 1848 the dual effect of glutted markets and altered trading patterns forced many businesses into bankruptcy. Lord Elgin estimated that at least half of the trading firms of Montreal had gone bankrupt between 1846 and 1848. Of course the general move to free trade affected lumbermen and timber merchants as well. There were firms in Quebec and Saint John that closed their offices and returned to England, or reopened on the Baltic. But grain dealers were Canadians, with no other home to which they might retire. They became a singularly desperate group by 1849. In that year, the price of flour was half what it had been five years earlier. Oats were selling for one third of their 1847 value.

As the worst seemed continually to worsen, the business community sought relief in panaceas. The first was free trade with the United States. But since northeastern manufacturing interests feared that Canada's close relations with Great Britain might lead to merchants dumping cheap British goods in the American West via the Great Lakes, New England businessmen were opposed to any such arrangement. Nevertheless, a free-trade bill did pass the House of Representatives before it was killed in the Senate. Governor Elgin despaired. He now believed that "the conviction that they would be better off if annexed [to the United States] is almost universal among the commercial classes at present."

Indeed, many traders did actively push for political union with the United States as their next best cure-all. In part, this was the result of political as well as economic frustration. In April of 1849 the Parliament of the United Province of Canada seemed to have repudiated loyalty to Britain even more thoroughly than the British had dissolved their colonial preference. In that year the Canadian Parliament passed the bill appropriating £100 000 to indemnify the sufferers in the rebellions, a Rebellion Losses Bill the governor general did not disallow. Since the recipients of the appropriation included some of the most notorious rebels, loyalists went on a rampage. They rioted. They set fire to the Parliament building and destroyed the homes of the most prominent members of the government. The Thistle Curling Club went so far as to strike the governor-general, Lord Elgin, from its roll of honorary members. The violence lasted several days but the returning quiet did not bring back the rioters' loyalty. Many felt that if Great Britain were no longer interested in preferring them they might as well follow their economic self-interest into the United States. Thus, an annexation movement developed over the summer of 1849.

On October 11, 1849, "An Address to the People of Canada" appeared as the manifesto of the annexationists. The document was short and surprisingly matter-of-fact, given the extremity of its purpose. "The reversal of the ancient policy of Great Britain whereby she withdraws from the colonies their wonted protection in her market" was identified as the cause of the crisis that "has produced the most disastrous effects upon Canada. In surveying the actual condition of the country, what but ruin or rapid decay meets the eye?" The evidence was impressive:

> "Our Provincial Government and civic corporations embarrassed, our banking and other securities greatly depreciated, our mercantile and agricultural interests alike unprosperous, real estate scarcely saleable upon any terms, our unrivalled rivers, lakes and canals almost unused; whilst commerce abandons our shores, the circulating capital amassed under a more favourable system is dissipated, with none from any quarter to replace it."

The "Address" posed six possible ways for Canada to extricate herself from such a dreadful situation. The first was "revival of protection in the markets of the United Kingdom." But the restoration of mercantilism was ruled out on grounds that the British would eventually stray back to free trade and "cheap food; and a second change from protection to free trade would complete that ruin which the first has done much to achieve." The second suggestion was for a Canadian tariff to "encourage the growth of a manufacturing interest in Canada." But the anticipated drawback to this policy was doubt that anybody outside Canada would buy such goods, and "from want of consumers, manufactures could not survive on the home market alone." A "Union of the British American provinces" was the third proposal, but the people in the "sister provinces" had the same surpluses as the Canadians, so this would only enlarge the scene of the suffering. On this account, a wider union was "no remedy." Nor was the "independence of the British North American colonies as a Federal Republic." This fourth possibility, with all that it entailed in developing the "acquirement of a name and character among the nations, would, we fear prove an over-match for the strength of the new republic." No non-nation could pretend to be a real nation and succeed. "Reciprocal free trade with the United States" was therefore attractive. But this had been proposed already and failed. Thus, only one choice was left: "This remedy consists of a friendly and peaceful separation from the British connection and a union upon equitable terms with the North American Confederacy of Sovereign States."

A long list of supposed benefits to the citizens of the State of Canada followed. First, "union would render Canada a field for American capital, into which it would enter as freely . . . as into any of the present states." Annexationists predicted that real estate values would rise, "probably doubling at once the entire present value of property in Canada . . ." The St. Lawrence would be alive with commercial shipping once again. Manufacturers would arise in "Lower Canada especially, where water power and labour are abundant and cheap." The production of raw materials would increase, "enhanced by free access to the American market." On it rolled, the long list of economic benefits that were supposed to follow from annexation.

Not one principle, not one moral intention was cited. Annexation arose from material self-interest and was so presented. Equally striking was the utter lack of self-confidence that the "Address" betrayed. The whole document, usually referred to as the Annexation Manifesto, was framed in a tone of sober acceptance of failure. The mother country had failed her colonies. The empire of the St. Lawrence had failed in its bid for commercial grandeur. And, in the future, without a substitute for Britain, Canadians did not see how they could even survive, not to mention compete. The annexationists were not only saying that British North America consisted of colonies that had not grown up; their prediction was that they could not become a national entity even with the passage of time.

The pessimism of the "Address" was thus noticeable; but it was also remarkable how prevalent this mood seems to have been among the population, especially the business community. The day the Annexation Manifesto appeared almost 400 people signified their agreement by signing their names to the document circulated as a petition. By October 18, one week after the "Address" had been issued, another 600 signatures had been secured. The first one thousand signers included many of the financial and political leaders of Montreal. The list included John and William Molson, the brewers, D.L. Macpherson, a future lieutenant governor of Ontario, and numerous other people prominent then and more so later. J.J.C. Abbott, the prime minister of Canada in 1891-92, is only the best example among many here. As the Annexation Association took form, a plan emerged to establish local committees beyond the city and form a party strong enough to control a majority in the Assembly. Since it was constitutionally permissable now that responsible government had arrived, the party would set policy on an annexationist course.

But it soon became evident that the French-speaking population of Canada East was distinctly cool to this scheme. Obviously the security of their culture, which had narrowly missed destruction by union with Canada West, would be even more endangered once Canada was submerged as only one state in the United States. In Canada West, similarly, the idea was almost equally unpopular. The government appealed to the ingrained loyalism of Upper Canada, saying "The mother country has now... been leaving to us powers of self-government, more ample than ever we asked, and it does appear a most impious return to select such a time for asking for a separation." Here the cause foundered. The businessmen-annexationists were nearly alone.

III.   A Decade of Unexpected Prosperity

At its peak, the annexation movement probably did not attract more than two thousand active adherents. Yet the discontent and uncertainty that gave rise to this extreme defeatism was not limited to one colony, nor was economic disappointment the only source of gloom. The immigration of the day was also distressing. This last great inflow of newcomers by timber ships arrived just as economic prospects dimmed, and the immigrants who landed were the most destitute yet seen. They were refugees from the Irish potato famines of 1845-48. More than 60 000 people, "penniless and in rags," appeared in one year at Quebec, the major port of entry. Nearly one third perished within one year of their arrival, and another third, probably "the healthiest and best off," moved south into the United States as soon as they touched land.

The diseases that killed the immigrants spread to the colonists as well, of course. In 1847 there were epidemics of typhoid fever from Saint John to Toronto, and more than 16 000 people died. In 1849 the plague was cholera; there were deaths by the thousands again. Many people responded to the crisis with compassion and useful service; as Lord Elgin himself reported, "Nothing can exceed the devotion of the nuns and Roman Catholic priests and the conduct of the clergy and many of the laity of other denominations has been most exemplary." Yet far more people responded with the baser reflexes of prejudice and panic. To discourage immigration, a head tax, a kind of entry fee, came into effect. To prevent the spread of disease, stricter quarantine was imposed, which meant prolonging the agony of immigrants in "foetid infections." This confinement of the apparently well with the obviously dying meant that newcomers could not spread infection among the established colonists, who considered their own lives more important than those of the immigrants. Yet it also reflected a virulent prejudice. Thus, Elgin also reported that the prospective employers of immigrants in Canada West were "unwilling to hire even the healthy immigrants" after their quarantine period had passed, and the newcomers began the adventure of making new lives for themselves in this land reputed to be a place of great opportunity. But unable to find work in British North America, many moved on to try their luck elsewhere, in the United States.

These recent immigrants were not alone in deserting the imperial connection. United States immigration figures for the period are incomplete, but if the numbers in the records that do survive are taken as a sample, rather than as a complete enumeration, it is possible to suggest trends over time. On this basis, it is possible that twice as many residents of British North America emigrated to the United States in 1846, the year that abandonment of British protection began, as in 1843, the heyday of mercantilism, given the Canada Corn Act. Furthermore, the tendency evident by 1846 continued on to the end of the decade. In 1849, emigration to the United States was three times that of 1843. In 1850 the tendency peaked with about five times the number leaving British North America as in 1843. In the 1850s emigration to the United States dwindled. Finally, in 1861, the year the Americans began their Civil War, the number fell back to the level of 1843. Thus, while some Canadians launched an annexation movement and registered their panic about the economic crisis brought on by the abandonment of mercantilism, many more expressed similar pessimism by migrating to the United States, a country with no end in sight to prosperity and no mother country to betray it.

Most of the people of British North America adjusted less dramatically. Here the case of New Brunswick is a prime illustration. In the first years after the end of the timber preference, merchants were caught in the grip of the same terrible panic as the Canadians. Lumbermen were encouraged to shift from timber-making to agriculture. At the same time, the businessmen cried out for the restoration of mercantilism, and failing that, a new mother country. Later, when the timber trade had shrunk to one third of its normal volume, the Saint John businessmen bagan to think that annexation to the United States was the answer. Thus, in April of 1849 the Saint John *Morning News* announced:

> "On Loyalty we cannot live.
> One Ounce of Bread it will not give,
> Clear the way for Annexation,
> Or we shall meet with starvation."

Workmen indicated support for the same escape by migration to the United States or emigration to Australia and New Zealand.

But the end of the protective tariff on New Brunswick timber proved to be a blessing in disguise. Of necessity, the province turned to shipbuilding as never before. They had always built some ships, but as long as the British market for timber was accessible and profitable, ship builders had to scramble for their lumber. Now they were an attractive market themselves, and the New Brunswick economy looked for a time as if it were beginning to develop independently of the metropolitan context. This tendency toward an inverse relationship between the amount of timber exported and the tonnage of ships built existed before 1840. But in the 1840s and after, it achieved new significance. In time, the blessing became a curse.

The wooden ship gradually replaced the imperial market as the invincible economic pivot. Just as the St. Lawrence merchants had once attributed omnipotence to their superior trading system, so did New Brunswick investors think that the superiority of their schooners and barques assured a future of unchanging profit. As the rest of the world was turning to iron ships and steam propulsion, Maritimers continued to invest their future in wooden sailing ships. When a Maritimer did go with the prevailing trend he was soon drawn elsewhere. Thus Samuel Cunard, a Nova Scotian, set his first "steamship on schedule" in 1840. But in 1845 he moved the western terminus of his transatlantic operation from Halifax to Boston. What might have been a real beginning proved instead to be a false start. A similar story applies to another beginning, that of coal oil. Kerosene was invented by Abraham Gesner of Nova Scotia as a means to utilize Cape Breton coal. But he could not interest local businessmen to back him in the commercial production of this new luminant. Halifax investors were quite happy with whale-oil lamps and a maritime economy. Gesner took his idea to New York and Maritimers continued to build and sail more rather than fewer wooden ships. From one standpoint, that of the heroic continuation of a tradition that was the very personification of a sturdy people making the best of challenging circumstances, well they might. Sailors the world over recognized the bluenose craft and crews without a second glance. Consider, for instance, this recognition of one such vessel overtaking quite a different ship somewhere between Australia and Africa:

> "... the stranger came storming up out of the west into plain sight. She was a big ship—a wooden three-master, black-hulled, heavily sparred, and deep laden—and she was forging through the long green seas with yards almost square . . . . This exhibition of sail-carrying in a heavy breeze, the well-set and well-trimmed masts and yards, the faultlessly stayed masts, and general spotless appearance of the ship evoked ... murmured admiration . . . . 'Hard packets these Bluenose ships. Worse than the Yankees, they say.' "

Nova Scotians built and sailed. New Brunswick built and sold. Together they reached the zenith in their development of the art early in the 1860s when nearly 700 vessels were built in a single year. But the rest of the world was already well advanced in turning to iron-hulled ships; and, year by year, this tendency caught up with New Brunswick and Nova Scotia. By the 1880s wooden shipbuilding was a sick and dying industry, with nothing having arisen to take its place. Thus, the Atlantic region, especially New Brunswick, was caught with a single-industry economy later just as it had been earlier. In the heyday of the schooner, as in the happy time of timber, there was too little willingness to diversify. Nor was there any apparent need to do so. For in 1854, the people of British North America as a whole rejoiced in a new imperial preference, this time, that of the United States.

Economic conditions in all the colonies had been improving since 1850 with an unexpected yet welcomed rise in the price of all staples. In part this was due to factors over which the colonists had no control: the California gold rush of 1849, and later the Crimean War between Russia and Great Britain allied with France. But the new preference was the result of local initiatives underway since 1849. At the height of the crisis over Britain's transition to free trade, William Hamilton Merritt, the Canadian entrepreneur of Welland Canal fame, persuaded New Brunswick to initiate the calling of an inter-colonial conference at Halifax. What followed was the first meeting between Canadian leaders and representatives of the Atlantic region to exchange views on matters of mutual concern. They discussed trade, of course, and more particularly what they might offer as enticement to the United States to win a reciprocity agreement that had been impossible to achieve by Canada alone. It was agreed that their best bargaining counter for free admission of Canadian staples would be unlimited access to the inshore fisheries of New Brunswick, Nova Scotia, and Prince Edward Island for the Americans. Although Nova Scotia was unenthusiastic, and Newfoundland initially refused to discuss the proposal at all (St. John's merchants felt they had everything to lose and absolutely nothing to gain from any free trade deal with the Yankees), reciprocity was in fact secured five years later in 1854, basically on the terms of the Halifax conference. It was negotiated in Washington by the charming governor general, Lord Elgin. The British conceded the inshore fisheries, the Americans allowed free entry of a broad spectrum of natural products including Newfoundland fish, Nova Scotia coal, New Brunswick lumber, and Canadian flour. Subsequently the treaty amplified an already encouragingly high level of prosperity. It also provided a psychological boost: reciprocity with the United States was not quite imperial preference, but to colonists who yearned for the supposed economic benefits of a mother country, the treaty was the comforting surrogate they desired.

IV. The Railway Mania

A good index to the optimism that accompanied the unexpected prosperity of the 1850s was the enthusiasm British North Americans developed for railways. In 1850 there was little in the way of commercial railway transport. By 1860 there were nearly two thousand miles of track in service and schemes in agitation for perhaps ten times that amount to build in the future. In fact the railway mania did not abate until about 1920, at which time Canada had more miles of track per capita than any other country in the world.

In part the railways were attractive because they could fill an important economic need. Unlike rivers, they could be made to run almost anywhere and in winter as well as in summer. Also they were a faster means of transport than steamships or sailing vessels. For the farmer more than twenty miles from navigable water, or for the merchant located on a waterway, forced to maintain a large inventory, owing to the impossibility of resupply after freeze up, a railway was a highly attractive alternative to wagon transport. Thomas Keefer, a Canadian civil engineer, went even further in his estimation of their economic importance. Writing in 1849, he said they were "now indispensible." "In conclusion," Keefer asserted, "as a people we may as well in the present age attempt to live without books or newspapers, as without Railroads. A continuous Railway from tide water to Huron upon the north side of the St. Lawrence, we *must* have, and as it will be the work of years we should lose no time in commencing it."

The United Province of Canada already had one of the finest systems of internal navigation in the world. The system of canals and harbors "from tide water to Huron" was in fact less than a year old when Keefer asserted that it needed to be paralleled by rail. In the context of the prosperous 1850s the wisdom of the project seemed inescapably obvious, no less so to Maritimers than to Canadians. They, for their part, wanted a rail connection between Halifax and Montreal. Saint John sought the same. From Halifax to Sarnia the idea spread like an obsession. The *Acadian Recorder* expressed the notion as well as any other paper or person. In one sentence it declared: "No nation can be great without a railroad."

The railway mania was exciting for reasons that went far beyond economics. In fact nearly all of the railway projects of the 1850s, and most that followed later, were economic disasters in the sense that they were built to generate profits for private investors, but attracted too little private investment to move beyond the stage of conception; after receiving enormous government subsidies to cover construction, they failed to make a profit once they were operational. Nevertheless, the railway's reputation for indispensability only increased. The waterways, which continued to carry most of the bulky cargo, receded in apparent importance. By the railway criterion, Canada went on to become the greatest country in the world.

In the Canadian context the railway had an important psychological function that would always redeem it from criticism based on cost-effectiveness (they were uneconomic) or politics (they were sources of collusion between businessmen and politicians). The railway was important because it seemed to abolish the cruelties of chance, which had dealt British North Americans vast expanses of topography too rugged for agriculture and winters severe enough to lay down sheets of ice more than three feet thick over every lake and slow-running river. This fact came first in Keefer's promotion of the railway: "Old winter is once more upon us, and our inland seas are 'dreary and inhospitable wastes' to the merchant and to the traveller;—our rivers are sealed fountains—and an embargo which no human power can remove is laid on our ports." But with a railway "to the most neglected districts" there will be "the daily scream of the steam whistle" of "the iron civilizer" as a reminder of "escape." Thus, Montreal joins Prescott and Halifax, Sarnia and Saint John, "since it is now universally admitted, that distances are virtually diminished in the precise ratio in which the times occupied in passing over them are diminished." So let us proceed, cried Keefer, we have no choice, "we must *use* what we have or *lose* what we already possess—capital, commerce, friends and children will abandon us for better furnished lands unless we at *once* arouse from our lethargy; we can no longer afford to loiter away our winter months, or slumber through the morning hours." Thus began the frantic boom that ran unabated past the end of the century.

The first railway was completed in 1853, less than four years after Thomas Keefer published his *Philosophy of Railroads*. The first line connected Montreal with the ice-free harbor of Portland, Maine; hence the name of the venture, the St. Lawrence and Atlantic Railway. The purpose of the link was reasonable enough, but for the sake of economy the roadbed and track were built so cheaply and hastily that the railway failed to make a profit due to one breakdown after another from the moment service began.

A rival scheme was the Intercolonial Railway. Rather than connecting Montreal with a nearby ice-free American port, this line was to run through a much longer distance of uninhabited territory and connect ultimately with Halifax. The idea for this railway was stillborn in the 1840s, however, because there were too many difficulties in gaining intercolonial cooperation on financing and deciding upon the route it should follow. The idea came up again in 1851 and died once more. Then in 1852 the British government, recognizing the utility of such a railroad from the standpoint of defense, called a conference of representatives from Nova Scotia, New Brunswick, and Canada to meet in London. Here Joseph Howe emerged as the Intercolonial's most eloquent champion. But despite his flamboyant rhetoric and good intentions, the colonists failed to agree on the two basic points: the location of the route and the terms of finance.

But Francis Hincks, one of the Canadian representatives, returned from the London conference hopeful that he might persuade his province to build a trans-Canada line, that is, a railway from Sarnia in the west to Quebec in the east. He proposed this as an entirely private venture. The public involvement would be no more than responsibility for chartering the line. Thus the Grand Trunk Railway was incorporated in 1852. The charter authorized a corporation with an initial capitalization of £9.5 million. Peto, Brassey, Jackson and Betts would do the building. Baring Brothers would handle finance. Both of these were reputable English firms. The railway could not fail.

In seven years the Grand Trunk was operational. The directors bought out the St. Lawrence and Atlantic, thus acquiring an ocean terminus ready-made. Then they extended the line to Quebec City in the east and to Sarnia in the west. When the railway was completed in 1859 it extended more than a thousand miles in length. Yet, by the time of its completion, the Grand Trunk proved so unattractive to private investors that the government of Canada was the primary guarantor of its solvency. In fact, the relationship of this private company to government was so much like that of hog to trough that critics stopped referring to the project as a railway. They called it the "Grand Trunk Pig."

Detractors were a minority, however. The Grand Trunk failed as a business, but it worked the psychological magic people demanded. Thus historians have tended to agree with J. M. S. Careless that "despite its costs in political scandals and bankrupt investors one could hardly imagine what the country would have been without the Grand Trunk." It was corrupt, it was extravagant, but it was thought to be indispensable. Mostly it was typical: an economic fiasco. Actually, of the half-dozen railways undertaken in the 1850s only one of them was not constructed ahead of demand. The one solvent road was the Great Western, which ran from Hamilton to Detroit in 1855 and soon extended as far east as Toronto. The key to its success was its route through heavily populated territory that was not already well served by water transport. By contrast, three-quarters of the Grand Trunk paralleled the waterway of the St. Lawrence. But all the railways, the most colossal failures as well as the one success, had one point in common: their building and their inauguration was the occasion for terrific enthusiasm. The railway boom and the optimism of their advertising joined British North America physically as no one before had even dreamed it could be unified. But this was a unity of proximity, not of mind. Each colony, now autonomous, was a "little nation" unto itself with a sense of a common British practice, but little awareness of a future with the others.

PART THREE

Nationality by Act of Parliament

CHAPTER TEN

Federal Union

1. From Expected Assimilation to Quasi-Federalism in the United Province of Canada

When the imperial authorities decided upon a union of the Canadas in 1840, they determined that harmony should prevail at almost any cost between the mother country and the colony, more specifically, between the governor and the Assembly. Lord John Russell, the colonial secretary at the time, had instructed the governor not to oppose the wishes of the local legislature except when "the honour of the Crown or the interests of the Empire were jeopardized." This policy of harmony was continued by Russell's successor, Lord Stanley. Here was the imperial context for the emergence of responsible government. The same British policy was decisively important for another constitutional development, that of federalism.

Federalist tendencies were inadvertent, however. To paraphrase Durham, the reason for the union was to keep the "French" quiet, and to make them British as speedily as possible. But in the period between 1841 and 1852 the two goals of harmony and assimilation proved irreconcilable. The reason was the problems that arose from assigning equal representation to each section of the Union, despite the fact that Canada West (Upper Canada) had but 450 000 population to Canada East's (Lower Canada's) 650 000. The architects of union had thought that the "English" voters from the upper half, together with those from the lower part, would be sufficient to "Swamp the French." But the immediate result was dualism, that is, quasi-federalism, rather than unity and the disappearance of French patterns in one common British mold.

The tendency to dualism was apparent from the very beginning of the

151

Union "experiment." Charles Thompson, Lord Sydenham, the first governor, presided over not one but two systems for administering justice.
Thus, there were two attorneys general. This expedient was considered
temporary but essential for the moment, because there were two systems
of law then in use. Chaos would have resulted from an overly abrupt transition to one. But assimilation was expected, and in fact legal provision had
been made to abolish French civil law—it remained only to be proclaimed
by a governor.

But no assimilationist policies were implemented in Sydenham's first
year as governor of the United Canadas, and the year, 1841, was also his
last. Sydenham's successor, Sir Charles Bagot (the official noted previously
as the governor who failed to hold the line against responsible government), is notable in the present context as one who also contributed to the
development of quasi-federalism. Within weeks of his assumption of
office in 1842, Bagot recognized a need for dual administration of the
different systems of education, and created two superintendents of education. At the same time, additional French Canadian members of the legislature were promoted to the provincial executive. Now Bagot realized that
the developing dualism implied federalism rather than fusion, and he
informed the colonial secretary that assimilation was no more feasible
than holding the line against responsible government. Lord Stanley was
not pleased—on either account.

But Charles Metcalfe, Bagot's successor and the governor chosen to turn
around the drift toward responsible government in its inadmissable sense,
emphatically agreed with his predecessor that assimilation was entirely
incompatible with a policy of harmony. "If the French Canadians are to be
ruled to their satisfaction," he said, "every attempt to metamorphose them
systemically into English must be abandoned . . . . " As a case in point,
Metcalfe cited the discrimination against the French language that was a
part of the Act of Union itself. The clause in question stipulated that
French could be used in debate but not in record. This denial of official status was a cause for considerable resentment, Metcalfe said. It was perceived as a brutal attempt "to destroy their nationality and anglify them
by Force." If such a rudimentary step by the imperial government in the
direction of assimilation were met by this hostility, then, Metcalfe reasoned, the acts of one half the province overtly to change the culture of the
other would excite much greater "bad feeling" and "be made use of by
designing Men for that purpose." Given Metcalfe's conservative inclina-
tions, inadvertent concessions to the fact of dualism looked wiser than
innovation in the direction of assimilation: "The course which I would
recommend would be to leave the French Race no pretext for
complaint . . . . " This meant abandoning the hope of anglicization; it also
entailed positive and "equal" promotion of representatives from both sec-

tions to the Executive Council. The dualism inherent in naming French members to the provincial cabinet was even more apparent after the attainment of responsible government. Then, and later, the ministries went by double, not single prime-ministerial names; the first, for instance, was the LaFontaine-Baldwin government. The precedent stuck. This was dualism at its starkest. It revealed the Union as a quasi-federal rather than a unitary state. Ironically, within three years of launching the "experiment" to assimilate the French by means of union, federalism, not anglicization, had resulted. Metcalfe was the first to recognize and to accept the fact. Eventually even Stanley, who had instructed Metcalfe to resist and "play the game which we recommended to Sir Charles Bagot," realized that nothing else was consistent with Russell's policy of harmony. Nobody chose federalism in this, its embryonic stage; but the alternative was brutal repression, perhaps even civil war.

II.   From Quasi-Federalism to Legislative Deadlock in the United Province of Canada

The governors and the colonial office aimed for harmony, but this is not to suggest that members of the legislature of the United Province dealt with one another harmoniously. In the first two years after the shift from expected assimilation to dualism and quasi-federalism between 1844 and 1846, there were no fewer than seventeen votes on matters pertaining to the domestic concerns of Lower Canada (items such as elections in Montreal, schools, and Jesuits' estates) that were decided by a majority consisting chiefly of members from Upper Canada. Louis LaFontaine, an unflagging supporter of the interests of *survivance* within the British imperial context, took careful note of each, and resented the interference bitterly. But later in the 1850s the tendency moved in the other direction, and Upper-Canada members began to complain of *French* domination. By then the population of the two sections was nearly equal and equal representation was no longer satisfactory to a majority of the Anglophones. The conflict intensified and resulted finally in political stalemate.

The beginning of deadlock in the United Province could be dated with the census of 1851, which disclosed that the population of the two sections, in round numbers, was 890 000 to 952 000. Since the more heavily populated section was Upper Canada, the disparity of equal representation now pinched those Canadians who called themselves English. This fact was flint on steel to members of the House who were already emitting sparks of protest over the members of one section joining with a minority from the other to impose their will beyond their own boundary.

Public support to Church-run schools was an example of one section legislating for another in a particularly sensitive area. In 1850, Canada East appeared to meddle in the affairs of Canada West when a School Act of that year increased state aid to Roman Catholic Schools in Upper Canada. The Irish, who benefited, were delighted at the assistance they received from their Lower-Canada allies. But the Protestant majority was furious. Their fury was most eloquently expressed in the pages of George Brown's Toronto *Globe*. This Presbyterian immigrant from Scotland grumbled first about the "entering wedge" of "priestly encroachment." Then he affirmed that "we can never have peace in Canada until the principle is acknowledged that every church is to stand on its own foundation without aid from government or legislature." Thus he revived the cause of religious voluntarism, the idea that the state is completely secular and without any ties to religion and that all churches are strictly voluntary associations supported exclusively by the cash contributions of their consenting members.

In 1853 Brown was in the provincial Parliament and giving full vent to this cry for "no sectarian schools." At the same time, as a means to this end, he moved for political reform to give him and his fellow "voluntaryists" their due representation in the house. Brown demanded abandonment of the principle of equal union in favor of representation on the basis of population, since more people now lived in Canada West than in Canada East. Subsequently, as "rep. by pop." became the rallying point for a new generation of reformers, new lines of political division followed.

Prior to the surfacing of this bitter ethnic and religious conflict there were radicals in the House, but the more important division was that between Tories and Reformers. Since 1848 this had been a nearly meaningless distinction, because the reforms of the Reformers were all in the past—the chief innovation, the one that gave rise to the reform label in the first place, was responsible government. The spirit of the old Reformers was spent, and the divisions between Reformers and Tories were less than those that set both apart from the new radicals. But the radicals before the arrival of George Brown and his fellow voluntaryists were not enough of a problem for the Tories and Reformers to realize their many similarities. The radicals before Brown were more of a lunatic fringe than a real threat to the status quo. They were the *Parti Rouge* based in Lower Canada, rabidly anti-British and anticlerical, pro-republican and nationalist. In Canada West, the radicals were Clear Grits, thoroughly tough advocates of "commonsense democracy." In a sense, both of these movements were more like hangovers from the 1830s than viable groups facing the future. But now came Brown's "voluntaryists" and the resurgence of a reform impulse with something like a mass following. Now the Reformers in power appeared especially passé since they were unwilling to act other than to conserve what they had already reformed. At this moment, logically enough, they joined with the Tories to make common cause against the new enemies. The step was taken in 1854 when Augustin-Norbert Morin, one-time republican and author of the *Ninety-two Resolutions*, joined with Sir Allan MacNab, one-time member of the Family Compact, as premiers of the province with the aim of heading off dogmatics of every hue. With Sir Allan declaring "my politics now are railways," Canadian "Liberal-Conservatism," the all-embracing center party, was born.

The MacNab-Morin alliance was followed by a union in Canada West of the Grits and Voluntarists. Earlier, George Brown had dismissed the Clear Grits as "bunkum-talking cormorants." But now a pragmatism of his own led him to join forces with his former rivals, and Brown of the Toronto *Globe* emerged as the grittiest champion of reform in Upper Canada. He still wanted "no sectarian schools" and as a means to this end he still sought "rep. by pop." But now for even more weaponry he joined in the cry for a broadening of democracy, demanding universal manhood suffrage, voting by ballot, and elections of new parliaments every two years. An aroused and enlarged Protestant electorate, with increased representation, would defeat those "vassals of French Canadian priesthood" now in power and in collusion with "jobbers" lobbying for the "Grand Trunk Pig." Remove the yoke of French domination; dissolve the corrupt bonds between business and government—this was George Brown's panacea for the public problems of Canada.

His cause became enormously popular in mainly Protestant Canada West. But very little thought was given toward joining with the *Rouges* of Lower Canada. Since the Clear Grits were as rabidly anti-French and anti-Catholic as the *Parti Rouge* was anti-British and anti-Protestant, it might be argued that there was too little mutuality of interest here for any merger to have occurred anyway. Furthermore, the *Rouges*, led by A. A. Dorion, continued to be a relatively unpopular, minor movement in Canada East. In numerical terms, there was not much strength to be gained from such a coalition. The strong party in Canada East continued to be the Lower Canada wing of the Liberal-Conservatives, the *Parti Bleu*.

Division along lines of ethnicity and reform was the structural pre-condition for deadlock, the danger of which increased directly with the popularity of reform in the two sections. So long as the *Bleus* were strong in Canada East, the Conservatives of Upper Canada, even if they were the minority party there, could still continue to govern by maintaining the coalition they had with their French Canadian allies. But if the Grits swept Canada West, and if the *Rouges* made significant gains in Lower Canada, then complete paralysis would follow from the inability of the two reform parties to compromise principles and function effectively in coalition.

The election of 1854 hinted that this was the case. The one of the 1857 repeated the message. The first time, Sir Allan MacNab and Augustin-Norbert Morin were able to manage a sadly divided Parliament by deft compromises and by cultivating the large patronage machine that attended their coalition and the Grand Trunk Railway. In this sense they were running a school for "trimmers" as much as a parliament of a country. Young opportunists such as John A. Macdonald could see that the safest path through the future was by day-to-day coalition-formation and thoughtful pursuit of short-run expediency. This is not to say John A. and company had no principles; merely, their principles were not sacred. Every value could be compromised a little. But in 1857, purity was more popular than pragmatism, and the electorate returned a House that was impossible to manage.

Economic crisis, brought on by another "panic" in international capitalism, and local scandals had increased the stock of reformers in Canada West. In fact, the Grits beat the Conservatives there by 33 to 28 seats. But, in Canada East, the *Rouges* won only 9 of the 65 seats. Even though the *Bleus* of Lower Canada in coalition with the Upper Canada Conservatives held an overall majority, the stability of this ministry depended upon the ability of the leaders of these two Conservative parties to make party discipline stronger than sectional jealousy. MacNab and Morin had both recently retired. The new leaders, John Alexander Macdonald and George Etienne Cartier, were comparatively young and inexperienced. Nevertheless, they soon confronted an issue so thorny and they handled it so masterfully that no one could doubt their professionalism as politicians.

In 1849 Montreal had been the capital of Canada. Since the burning of the Parliament buildings in the rioting over the Rebellion Losses Bill, the government had been "perambulating" between Quebec and Toronto, session by session. The issue was where to locate the seat of government in the future. After ten years of indecision, and after submitting the matter to royal arbitration, the matter reached a crisis in the summer of 1858 when Queen Victoria indicated Ottawa had been nominated as the site for the new capital. *Rouge* members moved for flat rejection of her selection; *Bleus* bolted their party to support the motion; and the government of John A. Macdonald and George Cartier was defeated sixty-four votes to fifty. They resigned. But this was not the end of the episode.

When the governor general invited George Brown to form a government in coalition with A. A. Dorion, Brown leaped at the opportunity, and the impossible coalition of Clear Grits and *Rouges* emerged as the government of Canada on Monday morning, August 2, 1858. Several hours later, one of the members of the opposition moved a motion of no confidence in the ministry because everyone knew Brown and Dorion were irreconcilable enemies. The debate dragged on until after midnight; then in the first hours of August 3, the government of George Brown and A. A. Dorin was defeated seventy-one votes to fifty. The governor general might have granted Brown's subsequent request for a dissolution, but the province had just had an election. Instead, he called back Macdonald, who reformed the old government and covered it by a bit of legal chicanery that George Brown denounced as the "Double Shuffle." The label stuck. By this means John A. Macdonald proved he was no amateur politician. But at the same time he also demonstrated that the best devices for keeping the United Province out of deadlock were legal tricks and supple maneuvers. People of all political groups began to wonder how workable was a union that depended upon trickery for the avoidance of stalemate. If the reality was deadlock, it was absurd to continue to regard the status quo as manageable. Now the Canadians began to think of a general confederation.

III.   Frustrated Visions of Expansion

There was another acute problem that Canada West wanted resolved and no combination of coalitions in the existing Union was competent to handle. This was territorial expansion. By 1857, the best of the agricultural land in Upper Canada was either settled or available only from speculators. There was little inviting soil in the remaining crown land. Thus, the farmers of the region found themselves against the Precambrian Shield, a mantle of rock, lakes, and bush, picturesque and rich in mineral reserves but useless for farming. In 1857 the people of the province also faced economic depression. Naturally, they looked to the country west of Lake Superior, the British West. Especially did they gaze westward when gold was discovered on the Fraser River in 1856.

Prior to the 1850s the whole western country received little notice from Upper Canada. Few Canadians were among those who settled in the West. This was the case with the Red River settlement at the time of the War of 1812, and that pattern of development independent of Upper Canada was repeated on the coast. The British territory that the Americans named Oregon had been lost to the United States in 1846, because Americans were the first white men to occupy the land, and the British were unwilling to risk war to expel them. In response, the Hudson's Bay Company which, by charter or licence from the British Crown, controlled the vast area from the Great Lakes to the Pacific decided to stake a stretegic outpost on Vancouver Island to claim what remained of British Columbia. They planted Fort Victoria with a handful of farmer-settlers directly from Britain. Then beginning in 1856 a throng of gold seekers from the United States rushed into the area around the Fraser River across the Strait of Georgia. James Douglas, the Hudson's Bay Company governor on Vancouver Island, proclaimed his authority over the newcomers. He was subsequently supported in this action by the British government. Thus another part of North America narrowly missed absorption by the United States.

It was due to a private non-Canadian interest, that of the Hudson's Bay Company, that all of British Columbia did not go the way of Oregon. It was the governor of Vancouver Island who was first fearful that the British West would pass to the United States if it were not occupied soon. But by the mid 1850s, Canadians of Upper Canada were becoming increasingly convinced that their little province had a western destiny as grandiose as that claimed by the United States. They were coming to view the whole territory north of the forty-ninth parallel and west to the Pacific as a vast treasure held in trust for them by the Hudson's Bay Company.

Periodically, the firm had to renew its title to the territory. Such occasions in the past had gone unnoticed in Canada, but not in 1857. This year the government of the United Province showed keen interest. In fact, Chief Justice Draper was sent to London to lobby, and Henry Hind was hired to go west, see the land, and report on its potential from his own observations. But this was all. The Canadians could only look and hope. Even if the government of Great Britain had been willing to transfer the bounty that was described in such glowing terms in Hind's report, Canada was unable to accept its annexation because only half the province wanted expansion and lustily demanded it. The other half, Canada East, with no territorial "birthright" beyond its own boundaries, resisted. The members for Canada East knew that annexation of the West would end forever the quality that existed, and since they were half the power of the House, under the current arrangement, annexation of the West to Canada at that time was impossible.

The United Province was thus restricted to internal, not western, directions. The Grand Trunk Railway, for instance, was pursued as a political as much as a commercial innovation. That is, in proportion to which other projects were impossible, the Grand Trunk received disproportionate attention. All the knavery and speculation that might have found an outlet in a western frontier experience went into this vast pork barrel instead. The result was extravagance and corruption, the full extent of which may never be completely known, but individual incidents are suggestive. At Sarnia, for instance, a certain acreage belonging to the British War Office was acquired for railway purposes for $825. But for some reason, the purchaser was not the Grand Trunk but the Canadian contractors, Gzowski, Macpherson & Co., and by the time the land passed from them to the railway the price had risen to $120 000. From the welter of this kind of enterprise the indebtedness of the firm by 1860 was $72 million, and receipts from operations were not enough to pay even the interest charges, not to mention a dividend to private investors who, of course, expected one. Just such a disappointed investor from Britain came all the way to Canada to inspect the railway himself, so appalled was he at the annual report. His inspection only served to convince him that "the Grand Trunk had not begun to be managed as a commercial carrying company . . . . " The railway was a political patronage machine.

But in 1861 a dramatic episode seemed to demonstrate the need for another railway even more uneconomic than the Grand Trunk. The reason was defense. The problem was a crisis in the relations between the United States and Great Britain, arising from the Americans' failure to observe Britain's freedom of the sea. The Civil War had just begun, and representatives of the separatist Confederacy of the South were on board the British mail steamer, *Trent*, bound for England to negotiate for aid in the war. Naturally the forces of the northern Union were anxious to prevent this assistance. What outraged the British was their action of stopping the *Trent* in international waters and taking the Confederate ambassadors into custody at gunpoint. Some British officials regarded the "Trent affair" as a cause for war and were prepared to act accordingly. Others advocated moderation, but everyone could agree it was wise to strengthen the defenses of British North America should war ensue. Thus, fourteen thousand troups were rushed to the colonies but they arrived too late in the year to steam up to the eastern terminus of the Grand Trunk on the St. Lawrence. Obviously the army could not disembark at the alternate terminus of the railway at Portland, Maine, so the men were unloaded at Saint John, and made their way overland through seven hundred miles of hip-deep snow. If the Intercolonial Railway, first proposed in 1852, had been undertaken with the same energy as the Grand Trunk, the whole trek would have been unnecessary.

But the building of the Intercolonial required the cooperation of more than one legislature. Furthermore, it was difficult to see how the transportation of ten thousand or twenty thousand troops from Halifax to Quebec on those rare occasions of winter war scare was enough justification to undertake the project—and defence against the United States would have to be the sole justification; if the Grand Trunk could generate only enough revenue to pay operating expenses and some of the interest charges on the outstanding indebtedness, a railway through the most sparsely settled parts of New Brunswick and Nova Scotia could not be expected to fare any better. Nevertheless, the enthusiasm of Saint John and Halifax businessmen knew no bounds, and for some Canadian politicians railways were the only political questions they relished. For a while, therefore, it appeared in 1861 and 1862 that the legislatures of the three provinces directly involved would cooperate with the imperial authorities in building the Intercolonial Railway as an entirely public project. Then Canada backed out, having just increased taxation to bolster the still faltering Grand Trunk Railway.

Maritimers seethed with anger when they learned in the autumn of 1863 that the Canadians would only commit themselves to sharing survey costs of the proposed venture. Saint John merchants consoled themselves by pursuing an alternate scheme that was attractive because it seemed more economic; but since this idea involved nothing more than the extension of a rail line to the State of Maine, it failed to spark the same enthusiasm or sense of British patriotism. Nor did "western extension" please the Nova Scotians. They proposed a solution more patriotic, and more thoroughly political. The Nova Scotians attempted to sell the idea of forming a maritime union.

Maritime union was not novel in 1863. It had been actively pursued several times before, and history did seem to be repealing the division of the region into many different provinces, which had occurred between 1769 and 1783. Cape Breton Island was a separate province until 1820, when it again became part of Nova Scotia. Now that the railway age was upon New Brunswick, they could think of nothing grander than "western extension" by themselves. United with the other Atlantic provinces grander schemes were possible. One united "Acadia" was not ludicrous; perhaps it was premature. Still, the first reaction was somewhat encouraging in the sense that the several provinces concerned reacted by debating the proposition, if only in their own provincial parliaments.

Then two events occurred in 1864 to sidetrack the movement to negotiate a maritime union. One was a revival of the Intercolonial Railway proposal when Canada announced its intention of beginning the project on its own to the extent of paying *all* the costs of surveying the route. The other event was the deadlock of the Canadian legislature and the formation of a coalition to seek a solution in a more general union, one that included all the provinces of British North America. Now the Canadians decided to attend a conference on maritime union and sell the idea that any argument in favor of this change was fulfilled even more by uniting all of British North America. But the movement for maritime union had not developed even to the extent of setting a date for such a conference. Still, the Canadians persisted. They asked for an invitation to the future conference anyway. Encouraged by the revival of the Intercolonial Railway and by some of the possibilities of union, maritimers agreed to have a meeting to which the Canadians might come. The date was set for September 1, 1864. The place was Charlottetown.

IV. The Idea of a Wider Federal Union

The Charlottetown conference, which only lasted six days, was still an enormously significant encounter. It was even more important for the nationalism the Canadian delegates defeated than for the nationalism they fostered. The Canadians *fought* nationalism in the sense that they talked representatives of autonomous provinces out of local patriotism in favor of continentalism. Surprisingly, the other delegates were receptive to this argument. The Maritime provinces were entitled to see themselves as nations; they each had their boundaries, autonomy, and a sense of pride in the independence they enjoyed. But some of their politicians disdained regionalism; Charles Tupper of Nova Scotia, for example, derided his "little province" as a "nation by itself." Nor was he alone in this attitude, so successful were the Canadians in persuading those at Charlottetown that their best future lay in a transcontinental British North America.

The Canadians were desperate. Ironically, theirs was the one province in all of British North America that lacked any national unity in its present circumstances. Canada, East and West, was deadlocked. The possibilities were complete separation, the creation of two "little provinces"; a federal union of the two with the prospect of deadlock between equal sides still as strong; or a wider merger on the supposition that every interest in this diverse agglomeration might enter a majority coalition enough of the time to make the alliance more or less permanent. That is, no one faction or ethnic group would be the predictable winner of everything, nor any one group the inevitable loser of all.

These political prospects, which appealed to the delegates as politicians, were still not as evident as another theme, that of Canadian continentalism. This was the belief that British North America had a common "destiny." It was an almost providential idea in that everyone assumed that there there was an over-riding imperative that gave "the races of man" cosmic purpose as they rallied to make "nations." Thus, to Charles Tupper for one, it was a perversion of history that the "little provinces" of British North America each had their own little legislatures, borders and customs officers. It made a mockery of the very idea of a nation. It was far grander for him, and for the other political leaders gathered at Charlottetown, to contemplate governing one "race" from sea to sea. Then they would lead the "Anglo Norman" people of North America. Surely this was their *proper* destiny. Thus as much as politics, it was this exercise in self-projection that occupied the delegates. Indoors and out, they heard and made great speeches about "moral courage." For the details of the union, the principle of which everyone embraced, the delegates agreed to meet again later that year at the capital of Canada, then Quebec. Meanwhile, a sense of destiny prevailed. Thus, in Halifax, for example, the *Witness* reported on September 24 that "a very manifest change has been creeping over the spirit of our leading politicians, and we believe of the people generally. There is less aversion to Canada. Indeed, there seems to be a positive desire for union."

What P. B. Waite has called an "authentic national spirit" pervaded the Charlottetown conference and lasted through the conference at Quebec which occurred in the last two weeks of October, 1864. But here more conspicuous than moralism was the hard bargaining over the actual terms of the union. This was, after all, a constitutional convention, the first in Canadian history (all previous events—1774, 1791 and 1840—were initiated, drafted, and passed by the outside influence of British officialdom and the Parliament of Great Britain). Now, however, in Seventy-two Resolutions, the delegations from the legislatures of all the provinces of British North America east of the Great Lakes agreed that a change in the constitution was due and they themselves settled upon the terms. They agreed upon a legislative union with a central government modeled after the form already existing in the autonomous provinces. That is, rather than imitating the American union with its system of controls balancing judicial, executive and legislative branches, in the proposed Canadian union there would be a House of Commons with representation according to population, and led by an executive responsible to that body itself. This potentially vigorous government was attractive to delegates who, fearful of the looser American system, sought to create the closest approximation to a unitary state that was possible. Furthermore, the representation-by-population aspect was pleasing to the reformers from Canada West. But vigorous central government and "rep. by pop." were both compromised to meet the objections of delegates who welcomed neither.

To pacify those who feared representation by population, because it seemed too populist or prejudicial to the provinces with small populations, an upper house, the Senate, was conceded. Here, representation would be equal, not proportional. That is, each region was promised the same number of senators regardless of population considerations, and it was agreed that Upper Canada, Lower Canada and the Maritimes should each receive 24; Newfoundland was promised 4, the number that would also be given to the West if and when it entered the confederation. And, since no act of the House of Commons could receive royal assent before receiving the confirmation of the Senate, small provinces were assured this safeguard. But there were two problems with the compromise. One was the obvious fact that Upper and Lower Canada were economically one region—the empire of the St. Lawrence—not two as was established for senatorial representation. Therefore, on economic questions that would bring the interests of the maritime region into conflict with the St. Lawrence area, the

Maritimers were going to be outvoted in the House, and by two to one in the Senate as well. To be sure, there was the possibility that Lower Canada and the Maritimes might join to oppose Upper Canada in the Senate on other matters, but this points out the other problem. Since the 1830s British North Americans had exhibited hostility to the very idea of bicameralism. After the concession of responsible government, an appointive upper house had no more freedom to kill legislation emanating from an elected legislature than a governor had free rein to veto acts of the Assembly. This was the nub of responsible government. The power of the crown and "aristocracy" became nice legal fictions, symbolic more than substantive. Nevertheless, the vacuousness of the proposal notwithstanding, the Senate is what the advocates of "rep. by pop." in Canada West were willing to concede to delegates from Prince Edward Island who felt equal to the Canadians in provincial stature, if not in numbers. Curiously, the Islanders accepted the compromise.

A similar series of problems followed from the compromise to accommodate cultural particularism. That is, in recognition of the real diversity between provinces in matters of religion, civil law, education, and language, it was agreed that the provinces would maintain their autonomy in matters of a "merely local or private nature." This was problematic since the implication conveyed by the word *merely* was that the provinces would retain their distinctiveness only on matters of little consequence. If this was so it would have been better to abolish the provinces altogether, and substitute something like the *departments* in France or the counties in England. But the fact then and later was the impossibility of such a reduction. The provinces were to continue because they were not guardians of trivial particularisms. The proposed union emerged paradoxically, then, because the central and the provincial governments were given exclusive jurisdiction over matters vitally important to both. The way around the apparent paradox of unity in diversity was to dismiss the sphere of the provinces as unimportant, even if this was self-deception. Still, it did indicate how the writers of the resolutions mediated the paradox inherent in the federal polity they were creating.

Bicameralism and federalism were the major compromises of the conference, which completed its work in less than two weeks. Now all that remained was for each delegation to return home and persuade the legislature that it was in their interest to compromise local pride and seek grandeur in the larger context. Each Assembly was to adopt an address to the queen praying for an Act of Union on the agreed terms. Since the conference was over before the end of October, 1864, it was possible that a united British America would come into existence within the year. But in the weeks and months that followed, the Seventy-two Resolutions of the Quebec conference sparked the enthusiasm of the western half of one province, Canada West, alone. In Canada East the English-speaking elite was at first completely skeptical, and some persons—such as the principal of McGill College—were actively opposed to the change. What they feared was isolation and subordination as a despised minority. McGill's principal said the "English dominion will be destroyed beyond redemption." Proponents of the Union successfully allayed this anxiety by pointing out that the powers of the provinces would be nothing compared with those of the central government. A. T. Galt dismissed the provinces as mere "municipalities of larger growth." But this assertion also served to support *Rouge* spokesmen, who denounced the union scheme as another attempt to suppress *canadiens*; it was the Durham union idea all over again. This prompted the *Bleus* to reply that the autonomy that was retained was in all the areas most precious: *sociale, civile et religieuse*. Thus, they won over the Catholic hierarchy without offending the elites Galt had courted; and, at the same time, the people of Canada East found themselves pioneers in the concept of coordinate power. The province was to be sovereign in the areas assigned to it, and the central government would be just as powerful in the material concerns of its jurisdiction. In this way, with English-speaking elites looking to the central authority and with clerical elites reassured about local sovereignty, opposition to the union was effectively checked. In Canada East, there was little enthusiasm for union but the anti-union forces were neutralized.

It was not Canada East that struck the death blow to confederation in 1864; that deed was done in the Atlantic provinces. One by one, every autonomous colony in the Atlantic region rejected the change. There were a variety of reasons but local nationalism was primary. Prince Edward Island was only one of several examples in this regard. This island community was a society of self-sufficient farmers all within "a day's drive" from the capital. They had suffered unhappy experiences in the past from absentee directors, and the people liked having the "independent powers" they now enjoyed. Why surrender or even compromise them? they asked. Or as a Nova Scotian put the same idea, emphasizing economic independence: "We have the trade of the world now open to us on nearly equal terms and why should we allow Canada to hamper us?" The reply: "We seek Union because we are, in reality, one people and ought to be one nationality . . . . " was a pious wish. Joseph Howe pointed to the obvious dualism of the United Province. It was clearly not a unity except by law. He keenly appreciated that the fact of duality had been stronger than constitutional unity. This, indeed, was the primary reason for the explicit federalism in the present proposal, and Howe disliked the dynamics of federal politics. He was certain that by "sticking together" the French would control the policy and legislation of the new union, even more than in the past. He predicted that "the English will split and divide as they always do, the French members will, in nine cases out of ten, be masters of the situation. But should a chance combination thwart them, then they will back their Local Legislature against the United Parliament . . . . "

Thus, Joseph Howe denounced the proposal, not only because he thought ethnicity would be the real basis for coalition formation, but also because it seemed to create a structure of competing authorities that invited disaster. Here, his proof was the Civil War, which had been raging in the United States since the spring of 1861 after the American federation split into its antithetical sectional components. "Have we not seen enough of federations . . .? Shall we not draw wisdom from the errors of others?" Thus, the Atlantic region held back, and eighteen months after the Quebec Resolutions were drafted, only Canada had approved them.

V.   The Enactment of Confederation

Although the courtship of the Atlantic governments by the Canadian cabinet was extraordinarily successful at the Charlottetown and the Quebec conferences, the romance failed to infect the populations at large. The Canadians had played on the politicians' sense of self-importance, and successfully persuaded them that they would be more important as the rulers of a nation than of "little provinces." But the simple fact remained that the concrete terms of the proposed union could not stand the questioning of ordinary people whose importance would be diminished by the change. The individual citizen of Prince Edward Island, for instance, could see himself as much more potent out of union than within. In his independent island, he was one in eighty-seven thousand; in confederation, the individual islander would be just one person in an artificial community of three million. What power ordained that bigger nations were inherently better? Thus, on this reasoning, the confederation scheme foundered. Were it not for two external factors, Great Britain and the United States, the cause of the confederates would have remained stillborn forever.

Intervention arose from the incredible fact that at the very moment the delegates were drafting resolutions of confederation at Quebec, soldiers of the southern Confederacy were robbing the banks in the little town of St. Albans, Vermont. The robbers slipped across the border to safety in Montreal, where most of the men and some of the money were apprehended. The Americans demanded extradition. Canada hesitated, and subsequently a judge dismissed all charges against the thieves. As the Confederate robbers went free, the full fury of the Americans was directed at British North America in general. The border was closed to everyone but passport holders and a movement developed in the United States Senate to abrogate the Reciprocity Treaty, which was up for renewal. Ultimately these senators succeeded. Thus, in the same period that the Atlantic provinces were rejecting confederation, the Americans were rejecting British North America—assuming that the free trade agreement in natural products had previously indicated acceptance. The War between the States was coming to an end; and American leaders such as the secretary of state, William Seward, and the senatorial leader, Charles Sumner, were beginning to think of remedies for the grievances between the Union and Great Britain that had grown out of the assistance the British had provided the Confederate states in the form of armament sales, including naval vessels such as the highly effective commerce raider, *Alabama*. For Seward and Sumner, the concession of British North America would cancel the debt of reparations owed the injured Union by John Bull.

The British took the St. Albans raid and the *Alabama* claims very seriously. They saw the Union's victory as an indication of a changed balance of power. Now the relative strength in North America of Britain and the United States was tipped so far in the direction of United States supremacy that the British chose to admit that superiority and withdraw, since their interests in North America were no longer great enough to warrant a strengthening of their own military presence to restore the balance. Thus was the mother country committed to confederation; a confederated British North America could be expected to shift for itself and Britain could concede American supremacy without losing face.

Great Britain not only encouraged Canada in her confederation scheme. Officials simmered with anger over the Atlantic region's reluctance to join the plan they had helped draft, a plan now blessed by the Colonial Office. Thus, W. E. Gladstone, a leading British politician soon to become prime minister, blustered that since "John Bull pays the piper in the matter of defense for the Lower Provinces, there is something almost ridiculous in the idea of their standing upon an opinion of their own in such a matter against ours, and against that of Canada with five or six times their population."

A year after the Quebec conference, Great Britain intervened to break the resistance of Nova Scotia and New Brunswick, the two maritime provinces indispensible to the Union. (Prince Edward Island and Newfoundland, out at sea in any event, could be left there indefinitely and picked up later; much later as it turned out in the case of Newfoundland, which did not join the confederation until 1949.) There were new instructions and, for Nova Scotia, a new governor. Finesse was required but also results were expected. The colonies must join.

Then came an exploitable crisis, a renewal of danger from the United States. The Fenian Order, an Irish patriotic society formed in 1858 to secure Ireland's independence from Great Britain, became a serious threat to British North America in 1866 when the order began to recruit immigrant Irish from the Union army now disbanding after the South's surrender in 1865. In such cities as Boston and New York, immigrant-Irish caught the vision of freeing their homeland by waging a successful flank attack upon the British by striking Britain's colonies in North America. The idea of an assault was made all the more attractive by the knowledge that one third to one half of the colonists were of Irish descent, presumably sympathetic to the cause of an independent Ireland. Although this sympathy was largely imaginary, the governments of the autonomous colonies grew increasingly anxious through the spring and summer of 1866. The Fenians gathered men and arms without active opposition from the United States, and in June actually invaded Canada with nearly one thousand men. Since Great Britain remained steadfastly determined to withdraw British defense forces from British North America, the Fenian threat was an exploitable crisis indeed.

In the face of the Fenian menace, mutual defense could be cited as a justification for confederation. At the precise moment that the threat was most critical in New Brunswick, Arthur Gordon, the governor of that province, maneuvered the local politicians into an election, only one year after the previous appeal to the electorate. In the earlier contest, candidates associated with the confederation scheme had been defeated. The anti-confederate victors had won thirty seats to the pro-confederates' eleven members. But the popular vote in New Brunswick had been extremely close in 1865; 15 556 pro-confederate to 15 949 anti-confederate votes. Now the Fenian crisis and generous cash support for Leonard Tilley's pro-confederation party were enough to tip the scale the other way. In June, 1866, Tilley was back in power with thirty-one seats in the assembly. Then came a resolution affirming support for confederation. A similar resolve came from Nova Scotia. Although the life of the legislature there had almost expired, Charles Tupper did not dare call an election, for confederation was still too odious for many voters. Nevertheless, with the governor inciting him to action, Tupper moved in the House; confederation, dormant since 1864, stirred back to life.

Once the threatened and actual Fenian invasion had subsided with the cover of winter, delegates from Canada, New Brunswick, and Nova Scotia met in London to draft the Quebec Resolutions into a bill for submission to Parliament. There the act was presented as a treaty to be accepted or rejected without alteration. Rejection was unthinkable, although one member of Parliament asserted it ought to be since he had petitions from Nova Scotia with 30 000 signatures indicating opposition to the idea; passage was rapid. On March 29, 1867, the British North America Act received royal assent and "one Dominion under the name of Canada" was legislated into being. Now Great Britain could recognize the United States formally as the supreme power in the Western Hemisphere by withdrawing her forces gracefully. But it remained to be seen how the Americans would recognize the new federation. The *Alabama* claims were still not settled, and the Americans still believed their "destiny" called for expansion from pole to pole in the Western Hemisphere. On the same day the British North America Act received royal assent, the expansive Union purchased Alaska, thus redefining the northern frontier of the United States. Was confederation merely a preparation for annexation? The question was germane in 1867—and later.

CHAPTER ELEVEN

Their Program Was Their Politics

I. The Significance of the Unpopularity of Confederation

Complex problems had driven British North America to confederation. In summary terms, the most critical were: political deadlock in the United Province; American abrogation of reciprocal trade and flirtation with annexation of the British West; the apparent need for an intercolonial railway; and finally the wish to provide some mutual defense now that Great Britain intended to withdraw her garrisons from North America. Confederation broke the deadlock by separating Upper Canada from Lower Canada (as Ontario and Quebec) while at the same time it created an intra-provincial authority to colonize "Rupert's Land and the North-Western Territory." As a further stipulation to the "consolidation of the Union," the BNA Act required work on an Intercolonial Railway from Montreal to Halifax to begin within six months and proceed "with all practicable speed" to completion.

The section of the BNA Act on the railway was understandable in light of the problems that gave rise to confederation, but this act of the British Parliament was also the constitution of the "Dominion." In this respect, Canada came into existence as the only federation in the world whose instrument of government defined its original unity in terms of iron rails and hand-hewn ties rather than in moral or ideological terms. Canada was launched as a collection of provinces to be joined by railway lines. It was not one nation joined by the will of its people.

Nor did it seem likely that Canada would become a unitary state in the future. In accordance with the Quebec Resolutions, characterized briefly in the previous chapter, the provinces retained a great deal of autonomy in "generally all matters of a merely local or private nature." The BNA Act enumerated sixteen classes of legislation in section 92 as "Executive Powers of Provincial Legislatures." The list covered nearly everything imaginable of a social, civil, or familial nature. And the next section went on to assign education "exclusively" to the provinces. By this means, each province was autonomous in everything pertinent to social character and in all matters having to do with nationality in the cultural sense. The central government, by contrast, received broad powers pertaining to material development. Section 91 defined the "Powers of Parliament" to give wide freedom for the government in Ottawa to build railways and canals, and to regulate trade, criminal law, and everything not exclusively assigned to the provinces. To make the distinction simply, perhaps crudely, one might suggest that while the provinces were supposed to look after everything sacred, the central government was to oversee anything of cash value. In this way, the division of sovereignty in Canada's constitution preserved the provinces as "little nations" and added a central Parliament to superintend matters of collective security, "peace, order, and good government." Therefore, confederation created a new country that was supplementary rather than successive; that is, the union was not a complete merger obliterating all the old linguistic and cultural diversities in one uniform Canada.

The federal aspect of the union was not very popular outside Quebec. But given the manner in which the change was made, the lack of popularity was irrelevant to its legitimacy. This was unusual. Most colonial societies that made the step from colonial status to nationality attempted to create a popular myth to explain their conception. Thus, in the United States, for instance, the preamble to their second constitution, which went into effect in 1789, began with the affirmation that "we the people . . . in order to form a more perfect Union . . . do ordain and establish this . . . . " Of course, the elite composed the phrases, but an elaborate ratifying procedure was stipulated to collect the voices of the people, at that time the male freeholders of each state. The problem with this mode of legitimizing a country was the tacit assumption that what the majority had a right to create, they also had the right to destroy, since the authority that justified separation from the mother country, the will of the people, was the same that legitimized the union. Consequently, separatism was endemic. In the United States it was threatened repeatedly; finally, in 1860 and 1861, "we the people" of the far southern states "solemnly declare the Union heretofore existing is dissolved . . . . " Civil war followed and force of arms cemented the union back together. Ultimately it was brutality rather than legality that made the Union permanent.

But in Canada, Confederation was enacted without a myth of

popularity—and this was no accident. It was entirely consistent with the ancient and self-conscious hostility to republicanism in British North America that insisted that sovereignty resided in the sovereign rather than in the voice of the people. This is why the governments of the provinces involved in the union project took their seventy-two resolutions to England and went through the ceremony of passage by Parliament and reception of royal assent to sanctify the change. To later, less monarchical generations of Canadians it might have seemed a rather superfluous bit of legalism. But in 1867, the monarchy was still a vital symbol of the way British North Americans placed themselves above the "slatternly republics" of the New World, and were it not for a wish to avoid offending the United States the new confederation would have been known as the *Kingdom* of Canada.

Predictably, legitimization by royal assent was a stabilizing influence in the first years of confederation. Just as the popularity of the change was not essential to its legitimacy, so the popularity of separatism was not sufficient to bring about secession. Consider the case of Nova Scotia. The vast majority of the Bluenoses did not want confederation. On July 1st, 1867, they mourned the passing of their independence more than they celebrated the launching of the Dominion; and, later, in September of 1867, there were elections in which this displeasure became manifest. In the contests for the local legislature, thirty-six of the thirty-eight seats were won by separatist candidates. For the Parliament in Ottawa, to which the electors were supposed to send nineteen members, they elected eighteen separatists.

Then, the first post-Confederation throne speech in Nova Scotia called for dissolution of the Union. In the context of the pre-Civil War United States this demonstration of popular resentment would have been enough to de-ratify the constitution. But the legal means of dissolving the Canadian union required repealing the BNA Act. For this, the government prayed to the queen. But in England, Prime Minister Disraeli agreed with the colonial secretary's view that "no legal ground of objection to the Confederation Act exists" because the measure "took place in accordance with the expressed desire of the people of all the Provinces expressed in the only known constitutional mode—through their respective legislatures." So the Crown refused to comply with the request of the new government of Nova Scotia acting alone. Now their choice was submission or rebellion. The scrupulously decorous "repealers" chose submission.

The demise of the Nova Scotia repeal movement indicated the potency of the Crown. Although the tie to the monarchy was ever more patently symbolic rather than substantive, the alternative myth was republicanism with its inherent instability. A republican rationalization of repeal would lack permanence. It conjured images of constitutional revolving doors:

what one government made, its successor could unmake—*ad infinitum*. With popularity as the determinative test, Nova Scotia would be continually coming and going, never being. The horror of this prospect, along with the prospect of ample federal cash, turned around even the most ardent repealers, including Joseph Howe who now entered the federal government. Thus, in 1869, with larger subsidies and generous patronage from Ottawa to sweeten the change, Nova Scotia became reconciled to Confederation. But the fact remained that it was allegiance at the top that united British North America, not a unity of moral purpose as to the destiny to follow in that common loyalty. Canada was a political—not an organic—nationality.

II   Macdonald and Company Acquire Rupert's Land

That the BNA Act provided a constitutional structure for an official rather than a spontaneous union was illustrated by the Nova Scotia repeal movement between 1867 and 1869. This matter-of-fact approach to nation building was also emphasized by the first projects embarked upon by the first Dominion government; they included railways, the promotion of fisheries, and territorial expansion, and indicated that Confederation was unfolding with about the same excitement as the incorporation and expansion of a joint-stock company. There were, it is true, those who protested against this lack and who struggled to define their country in more heroic terms. But their voice was weak, and the effect was only to underline yet more starkly the lack of ideological commitment as a determinative factor in Canadian history.

While John A. Macdonald, the chairman of the board, presided over Parliament, only a tiny group of ideologists met together to preside over the creation of a national myth. The motto of the group was "Canada First" to convey the idea that they were united to put the cause of nationalism above all other causes. They felt Confederation was incomplete until a strong out-pouring of "national sentiment" emerged to unify the country as "one nation of brothers." This attitude was predictable enough. Something like Canada First would have had to blossom if Confederation had arisen from any "national spirit" at all. But Confederation had not developed out of a drive toward consolidation and centralization, struggles that made nations out of the principalities of Italy and Germany, or a nation out of the federation of the United States. In the nineteenth century, in those countries, a bevy of poets, demagogues, and other national myth-makers had attended the actions of the generals and the politicians to attribute cosmic significance to the changes that were taking place. By contrast, in British North America before Canada First, the "Fathers of Confederation" had little more than D'Arcy McGee to play this role, and his orations were more bombast than mythical nationalism. When the delegates emerged from the Quebec conference, for instance, everyone felt like hearing some stirring words to herald the great moment. There were shouts for "McGee! McGee!" And, according to P. B. Waite, this is what "deserves to be remembered" from the speech that followed:

> "They had not gone into the Chamber to invent any new system of Government, but had entered it in a reverent spirit to consult the oracles of the history of their race. They had gone there to build, if they had to build, upon the old foundation—(cheers)—not a showy edifice for themselves, with a stucco front, and a lath and plaster continuation—(laughter)—but a piece of solid British masonry, as solid as the foundations of Eddystone, which would bear the whole force of democratic winds and waves, and resist the effect of our corroding political atmosphere, consolidate our interests, and prove the legitimacy of our origin. (Loud cheering)."

When McGee was assassinated in April of 1868, five young Ottawa intellectuals were among the thousands who felt wounded by the loss of "the prophet of confederation." They resolved to carry on where McGee had led; hence the motto, *Canada First*. They dedicated themselves to infusing some spirit into a country that seemed to them "to crawl into existence in a humdrum, commonplace, matter-of-fact way" rather than by "fiery ordeals."

The Canada Firsters felt that the path of glory could yet be trod if only the people could be moved to take it. The mission chosen by these five writers, therefore, was to reveal to Canadians their racial superiority in the world at large and in North America in particular. The people needed to be told, they thought, that Canadians, regardless of province, were all descended from the "Aryan tribes" of Northern Europe and were therefore of good stock for starting a virile new land. Unlike the United States, which had sprung from similar origins, the Canadians were sturdier for having been nursed on "the icy bosom of the frozen North." They, the "Northmen of the New World," were foreordained to greatness. One day there would be a great "rattling war" with the then "weak and effeminate" Americans, and at that appointed hour the "defensively warlike" Canadians would emerge triumphant, "a single nation of brothers." Thus emerged the myth of "The True North Strong and Free." It was hardly more racist or juvenile than the myths born of the other movements that accompanied nineteenth-century drives for national consolidation. What seems significant about the Canadian case was the subsequent failure of the ardent nationalists to propagate their frothy nationalism. What McGee had attempted to begin, and what Charles Mair, William Foster, George Denison, Robert Haliburton, and Henry Morgan attempted to continue, popped briefly, fizzled, and vanished almost completely by 1880.

Their failure was emphasized by the fact that Canada First had had an apparently ideal opportunity to impress itself upon the national consciousness near the end of 1869. The firm of John A. Macdonald, the government of Canada, had successfully completed the humdrum negotiations with the Hudson's Bay Company for the transfer of the West. The arrangement was a business proposition from first paragraph to last. For £300 000 cash and one twentieth of all the land surveyed for settlement, the Hudson's Bay Company agreed to relinquish all rights to governance and colonization. All that remained to complete the transaction by November of 1869 was the formal transfer of authority, and the establishment of a provisional government to administer the territory as a colony of the Dominion. In the hazy future, after the conquest of western primitivism by the steady hand of civilization, provinces would emerge. But provincial status would occur only after the influx of proper colonists; it would not occur at the same time as the transfer since the western population then was primarily made up of Indians and Métis who were considered "inferior races."

Unexpectedly, the people already in the vicinity of Red River resented the government's conspicuous disregard of their attitudes toward the transfer of authority from the Hudson's Bay Company to Canada. Canada's action in sending surveyors west was another cause of resentment. But initially, the Métis of the district felt rather helpless to influence either of these developments. It was then that vital leadership was provided when one of their own, who had been sent for education to the seminaries of Quebec, returned to Red River. This savior was Louis Riel, the very antithesis of Canada First nationalism, yet in his own way no less romantic nor less racist in the feeling he embodied and projected. He traced his French Canadian and Cree Indian origins to the Métis buffalo hunters, a distinctly New-World type as easy to romanticize as any of the "Aryan tribes" of Europe.

Riel felt a divine mission to defend the life of the buffalo hunt, subsistence farming, and barter as a positive good ordained by God for men to pursue with one another, along with the cyclical round of seasons and Roman Catholic sacraments. But mostly Riel spoke as a charismatic political leader, affirming that the people of the Red River settlements deserved to be consulted before they were brought into Confederation—and with the status of a province, rather than as a colony. Thus, Riel and his followers interrupted the apparently inexorable transfer of authority from the Hudson's Bay Company to Canada by forbidding the entry of the colonial governor, William McDougall, on November 16, 1869.

The government now found itself in a dilemma. Two courses of action were open. Macdonald could declare war or negotiate a settlement. From the standpoint of Canada First a show of force was justified, indeed, desirable. But Macdonald chose negotiation, and for more reasons than humanitarianism. First, the Red River resistance had not violated any law. To be sure, they resisted the goverment of Canada, but technically this authority had no business in Hudson's Bay Company territory until the queen ratified the transfer, which had not occurred by November 16. Still, the company's authority had lapsed. Therefore, the people were without formal government and, it might be argued, were justified from the standpoint of international law in establishing a provisional government of their own.

Another of Macdonald's considerations in rejecting force was the political danger to central Canada of launching a crusade in the West that would be a religious-ethnic war. The already fragile union could not bear the additional strain of French-speaking Catholics versus English-speaking Protestants, certain to occur in any repression of the French-speaking Catholic Métis around Red River. For these reasons it was decided to send an ambassador rather than an army. Donald Smith, the Hudson's Bay Company official chosen for the task, arrived on the spot at the end of December. With the new year, an extraordinary series of events unfolded. To determine whether Red River would negotiate entry into Confederation or pursue an independent course like the other provinces who were refusing to compromise their independence (Newfoundland and Prince Edward Island, most notably), it was decided to hold a mass meeting with everyone invited to join in the decision. On January 19 and 20, 1870, about one thousand adults gathered near Fort Garry under a china-blue sky, with temperatures so low that breath condensed and froze on beards and eyebrows; but the sturdy thousand patiently listened to the speeches for hours. Donald Smith persuaded the crowd that Canada sought union "peaceably" and without prejudice to any "class of people of this land." Then the community entrusted its future to the deliberations of a committee of forty.

Before the mass meeting dispersed, however, Louis Riel made a final speech in which he expressed the mood of the previous deliberations and the aim of the negotiations to follow. "Most of us are half-breeds," he began, "but we all have rights. We claim no half rights,... but all the rights we are entitled to. Those rights will be set forth by our representatives, and what is more . . . we will get them." There were loud cheers. Then everyone went home.

Two developments followed the decision to enter Confederation. One was growing resentment in Ontario. The other was increasing satisfaction in Quebec. The legislation that brought the Red River settlements into

Confederation in 1870 with the Indian name of Manitoba indicated that the new province was not going to develop in the image of its nearest neighbors, Ontario and the United States. The existing population, although "inferior" in race, was promised superiority on the land where they were rather than the inferiority of a reserve in the bush. Similarly, Roman Catholicism was protected by assurances of support from the public treasury for denominational schools. Finally, the proceedings of the bicameral legislature and all sections of the courts would be conducted in French as well as in English. Thus, the Red River settlements entered Confederation on June 12, 1870 in a manner that seemed to assure survival for this distinct community of 12 000 persons.

But while the Manitoba Act was a happy portent to the Quebec leaders, Ontario had grown accustomed to speaking of the western territory as its "birthright." Unfortunately, Quebec's happiness in this, as in many later episodes, was only an indicator of the strength of Ontario's anger.

The Protestant majority of former Upper Canada was resentful at the frustration of their plans for western colonization. They were also angered because they said the French-speaking Métis were not being rightly punished for murder. On March 4, 1870, the "rebel government" quartered at Fort Garry had executed one Thomas Scott in the courtyard of the fort for resisting the Métis authority. Although Scott was certainly a troublemaker, he probably did not deserve death by firing squad for his crimes. At least, that was the consensus in Ontario, when Scott's brother and another Upper Canada immigrant to Red River returned home to spread the news that a brother in the Loyal Orange Association of British North America had been brutally slain on orders from a half-breed papist usurping Ontario's destiny. The premier of the province, Edward Blake, rose to the occasion by offering $5 000 reward for the apprehension of Scott's killers. But Ontario wanted more than an eye for an eye. The people seem generally to have been itching for a little war against the whole population of Manitoba. Now Canada Firsters gained their first and last large audience. But outside Ontario their outcry came through as Ontario First rather than anything pertinent to the national interest. Cry out they did nonetheless.

Demands for "Riel's head in a sack" were so strident that the federal government was encouraged to send a military expedition to Red River. Not only would it check American annexationists and reassure the Plains Indians, it would also head off an independent expedition of revenge from Ontario. Even so, the Ontario contingent in the Ottawa force was large; fully two thirds of the volunteers came from the province, determined to make an example of the Métis. But when they arrived at Fort Garry under Colonel Wolseley in August, Riel was no longer on the scene and there was no resistance from any of the people who remained. There was no blood bath, only broken promises. It had been believed in Red River that amnesty had been promised, but in the end the federal government refused to pardon Scott's "murderers." Manitobans were resentful and wondered what other promises would be broken in the future. But the Canada Firsters were also disappointed. Wolseley may have reported that he had "routed the banditti" upon his arrival but not one shot had been fired at any rebels. There was not even a *little* rattling war. In yet another way—to Ontario First nationalism—Canada was appearing to "crawl into existence," without "fiery ordeals" or glory.

III.   Further Territorial Acquisitions and Negotiations with the United States

The same businesslike approach to nation building was to be seen in the case of British Columbia, which merged with Canada at almost the same time as Manitoba, and with even less drama. The Colonial Office simply instructed the governor and he moved the executive and legislative councils in the direction of Confederation (as there was no legislature as yet, there was no responsible government to get in the way of the project). But councillors did reflect their customary resentment of the strangers east of the mountains (too many Scots, therefore the English of British Columbia tended to dismiss the Canadians as 'Oatmeal Chinamen'). Still, for the right price, they would join. The price the legislative council established was high, very high indeed. On March 12, 1870, they agreed that if Canada would assume the colony's debt and responsibility for certain transportation projects, they would come into the federation. They wanted a carriage road all the way to the head of Lake Superior and promises that a railway to the Pacific would replace the wagon road soon thereafter.

Three persons took British Columbia's terms to Ottawa in the summer of 1870. Macdonald was too exhausted from the Manitoba business to deal with them himself so Cartier did the dickering for Canada. Cartier's bargain was assumption of the debt, subsidies for local public works, and a railway from eastern Canada over the north shore of the lakes, across the prairies, though the mountains and terminating on the Pacific coast, to be started within two years of British Columbia's entrance into Confederation and to be completed within ten. The British Columbians were dumbfounded. They described Cartier's terms as "outstandingly better . . . than what we asked for. And the Railway, Credat Judaeus! is *guaranteed* without a reservation!" On the delegates' return to Victoria the council ratified the agreement unanimously.

Now in the summer of 1870 the Macdonald government could claim to have completed the great work of territorial consolidation that was its first major objective. Section 146 of the BNA Act empowered the central government to add "other colonies" and this had certainly been done. In 1867, Canada extended only halfway to the Pacific Ocean. The hold on the Atlantic shore was uncertain. But the Nova Scotia repealers had been pacified and the West was admitted without war. Still, it took the promise of a railway to purchase the goodwill of British Columbia. But even this Macdonald could turn to the political advantage of his party. Since there would have to be a general election in 1872, the railway could be launched in time to provide a focus of national purpose that would make the second election the kind of plebiscite the first had been. By the same convenient timing the railway might be used to guarantee a third Macdonald victory in 1878, assuming he lived that long (the Conservative leader was by this time an aging alcoholic). On the other hand, if the Pacific railway happened to prove impossible, the party in power might still survive by disassociating itself from George Cartier. It could be suggested that it was the impetuous Cartier, not Macdonald, who was "the principal architect, indeed the rash begetter, of the policy of rapid construction of the Pacific railway, . . ." Either way, the government was in a nice position for reelection in the summer of 1870.

But then an unexpected dilemma arose that threatened to destroy the calm setting necessary for business, and presented as much potential difficulty as anything Macdonald had encountered since launching Canada in the first place. This problem was an invitation at the end of 1870 for Canada to participate in a treaty-making conference to be held in Washington in the spring of 1871. The purpose of the meeting was to resolve the tangle of diplomatic loose ends that had complicated Anglo-American relations since the War between the States. In one sense, the agenda involved the United States and Great Britain alone. Those two countries had shown before that they could settle disputes between themselves at the expense of Canada, and therefore Macdonald could hardly refuse the invitation to participate. But since he was to be one negotiator among eight (four Americans, three British, and one Canadian), he would be powerless to defend his country's interests. Naturally the Canadian prime minister was embarrassed by the appointment; if he accepted, he was sure to be denounced for any concessions; if he refused, he was sure to be criticized for giving up without a fight. Either way, an ordinary politician would have emerged a loser.

John A. Macdonald was no ordinary person. He was a brilliant politician, nearly a magician. He could not turn water into gin (as he might have wished), but he had shown himself capable of giving independent provinces the appearance of nationality. Now his challenge was to make humiliation—the Washington conference was inevitably humiliating— look like triumph. The Americans won compensation for the *Alabama* claims and free access to the inshore fisheries of the Atlantic provinces from which American fishermen had been excluded since the United States abrogated the Reciprocity Agreement in 1866. Great Britain, for her part, won the point that the *Alabama* claims would be no more than a cash settlement to be awarded later by a board of arbitration. Canada, it seemed had won nothing at all. Macdonald had dared to hope that the British might join him to secure reparations for the Fenian raids. They did not. He had also hoped they would work with him to restore reciprocal free trade with the United States. The British failed him there as well. In the end, Macdonald had to settle for free navigation of Alaskan rivers. The Americans gained the inshore fisheries, Canadians won free access to the mighty Porcupine. Thus, Canada paid for Great Britain's policy in a manner that left Macdonald disgusted with the "squeezeable" British. Privately, he said he was disgraced; publicly, he said not a word.

The Opposition was not so reticent. When the terms were made public in May of 1871, they moved immediately to publicize the treaty as a disgraceful humiliation. For one entire year thereafter, the Opposition newspapers hammered away at what they characterized as the latest blunder. Nor were they silent on other issues. They said the construction of the Intercolonial Railway from Montreal to Halifax was costing too much and taking too long. The promise of a railway to British Columbia, they said, was impossible to fulfil. The recent negotiations with the Manitobans they denounced as a national insult. And now, the capstone: the ocean treasury of the Atlantic region had been thrown away.

The Opposition charged into the last session of Canada's first Parliament thirsting for Macdonald's blood. They listened to the throne speech, which called for ratification of the treaty and passage of a bill to build the Pacific Railway, certain that the debate that followed would sorely embarrass if not defeat the government. But even as the debate began in its full fury, Macdonald said not a word. Then everyone discovered the reason for his apparent smugness. In consideration for Canada's ratification of the Washington Treaty, the British government would agree to guarantee the financing of the Pacific railway to the extent of £2.5 million. Furthermore, the fisheries were not to be thrown away for nothing. Only the system of licenses would be modified. Canada was to receive a lump sum rather than a payment per ton for American ships that fished in Canadian waters. But this was a trifle compared to the railway loan. The prime minister seemed to have played a pivotal role in solving two problems at once; he had contributed to the resolution of difficult Anglo-American relations, and at the same time he had restored the confidence that business would proceed smoothly by significantly diminishing the risks involved in the Pacific railway. To all appearances, then, the Washington Conference was a triumph, not a humiliation.

Privately, however, Macdonald continued to feel humiliated even though he knew he had played a stealthy game. He had signed the treaty in Washington, but informed his British colleagues at the time that his signature was meaningless without ratification by the Canadian Parliament, and that, he said, was impossible without something to sweeten the pot, such as a subsidy for the railway. Originally he demanded £4 million, but finally settled for £2.5 million. Even his blackmail was only partly successful.

But publicly, all was glory. In the election campaign that followed, Macdonald was reported to have said in one exuberant speech that "if he wished to have any record on his tombstone, it was this, that he had been a party in the making of the Treaty of Washington." And, in this pose, that of the conquering hero, "the Father and Founder of the Dominion" won another majority for another five years.

IV. Scandal

The election of 1872 was bitterly contested. The earlier campaign had been four local plebiscites over Confederation. With the exception of Nova Scotia, most voters seemed to have approved of the *fait accompli* that confronted them. Thus, the Liberal-Conservative coalition that carried the union, carried the election as well. But in 1872, Macdonald's party were legislators with a record less lofty than the BNA Act. To be sure, the government's strategy was to pose as nation builders first and partisans second. All they wanted was another five years to round out the great work launched in 1867, carried forward to date but not yet quite complete. Confederation was now only "in the gristle," more time was needed before the union would have "hardened into bone, and . . . taken such root as to be able to stand the storm."

But the buffeting current was not directed against the union. It was the government of that union that was under attack. One of the primary causes of resentment was the extravagance to be lavished upon British Columbia in the building of the Pacific Railway. The enormity of the project was attractive to some businessmen, land speculators, and workers who would benefit directly from its building. But others were more inclined to regard the idea as a public work that should be undertaken over a longer period and with less direct government involvement. The first two government-subsidized railways, the Grand Trunk and the Intercolonial, were bad enough. The new pork barrel was far deeper. In George Brown's opinion, it was a "rash and maybe disastrous step."

Nevertheless, the railway bill, which Macdonald had pushed through the House just before dissolution, provided thirty million dollars and fifty million acres to the private company that could complete the work from the Pacific Ocean to a point about two hundred miles directly north of Toronto within ten years of July 20, 1871. Another feature of the legislation was the discretion left to the government in awarding the charter. Parliament left it to the cabinet alone to dispense this, the greatest piece of patronage in Canadian history.

By 1872, there were two rivals contending for the prize. The Grand Trunk, the firm most likely to receive the reward, given its past close association with government, was not one of the competitors. Most of the directors were skeptical about the practicality of blasting a railway through the Canadian Shield and, supposing it was possible to do the work, the wisdom of a line through so much emptiness. Nevertheless, some Grand Trunk directors were enthusiastic capitalists who liked this project simply because of its enormity and government backing. In Toronto, they gathered around Senator D. L. Macpherson, a repentant signer of the Annexation Manifesto of 1849. The other rivals were centered in the other commercial capital of Canada. They were a Montreal conglomerate gathered around Sir Hugh Allen and allied with American railway promoters in Chicago and Minneapolis.

Macdonald wanted the Allan group to jettison its American affiliation and combine with Macpherson to make one Canadian firm. For obvious political reasons this was far more attractive than picking one over the other. When they refused to look beyond their own narrow interests, the prime minister hesitated to award the charter to either—in an election year. The risk of alienating the section of the loser was simply too great. Thus, the decision was postponed until after the election.

In the campaign itself, however, the expectations of would-be promoters were exploited to full advantage by Macdonald in order to obtain money to pay for the hard-fought contests. It is not clear how much cash was generated from the Macpherson group; but, after the victory, the government's dealings with Allan came out in lurid detail. The reason was simple: Allan and company had contributed enormous sums to Macdonald and company in the expectation of buying the government, but the government of Canada betrayed this implicit trust and refused to stay bought.

The railway charter was awarded to a forced conglomeration of Canadian business and Sir Hugh Allan was obliged to disassociate himself from his American backers before being named president of the Pacific Railway. The Americans were furious. Details of their political contributions were leaked to the Opposition, who dutifully confronted the prime minister with charges of bribery. Thus began the first volley of recrimination and counter-recrimination that ran nearly unabated from April through October of 1873.

In this, the Pacific Scandal, there were two issues. Indirectly, one was nationalism in the sense that Sir John A. Macdonald was caught with his hand extended across the border. He was getting campaign contributions from Americans as well as from Canadians. The other issue was the question of corruption, the morality of soliciting favors from expectant recipients of government patronage. Parliament and the country were exceedingly sensitive on both matters. In the summer, Macdonald diverted attention by charming Prince Edward Island into Confederation (with the promise of a railway, of course). But the scandal kept resurfacing. By the autumn, the prime minister had met his nemesis.

Heightened sensitivity on matters of national and political integrity brought about Macdonald's defeat. Ironically enough it was due to his successes in the years before. When he became prime minister of Canada in 1867 there was no national integrity to be violated. At best, the country was four provinces that had agreed to disagree in Parliament buildings on the neutral ground of Ottawa. But by 1873, there was the appearance of national purpose, and the Opposition was able to denounce a national scandal. Virtue triumphed. John A. Macdonald resigned on November 5th.

Lord Dufferin, the governor general, believed that there was "no one in the country capable of administering its affairs to greater advantage" than Sir John; but, in 1873, Macdonald appeared to be a patronage boss who could pursue only short-run expedients. He did not inspire confidence as a preceptor and national moralist. And that, precisely, was what the Parliament and the country now demanded.

A new government, that of the Liberal party under Alexander Mackenzie, assumed control of the House; and in the subsequent general election John A. Macdonald's party was routed. But in 1874 it remained to be seen how successfully a party could govern the provinces from Ottawa if it formulated its mandate in moral rather than in practical terms. It did not take long to learn and the lesson was learned well. After 1874, it was eighty-three years before another government was elected on the same stony ground of "Canadian virtue."

CHAPTER TWELVE

Their Principles
Were Their Politics

I.   Liberals with "Sound Principles"

Soon after John A. Macdonald resigned in disgrace over the Pacific Scandal, the new government went to the people in a general election. This, the third since 1867, was more significant than either predecessor, at least from the standpoint of the history of political parties. The contest of 1874 was the first time candidates confronted one another as combatants for two national political organizations. Macdonald's party, labeled *Liberal-Conservatives*, was well developed from the start, but the other parties—Anticonfederates, Anti-Ministerialists, Reformers, and others— were simply the Opposition. It was not until the Pacific Scandal that all elements united to choose a nominal leader. Alexander Mackenzie then emerged as the leader of one party that was labeled *Reformer-Liberals*. It was therefore Mackenzie who formed the new government when Macdonald resigned on November 5, and also Mackenzie who was chiefly responsible for dramatizing the differences between those on his side of the House and those of the other group in the election of 1874.

When Mackenzie addressed his own electors in Lambton County, Ontario, he suggested that the major difference between the two parties was morality rather than ideology. The two parties professed similar truths, but the previous government was distinguishable by its immorality, its "members were elected by the corrupt use of Sir Hugh Allan's money." His Reformer-Liberals, by contrast, were morally upright; they were the ones who were true to "sound principles." They could be counted upon to "elevate the standard of public morality... and ... conduct public affairs upon principles of which honest men can approve, and by practices which will bear the light of day." Mackenzie denounced Macdonald's method of nation building as one of giving bribes to provinces with public money and taking bribes from contractors. The new prime minister promised to dismantle some of his predecessor's projects. He would renegotiate the "impossible" railway promise to British Columbia, for instance. Instead of projects, Mackenzie promised reform. Thus, the program of his party would be its purity.

There were three kinds of reform indicated in the Lambton Address. One was electoral reform. The other was constitutional. The third was fiscal. With regard to the first, honest elections were promised by changes providing for simultaneous voting, on the assumption that if everyone voted on the same day an incumbent government would be less able to resort to the corrupt practice of bowling over critical constituencies, one by one, as was the case previously. This was not all. Other reforms of election procedure included repudiation of the "manly" practice of open voting in favor of secret ballot, extension of the franchise beyond property owners, and investigation of controverted elections by a judge, instead of by a House committee, a practice that gave the incumbent government a built-in advantage.

The constitutional reforms Mackenzie promised in his Lambton Address were two. One was a revision of the militia system, intended to make Canada more self-reliant now that Britain had completed the withdrawal of the last of the army garrisons in 1871. The other constitutional reform pertained to the legal system. He promised to create a Canadian Supreme Court, and so abolish appeals to the judicial committee of the British Privy Council as a court of last appeal.

The promised fiscal reforms pertained to public and private spending. Mackenzie asserted a need for an "insolvency law" to facilitate the declaration of personal bankruptcy without consequent imprisonment for debt. But at the same time, to set a good example of the way to avoid bankruptcy in the first place, Mackenzie promised to scale down the level of government spending. He denounced Macdonald's railway plans as particularly extravagant. These would be cut, and the government's need for revenues would be reduced accordingly. Thus, the voters were led to expect that the government's prime source of income, the tariff, would be lowered significantly. Honest and frugal government would relieve everyone—a little. Invigorated honesty and pride would raise Canada in spirit. This was Alexander Mackenzie's promise to his own electors, and although it was a slower way to build a nation, it was, in the new prime minister's opinion, the only proper method.

The electorate responded. Mackenzie triumphed in Lambton. Reformer-Liberals triumphed elsewhere as well. Macdonald's Conservatives were reduced to 67 seats in the House of Commons. The Reformer-Liberals received a two-to-one majority with their 138 seats. Since this result occurred in every province except British Columbia ("the spoiled child of confederation"), Alexander Mackenzie expressed pious satisfaction over the conquest: "Now, the country has pronounced its condemnation of the Pacific Scandal." Now everything the Opposition had yearned to accomplish before November of 1873 might be attained because the country was united in its preference for virtue over bribery.

But men of virtue come in different denominations. Among the Reformer-Liberals there were no less than four strains of "sound principles" pulling at the unity of one nominal party. From Ontario, the oldest and most outspoken of the Liberal-moralists were former Clear Grits, such as the leader himself and George Brown, out of Parliament but still active in politics through his ownership of the most formidable newspaper in Canada, the Toronto *Globe*. The distinguishing characteristic of this liberalism was its assumption that society was nothing more than an agglomeration of individuals; and an ideal government was just a good referee in any dispute that might arise between interest groups as they associated for this or that end. Thus, the power of government was to be used in a negative way, for instance, acting to prevent combinations of wage earners from forcing their will upon the individuals who employed them. Ideally, the state did not favor particular individuals or groups in their private projects, for instance, in railways. Government had one frugal, self-denying role to play. According to Mackenzie, this was seeing that every man "has the same opportunity, by exercising the talents [with] which God has blessed him, of rising in the world . . . . "

Another kind of liberalism was the Quebec variety for which A.A. Dorion was the most venerable spokesman. This liberalism was the old *Rouge* position, now more temperate in its republicanism, but only slightly more compatible with the ancients of the Clear Grit persuasion. This liberalism was ardently anti-Protestant and hypersensitive to insults from Protestant nationalists. But their chief enmity in this period was directed toward the clergy in Quebec. The mid-century Roman Catholic Church was at the apex of its power and prestige, outspoken in political matters and extraordinarily ultramontane, that is, oriented to Rome rather than to local secular or clerical leaders. Clerical ascendancy and ultramontanism was a source of enormous controversy in Quebec. The most outspoken young Liberals associated in a literary society that called itself the *Institut Canadien*. The Bishop of Montreal denounced them for propagating ideas from the pope's list of forbidden books. When Liberals denounced Bishop Bourget as a meddler, Bourget brandished threats of excommunication. The animosity reached crisis proportions in 1874 when an excommunicated Liberal, five years dead, and a former member of the *Institut*, was denied Catholic burial. His family gained a court injunction to bury him in consecrated ground and backed by court orders and troops, Joseph Guibord was entombed in reinforced concrete, only to have Bourget de-consecrate that portion of the cemetery. The Quebec alliance between Church and Conservatives emerged the stronger; Quebec Liberals found themselves allied with Mackenzie to oppose Cartier and the Catholic Church. But there were no strong positive links between themselves, perpetuating the *Rouge* tradition, and Mackenzie representing the Clear Grit style of Ontario. This was a case of one's political friends following from common enmities rather than by shared constructive purposes.

The tendency toward liberalism by circumstance was even more pronounced among the other two strains of 1874 liberalism. The first were those independent nationalists illustrated best by the little group of intellectuals that called themselves Canada Firsters. Such persons might be revolted by Macdonald's determination to build a nation by "sordid and mercenary means" rather than on "some other and truer ground." But at least he was building; he did provide vigorous government leadership, especially when it came to extensive railway construction. Mackenzie seemed unwilling to drive ahead to nationhood, and so the nationalists' enthusiasm for the new government did not last long.

The second of the remaining strains was that of the Conservatives who had changed party in the aftermath of the Pacific Scandal. This grouping could hardly be expected to contribute to one harmonious consensus—not even if it included Richard Cartwright, the former Conservative, who now appeared as one of the most prominent Liberals. Basically, his quarrel with the Conservative Party was with its leadership and one of its projects. If the Conservatives dropped Sir John A. Macdonald and espoused free trade, then Cartwright might have abandoned the Liberals.

Macdonald-hating conservatism, Canada First nationalism, parochial anticlericalism, and classical liberalism were the strains that threatened the cohesion of the Liberal Party's majority in Canada's third Parliament. But it was not the width of opinion so much as the dogmatism of the various kinds of Liberals that threatened party unity. There were opinions and divisions in Macdonald's party, too, but pragmatism had emerged as the proven method of accommodating diversity. This was Sir John A. Macdonald's style and strength. It was also his undoing, for in 1874, virtue was an obsession. Edward Blake expressed this emotion best, perhaps, when he said "we must find some other and truer ground for Union than that by which the late government sought to buy love and purchase peace." Everyone was to stand on principle. But the stand on virtue entailed one region imposing its principles upon the rest of Canada, or else coexisting with conflicting principles but abdicating leadership.

II. A Railway in Principle

To Alexander Mackenzie, inactive government was no failing. He led a coalition that was a pious pilgrimage consciously avoiding lavish projects. He chose only one clear direction and that was toward those reforms he had promised the electors of Lambton. Simultaneous voting, the secret ballot, and something resembling a Supreme Court, but without the abolition of appeals to the British Judicial Committee, were all established. Beyond these matters on which morality was the issue, the leader could not count on consensus, and so his party simply did not act.

Mackenzie's railway policy was the prime illustration of inaction and paralysis. The prime minister's strongest impulse was to abandon this "impossible" project entirely, but too many Liberals refused to cooperate in this act of repudiation. Still, Mackenzie could not accept the inevitable debauchery that would attend rapid construction with large government subsidies, and so he himself took the Minister of Public Works portfolio and throttled most of the building that had been planned earlier. Here, though, he struck upon an alternative to the Conservatives' railway. Furthermore, by his personal supervision he kept the project free of scandal. It was neither corrupt nor extravagant. In this sense, Mackenzie succeeded. But more to the point, the transportation system that resulted was a shambles.

The Conservatives' idea was to build a line from British Columbia to eastern Canada over a period of ten years. Mackenzie considered this proposition ludicrous. Not only was it a railway ahead of demand, it was also beyond the means of a country with such a small population as Canada. What Mackenzie advocated in principle was piecemeal construction, following rather than advancing the line of settlement. Also, in principle, the railway would supplement rather than supersede "water stretches." East-west transportation would move by boat over the Great Lakes as far as Port Arthur. Here a railway would run to the chain of lakes fifty miles west. Then it was back to boats for 270 miles over Shebandowan Lake, Lac de Milles Lacs, Rainy Lake, Rainy River and the Lake of the Woods. At the northwest corner of the last lake, the railway would resume, and by this means cargo would be transported the remaining 115 miles to Red River. For the foreseeable future, this terminus, roughly the site of present-day Winnipeg, would be the western terminus of the Pacific Railway as well. Gone was the expensive line over the mountains of British Columbia, the long stretch over the empty prairies to Manitoba, and the astronomically expensive section traversing the north shore of Lake Superior. Thus, Alexander Mackenzie's project was a Pacific Railway only in principle.

But Mackenzie's alternative might have worked had it been pursued less in theory and more in practice. His idea was not impossible, only the implementation. The government pretended that the 270 miles of water from Lake Shebandowan to Lake of the Woods was "virtually" uninterrupted. But as a matter of backbreaking fact there were over seventy portages that had to be made around obstacles such as rapids and waterfalls. It was absurd to imagine that this was of little importance. Had the government been more concerned with water transportation and less with merely a theoretical alternative a great opportunity might have been taken.

Recent research has suggested that economic growth and extended settlement in nineteenth-century America might have been just as feasible by using improved water routes as it was by railways. To some extent Mackenzie anticipated this finding. He could point out to his contemporaries that the railways in the already settled part of Canada as late as 1860 carried less freight than the water-borne carriers; assert that the West possessed a system of natural waterways almost as attractive as the St. Lawrence; then point the accusing finger at the other side of the House to indicate that those "members elected by the corrupt use of Sir Hugh Allan's money" were railway promoters first, Fathers of Confederation second, and opportunists always. The Liberals, on the other hand, would pursue Canada's western destiny through her northern waters. Mackenzie's Liberals would make the St. Lawrence navigable from tidewater to the Rocky Mountains. The big project would be a canal from Port Arthur to Lake Shebandowan, and improvements around the seventy-odd portages to Lake of the Woods. Then, rather than moving overland, the route of the fur traders over the Winnipeg River to Lake Winnipeg would be followed. From here, north was the Nelson, south the Red, and westerly the Assiniboine and Saskatchewan. Later, as settlement advanced from the rivers of the west and as capital accumulated in enterprising hands, there would be railways as well, but not with the extravagant subsidies that were required to build them ahead of demand.

The one flaw in this scenario was its impossibility. Mackenzie was no more interested in Liberal seaways than Conservative railways. Nor were many of his party any less infected with the railway mania than the Conservatives. What concerned Mackenzie, and mightily, was cost. This was the ground for his policy of railway connection between fictitious "water stretches," the non-policy in practice. It could not work without improvements to the waterways as they were. And these improvements were only relatively inexpensive, cheaper than railways but not cheap in absolute terms.

In the end, Mackenzie's government admitted its water stretches policy was merely a tactic to avoid action when it decided, in its last year, to begin two all-rail connections with Manitoba. One was a route leading east from Winnipeg to Port Arthur; the other line was to run south, from Winnipeg to Emerson. The Pembina Branch, as the second line was called, was completed first, of course, since it was far shorter and ran over loamy, level ground for the entire distance. In 1879 the connection was completed at the border with the Canadian-controlled St. Paul, Minneapolis and Manitoba Railroad. From this date, the Pembina Branch functioned as the main link between Manitoba and the rest of the world. The other line to Port Arthur was continued but over much more difficult terrain and for a longer distance. This east-west link did not come into service until several years later.

Future settlers and their freight traveling west from Ontario before 1883 would take ship as far as Duluth, and then take the train through the United States. Once in Winnipeg, having arrived by the Pembina Branch, they could, if they intended to settle in the west beyond Manitoba, board the steamer *Northcote* in Winnipeg and travel out via the Saskatchewan River, in its unimproved state, nearly as far as Edmonton. In a sense, this was a "water stretches" transportation system. But it was not the one that might have been, nor even the scheme the government espoused in principle.

III.   Four Treaties

Mackenzie was more active in clearing Canadian title to the West than in promoting transportation improvements for its settlement. Macdonald's government had purchased title to Rupert's Land and the Northwest Territories from the British Hudson's Bay Company, but they were only one claimant. The people actually in possession of the land were the Indians and in 1869 they had no intention of selling.

When representatives of Canada made their first overtures of bargaining with the native people they were rebuffed by Indian chiefs who well suspected what the government was after. At Fort Frances in 1870, for instance, Colonel Wolseley offered gaudy presents to one chief who rejected them on the spot, saying: "Am I a pike to be caught with such a bait as that? Shall I sell my land for a bit of red cloth? We will let the pale-faces pass through our country, but we will sell them none of our land, nor have any of them to live amongst us." Similarly, another chief further west rejected comparable gifts on the same logic: "We want none of the Queen's presents; when we set a foxtrap we scatter pieces of meat all round, but when the fox gets into the trap, we knock him on the head..."

Nevertheless, it was in the period of Alexander Mackenzie, between

1874 and 1877, that most of the Indian lands between Manitoba and the Rocky Mountains south of latitude 60 degrees north were transferred by treaty from the native people at almost no cost to the government of Canada. Military force was not the reason. In fact, the only soldiers Canada had sent were paramilitary constables, the (Royal) North West Mounted Police, whom the Indian chiefs tended to welcome because they were a force to discipline the whiskey traders, interlopers mainly from the United States. But the Mounties were not present in large numbers. The force as it was originally constituted in 1873 contained only 150 constables. When Mackenzie's government sent them west from Manitoba to what is now southern Alberta in 1874, the force was increased by only 300 since the prime minister was no more inclined to extravagance in budgeting for the national police than for national transportation.

Nor was encroaching settlement and the force of vigilantism the reason behind the Indian capitulation. In the decade between 1870 and 1880 there were no more than a few thousand settlers west of Manitoba. Most people went no further than the rich farm lands of the Red River area, which began to prove their potential for wheat production as early as 1876 when the first surplus of Red Fife wheat was shipped by way of Minnesota for milling in Ontario. The few pioneers who did ride the *Northcote* west tended to locate themselves in compact settlements on the banks of the great river system that was their highway. Thus Protestant Prince Albert came into existence. Similarily, a number of Métis villages appeared in the same vicinity, populated by the people who had become discouraged and fled Manitoba since that province was taking on an increasingly Ontario-cast, a result of the influx of thousands of Red Fife growers. The Métis were buffalo hunters and the buffalo were rapidly disappearing. Hunters followed the herds west and north accordingly.

Soon, however, the buffalo began to disappear everywhere. This, and the decimation of native people by smallpox, was why so many Indians surrendered themselves and their lands to be wards of the government of Canada between 1874 and 1877. Pestilence came first. At least half of the Indians in what is now Saskatchewan and Alberta died of smallpox in the early 1870s. The Indians who survived the epidemic then faced the crisis created by the disappearance of the buffalo. Systematic extermination of the beasts that provided the Plains Indians with their food, clothing, shelter, and even fuel was begun in the United States to clear the land of obstacles to railways and agriculture. There were perhaps sixty million buffalo milling back and forth over the invisible border when the slaughtering started. By 1875 the herds had dwindled enough to threaten famine. By 1885 they were virtually extinct. As starvation followed disease, the will to resist was broken.

There were no wars in Canada that preceded the making of treaties. The decimation by smallpox and threatened starvation "did more to win an empire for the whites," according to J. K. Howard, "than bullets could." It is possible that "bullets could never have done it alone."

Between 1874 and 1877, the once proud rulers of the prairies in what is now Saskatchewan and Alberta surrendered without having been defeated in war or swamped by large-scale settlement. In all, there were four treaties negotiated between 1874 and 1877, one each year. The last two were the most difficult as well as the most significant. The two final treaties were negotiated with the Alberta Cree and Blackfoot, the people previously most averse to giving up their land. It was significant that they now wished to sell. But their price—apparently minimal for the moment—could be enormous in the future. In addition to the usual guarantees of land reserves and government annuities, the Cree and the Blackfoot demanded that Canada maintain them in times of pestilence or famine, should either misfortune strike in the future. The commissioners agreed, although the Minister of the Interior, back in Ottawa, consistent with the general miserliness of the Mackenzie regime, objected that this guarantee might prove burdensome later. Nevertheless, for the moment, the land was won for next to nothing. Of this, Mackenzie could be proud. But it was small consolation to him in 1877. By this time, the Opposition had revived in voice if not in numbers. Non-confidence motions were being served for breakfast, lunch, and dinner from the benches of the other side of the House.

IV. The Revitalization of Smiling Pragmatism

In his first two years in Opposition John A. Macdonald languished like a warrior with mortal wounds. In 1873 he was sixty years old. He had good reason to think his political career had ended. Macdonald retreated. He rarely attended Parliament and relaxed his discipline over the party. For two years he avoided the game of opposition for its own sake. When he participated in parliamentary debate at all it was to offer cordial amendments, calm suggestions, and none of the flourishes of an expectant leader.

Near the end of 1875, however, by-election results suggested that public opinion was beginning to swing away from the party of principle. Increasingly, it seemed, Macdonald's party was remembered more for its flair in action than for asking Americans for campaign contributions. But in 1875, Macdonald had not yet defined his program. It could not be the railway by itself.

The harsh reality for the Mackenzie years was financial stringency, a lack of government revenue that would have handicapped even Macdonald had he returned to power in 1875. The source of about three quarters of the government's revenue was the customs, a fact that continued until the personal income tax appeared in 1917. Originally, the tariff was set at 15 percent of the value of imports, and this seemed adequate until the volume of imports began to decline after 1873.

In part, reduced imports were due to a downturn in the business cycle. But import reductions also stemmed from the growth of Canadian manufacturing, which expanded remarkably well to take advantage of the wider market that came with Confederation. The makers of agricultural implements, for example, prospered by copying American designs and patents and producing them at lower cost in central Canada for sale in the Maritime Provinces. One implement maker reported that "wherever" he expanded "the American manufacturers have retired from the field for the reason that we can undersell them. They make a very nice machine; it is the same machine . . . that we sell." But where Americans charged $100, this Canadian sold his product for $75. That margin was significant. It suggests that the tariff was not essential to this Canadian manufacturer's survival; Canadian consumers could purchase Canadian hardware for reasons of economic self-interest as well as for economic nationalism; but the margin of difference also suggests how the treasury of Canada lost $15 every time a farmer bought this implement from a Canadian rather than from an American manufacturer.

Year by year the Mackenzie government faced declining revenues. There were two conventional methods of halting the decline. One would be an excise tax on domestic manufacturing. The other would follow from an increase in the tariff. But Mackenzie's finance minister, Richard Cartwright, had already compromised his free-trade scruples more than he had ever intended. He had inherited a 15 percent tariff. In 1874 it was raised to 17.5 percent. He opposed any more tax increases, in any form. Cartwright was keenly aware that the Liberals had inherited a national debt of $134 million that was carried with annual interest charges of $6 million, and that the national revenue had declined from twenty million to seventeen million dollars between 1873 and 1876. But with more than one third of all receipts budgeted "just to stand still," Cartwright felt that the country needed sermons, not higher taxes or increased spending. This was a moral problem. The present government would "atone for past extravagance and folly;" it would practice "prudence and economy until this present trial is passed."

Here was the opportunity for which Macdonald had been waiting. The Liberals were espousing yet more inaction on principle. But here action was inviting, simple, and dramatic. Even though Macdonald had never clarified any position on tariff policy before, as soon as it became clear that the Liberals would keep the tariff low regardless of declining revenues, Macdonald stood unequivocally on the side of a dramatic increase. He produced a motion in mid-March of 1876 for a much larger tariff, not simply for revenue to subsidize such projects as railways, but also to encourage manufacturing in Canada.

Existing firms were not clamoring for such a boost, but certainly the wider profit margin it assured was no cause for protest either. Then, too, those would-be manufacturers intending to start a business with prices in excess of world prices could find real comfort in a tariff subsidy. Nor would labor oppose a fiscal policy that promised to protect them from the competition of workers who were supposed to be employed at starvation wages in Europe. Even farmers could find an interest in a scheme that would tend to encourage apple rather than orange consumption. Thus, Macdonald found a panacea that he called the National Policy: a tariff adjustment to afford permanent protection to "the struggling manufacturers and industries as well as the agricultural productions of the country."

Macdonald also found a convenient vehicle for conveying the National Policy to the public. This was the political picnic, meetings of voters and their families in parks on sunny summer afternoons to feast upon sandwiches, lemonade, beer, and political talk. Later, others—even Conservatives—would come to find these occasions "nothing but a lot of people walking about a field and some nasty provisions spoiling on a long table in the sun." But for John A. Macdonald, "a happy soul whom everybody likes, " they were a lovely way to get drunk on ale, conviviality, and rhetoric. Mackenzie had to respond with picnics of his own. "But he could never be taught these little arts... There was no gin and talk about Mac."

Mackenzie preferred to remain true to his promises of delivering reform. In the last session before dissolution he delivered one last cleansing measure. He enacted a prohibition law, an outrageously unpopular "Temperance Act" by which local authorities could impose complete abstinence on the picnickers, drunks, and tipplers of a whole district. Its very unpopularity was a sure sign that this was Mackenzie's last reforming gasp.

A third summer of political picnicking preceded the election that defeated the party whose principles were their politics. John A. Macdonald's party had a clear program. But unlike the earlier matter-of-fact, even crass, consolidation of national boundaries by cash promises and railway schemes, the new program, no less concrete, was calculated to arouse a "national sentiment." Macdonald marketed his new project brimful of nationalism. "There has arisen in this country a Canadian party," he said, "which declares we must have Canada for the Canadians." This was not the ideological, racial nationalism of Canada First. It was economic nationalism, an affirmation that reciprocity was a dead end. "You cannot get anything by kissing the feet of the people of the United States." On the contrary, the way to the better future was along the path where Great Britain pioneered. "England, gentlemen, was the greatest protectionist country in the world until she got possession of the markets of the world . . . . " The tariff would work that magic; Macdonald promised it would "give a sprat to catch a mackerel."

Liberals denounced economic nationalism as so much "humbug." Cartwright attempted to ridicule the proposition because it benefited only the rich, "the poor and needy manufacturers who occupy those squalid hovels which adorn the suburbs of Montreal, Hamilton, and every city of the Dominion." It was a tax upon 95 percent of the people chiefly to benefit the top five percent. But the electorate was tired of pious inactivity. In 1878 the Liberals were routed. "Nothing has happened in my time so astonishing," Mackenzie complained. There was bitterness as well as truth in his observation that "Canada does not care for rigid adherence to principle in government."

But Macdonald knew that Canadians did not care for bribery either. Obviously, the winning formula was to cover matter-of-fact intention with language that suggested some cosmic purpose. This was the lesson he learned from the Pacific Scandal and his two years of observing a government whose politics were their principles rather than their programs. Such politicians made admirable critics, but in a country as diverse as Canada, rigid adherence to principle spelled incapacity in leadership. In Macdonald's party, on the other hand, almost any policy was possible, so long as it continued to work.

CHAPTER THIRTEEN

Years of Crisis

I. A Tariff and a Railway

Although the National Policy had been popularized in rhetorical flourishes that decorous Liberals called "humbug," the program itself was not a sham. It was not simply an image for an election and then forgotten. For good or ill, the tariff Macdonald promised was the most conspicuous and controversial feature of his first budget, submitted to Parliament on March 14, 1879.

It had taken the finance minister, Leonard Tilley, nearly three months to make all the adjustments for the new schedule of duties. Some items, such as raw cotton and the machinery for manufacturing processes such as textile production, were exempted from any duty at all. Other items, without particular pattern, were taxed to the sky. The rule was completely arbitrary. Any manufacturer who wanted protection had simply to ask for it. This made Tilley's work harrowing and endless since protection seekers were said to have "waylaid him by night, taken up his time by day . . . . " Ultimately, a statistician skilled in the chaos of tariff schedules had to be employed. Depending upon the article, the final rates ranged from zero to 35 percent, most falling around the 25 percent level.

Such significant increases were bound to generate enormous debate. The wrangling began on the evening of March 14, and ran nearly nonstop to the end of April. All arguments were aired. But the 64 members of the Opposition were helpless to prevent Macdonald's 142 colleagues from having their way.

What the government enacted was not simply a scheme for increasing revenue. They also embraced a policy of indirect subsidies to Canadian industry on the stated premise that it was impossible for a large Canadian manufacturing plant to exist otherwise. It was true that some manufacturers had asked for protection and asserted that "we must make the policy a permanent policy." If this need was general, Macdonald's tariff was indeed a National Policy. But the prime minister did not bother to study the problem of need since he knew he had a good issue. One fact was certain: the party that insisted on the tariff's "permanency" could count on the permanent support of business.

The identification of nation building with business promotion became even more evident in the resurrection of the Pacific Railway project. The House adopted a resolution in 1879 that authorized the government to offer one hundred million acres of western land to prospective builders of the line. Unlike the 1872 offer, this one did not promise money, but the acreage offered was more than three times the previous land grant. When this proved insufficient, the government began a western section of the railway as a public works project, and approached George Stephen, the man who was supposed to be the richest person in Canada's wealthiest city.

Stephen was Canada's living example of the success myth, the dream that the New World was an open-ended universe in which any immigrant could rise to lofty preeminence with luck and work. In 1850, Stephen started as a newly arrived Scot clerking in a dry goods store. Through shrewd dealing and fortunate family connections he had become a wealthy textile manufacturer by 1872. Now, in 1879, with his cousin Donald Smith, he was a multimillionaire and deeply involved in railways. It was Smith and Stephen, with American associates, who made the St. Paul, Minneapolis and Manitoba Railroad the first railway link between Canada's West and East by connecting Winnipeg with Lake Superior over United States territory from Pembina to Duluth.

Stephen and Smith agreed to build the Canadian Pacific Railway, but the terms they proposed were so extraordinary that any government accepting them would have to persuade Parliament that the country faced a do-or-die challenge. The political problem was to make rapid construction of the CPR analogous to a national emergency. Not only did Stephen and Smith demand an immediate cash subsidy of $25 million, almost equivalent to two years of the whole national revenue; not only did they demand title to arable land equivalent to a belt twenty-four miles wide on either side of the CPR mainline from Winnipeg to the Rockies; not only did they demand title to the three sections of Pacific railway already completed or under contract—in all, 730 miles valued at $31.5 million; they also demanded perpetual exemption from all taxation and a traffic monopoly until the year 1900. In return, Stephen and Smith promised to build 650 miles of railway from Port Arthur to Callender and 900 miles from Winnipeg to Kamloops by May 1, 1891.

In December, 1880, Macdonald brought this proposal before Parliament, thinking that he could secure ratification before the New Year. He miscalculated. The Liberals attacked this project even more vehemently than the tariff, using every argument and stratagem to persuade the government to revise the terms. The debate did not end with the Christmas recess. It resumed in January and continued to the end of the month.

The Opposition's arguments—including Edward Blake's five-hour speech—elaborated two propositions. One was that the contract was extravagant; the other, that it was sinister. Both objections would be met if Macdonald abandoned his obsession with rapid construction. Liberals preferred building the "prairie section as fast as settlement demands," and indefinite "postponement" of the western and eastern sections. A slower pace would permit greater economy and obviate the need to offer such lavish incentives to private builders, who would probably fail anyway and "ruin the public credit" in their downfall. The Opposition also saw the railway as a threat to western freedom, since the land and monopoly clauses transformed the West into a fief of "the Syndicate." Stephen and Smith were proposing to become the landlords of most settlers and the carriers for all.

Of the two roles, the monopoly privilege was the more hated. Manitobans already felt the sting of sharp businessmen and their capricious freight rates. In 1880, for instance, wheat was selling in Toronto for $1.10 a bushel; the freight from Manitoba to that market by way of St. Paul took almost half the price the farmers received, and the first one third of the trip, over Stephen and Smith's existing monopoly, accounted for most of the freight charges. Manitobans were anxious to see the rail line to Lake Superior operated competitively. But, to their horror, the CPR was going to the same businessmen who were already gouging them.

Western hopes that the Opposition in Ottawa could save them availed nothing. A score of amendments was proposed, but every one was defeated. The CPR contract was passed by Parliament and received royal assent. Construction began in February, 1881.

By this time, another election was looming. Macdonald could hope that the tariff adjustment and the reinvigorated Pacific Railway might assure his return. But he aimed to take advantage of a redistribution of federal seats to make that assurance even more secure. The BNA Act stipulated that Quebec was always to have 65 members, and that each province's quota was to be based upon its population as compared with Quebec's; thus, provinces would gain or lose seats as they gained or lost population relative to the movement of Quebec's. 1881 was a census year, and it became possible to note how the country's settlement was changing. In the ten years since the previous census, Manitoba and Ontario had gained people at a greater rate than Quebec. Thus Manitoba was now entitled to five rather than four members of Parliament, and Ontario to ninety-two instead of eighty-eight. The entitlement of the other provinces did not change.

The need for redistribution presented Macdonald with a golden pre-election opportunity since nearly half of the Opposition was returned by Ontario alone. The census entitled that province to its four additional seats, but the government was free to create these new constituencies as Macdonald pleased. Furthermore, he might redraw every electoral boundary in the province to find them. He did. Electoral boundaries were run to make each Conservative vote count for more and each Liberal vote for less. In other words, constituencies that previously returned Liberals by slim margins had their boundaries redrawn to increase the chances of them returning Conservatives in the coming election.

Where the tariff had generated a debate and the railway contract a near filibuster, the Redistribution Act of 1882 provoked something that is best described as a sustained howl. Soon others became aroused to indignant protest, and Macdonald's party did worse at the polls in 1882 than in 1878. Even so, the prime minister did win an overall majority, even from Ontario. The regions had watched Macdonald spend the past five years translating his image of a National Policy into a reality of protection and railway construction. The electorate seemed reconciled to paying the higher prices that the tariff and the CPR would entail. They also seemed to tolerate the idea of a transcontinental railway constructed as an emergency, with all the extravagance that involved. In tariff protection and national mobilization Canadians seemed to perceive the appearance of nationality without needing to resolve or even think about any of the regional differences that would remain untouched by either. Macdonald demanded sacrifice; and sacrifice was supposed to bring countries together. Thus the people gained their first taste of what later generations would call "the price of being Canadian," and they seemed to approve.

II.   Mobilization for the CPR

If the CPR's launching resembled a mobilization for national emergency, the frenzied construction that followed was the appropriate continuation. Two hundred and seventy-five miles of track were laid in 1881 and William Cornelius Van Horne was recruited from his superintendancy of an American railroad to fill the position of Engineer-in-Chief to make the distance covered in 1882 an even five hundred miles. He succeeded. By the end of the construction season, the crews were pushed to within twenty-five miles of Medicine Hat.

Frantic building required logistics of supply similar to those of the two world wars of the next century. In the case of the CPR, however, the enemy was nature and the battlefields were all in the Shield, on the prairies, and the Rockies. Also, the allies included Germany as well as the United States and Great Britain. The Krupp family provided the rails, Canada and China provided the troops. In this pattern of international cooperation, the wilderness of Western Canada was forced into armistice and unconditional surrender.

At the same time, however, it should be remembered that the railway was a private company's source of profits as much as the realization of a "national dream." It was a syndicate of businessmen who received the public's money and looked after themselves first, the public interest following incidentally. The best indication of company profiteering was the decision to change from the commonsense route through the rolling agricultural land of the Saskatchewan River system and move the mainline far to the south close to the American border through the near desert of the Palliser Triangle. Since settlement followed where the railway led this was to have dire future consequences. But the directors were determined upon the change for two reasons, both related directly to profits. First, they wanted their mainline as close to the American border as possible, in anticipation of the future competition with the Northern Pacific Railroad then under construction through Montana and bound for Seattle. The monopoly clause would run for only twenty years. After that time, the NPR might have branch lines running across the border like pickets in a fence; the greater the distance between the two mainlines, the more threatening the branches.

But future American competition may not have been as determinative as the other factor, the activity of Canadian land speculators who expected the more reasonable, northerly course. The CPR directors were also land dealers themselves. It was in their interest to have as much empty right of way as possible. Where the railway ran, land values would soar. By opting for the southerly route they bypassed existing settlement and ran through the most empty, therefore the most exclusively CPR-country possible. CPR branch lines would take care of the northern settlements in due course. This would mean longer hauls for them, but more revenue—hence profits—for the company.

While the railway directors used every method to maximize income, they were also well aware that no matter how prodigal they were in rushing construction or in buying ready-made railways in the East to connect with Atlantic ports, Macdonald's government could not afford to see the railway falter should it fail in attempts to recruit private capital. Thus, Van Horne would boast one day that he "never estimated the cost of any work," and Stephen would demand greater government subsidy the next.

In 1884 the CPR demanded $30 million over the contract price. Macdonald did not declare the company forfeit. He complied with $23 million. One year later, the directors returned for a further $35 million. This time, Macdonald's fellow cabinet ministers, the members of Parliament most likely to support the project, rebelled. Macdonald despaired, but he had no choice. He did not have the power to force such a grant in 1885. He therefore refused the directors' petition and on March 26, the CPR was finished. It was technically bankrupt. But Macdonald's amazing luck held, and when all seemed darkest he was unexpectedly, not to say ironically, delivered.

Seven years of studied neglect of Western problems had caused the region first to protest, then to threaten, and finally to rebel. On the prairies there were no less than three groups antagonistic to Ottawa. The first consisted of white settlers on the Saskatchewan, suffering an interruption of their expectations that they would play a role as land speculators and cash-crop farmers by the changed direction of the CPR far to the south. They were only protesters, however; they were not conspicuous among the rebels. The actual rebellion was launched by Métis and Indians. The two years immediately following Macdonald's return to power was a period of crisis for Indians nearly as awful as the smallpox epidemics earlier. These were two years of famine—caused by the extermination of the buffalo—neither controlled nor relieved by the government largesse that had been promised in the last two treaties negotiated between 1876 and '77. Instead of welfare, the government responded with instructions that the Indians be moved to reserves; there they were starved one day and fed the next on the assumption that this was the right incentive to turn them into self-supporting farmers.

In a particularly well-chosen metaphor, the Indians replied that "you cannot make an ox of a deer." Their point was primarily that they feared they would no longer be Indians if they became farmers. But as the metaphor implied, they also feared for their humanity, since they knew it was impossible to make an ox of a bull without first making him a steer. From their standpoint, they had exchanged title to their land for guarantees against famine and pestilence. Now they were starving and it was time for Canada to keep its side of the bargain. The Minister of the Interior, Sir John A. Macdonald, did not say yes. He did not say no. But his "vexatious delay," or what one Indian agent termed "endless procrastination," transformed the Indians' misery first into resentment and finally into hate.

The disappearance of the buffalo affected the Métis nearly as much as it hurt the Indians. But the Métis were more willing to make the transition to the sedentary existence farming demanded. Their problem was getting title to the land onto which they had drifted. By the Dominion Lands Act of 1872, a grid of townships, each containing thirty-six sections and starting at longitude 95 degrees west and latitude 49 degrees north (the southeast corner of present-day Manitoba), was extended westward making it possible to identify every acre for whatever purpose. For a ten-dollar registration fee, any male adult was supposed to be able to secure patents for any quarter of any even-numbered section. But there were qualifications and exceptions: a person had to live and work on his land for three years. Furthermore, no amount of work or residency could entitle a person to land on sections 8 and 26, which were reserved for the speculative purposes of the Hudson's Bay Company; nor were any of the odd-numbered sections open for settlement. These were set aside for railways and schools, mostly the former (only sections 11 and 19 were the school reserve). From the standpoint of the government, this pattern of orderly survey assured orderly development. But from the Métis' point of view it was checkerboard madness. It failed to take the course of rivers into account, and they wanted their land in the traditional river-front lots. When they petitioned for a revision of the law, they were met with silence. They had suffered similar insecurity before, in what had since become Manitoba. Louis Riel had helped them then. If he had helped them once, the Métis could call upon him again to organize a second resistance.

Since 1874, Riel had been living as a hunted villain and a haunted visionary. First there had been no amnesty, only a price on his head. Then he was told he could return to Canada after five years of exile. In 1878 he finally settled in a Métis community in Montana, married, worked as a school teacher and became a citizen of the United States. Now, in June of 1884, riders appeared in his village and asked him to return with them to organize their protest in the country at the forks of the Saskatchewan. He accepted the invitation and on March 19, 1885, the Red River republic was reborn on the Saskatchewan, with Riel as president and pope, the Ten Commandments as the only law, and the Métis cavalry as the sole security.

On March 22, General Frederick Middleton and 8000 militia were ordered on the alert. Then on March 26, the very day the CPR loan was refused, skirmishing occurred between the Métis cavalry and the North West Mounted Police. Now the Indians rose. Civil war had begun and the troops were ordered west.

It was now that Macdonald could win support and votes for the railway. In 1870 Wolseley and his men had had a terrible time getting as far as Red River. Now, a short fifteen years later, a more serious threat much further west had been dealt with promptly and easily, thanks to the railway that whisked the troops to the scene. By May 15, Louis Riel had surrendered; by May 26, the last Indian resistance had ended. Canada's first war had been a resounding success, and, in the mood of euphoria it generated, there was no difficulty in persuading Parliament to vote the additional funds demanded by the railway's directors.

III.   Disunity

With a fresh infusion of the government subsidy, the CPR moved quickly to completion. By the end of the 1885 construction season the long lines of steel met in British Columbia. On November 7, there was a last-spike ceremony at which Donald Smith was photographed like a hammer-swinging Father Time to commemorate the moment at which the country was "stitched down." The moment was not unimportant. But it seems rather an exaggeration to join P. B. Waite in referring to the completion of the CPR as "a greater contribution to pulling the country together than any other single event," or to go even further and assign it supernatural power saying with Waite that the railway "alone could nail the country together." This is the hero theory of history applied to objects rather than to persons.

The railway may have brought the provinces into physical proximity. But regional diversity was still a fact, and indeed it was given fresh vitality in the aftermath of the Northwest Rebellion. Whatever glory there was in driving the last spike vanished in the long shadow cast by the Regina scaffold where an execution occurred nine days later. John A. Macdonald had no intention of assuming responsibility for the rebellion himself. Although seven years of neglect had magnified simple questions over land titles and government treaty obligations into such monumental frustrations that the people concerned finally threw all regard for law to the wind, and rose in arms to demand recognition by force, the government intended to put the burden of villainy entirely upon the shoulders of the rebels, and on one rebel in particular, Louis Riel.

A number of leaders were captured, but Riel was the only one charged with high treason as defined by the fourteenth century English "Statute of Treasons." Riel's life hung on the question of whether he did "most wickedly, maliciously, traitorously ... levy and make war against our said Lady the Queen . . . . " Since his participation—indeed his leadership—was beyond doubt, the matter appeared settled before the court convened. But the issue at the trial was Riel's sanity. If he was found to be insane, then the government was morally bound to pity rather than to punish him. Riel himself denied that he was mad. He declared "humbly through the grace of God I believe I am the prophet of the new world." Riel was delighted that the government found this reasonable. His jury of six was not so easily persuaded; they found him guilty, but they they did recommend mercy. On instructions from the justice minister, however, the magistrate was bound to ignore the recommendation for clemency and ordered execution by hanging. There were appeals, of course. When they all failed—as they had to fail—the man who was held accountable for the rebellion paid the full price with his life on November 16. Sir John A. Macdonald, the minister responsible, held on for more than half a decade longer.

To many Protestants, Riel's execution was just punishment for two rebellions. Even if he had not been completely sane in 1885, he had been lucid enough in 1870, and Protestant Ontario still considered the Red River Resistance no less a rebellion than the later episode. So there would be no regrets in Ontario over the execution of the troublemaker who kept returning. All rebels had to be equal before the law. The Toronto *Mail* preferred to see Ontario "smash confederation" on this point rather than compromise the legal principle.

Quebec spokesmen were quick to reply that Riel was not the only person involved in the uprising, and wondered aloud why he was the only victim of the hangman. Their conclusion was that the real motive for the hanging was Protestant resentment of the compassion Riel had won from French-speaking Catholics in and out of Quebec. Protestant bigotry blinded Ontario to Riel's madness and the jury's recommendation for clemency. Quebec demanded nothing more for Riel than for any other lunatic. The man deserved to be pitied, not punished.

The storm of controversy raged for nearly six months before Macdonald felt it was calm enough to reconvene Parliament. Then the controversy resumed all over again. The prime minister kept silent, but he did permit—in fact, he promoted—a demonstration of anger by Quebec Conservatives. As soon as the House reconvened, A.G.P.R. Landry, the president of the Quebec Conservative Association, moved a resolution that the House express its regret that Louis Riel had been executed. In the debate that followed, Edward Blake, the provincial leader who had put a price on Riel's head in 1870 and who was now leader of the federal Liberals, elaborated a position that he did not propose to "construct a political platform out of the Regina Scaffold." This default enabled Wilfrid Laurier to become the rising star of the Liberal party with a speech that was poignant without being maudlin, and scathing without being unseemly or opportunistic. He offered an indictment which hinted that the government had been playing a political game all along: "Had they taken as much pains to do right, as they have taken to punish wrong, they never would have had any occasion to convince those people that the law cannot be violated with impunity, because the law would never have been violated at all." Macdonald said nothing in reply, not one word to confirm or deny the charge. Ultimately, the Landry motion was defeated. Only 52 members expressed regret; 146 voted that they approved of the execution. This was very nearly a free vote, and therefore it was a good measure of real feelings. About one third of the Liberals voted with the Conservatives and approved the hanging. Nearly half of the Quebec Conservatives either abstained or voted with the regretters, thereby censuring the government.

In Quebec itself, opinion was divided in similar proportions, half-approving and half-regretting. At the time of the execution, Honoré Mercier, leader of the Quebec Liberal party, denounced the event as a direct insult to the integrity of the people of his province, and began to call for the creation of a new political party, one with no pretensions beyond Quebec, neither Liberal nor Conservative but a *parti national*. He did not stop hammering away at his theme until the provincial election, which occurred in the autumn of 1886, at which time Mercier's *nationaliste* party gained control of the provincial legislature.

The return to nationalism in Quebec was consistent with a general drive toward provincial autonomy. There were elections of new legislatures in every province in 1886, and anti-Macdonald governments were triumphant everywhere except on the fringes of the federation. Only Prince Edward Island and British Columbia were complacently tolerant of the image of the future nation the Conservatives were pursuing.

The resentment in the rest of Canada arose from complaints over more than the Riel incident, however. In Nova Scotia, for instance, dissatisfaction stemmed from the appearance of growing regional disparity. By 1886 wooden ships had no future, but a new economy oriented toward coal mining was providing nothing more than a marginal substitute. It was relatively simple to blame Confederation for steadily declining economic fortunes. Premier Fielding threatened separatism if more revenue for local development was not diverted from other regions to the Maritime Provinces. Fielding argued that Confederation had brought Maritimers a tariff and the loss of the United States market. He reasoned that Macdonald was therefore obliged to make up the difference, or sanction the Maritime Provinces' withdrawal from an arrangement that was proving to be a bad bargain. This threat of separatism on economic grounds was enormously popular. In the election of June, 1886, Fielding was returned with a significantly strengthened majority.

In Ontario, anger arose from disputes over the division of sovereignty. The issue was status more than dollars. The government was Oliver Mowat's and provincial autonomy had been his favorite theme since the early 1880s. It was similar to the affirmation of loyalty to province that was current in Quebec, but the more decorous Ontarians had gained legal decisions against the Dominion from the highest level. The most important of the court battles was a case arising from Archibald Hodge's pool tables.

Ontario had a law that tavern games had to end when the drinking stopped. But on May 7, 1881, Hodge's customers went on shooting pool after the 7 P.M. Saturday drinking ended. Constables took note of this scandalous gaming and did their duty accordingly. Hodge was fined twenty dollars but appealed his case all the way to the Judicial Committee of the

Privy Council of Great Britain. Hodge's lawyers contended that the Ontario government had no power to regulate commerce in the course of granting licenses. The British Law Lords disagreed. Here is where the issue rose above Hodge's billiards. The Judicial Committee asserted that any province was competent to make such stipulations in the course of exercising their power to grant licenses under section 92, despite the apparent conflict in this case with the central government's power to regulate commerce. Thus, the case of *Hodge* v. *the Queen* confirmed the federal nature of the Canadian union by asserting that the provinces were in no sense merely the administrative districts of a government in Ottawa, but had "authority as plenary and ample within the limits prescribed by section 92, as the imperial parliament, in the plenitude of its power, possessed and could bestow." In other words, Mercier's Quebec, Fielding's Nova Scotia, Mowat's Ontario and all the others were coordinate with, not subordinate to, Macdonald's Ottawa.

By the end of 1886, five out of seven of the provincial premiers thought it might be possible to establish coordinate power even more broadly than was enumerated in the clauses of section 92. As a result, they gathered for a second Quebec conference in October of 1887, in order to discuss resolutions affirming coordinate power. They wanted to reverse the tide of centralization that had been running with Macdonald since 1867, but which was now apparently beginning to run the other way—at least on the provincial level. Most conspicuously, they demanded a greater share of the national revenue and abandonment of the principle that Ottawa had a right to disallow provincial legislation. The provincial premiers wanted a federation that was even looser than that provided by even the widest interpretation of the BNA Act. Naturally Macdonald denounced the resolutions as the emanations of a party gathering, for, after all, only one of the attending premiers was from Macdonald's party. But the fact was inescapable that with only Prince Edward Island and British Columbia prepared to stand by the prime minister's conception of confederation, and with the five most populous provinces having declared against him, a significant protest had been made against centralism.

Even so, the check to Macdonald's design must not be overemphasized. There was no uniform pattern of support for one level of government. In Nova Scotia, for example, the voters who approved Fielding's separatist resolution overwhelmingly in June of 1886, had the opportunity to return twenty-one like-minded candidates to Ottawa in the federal election of February 1887. But they did not. On the contrary, they voted overwhelmingly in favor of Macdonald's party. Nova Scotia was not unusual in this regard. Every other province that was represented at the Quebec conference exhibited the *same* tendency. The voters affirmed that they wanted the staunch proponents of provincial autonomy running the local scene, and

Macdonald, the arch-proponent of dominion power, governing in Ottawa. It was perverse; in a sense, even schizophrenic. But it proved that Canadians wanted a national as well as a regional identification; a strong country as well as a vital province.

This pattern was evident in the election of 1891 as well. This contest was a plebiscite on the National Policy versus Continentalism. The Liberals, now led by Wilfrid Laurier, advocated abandonment of the protective tariff in favor of unrestricted reciprocity with the United States, a position that was consistent with the provincial autonomy of the Liberal premiers. Conservatives asserted that reciprocity would threaten Canadian autonomy, and some Liberals agreed that "political union with the United States, though becoming more probable, is by no means our ideal, or as yet our inevitable future." Thus, they refused to support their party's policy on these grounds. Others asserted that free trade was not a first step to annexation. But they were confounded by the Conservatives, who appealed to loyalty to Macdonald, to the British allegiance, and to the opinion that the tariff was indispensable to national survival. The election was close; 51 percent of the votes went to Macdonald's Conservatives, and 49 percent to the Opposition.

Within weeks of the election, however, Macdonald began to suffer a series of paralytic strokes. In June, they killed him. Now that John A. was gone there was no one in his party with the ingenuity to replace him, and this was more than a problem for the Conservatives. Macdonald's death was also a crisis for Canada because, more than any other single person or project, it was the force of his amiable personality that had secured the union of diverse provinces in the first instance, and it was his constant attention that had given them the semblance of nationality in the two decades that followed. The man was mortal; so also perhaps was the union.

IV.   Bigotry

The first to suffer the effects of Macdonald's demise were the leaderless Conservatives, a party that now drifted dangerously toward a newly-militant Ontario Protestantism that Macdonald had done much to dampen. Two years before his death, in March of 1889, it had been moved in the Commons that the Dominion government should be used to disallow a recent provincial statute of Quebec that was inimical to the national integrity because it set a precedent for intervention by an authority unknown to the British Crown. The provincial law in question was the Jesuits' Estate

Act, passed to award $400 000 to the Pope as a token compensation for Jesuit properties lost by the Church at the time of the Conquest. The Vatican, in turn, would decide how the money would be apportioned to Catholic institutions in the province. After several days of debate, the federal motion was defeated by 188 votes to 13.

Here the matter might have remained, but in the course of the debate the Toronto *Mail* asserted that "the abandonment of Quebec to the Ultramontane and the Jesuit will be the death of Canadian nationality . . . . " This struck a sensitive nerve in Ontario, a nerve that the "Noble Thirteen," the members of Parliament who had raised the issue, had failed to arouse in the House. When they failed in Parliament, D'Alton McCarthy led an appeal to the people. Thus, the Equal Rights Association was formed in Toronto in June.

The demand for equal rights for all religious denominations and special privileges for none was an old slogan in Ontario, and it was a liberal-democratic doctrine that sounded lofty in principle. In this case, however, majority rule meant repression of minorities on a national scale. First, it involved withdrawal of the long-established public support to Catholic schools, then withdrawal of the customary toleration that was sometimes accorded the French language outside Quebec in New Brunswick, Ottawa, and most recently, by statute, in the West. Ultimately, majority rule would lead to the use of dominion power to coerce the provinces because eventually French-speaking Canadians would seek refuge in a militantly defensive Quebec. There, at the last ditch, they would outnumber English-speaking Protestants, and by the same doctrine of majority rule, they could tell the English to attend schools and speak the language that accorded with the majority. But since Ottawa could claim that the English-speaking people of Quebec were part of the wider Canadian majority, in this sense not a minority at all, they would say, in McCarthy's words: "No. This is a nation, the provinces have great powers for local government, but all these must be subject to unwritten laws which must regulate the whole Dominion." In time, according to McCarthy's most pious wish, Canada would be one centralized British state united by common language and outlook.

It was against the background of this gathering storm that the Tory leadership passed (after an interregnum presided over by J.J.C. Abbott who admitted that "I am here because I am not particularly obnoxious to anybody") to Sir John Thompson. His position was a painful one. Thompson was seen by many of the Protestant camp as a "pervert," for he was a lapsed Methodist and a convert to Roman Catholicism. He was aware that he was the first Roman Catholic prime minister, and that everyone in Protestant Canada, especially those in the Orange Order, would be watching for signs that he was favoring his co-religionists. He therefore "bent over backwards to avoid even the appearance" of favoring Catholics, and, accordingly to Lovell Clark, "he did them less than justice" as a result.

Thompson's overcompensation was well seen in his handling of the Manitoba Schools Question. By the late 1880s Manitoba had received many new settlers. The vast majority of them were from Ontario, for the expected migration from Quebec had not occurred. The result was that the French-English dualism of 1870 disappeared, and the strongly Orange sentiments of the newcomers, inflamed by a violent speech at Portage la Prairie given by D'Alton McCarthy late in the summer of 1889, was directed against Francophone institutions, notably the official status of the French language and the Catholic school system.

Education rights caused the most controversy, and a series of legal cases and appeals made their tortuous way through the courts over the next half decade. The basis of the French-Catholic case was that the BNA Act had given them the right to their schools; section 93 (1) stipulated that "nothing . . . shall prejudicially affect any right or privilege with respect to denominational schools which any class of persons have by law in the Province at the Union." Unfortunately for them, it was held by the Judicial Committee of the Privy Council that the rights of French Catholics in 1870 had not amounted to a system established in law; their schools had been private institutions supported by gifts rather than by taxation. Accordingly, section 92 (1) could not be invoked to protect minority rights in Manitoba.

Thompson was not in a position to resolve such a dispute. He died in 1894. His successor, Mackenzie Bowell, was a character even more flaccid than Abbott; worse still, he was a prominent Orangeman. When the leadership of the Conservatives passed to Sir Charles Tupper in 1896, the situation was out of hand and it was too late for his pragmatic approach to be effective. By this time the embattled minority in Manitoba had long before exhausted the appeal process. The only remedy that remained was that provided by section 93 (4) of the BNA Act, which permitted the government of Canada to enact "remedial laws" to preserve "any right or privilege of the Protestant or Roman Catholic minority . . . in relation to education." It was a course of action from which the Tories shrank; to implement remedial legislation was to offend the notion of provincial autonomy and to antagonize the Protestant party and majoritarians; to deny remedial legislation was to confirm Quebeckers' worst fears that they had no future beyond their own province and that the party of Macdonald and Cartier was as dead as its former leaders.

It was against such background that the election of 1896 was fought. Here the Conservatives met defeat. One dynasty ended. Another was about to begin.

PART FOUR

Nationality
Short of
Independence

CHAPTER FOURTEEN

Illusions of Change

I.   Laurier—Macdonald's Successor

The election of 1896 seemed to mark a decisive change in Canadian politics. After an eternity in the wilderness (only five years in office since Confederation) the Liberal party had come to power, and there they stayed for the next fifteen years. But the change was primarily a change in names, not of policies or styles of leadership. Even the election that brought Laurier to power suggested continuity with Macdonald, rather than a change.

The primary issue in the contest of 1896 was the Manitoba Schools Question, in the handling of which it was Laurier, not Tupper, who was seen as the true heir to Macdonald's smiling pragmatism. The Liberal leader showed that he had learned well from his former opponent. As far back as 1893 Laurier had written to a friend that he preferred tax-supported schools on nonsectarian lines, but where Catholic children were already instructed by Catholic authorities the pattern should be retained. In 1893 Laurier was espousing something of a compromise, one that avoided full-blown separate schools as much as suddenly imposed nonsectarian education.

This flexibility itself was revealing. But perhaps even more significant was Laurier's refusal to make this position public. Whereas others, notably Blake, his predecessor as Liberal leader, would have rushed forward with an open avowal of conviction, Laurier preferred to keep quiet; as he put it in 1895, "I fully realize that a good many of our friends are not satisfied with my course . . . . But under existing circumstances it was impossible to make a bold and well defined attitude without breaking the unity of the party. . . . . My aim therefore was to keep and maintain the party unity, whilst the government was hopelessly divided." Here, too, Laurier had learned from the master. In matters of political style Laurier and Macdonald were successor and predecessor, not opposites or even contrasts.

In the 1896 election itself, both parties seemed to be claiming the mantle of Macdonald. At the last minute Tupper introduced a Remedial Bill, allowed Parliament to debate it for seven weeks, and then went to the people. During the campaign the measure was identified with him, while the party tailored its position to the conscience of individual members riding by riding. In a sense this was a compromise, because the full might of party discipline was not brought to bear on independent Conservatives who furiously opposed the Remedial Bill. The tactic saved the party, but lost the election.

More successful was Laurier's handling of the awkward problem. He implied rather than specified; "sunny ways" would be more effective than Tupper's harsh remedy. Naturally such glibness did not please everyone; the Catholic hierarchy and the Ultramontanes in general were antagonistic to this style, preferring Tupper's belated but strong Remedial Bill. This publicly declared preference of the Church only made Tupper more odious in Protestant Canada; and the official position of clerical spokesmen failed to persuade most Quebeckers, who went solidly for Laurier. The sincerity of the Conservatives was questioned, in part, by remembrances of the Riel affair. Others were simply charmed with the possibility of electing a French Canadian prime minister. A minority of the rest of Canada and a majority of Quebeckers thus combined to defeat Tupper and the Conservatives. In this sense, it would perhaps be true to say that the Conservatives lost the election of 1896 rather than to say that the Liberals won it.

Macdonald's party without Macdonald appeared cynical or simply clever. The Liberals under Laurier appeared to be the Liberal-Conservatives of Macdonald's prime. And, as the successful defusing of the Manitoba Schools Question in the next few years indicated, Laurier's was a pragmatism that brought results. In keeping with his preelection promises he negotiated with the provincial authorities in Manitoba, thus preserving the principle of provincial autonomy in educational matters. The negotiations went well, helped by the fact that Clifford Sifton, Manitoba's attorney general, was appointed to the federal cabinet, and that this prize was made conditional upon the outcome of the negotiations. As a result, the Manitoba Schools Act was amended: an urban school with 40 Catholic pupils and a rural school with 10 could demand a Catholic teacher; ten heads of families could demand religious instruction by a priest or minister in the last half hour of the school day; finally, where the pupils spoke a language other than English, teaching could be bilingual. This last clause was passed with the French language in mind, but was to have unforeseen consequences when Central- and Eastern-European migration to Manitoba boomed in the years ahead.

For the moment, it was enough that Manitoba had cooperated in a popular compromise, and in the next election, that of 1900, 52 percent of Manitoban voters preferred Laurier Liberals. This was quite a change. In 1896, Manitobans had been so opposed to meddling that they had opted for Tupper's party and the pledge of overt intervention, on the confident assumption that he would drop the question entirely once the election was over and as it became clear just how divided the Conservatives were. But after Laurier's ascendancy and following negotiations which Manitobans found satisfactory beyond expectation, they responded appropriately by joining the rest of the country in the renewal of Laurier's mandate. Thus were the wily arts of opportunistic politics reaffirmed and the "sunny ways" of Macdonald firmly restored.

II.   A Tariff and More Railways

Essential continuity rather than decisive change was also to be seen in the debate—or lack of it—over the tariff. Until 1891 Laurier had been a convinced freetrader, and had eagerly spoken out against the National Policy. But by 1893 the Liberals had come to accept the political benefits of protection. Thus, in the 1896 election, Laurier and his party were conspicuously silent on the issue of free trade. Then, after the election, expediency dictated retention of the tariff more or less as it was inherited. In April of 1897, the House that perused Laurier's first budget was treated with a schedule of duties essentially the same as Macdonald's. As a token gesture toward farmers there were some reductions on tariffs on their machinery. And as a nod in the direction of the party's free trade past a 5 percent general reduction was offered to any other country willing to reciprocate. Basically, however, the 25 percent *ad valorem* structure was to remain as Macdonald's government had set it in 1879.

When prosperity followed, Laurier's embrace of the Old National Policy was seen as statesmanlike rather than as opportunistic; his conversion appeared to be good for the country. The dramatic upswing in the value of Canadian staples, which occurred almost immediately upon Laurier's taking office, was merely coincidental, of course; but the boom that followed was an event for which the prime minister and his newly oriented party were only too happy to take full credit.

Several factors explain the boom. First, an infusion of gold from newly opened mines in South Africa and Canada in large enough volume to cause inflation on a global scale made the price of Canadian staples rise accordingly. Between 1896 and 1914 the index of staple commodity prices rose 32 percent. Foodstuffs—particularly grains—nearly doubled in cost because of the concentration of the European population in cities and a relative decline in European production.

Another factor contributing to the boom was technological change, which invited Canadians to exploit completely *new* staples. There were innovations in hard-rock mining, for instance, that gave new value to "the land God gave Cain." Previously, the Shield was either a source of fur or simply an obstacle to agriculture. Now it became a treasure-trove of minerals such as silver and nickel. Other technological changes led to new uses for the forests and water of the same previously economically valueless territory. There were beginnings in hydroelectric production. But more immediately important was the development of a technique for making paper from wood fiber.

Prior to the introduction of the new material all the world's paper was manufactured from cotton and linen rags. The old product was satisfactory in every respect but price. The new wood-pulp paper was infinitely less durable but proportionately cheaper, and any country with trees unsuitable for lumber could lead in its production. Thus, the jack-pine forests of the Shield began to fall before the pulp-makers' cutters just as the larger trees once fell to British timber buyers, and an industry that did not even exist at the time of Confederation emerged suddenly as one of the leading edges of economic growth. In fact, no other country turned to the new staple with the same vengeance as the Canadians, who began turning their forests to pulp. Almost overnight, Canada became the leading exporter of wood fiber.

All the staples, new as well as old, were commodities that were sold oceans away in their raw or semi-finished form. And, since all were of low value relative to bulk, their production was highly susceptible to even slight changes in shipping charges. The third factor that supported the boom was, therefore, the dramatic fall in transoceanic freight rates that accompanied the completion of the world's shift from wooden-hulled sailing vessels, which leaked and required large crews, to the "tramp steamers," which were tighter and less heavily manned.

Together, all these factors created and sustained a new commerce and prosperity, which, in turn, stimulated both immigration and settlement. Earlier, between 1878 and 1891, immigrants moved into Canada at the rate of about 50 000 per year. Now in the period of the Laurier boom, the rate of immigration was four times that of the earlier years. Almost 2 million people arrived between 1897 and 1911. Most settled in cities, but many of the newcomers seem to have emigrated with the free land of the prairie West as their goal. New farms were created at the rate of about 30 000 per year, a process eased by the simpler claim registration and title-securing procedures instituted by the new Minister of the Interior, Clifford Sifton. This vast inflow of settlers, coupled with the other factors mentioned earlier, resulted in spectacular growth in the output of agricultural staples, particularly wheat. Production of wheat tripled every five years between 1896 and 1911. In 1896, output stood at 8 million bushels; by 1912 it had reached 232 million bushels. With the increased volume of freight, the CPR groaned under the burden of the annual harvest.

In 1882, critics had complained that a transcontinental railway through empty land would not generate enough revenue to pay even for its axle grease. But by 1899, Manitobans were saying that no amount of railways was sufficient: "We want all the railways we can get." In 1903, Laurier complied and came down with a nearly fatal case of railway enthusiasm by deciding to back vast additional systems. There were two firms that vied for the privilege of building the one additional transcontinental line that was apparently needed. One firm was the creation of William Mackenzie and Donald Mann, speculators and tycoons who were the very epitome of that reckless optimism that Americans call the "can-do spirit." Their railway, the Canadian Northern, was a hodgepodge of branch lines put together by joining areas in the West that the CPR had declined to serve. By 1901, Mackenzie and Mann were ready to build across the Shield from Port Arthur to Montreal and they wanted government sanction to do so. At the same time, from the east, the Grand Trunk vied for the identical favor—but wanted to build from the opposite direction.

The reasonable policy in 1903 would have been to force a merger of the Canadian Northern and the Grand Trunk. This would have required one short and expensive connection around Lake Superior; but the result would be the benefit of a second transcontinental railway at a fraction of what the CPR had cost in subsidies. The problem with a merger was that neither the directors of the firms nor the leaders in government were willing to create it.

Caught between businessmen and his cabinet, Laurier paled at the thought of attempting to coerce either. But he was just as reluctant to turn down the two firms and confront the public with a least-growth option. As a result, Laurier said yes to everyone but his closest advisers. The Grand Trunk was authorized to strike out across the prairies; Mackenzie and Mann were sanctioned to head for the Atlantic. And there was more. Since the existing Grand Trunk was all in the south, a third railway was to be built by the government from Moncton, through northern Quebec and Ontario, to Winnipeg. It would be called the National Transcontinental and would be leased to the Grand Trunk upon completion. Thus, in the beginning two firms competed for one line, but in the end, Laurier gave his consent to both and threw in one more railway for good measure. Here was railway policy in the grand manner. Laurier had acted contrary to advice from his cabinet; in fact, the Minister of Railways and Canals resigned in anger over the decision. But the prime minister had acted in the style he knew was popular, a style that was also becoming customary for the governments of the most rapidly industrializing provinces.

By one form of subsidy or another, vast projects were being underwritten by public treasuries. And yet, as H. V. Nelles has pointed out with regard to Ontario, the politicians failed to pursue "the logic of responsible government into the industrial age" by following up their financial risks with regulation and controls to safeguard the public interest. Governments subsidized; they did not control business. Considering the strength of the respect for the privacy of enterprise, however, control was probably impossible. At the very least, voters would have interpreted intervention as meddlesome. More likely, they would have believed the spokesmen for businessmen's associations, who would have spread the alarm that controls were unprogressive. And, since this was the age of "progress," the kind of responsibility that Nelles defined did not occur. What did attend the launching of vast subsidized projects was political bombast, the sort of rhetoric that led Laurier to describe Canada as "the star towards which all men who love progress and freedom shall come for the next hundred years." He said it with such amiable assurance that one Toronto newspaper recognized just how completely he had "that strange and mysterious gift, which Sir John Macdonald possessed in almost equal degree . . . . " Like his predecessor, Laurier appreciated that economic nationalism and the growth of the economy were the topics on which Canadians could always be expected to agree. Thus, the National Policy introduced by Macdonald was carried to apparent fulfillment by Laurier, and the whole country thrilled to Laurier's pronouncement that "the twentieth century shall be the century of Canada."

III. The Consequences of Long–term Tariff–Protection

Even in the age of progress, however, it might have been asked whether different kinds of encouragement to private enterprise were more appropriate. Subsidies for railways or indirect payments in the form of the tariffs could be dramatized as attractive means of developing a new nation, but surely a country would eventually approach a point of diminishing returns in railway construction or even in the recruitment of more population. By 1905 there were provinces from sea to sea, and—in this sense—the country had "grown up." In another respect Canada was coming of age: the annual value of industrial production was approaching parity with that of agriculture. Perhaps Canada was no longer such a new country, and it was no longer appropriate to devote so much energy toward rapid growth regardless of cost or means.

The idea behind the Macdonald-Laurier tariff, apart from winning elections, was to attract industry and people, both foreign. In one way, this was a strange "protection" for it was aimed at bringing to Canada those people and factories against which Canadian workers and businessmen were supposed to need protection. But in the age of progress everyone seemed to agree that the chief duty of government was to provide a stage on which capitalists might produce their profit-motive drama with as large a cast as possible. Since a businessman who was persuaded to build a factory in a small town brought the promise of employment and auxiliary commerce with him, it mattered little that he came from afar and left his allegiance abroad. As villages became cities, and provinces filled with people, Canada would become rich and powerful—a nation in a sense.

There was ample *room* to pursue this path: Canada was the second largest country in the world in geographical terms. And by the time of the second census in the twentieth century there were indications that Canada was on the threshold of greatness in population as well as in economic terms. From a total of 4.8 million people in 1891, the country had grown beyond 7 million by 1911. The gross national product, which stood at $803 million in 1890, shot up to $2 235 million twenty years later. Then as now it was impossible not to be impressed with the sheer magnitude of these increases in such a short span of time.

Closer examination, however, raises awkward questions about long-term side effects of the National Policy. This was a "nationalism" that intentionally encouraged foreign ownership as the means of developing industrial capacity most rapidly. The tariff, patent laws, and schemes for "bonusing" were policies employed at all levels of government with the aim of making Canada as attractive as possible to *foreign* investors. The tariff was an incentive in the sense that it taxed finished manufactured goods to the sky, but permitted the free entry of parts for assembly. Patent laws of 1872 and 1903 went even further by refusing to recognize foreign copyrights unless foreign manufacturers licensed a Canadian producer or built a branch plant themselves. But the systems of bonusing were the most brazen encouragement of all; by outright grants of land, or tax exemptions, or promises of free utilities (or all three), provinces and municipalities bribed foreigners to establish branch plants within their jurisdictions.

These incentives, which were in place by 1879, all began to have noticeable effects in the 1880s. The first foreigners, Singer Sewing Machine, Bell Telephone, and the aptly named American Screw Corporation were joined by nearly fifty other foreign-owned companies before 1890. By 1912 Coca-Cola and two hundred other products were being "made in Canada," and the Canadian Manufacturers' Association proudly announced that every town of any size had an American subsidiary assuring its growth. In their view, it was the tariff that was primarily responsible for this wonderful development. "Hence a strong argument exists for not meddling overmuch with the duties."

Canada's new dependence on foreign investment represented a remarkable shift from the previous century. Before the National Policy between 1850 and 1878, foreigners were viewed primarily as a source of capital with which to build a Canadian empire. But now the borders were opened for the foreigners to play the role of the empire-builders themselves, as in the heyday of the timber trade between 1807 and 1850. Equally remarkable was the increasing tendency for the nationality of these direct—rather than portfolio—investors to be American rather than British. By 1913 the Americans held $835 million worth of Canadian assets. The British share was $3 billion. But the British branch-plant operations represented less than one-tenth of their interests in Canada. Five-eighths of the American capital was in direct investment, in that aggregation of 200-odd branch plants.

The proliferation of American subsidiaries had important consequences. First, in the area of secondary manufacturing, industrialization following the tariff incentive meant an extraordinarily large number of uneconomic assembly operations. Singer, Westinghouse, Gillette and the others pole-vaulted the tariff barrier because they were attracted by the higher profits the Canadian government guaranteed by the protected market. But sewing machines and safety razors had their "made in Canada" labels at the expense of workers who now had to pay more for consumer goods. In this way, although the times were prosperous, life grew no less harsh for the urban poor. In Montreal, for example, the typical working-class family in 1897 consisted of five people, crowded into a small cold-water apartment. Children as well as parents worked in an effort to keep up with the widening gap between bare subsistence and working-class "prosperity." But there could be no improvement in their living conditions so long as prices increased faster than real wages.

The lowered standard of living was only one regressive consequence of foreign investment. Foreign ownership of primary industry was even more detrimental to development. In this sphere the normal pattern was for the large foreign corporations to view Canada as a supplier of raw materials to support their manufacturing elsewhere. Thus, American newspapers, which owned paper mills, cut pulpwood to supply their paper factories in the United States, and metal producers mined ore to supply refineries and factories, also in the "mother country." The production and export of staples in their raw form was so vast that governments imposed export duties in the 1880s and 1890s to compel foreigners to invest in lumber milling and pulp milling as well as timber cutting, and in smelting in addition to mining. Whether such industrialization contributed to "national" development is debatable. But even more clear was the failure along these lines; by 1910 Canada was twice as committed to the export of raw staples as in 1879. In this sense, Canada's economy relative to the world's was that of a supply base more than that of an industrial state. The economy had grown, but not matured.

But a lowered standard of living and an economy tending ever further toward a mere supply-base level were not the only drawbacks. Two further disadvantages flowing from the National Policy were an underscoring of the traditionally weak Canadian entrepreneurism and *increased* out-migration of population. Although neither of these tendencies has been researched in full, there is interesting speculation in support of both. With regard to the first, R. T. Naylor has suggested that pre-National Policy Canadians were more interested in merchant capitalism (banking, land speculation and merchandizing) than in industrial capitalism (investment in primary or secondary manufacturing). Since the tariff was "explicitly intended to attract foreign capitalists" to develop industry, Naylor says it follows that "it was not industrialists who initiated this policy but the more numerous" and more influential "merchant capitalist class" and in the long-term this was self-defeating because in "previously open sectors where no secondary industry existed, the future potential of the local industrialist is reduced by the establishment of foreign branch plants." Thus, an even greater "stultification of indigenous industrial capital" followed. As in the days of the square timber trade, the "industrial capitalists" were foreigners exploiting Canadian resources to their advantage; local businessmen who viewed timber production as essentially a gambling trade continued land speculation and forwarding operations. In the twentieth century, their counterparts were bankers, railway owners, merchants, and land speculators and the role of the British was passed to the Americans. In the Canadian case, "the more things changed, the more they remained the same."

A similar conclusion follows from scrutiny of population migration. Since the original proponents of the National Policy justified their tariff on the grounds that "we have no manufacturers . . . . our work people have gone off to the United States," it seems particularly self-defeating that the tariff actually increased the incentive for Canadians to leave. The speculation that this was the case stems from J. H. Dales' observation that the 25 percent tariff drove real wages about 20 percent below those of the United States, that this was an even stronger push to migration than the original lack of jobs in manufacturing. Fragmentary data in the historical statistics of the United States tend to confirm the hypothesis; in the Canadian pre-industrial period between 1854 and 1874, American officials recorded the entry of 345 000 Canadians. If they had not migrated—all other factors being equal—the population of Canada in 1874 would have been 9 percent greater. But in the years of rapid industrialization and relative decline in the standard of living between 1896 and 1926, more than 1.5 million Canadians were recorded as immigrants by United States officials. Had *this* group remained in the land of their birth, the 1926 population would have been 16 percent greater. But since the Canadian standard of living never fell below that of Europe, Canada continued to be an attractive destination for European immigrants; therefore, as the born-in-Canada Canadians moved out, the burgeoning branch plants made good their shortage by recruitment from Europe. In this way, the National Policy operated as Canada's first venture into foreign aid because the encouragement it offered to the native born to move out only made it easier for new Canadians to move in. But here is the ironic and self-defeating aspect: the "National Policy" to keep Canadians at home and to "protect native labour from the competition of cheap foreign labour" actually provided greater incentive for Canadians to leave, and eventually brought the cheap foreign labor to Canada itself, since the influx of newcomers more than outweighed the attrition of population to the United States.

Thus, Canada's National Policy, which invited foreigners to build the industrial base and man the factories while tacitly encouraging Canadians to seek better paying jobs elsewhere, was self-defeating. But in 1910 no thought was given to alternative policies. The striking fact was growth and since this was the primary value, the National Policy acquired a moral as well as a political value. Given its anti-American orientation (political speakers continued to oppose all Yankees except those who moved to Canada) the tariff appealed on patriotic grounds as well. The National Policy seemed a good hedge against continentalism in a time when most Canadians still believed that "in order to be Canadian one must be British." Thus, any attack upon the tariff—like any other interference with the privacy of business—was seen as at least "meddlesome" if not "veiled treason" and therefore an attack upon Canada itself. Under these circumstances, criticism of the tariff never succeeded; it hardly even began.

IV   Ethnic Conflict

What did worry some Canadians—and greatly—was the impact of the vast new immigration from sources hitherto unknown. That huge tide of immigrants mentioned earlier came mostly from Central and Eastern Europe, and since these newcomers tended to go to the West, a part of the country whose social forms and institutional life had not yet taken settled form, their arrival posed uncertainties, particularly for the future of Western Canada. To be sure, in its earliest years in Confederation, this region was supposed to give equal status to French- and English-speaking Canadians. The Manitoba Act of 1870 and the ordinances that regulated the Northwest Territories after 1875 both assured this equality.

But very early in the history of Manitoba, Ontario-born settlers moved into the new province and overshadowed the French (this was evident in the balance of population by 1881). By 1890 these new Manitobans were preparing themselves to disregard the provisions of the Manitoba Act for support of denominational schools and the status of French as an official language. Now Manitoba would be uniformly "British." Soon similar changes were made to the ordinances that gave institutional shape to the territories. Thus, the blueprint for the West was shifted from dualism to monoculture. By 1890, the newly ascendant Westerners looked forward to the day when the whole region of the prairies would be recognized with the status of provinces on a par with Ontario.

Then came the new immigration from Central and Eastern Europe to upset this vision of monoculture. The city of Winnipeg, which barely existed in 1870, numbered 26 000 people in 1891. It was 70 percent Protestant and 60 percent "British" ("British" meant a person born in Ontario or in the British Isles). But in the next twenty years Winnipeg more than quadrupled; it grew from the 26 000 of 1891 to more than 136 000 in 1911. At the same time, the city lost any sense of homogeneity. By 1911 the majority of Winnipeggers were foreign-born. The British, the Irish, and even the "acceptable" Scandinavians were a minority by themselves, since the newcomers who made up 55 percent of the city's population were "of radically different race," mostly Slavs. According to the Winnipeg *Telegram* in 1901, "there are few people who will affirm that Slavonic immigrants are desirable settlers, or that they are welcomed by the white people of Western Canada . . . . " Now the Manitoba Schools settlement of 1899 began to have unforeseen consequences as the newcomers claimed their statutory right to education in their own language. By 1907, Winnipeg schools offered instruction in thirteen different languages. To many of the Ontario newcomers of the previous decades, this "absurdity" had to stop. They demanded assimilation, and the crux of that policy was fluency in one language, namely English.

Many of the immigrants were happy to deliver even more than the "English" demanded. It was obvious to many of the ghettoized immigrants of Winnipeg's North End that they had to become "Canadian" the more fully to realize the cash value of the New World. Since "when you're English it's the same as bein' Canadian," many young lads learned English without an accent, and went on to mask their ethnicity behind British-sounding surnames. Thus, the Royal Society of Canada was informed by the Reverend George Bryce in 1910 that "the children sing the patriotic songs of Britain and Canada and the reading books are full of patriotic selections. There is no honour more regarded by these young foreigners than to be called Canadians." But as the Sandor Hunyadis became the Alex Hunters the "real English" faced the problem of "racial imposture." They wanted assimilation in the sense of structural adaptation (meaning fluency in English) but at the same time, the economic and social elite preferred such outsiders to stay in their place (that is, avoid pretensions of being 'white'). Thus, a man could change his name but not his ethnicity. Hunyadi as Hunter was still a "hunky." Here was "race" prejudice that would have important consequences in the future.

But in 1910 or later, there was one point on which the ethnic newcomers and the established elite always agreed; the French were simply another language group with no more rights than any other non-English minority. Furthermore, even though there were disagreements between the ethnics and the British as to the meaning of assimilation and how far it should be encouraged—or permitted—it was tacitly assumed by everyone, except the communitarians such as Hutterites and Doukhobors who lived in rural isolation, that any non-English person who wished to get ahead would have to learn English; government and business naturally recognized English as the only official language. In this way, the vision of a dual society, which was sidetracked first by Ontario-born newcomers in the 1880s, was dashed completely by later arrivals; if the French deserved special status, so also did the other ethnic groups; if not all, then none. Western Canada emerged, then, as incipiently multicultural but with English primacy. Monoculture was the more robust of the two ideals.

That the majority of the rest of Canada also supported the monocultural model was shown when Parliament carved two provinces out of the southern part of the Northwest Territories. The legal instruments for this creation of Alberta and Saskatchewan were the Autonomy Bills of 1905; naturally their passage was the occasion for intense debate over the "autonomy" that would follow. Either the new provinces would be as autonomous as the original four, in which case they would have control over their natural resources and a free hand in education, or the autonomy would be qualified, in which case they would continue to see their crown lands controlled from Ottawa by such statutes as the Dominion Lands Act of 1872, and education would be set up in accordance with federal policy, returning, perhaps to dualism. The Autonomy Bill did limit autonomy, and at first it was intended to divert the western provinces away from monoculturalism or incipient multiculturalism back to dualism. Thus Laurier sought special protection for the western French Catholic minority and continued control of western resources as a matter of *national* policy. But he was successful only in the latter. One compromise followed another, and Alberta and Saskatchewan entered Confederation as the colonies of the central government regarding economic development, but as free as Ontario to impose the cultural conformity they desired.

In this sense, the settlement and expansion of the West was a breach of what some—especially French Canadians—had seen as the promise of Confederation. And that had dark consequences for the future of the federation itself, because Quebec and English Canada were coming to a showdown on another fundamental question, that of British imperial relations. Once this was resolved in accordance with the English majority's wishes, the tendency for Quebeckers to brood over domestic betrayals was greater and more bitter than ever before.

CHAPTER FIFTEEN

Imperialism and the National Policy

I. The Beginning of External Affairs

Throughout most of the nineteenth century, Canadians enjoyed a splendid insulation from the crises of the world beyond their own borders. They had little to fear beyond their own continent since Canada enjoyed the security and even some of the prestige of an imperial power. Britain might have withdrawn her garrisons in 1870, but the Canadians were not totally abandoned. The later nineteenth century was the time of British naval supremacy, and so long as the mother country maintained a powerful fleet, Canada would be protected by it.

Such a state of affairs was particularly attractive to Canadians, for this kind of protection was provided entirely by the British taxpayer; Canada had no tribute to pay, only allegiance. Unfortunately, as the century drew to a close the cost to the British taxpayer was mounting steeply. This was the time when other countries were emerging as industrial powers and beginning to develop colonial ambitions of their own. Germany in particular was challenging Britain's lead, and the German naval programme of the 1890s called for a corresponding expansion on the part of Britain. In the face of the costs involved, British politicians began to wonder, as in 1763, if the time had not come for colonials to contribute their mite to the imperial effort.

The issue surfaced in 1897. That year was the diamond jubilee of Queen Victoria, and colonial leaders were gathered in London to help celebrate sixty years of imperial expansion and consolidation. Laurier was present, and he was asked if he would consider Canadian contributions to the defense of empire. Sir Wilfrid demurred. However, the request had been hardly more than a hint; England seemed securely at peace, and there was no resentment on either side.

But within a few years two issues arose that demanded Laurier take a more committed position. Unfortunately for the pragmatist, these issues provoked conflicting responses among Canadians and posed a serious challenge to Laurier's powers of accommodation.

The first arose only two years after the diamond jubilee. In 1899 Great Britain went to war with the Boers of South Africa. Laurier was asked to participate. At first he responded by pointing out that the conflict in South Africa posed "no menace to Canada" and therefore did not require the sending of Canadian soldiers. But the Canadians who felt "we must be British... in order to be Canadian" demanded participation. In the imperialists' view, Laurier's timidity was the height of ingratitude. They protested so loudly that the prime minister stated a week after his first announcement that he was now aware of a "desire of a great many Canadians who are ready to take service," and therefore reversed himself. Within days of arguing that the South African war was none of Canada's business, Laurier now called for one thousand volunteers to assist in the adventure because it was British.

Canada's enthusiasm for the Boer War proved keener than the opportunity. In the end, no fewer than seven thousand Canadians enlisted in the name of imperial solidarity. This was enough to provoke rumblings of protest from anti-imperialists, and other nationalists who suspected that the adventure set a dangerous precedent for larger and more foolish adventures in the future. Laurier asserted flatly that this episode "cannot be regarded as a departure... nor construed as a precedent for future action." But Henri Bourassa, the leader of the bloc known as the *autonomistes* and a rising force in Quebec politics, repudiated such an argument: "the precedent," Bourassa retorted, "is the accomplished fact."

Resentment in Quebec over imperial involvement was a foretaste of worse to come. But at the time Laurier sensed that its proportions were not threatening and that the mood of imperial identification was a dominant one. However the second issue soon arose, one that left Canadians not nearly so sure of their attitude toward the mother country. This was the Alaska Boundary Dispute of 1903.

There had never been a clear boundary between Canada and Alaska, but since gold had just been discovered in the Yukon it became a matter of signal importance to settle the matter quickly. The best access to the gold fields was through the ports of Dyea and Skagway. If these ports were Canadian, the development of the Klondike would elevate Vancouver to metropolitan stature; otherwise, Seattle would become the jumping-off point for gold seekers and their business. In 1903, the United States, Canada, and Great Britain agreed that a committee of six "impartial jurists" would decide the boundary. There would be three Americans, one Englishman and two Canadians. Predictably, the representatives of the United States promoted the American case, the Canadians promoted that of their country, and Lord Alverstone looked after Britain's interest. Alverstone sided with the Americans and Dyea and Skagway became American ports. Once again, according to Clifford Sifton, the British had "deliberately decided... to sacrifice our interest at any cost, for the sake of pleasing the United States.".

Canada, and the federal government in particular, had been humiliated. Laurier was obliged to conclude that future jumps upon the imperial bandwagon would have to be handled in a much more thoughtful fashion than in the past. It was clear that British gratitude for Canadian cooperation was a fleeting thing. British policy makers would always be more preoccupied with geopolitics than with small bits of Canadian real estate. On this basis, Laurier decided that, insofar as Canada had other external interests, Canadians would be better advised to "ask Parliament for more extensive powers so that if ever we have to deal with matters of a similar nature, we shall deal with them in our own way."

II. A "Tin Pot" Navy

The loosening of the ties with Britain did not immediately follow, however. There were two reasons. The first was well summarized by Governor General Minto when he pointed out shortly after the Alaskan boundary arbitration that "if Canada wishes to possess complete treaty-making powers she must be prepared to back her claims with her own forces." In other words, Canada would conduct her own foreign policy only if Canadians were prepared to fight the wars that might follow. In 1903, in any showdown over the Alaskan boundary six million Canadians were not likely to win much against eighty-one million Americans. Nor was the most skillful *quiet* diplomacy likely to prevail in the face of the United States' president, Teddy Roosevelt, who bragged about speaking softly while carrying a big stick.

The new aggressiveness of the Americans was the second reason for accepting British tutelage in external affairs. Although Canadian nationalists had reason to feel betrayed by Alverstone's behavior in the latest British negotiating, there was reason to regard the United States with a much stronger emotion. Even while the arbitration tribunal was meeting, Roosevelt sent marines to Alaska, and announced his intention of persuading Congress to declare war and "run the line as we claim it" if Americans could not talk the Canadians out of their version of the boundary. Any questioning of the imperial tie was thus countered by dislike of the Yankees. Nevertheless, Laurier had to maneuver carefully. In 1904 he made a small move towards increasing Canada's control of her own destiny when he nationalized the militia. Previously the General Officer Commanding had been British; henceforth he was to be Canadian. However, even this small step was provocative, as was made plain when the last British commander's departing injunction, "Men of Canada, keep both hands on the Union Jack", drew forth loud applause. Laurier realized that further moves in this direction would be unwise, and he was happy to have public attention concentrate for the moment upon economic growth and railways.

But by 1909 the issue could no longer be dodged. The first Lord of the Admiralty had just announced in Britain that naval supremacy was being lost to Germany, and that an immediate crash program of dreadnought building would have to be undertaken; "we want eight and we won't wait" became the vociferous slogan. Here was an imperial emergency, and there were Canadians ready to respond. It was moved in Canada that the country "should no longer delay in assuming her proper share of the responsibility and financial burden incidental to the suitable protection of her exposed coast line and sea ports." In other words, Canada should stop fussing over petty concerns and start recognizing that she benefited as part of a stronger empire.

Laurier responded with a substitute motion that repudiated the idea of cash tribute and proposed the launching of a Canadian navy instead. This seemed to satisfy his party, who held the majority in the House by a margin of nearly two to one. On this basis, for the moment, the proposal of a Canadian navy to cooperate with the British seemed to be the happy compromise.

The debate over Laurier's naval service bill was a good gauge of a developing crisis over the nature of Canadian nationality, however. On one side, there were English-speaking opponents who denounced the scheme as a flaccid gesture that divided the empire. On the other side, French-speaking Canadians suspected that any naval force that was affiliated with the British Admiralty at all was a dangerous precedent akin to the contribution of troops to the Boer War. Since Laurier's compromise seemed to only separate extremes still further, the prime minister was bewildered to say the least. In the year before, he had observed that Canada's existence was fearfully "anomalous," in the sense that "we are British subjects but we are an autonomous nation; we are divided into provinces, we are divided into races, and out of these confused elements the man at the head of affairs has to sail the ship onwards, and to do this safely." To reach the goal, Laurier had tried to find "the policy which can appeal ... to all sections of the community." But now in 1910, the politics of accommodation were breaking down on the question of imperial obligations.

Robert Borden, the leader of the Conservatives since Tupper's retirement in 1902, solved the problem for his party by advocating the position that would appeal to the majority of the population. He did not even try to formulate an alternative that would prove acceptable to a majority of French-speaking Canadians as well as the majority of English-speakers. Instead, Borden advocated the imperial plan of cash contributions, in the confident assumption that this was the approach preferred by the larger part of the dominant majority; and if the minority could not be made to like it, they were still powerless to prevent it.

At the end of the 1910 session, it was Laurier's compromise proposal that prevailed. With imperialists ridiculing the idea of the creation of a "tin pot navy," and with the editor of *Le Devoir*, Henri Bourassa, Laurier's old critic, warning that even this small force posed a danger for the future, the country showed signs of beginning to break along the lines of its primary antithesis. It was not a question of one side being weak on nationalism. The imperialists and *autonomistes* were each nationalists in their own way. What divided them was the method for acquiring a greater Canadian influence, and at the same time the definition of the purposes for which those new powers would be used.

II.   A New Direction in Tariff Policy

Laurier's naval service bill was a half-hearted response to the demand to assist Great Britain in the arms race with Germany and was denounced by all sides on that account. By the end of the session Laurier was tired of controversy and in need of escape. Accordingly, the aging prime minister went west in the hope of gaining some approval, if not unqualified recognition, for the fruits of his other policies. The prairies had come into booming prosperity since he had come into power, and provincial autonomy was well received by Alberta and Saskatchewan. Thus, the West was one region of the country in which he was still likely to receive the hero's welcome that was no longer forthcoming elsewhere. The cheering of the crowds that greeted Sir Wilfrid from June to September as he paraded from Winnipeg to Vancouver and back was just the tonic the old man needed.

But all was not approval and recognition. At nearly every stop along this regal progression there were also angry petitioners—farmers who were not satisfied that their share of the prosperity was all that it might or ought to have been. No group is as likely to complain as loudly or as sharply as the businessmen with rising expectations that are not being realized as fast or as fully as they hope. The farmers, the country businessmen of Western Canada, were no exception to this rule. They did not complain that they were impoverished, but they did suggest that their present income was only a shadow of what was possible if government would only accord them guarantees for such necessities as equitable freight rates, or more rational storage and marketing of their staple grains. But most of all they denounced Laurier's perpetuation of the protective tariff.

At Saskatoon, one farmer asked Laurier directly what had happened to all the Grit in the Liberal Party. He reminded the prime minister that it was Laurier who once promised "to skin the Tory bear of protection." This Liberal wanted to know "what you have done with the hide." The accusation put Laurier completely off balance. He could say only that his "blood is a little cooler now." But that confirmed what Westerners suspected, and they were not pleased with the confirmation that they had little to choose between Liberals and Conservatives.

In September, the prime minister returned to Ottawa with angry protests as well as the crowds' cheering still ringing in his ears. In that region of the country where the position of his party was expected to be fairly secure, the results of face-to-face meetings with the people were mixed, and therefore disappointing.

There was also proof of faltering popularity in his home province. Quebec had cast the majority of its votes for Liberals for the first time in 1896 on the strength of Laurier's approach to the Manitoba Schools Question. They had given him increasing support in each election since that time. In the most recent contest, that of 1908, the Liberal candidates took almost 60 percent of the Quebec votes. But in November of 1910, the voters had their first opportunity to express their attitude toward the idea of a Canadian navy in a by-election, held in a riding that Liberals had previously won with ease. But this time the Liberal candidate was defeated by an *autonomiste* critic of Laurier's half-step toward imperialism. The victor was an unknown politician supported initially by the powerful pen of Henri Bourassa. Thus, Laurier's stock appeared to be declining even in his home province.

Soon after the defeat in the Drummond-Arthabaska riding, the farm protest resumed. This time one thousand protestors from the Canadian Council of Agriculture, represented by every region of the country, descended upon Ottawa, demanding action on all the measures that had been called for in a less organized fashion during the prime ministerial tour the previous summer. Laurier's response was cordial, yet evasive. He found demands for such action as government encouragement of farmers' cooperatives and public ownership of the grain elevators "too radical," but there was one concession he might make. Although Laurier announced nothing definite at the time, negotiations were underway and by December, at an advanced stage, for a general relaxation of the tariff, particularly as it related to agriculture. Americans had just proposed full-scale discussion of the question of reciprocal free trade between the two countries, but Laurier was at first hesitant. He became progressively more interested, as such a bold new policy seemed likely to divert public attention from the imperialism controversy and bolster support for Laurier's Liberals in those regions where they were faltering and most dependent—the West, Quebec, and the Maritimes.

By mid-January the negotiations between the two heads of state resulted in an agreement that was to be implemented by concurrent legislation passed by the Congress and the Canadian Parliament. Fielding, the long-time finance minister and life-long advocate of free trade, was positively giddy when he reported the proposal to Parliament on January 26. As soon as the legislatures of the United States and Canada enacted it, there would be free trade in natural products, manufactured items such as farm machinery, and a much lower rate of duty on some other products.

At first, the Opposition was stunned and stupefied. Anticipating an election soon, Borden observed that there was "the deepest dejection" among Conservatives, since they feared "the government's proposals . . . would give it another term in office." Indeed, Liberals and Conservatives alike welcomed the idea of a restoration of that same reciprocity that was supposed to have made the decade after 1854 so prosperous. Renewal of reciprocal free trade had been a shared goal of every Canadian political leader at one time or another since the original agreement's abrogation by the Americans in 1865. As late as 1891 even John A. Macdonald, the father and guardian of the National Policy, had explored the possibility of freer trade with the United States in order to undercut the Liberal's war cry that year. After he found the Americans unresponsive, tariff protection was seen again as indispensable and patriotic. The cry of patriotism in 1891 foreshadowed what was to follow in 1911. Still, the Conservatives' initial reaction was to rejoice in the agreement for its economic implications. Their only lament on the day of its announcement was that reciprocity was a Liberal rather than a Conservative coup.

IV. Laurier's Defeat

The lead of Toronto businessmen proved decisively important in finding good ground on which to oppose reciprocity. Sir Edmund Walker, the president of the Canadian Bank of Commerce, now known as the Canadian Imperial Bank of Commerce, led the way when he addressed the Toronto Board of Trade to criticize the tariff agreement because it put continentalism ahead of the British connection. Four days later, eighteen prominent businessmen, who identified themselves as Liberals, echoed the same theme when they issued an open letter to the public denouncing the agreement because it would tend to "weaken the ties which bind Canada to the Empire." Thus, Ontario businessmen, who had little to fear from a relaxation of trade restrictions on commodities covered by this proposal, nevertheless opposed the change. They may have feared that one relaxation of the tariff would be the first of many to follow, until eventually the principle of protection would be entirely repudiated. It was convenient for them to pitch freer trade onto the lofty plane of principle and, by drawing attention to the naval service bill, suggest that the two issues together pointed to a sinister "inner" meaning. In this way, reciprocity became inextricably entangled with imperial relations and the ideal ground of opposition for politicians who followed.

Soon afterwards, Clifford Sifton announced that he was leaving the Liberal Party to fight reciprocity. Other Liberals—ready to make the same move after the militia bill of 1904, the 1905 legislation that created Saskatchewan and Alberta, the naval service bill, or the host of little personal grudges bound to accumulate around a government fifteen years in power—took the occasion of the reciprocity controversy to get clear of Laurier and contribute, if possible, to his downfall.

Robert Borden's mood of defeat shifted accordingly to quiet confidence. The Conservatives decided to filibuster the passage of the trade bill, and thus force the government into an election that Borden thought he was bound to win. The debate therefore dragged on through March and April, and then adjourned for two months so that Laurier could attend still another of those nearly annual conferences in Britain. After the "chit-chat" had resumed in July, the prime minister decided to challenge the Opposition to a September election, a contest Sir Wilfrid was confident of winning.

From an economic standpoint, the case for reciprocity was strong. No abrupt repudiation of protection was contemplated, and therefore the branch-plant economy was not jeopardized by the withdrawal of the incentives for maintaining Canadian assembly plants for American products. There were economic benefits promised to fishermen, miners, forest workers, and most cash-crop farmers. In the long run, this might lead to even greater benefits. It might encourage more rapid development of domestically owned staple-related secondary manufacturing as larger profits accrued to staple producers, who would gain better access to closer markets and who might predictably seek even richer fields of profit in a more sophisticated industrial structure.

But these were analyses that looked to the long-term benefits. In a mass democracy, it is the short-run that is more evident. The arguments that warned British Columbian fruit growers that they would face stiff competition from American producers, and that warned railway workers everywhere of massive lay-offs if the east-west transcontinentals were sacrificed to a new trading pattern that ran increasingly in a north-south direction, were powerful. Then, too, Premier Roblin of Manitoba could point out that the frustrations of wheat farmers might even be worse in a wider union than they already were in Canada; he pointed out that Minneapolis would become as much a buyer's market as Port Arthur if Canadian staples were diverted south by free trade. And finally there was the fact that in 1911 the country was prosperous and many people—even farmers—could doubt the wisdom of tampering with the status quo. But all this was somewhat peripheral. What defeated reciprocity was not so much the economic as the emotional arguments. Latent anti-Americanism erupted into open hostility. In this, Americans contributed to their own undoing. They treated Canadian voters to startling speeches, and no less a leader than the Speaker of the House of Representatives expressed his "hope to see the day when the American flag will float over every square foot of the British North American possessions, clear to the North Pole."

This was precisely the point the Conservatives were beginning to make *ad nauseum*. They said that closer trade relations would not only weaken the empire, but that the reciprocity deal would probably mean the end of Canada as well. George Foster denounced freer trade as "veiled treason", and challenged the government to "tell the Sons of the Blood what it is" if not subversive. It became pointless for Laurier's defenders, such as Premier Scott of Saskatchewan, to answer that "we may remain loyal, while sending our flax crop over a high tariff wall into the United States, but if the wall be removed and we obtain consequent higher prices for our flax we become disloyal." More important was the Conservative promise of "No truck nor trade with the Yankees" and the implication that the Canadian voter now had the opportunity to exercise a power with his vote that he might never have again. The Americans apparently wanted something from Canada, a favor—vague perhaps—but a favor nonetheless. Congress had convened a special session just to deal with the Canadian business. The President had assented, and now Laurier's Liberals were asking for permission to finish the work. But if the electorate struck down Laurier, they would defeat the Congress and the President of the United States by the same swift stroke. To be sure, the punch would fall on the head of their own prime minister, but the swing would hit Uncle Sam indirectly. In the words of the University of Toronto student newspaper, Canadians had a chance to "wipe the eye of the United States"; they took it.

In a reaction against reciprocity, the country, apart from Quebec, repudiated Laurier; Borden's Conservatives needed 111 seats to have a majority plus one; the predominantly English-speaking provinces gave him 107. At the Conservatives' weakest, in 1900, they still returned eight members from Laurier's province. But there was never as much reason for Quebec to oppose the Conservatives as now in 1911. Laurier's naval policy was less than satisfactory, to be sure, but from the standpoint of *autonomistes,* Borden's was brazenly imperialist. From this perspective, Quebeckers should have united solidly behind Sir Wilfrid as the lesser of two evils. If they had, the Parliamentary tally would have been 114 Liberals to 107 Conservatives. But Quebec voted to the contrary, and this fact gives the election of 1911 an especially interesting as well as important, twist.

Henri Bourassa, probably the most influential individual in Quebec, planned to defeat Laurier's naval policy without furthering Borden's. His plan was to work for the election of a block of *autonomiste* candidates who would be independent of the Conservatives as well as of the Liberals, yet would be a large enough force to hold the balance of power in the House of Commons. Bourassa assumed that Laurier would win less than a majority from the rest of Canada because he predicted that Borden's Conservatives were going to win more of Ontario than ever before. Bourassa's strategy was to fight a contest against Laurier in Quebec. By this means a minority government—Liberal or Conservative—would emerge, with Bourassa holding the ace to force revisions of the hated naval service bill.

Bourassa's strategy was reasonable in June. It was sound even in August. The confirmation of this was Borden's willingness to cooperate in the scheme, even though it seemed to promise him no more than minority government. Accordingly, the Conservatives agreed to nominate candidates only in the Eastern Townships and in the English-speaking ridings of Montreal. The rest was to be left as a clear field for Bourassa's and Laurier's candidates.

The failure of Bourassa's strategy became clear in the last week of the campaign as Laurier's sagging support became evident outside Quebec. By this time the outcome of the election in Quebec was fairly predictable. By election day, votes for Bourassa were votes for Borden and, in the language of *La Presse,* "a vote for imperialism with a vengeance." But Bourassa would not concede this fact and throw his support behind his one time friend. Two days before the election, Laurier knew he had lost.

And so he had. But so had Bourassa. It was a Borden majority government that took the seals of office in the autumn of 1911. The era of the politics of accommodation appeared to have passed. Government for the imperialist, "progressive" majority was now to follow.

CHAPTER SIXTEEN

The Imperial Tragedy

I. Pre-War Progressivism

The change from Laurier to Borden in 1911 was reminiscent of the shift from Macdonald to Mackenzie in 1873. Both new leaders were swept into power on a wave of moral indignation. Both were pledged to undo the work of their predecessors and thus "to elevate the standard of public morality . . . and to conduct affairs . . . by practices which will bear the light of day."

Although Mackenzie called his program honesty while Borden labeled his progressivism, both were moralists and reformers. The progressive impulse was a moral perspective similar to Mackenzie's, but more far-ranging in the sense that the evils of industrialism were as much the objects of concern as the morality of politicians and their practices in government. In the cities the progressives sought pure water, for example. Since the water would be piped into all homes and buildings from a central source, this innovation would serve to eliminate the periodic ravages of typhoid and cholera. Similarly, the same quest for purity inspired crusades against privies, saloons, prostitution, and a franchise that allowed men to vote, including immigrants although all women were excluded. Beyond these concerns, there were other dimensions to progressivism that implied no more than a pragmatic desire to make society work more efficiently. Thus, police forces were expanded to enforce a whole new category of laws—ordinances that regulated behavior more than they defined offenders by their victims. Laws against drunkenness in public places, admittance of underage persons to pool rooms, and gambling typified this quest for a higher degree of social order enforced by bureaucratic means. In this spirit—without espousing doctrines of socialism—some reformers advocated municipal ownership of public utilities, pointing out that gas, water and telephone companies were all natural monopolies, and public involvement was the most efficient way to protect the public interest from otherwise private monopolists. But in the early 1900s only a small number of Canadians were so easily persuaded. Most of the new reformers were more interested in having a government that imitated—rather than one that supplanted—private business. All across Canada, citizens expressed a need for government based on "sound business principles." This heightened zeal for bureaucracy, pragmatism, and efficiency is what distinguished the new from the old reformers—the Robert Bordens from the Alexander Mackenzies. In this way, although Laurier's successor was a moralist and a reformer, there were many principles that the new prime minister was willing to compromise.

Borden's flexibility was demonstrated immediately by the new government's retreat from the promised reversal of continentalist tendencies. The promise of "No truck nor trade with the Yankees" during the election campaign implied repudiation of reciprocity, and a lot more besides. But Borden was quick to assure the United States that, even though Canada was not ratifying the reciprocity agreement, American investment was still secure and welcome in Canada. The Americans, for their part, stepped up the level of investment to record proportions between 1911 and 1913. They also decided that, since Canadian raw materials were so useful to the American capital plants the unprocessed staples of Canada should be granted nearly duty-free entrance by the American tariff, which was revised in 1913.

That same pragmatism, which enabled the party that campaigned on anti-Americanism to welcome continentalism, extended to domestic policy. The West was newly-won Conservative territory, and Borden intended to keep it on his side by experimenting with progressive changes; for instance, by giving federal subsidies to build provincial highways, provide free rural mail delivery and agricultural education, and by enforcing government rationalization of the grain trade. In two ways this commitment was innovative and reforming. First, Borden's reforms provided greater direct government involvement through public ownership of grain elevators and the regulation of the grain trade itself. And secondly, tradition was broken by making federal grants conditional. In the past, subsidies were disbursed like ransom payments without coherent pattern or purpose other than that of keeping a province happy in confederation. But now subsidies would be increasingly contingent upon particular uses. Here was a rationalization of provincial-dominion relations, and another indication of Borden's pragmatic progressivism; it was expedient to provide grants, but now they had to be rationalized.

However, the pragmatism of Borden's approach to reform halted in the face of two principles that he clung to as rigidly as any defended by Mackenzie. One principle was the notion that the majority rules. The other was the view that Canada was a partner in a wider empire, a position that implied responsibilities as well as privileges.

The first evidence of dogmatic majoritarianism was a reform of the rules to streamline debate in the House of Commons. The old rules permitted filibuster, a method by which a howling minority could obstruct the House to the point of dissolution if necessary (the most recent example had been the one led by Borden in the opposition to reciprocity). Now in power, however, the Conservatives wanted to bring the Canadian Parliament into line with British practice. There, a recent rule had dictated that debate could be closed as soon as further talk seemed obstructionist; the final reading of the bill would follow. Thus the majority could speed up the processing of one measure, and proceed without further delay to other business. This implied that Parliament was a kind of factory for legislation and that the important thing was to keep the assembly line moving. The image appealed to Borden's progressive side; the rules were changed accordingly.

The new closure rule was used for the first time to further Borden's dogmatic adherence to imperialism. In March of 1912 the government announced its intention of revising Laurier's naval service bill. Borden then consulted his closest advisers for assurance that a money gift to Great Britain was both "necessary" and "expedient". When the Quebec Conservatives replied that a contribution was justified only in the event of proven necessity and that they were "not agreed on the fact of emergency," the prime minister went to England and talked to Winston Churchill at the Admiralty. The meeting, according to Borden's private notes, proved "quite satisfactory. He is quite willing to play the game. Will give assurance as to necessity." Then, with Churchill's letter confirming Britain's need, legislation was drafted for appropriating $35 million to the Royal Navy for the construction of three dreadnoughts in Britain. The bill was introduced at the end of 1912 and debated through April of the next year. After five months of argument, the government invoked closure and the measure then passed the House of Commons on May 13.

The Liberals had prepared themselves to keep talking until Borden's mandate or his patience expired. They did not believe the government would dare to move closure on such an important matter. When they did, the Opposition decided to play a trump card of its own. The naval aid bill had to pass the scrutiny of the Senate, a body well stocked with Liberals from the previous fifteen years of Laurier government. Since the Conservatives had violated one tradition with closure, the Senate decided to violate another—the tradition of senatorial deference to the will of the lower House. The senators refused assent to Borden's navy bill "until it is submitted to the judgement of the people." Here the matter died.

Borden was reluctant to call an election. He feared that popular judgment would be too severe. By now the economy had begun a downward spiral with no sign of leveling off by the end of 1913. Unemployment plagued the cities. Farmers faced threats of foreclosure from mortgage holders. The new railways teetered on the edge of bankruptcy. Although the railway companies were bolstered by government loans, there was no sign of relief for the unemployed factory workers or for the bankrupt farmer.

But just as Borden began to contemplate the spectre of defeat in a forthcoming election, the Austrian heir presumptive was killed by an assassin's bullet, and most of Europe, including Great Britain, was at war by August of 1914. Canada, as part of the British empire, was automatically caught up in that war that stemmed from such remote causes and, with this fortuitous distraction the declining stock of an imperialistically-minded government began to rise.

II.   The Unifying Impact of the War

As with the response to the call for volunteers to fight in the Boer War, there were far more recruits, initially, than places in the ranks of the contingent to be sent. Nobody suspected that this adventure was going to be any less exciting than the South African affair. Nobody could tell that Canada was now plunging into the most tragic episode in Canadian history.

There were two tragedies, in fact, each very different from one another. The first was the tragedy of war itself: the numbing effect of a mindless slaughter that kept up for over four years. And yet out of this waste, it was possible to extract a measure of heroism and self-discovery, so that Canadians as a whole drew closer together in national pride. It is with this first tragedy that the remainder of this section is concerned.

The unifying sense of danger in all previous emergencies was artificial by comparison with that of 1914. Before, as in the case of John A. Macdonald's attempt to create an atmosphere of national urgency to build the CPR, the artificiality of the unity had been only too transparent. But the unity that surrounded Canada's entry into World War I, initially at least, was the most emotional and spontaneous expression of common cause that had ever occurred. Borden pledged "every effort and . . . every sacrifice." He believed that "the manhood of Canada stands ready to fight beyond the seas" to the last individual if necessary. Similarly, Laurier, for his part in August of 1914, affirmed that "when the call goes out, our answer goes at once, and, it goes in the classical language of the British answer to the call of duty: 'Ready, Aye Ready." There would be no opposition from his side of the House; as Laurier said "We shall offer no criticism as long as there is danger at the front."

It could be charged that these affirmations were hollow in the light of what eventually followed, but one must repeat that no one knew in 1914 that the war would drag on for four years. Even then, enthusiasm did not waver for one entire year, and the major signs of disunity did not unfold until near the end, at the time of the conscription crisis. From this standpoint, there were three years of spontaneous and intense nationalism and *that* had never happened before.

The self-sacrifice involved more than young adventurers flocking to the Union Jack. It also led to voluntary contributions of enormous amounts of time and money for the war effort at home. Every association from the I.O.D.E. to the Y.M.C.A. had wartime projects. But the most important contribution in this regard was probably the work of the Canadian Patriotic Fund, an association chartered in 1914 with the purpose of "preserving the families' economic status in comfort and decency, as a partial recognition of the services of the soldiers overseas." The idea was to raise money for distribution to the families of enlisted men, in the hope of bridging the discrepancy between what a man could expect from his peacetime work and what he now received as his soldier's pay. Although the project was overly ambitious, the volunteer workers and contributors almost realized their ideal. Before the war, the average wage for factory workers was about $80 per month; and the Canadian Patriotic Fund almost succeeded in guaranteeing this minimum to the dependent families of men overseas.

Voluntary contributions at home were enormous because the sacrifices of the men in the trenches were astronomical. In the spring of 1915 the soldiers received their first dose of the indescribable misery that would characterize the whole war to follow, with its poison gas, waist-deep mud, and suicidal frontal assaults across open ground swept by murderous artillery barrages and lethal bursts of machine-gun fire. When they arrived in the field, Canada's first division contained about 100 000 men. But in May and June, nearly one quarter of them were casualties.

Still, the willingness to participate on an even larger scale remained in 1915. Thus, Borden announced his personal decision to augment the Canadian contribution to a corps of 500 000, and there was no outcry of protest. To be sure, there were signs that enthusiasm was beginning to falter here and there. But the Canadian majority continued to be confident that the pressure of public opinion by an aroused democracy could keep the volunteers coming without formal government coercion.

The worst fighting was still in the future. The four Canadian divisions were up to full strength by 1916, in time to expect imminent victory.

Unfortunately, increased numbers on one side were always balanced by strengthened forces on the other. Thus the triumph expected from each new push vanished in high casualties, misery, and stalemate. For the men in the field, it was discouraging to say the least. "How I hate this country," one young captain wrote home in the autumn. The whole war seemed futile to him since "hundreds of men work all night in the rain to do a piece of trench, and the next day the Germans throw a thousand shells or so at it and flatten it out." Then, too, there was the constant misery of the mud. "It is so deep that it is not possible to walk in it. Men lie on their bellies and wallow and wiggle through it . . . they are exhausted before the real attack starts." But in 1917, under conditions like these, the Canadians won a victory which their Canadian commander, Sir Arthur Currie, described as "the grandest day the Corps has ever had."

For over two weeks before Easter Monday, about half of all the available artillery had been pounding a low hill three miles long. Then that dawn the allies began a barrage with every gun in range. The whole area was suddenly one trembling field of exploding artillery shells. Below the surface, tunnels connected three lines of trenches. At the top of the hill there were gun emplacements protected by reinforced concrete. It was these German guns, whose ammunition was supplied by a subterranean railway, that the Canadians were supposed to silence—but not with artillery; the top of Vimy Ridge had to be taken by hand-to-hand fighting through the three lines of trenches below.

At 5:30 A.M. the artillery stopped and all four divisions of the Canadian corps came running in the direction of Vimy Ridge. Then at 5:33, everyone fell to the ground, and the most colossal artillery bombardment ever let loose on a battle front resumed. Soon it lifted and the Canadians, shivering in the sleet and from the proximity of the explosions, continued their uphill rush. Thus they advanced through closely timed artillery barrages, fought their way through the three systems of trenches, and placed their own machine guns at the top to command the other side of the hill. But over the 4.5 square miles of battlefield below lay the thousands of men in the "awkward humpbacked posture" of death. A soldier who was there said, "It is no exaggeration to say that the ground at the crest of the Ridge and for rods behind it looked . . . like nothing so much as a rich plum-pudding before it goes to boiling."

Since the taking of Vimy Ridge had been planned and executed by Canadians and since the battle was one of the most dramatic events of the war, it was a source of enormous pride for everyone who believed the war would amount to more than mere slaughter. For the true believers, this battle was more than "the grandest day the Corps has ever had"; it was a triumphant moment for Canada as a whole. Roger Graham, the historian, **was only** stating a fact when he observed in the 1960s that "Vimy Ridge became a symbol of Canadian achievement." But Graham was also echoing the piety of succeeding generations of historians when he went on to assert that "the pride engendered on the bloody slopes of that commanding hill did much to bring Canada to full nationhood." It was a fiery ordeal such as the Canada Firsters had wanted, and it worked some of the magic supposed to follow from mutual sacrifice. As one veteran put it: "We went up Vimy Ridge as Albertans and Nova Scotians. We came down as Canadians."

Unfortunately Vimy was not the last battle, and the worst was still to come. Casualties outnumbered enlistments and conscription had to follow. As criticism of that policy accelerated, the government moved in the direction of conscripting wealth as well as men. There was already a business profits tax, but this had been imposed in the year before to meet a fiscal more than a political need. Now there had to be a gesture to satisfy the outcry for conscripting income as well as service. "There has arisen," the minister of finance reported, "a very natural and, in my view a very just, sentiment that those who are in the enjoyment of substantial incomes should substantially and directly contribute to the growing war expenditure . . . " Thus came the progressive income tax. Persons with average incomes were not affected, but professional and managerial people, those whose incomes had increased enormously in the wartime prosperity, were taxed significantly. A professional man receiving $10 000 per year, for instance, would pay $420 income tax. A tycoon netting $200 000 was supposed to pay nearly $44 000 tax.

The shift from voluntary enlistment and voluntary cash contributions to conscription and the income tax signified a decline in voluntary support. And, although the income tax did nothing to mend the growing rift between Quebec and the rest of the country, it did tend to reverse the class resentments that conscription had triggered. But the income tax was too small to satisfy labor for long. Fortunately, the war was drawing toward its final agony.

In the spring of 1918, the German command launched one last desperate offensive. The Allies were driven back almost to Paris, but they counter-attacked and by November 11 both sides agreed to stop fighting and begin negotiating. At this moment of the Armistice, the Canadian corps was on the e ge of a little town in Belgium, only yards away from the exact spot wh e some of those men had first begun their "great adventure" over three years before—except that many no longer believed there was anything adventuresome about the war they had fought. For the most embittered of the soldiers, "the things that were glorious had no glory," and the sacrifices were like those of stock-yards "if nothing was done with the meat except to bury it."

But Canada had expended too much on the Great War for such cynicism to be general. Over 230 000 (̲ ̲ ̲ ̲)ad been killed or maimed. About one quarter of the entire male population of service age was a casualty of one sort or another. The country had sacrificed too much to say that it was all for nothing.

Canadians in 1918, and historians since, have tended to agree that the tragedy of *World War I* was a price that was paid for the immeasurably valuable prize of international recognition. Having fought so well and having contributed so generously, Canada was no longer a colony in fact or image; the country "could no longer be what she no longer felt she was." Thus, the Dominion was accorded the status of full nationality by securing membership as an independent nation within the council of the League of Nations when that body was formed in the wake of the peace settlement in 1919.

In this sense, *World War I* was "Canada's equivalent of the War of Independence." It "gave a nation its soul." But this conclusion only follows from one side of the story, from those tragedies that are fit to be commemorated. That second tragedy alluded to above was too bitter to celebrate, for it brought the country close to destruction; it is, therefore, too important to ignore.

III.   Wartime Disunity

Among the first to experience disillusionment amid the pride was none other than the prime minister himself, when he was forced to realize that Canada had chosen to participate as a principal without receiving a proportionate share of the war's direction. In the summer of 1915, Borden went to England to attempt to resolve this and other points. But rather than resolution, the Canadian prime minister only found greater difficulties. There was a frustrating lack of direction in the British approach to the war, and British politicians were consistently supercilious in evading Borden's questions. The Canadian prime minister returned home hurt and angered, but his subsequent actions were curious if not childish in light of what went before. Rather than deciding to curtail Canada's involvement on grounds that limited control warranted nothing more than limited liability, Borden decided to double the commitment, which had already grown ten times over the original contingent. The first call in August of 1914 was for 25 000 volunteers, which was three times more than had fought in the Boer War. But even before Borden's trip abroad the call had risen to 250 000. Now the prime minister promised to field a

500 000-man army as Canada's total commitment. By this tragic decision, Sir Robert hoped to prove that Canada was too valuable to treat lightly. He would show Britain—and the world—that his country was no mere colony.

But Borden's decision to maintain an army of 500 000 volunteers was impossible as well as vain. It defied simple arithmetic. The total population then was just under eight million. The total number of seventeen-year-old to forty-year-old males was probably no more than 1.5 million. If half of these men were engaged in essential services such as food production, running the transportation network, and producing munitions, then there were barely more than 700 000 who were eligible overall. That allowed for only 200 000 casualties, assuming anyone who was not engaged in an essential service was willing to join.

The numbers that impressed Borden and many others were the levels of enlistment before New Year's Day, 1916, which was the moment the decision was announced by Borden without prior discussion in cabinet. But even these numbers provided reason for caution, a suggestion of future tragedy in any commitment of the size that the prime minister tossed out on his own initiative. Most of the early enlistments were unmarried immigrants from the British Isles. Less than one-third of the first volunteers were Canadian-born; nor was this Canadian portion evenly distributed over the whole country. The Canadians who were most likely to volunteer were the unemployed single men of urban Ontario. The least likely were western farmers and anyone from French-speaking Quebec. Thus, the unity that was apparent in the first rush to enlist was illusory. But the 500 000-man army was a commitment Borden refused to compromise.

Predictably, the pressure for enlistments seemed to exhaust the number of readily available volunteers. Urban Ontario began to wonder about the rest of the country, and this distress was echoed by urban Manitoba where Winnipeggers were distressed at the way "enemy aliens" had only developed a love of Canada and no proportionate attachment to Britain.

The governments of Ontario and Manitoba struck out at persons of suspicious ethnicity in the easiest and most sanctimonious way possible. They imposed unilingual instruction on their schools in accordance with the popular exhortation in Charles Sellar's book, *The Tragedy of Quebec*: "The issue . . . is fundamental and admits of no compromise, it is one that is not local but affects the future of the entire Dominion. It is simply whether this Canada of ours is to be British, and nothing else than British, or whether it is to be a mongrel land, with two official languages and ruled by a divided authority."

Such bigotry was bound to provoke tragic disunity. French-speaking Canadians now began to question the fundamental premise on which unlimited involvement rested. Borden and his imperialist supporters had gone to war initially because Britain was at war. But this was no argument for unlimited liability. For that, Borden and company had asserted that the cause was just; the civilized nations of the world were standing together to resist "Prussianism." This was the premise French Canadians began to challenge in 1916. Provincial governments had launched overt discrimination against minorities, and the federal government had a War Measures Act, which sanctioned dictatorship so long as the struggle continued. Bourassa began to suggest "Prussianism" was as rampant on one side as on another.

Another reason for minorities to remain aloof from the war effort was the absence of anything but English-speaking units in the Canadian corps. The Royal 22nd Regiment was created, ostensibly to fill this need with regard to Quebeckers, but there were few French-speaking officers and thus it was simply another unit like the others. The crowning insult to Quebec was the appointment of a Protestant clergyman to supervise recruiting in that province.

Not having units of their own, and skeptical that the war aims touched them directly, French-speaking Canadians began to participate in an informal boycott of enlistments in 1916. By 1917, the number of volunteers elsewhere had fallen sharply as well. The number of recruits fell sadly behind the record of casualties in each month of the first half of 1917. Now Borden faced a difficult choice. He could reduce the level of Canada's commitment to that supported by the new rate of enlistments, or he could resort to coercion and impose conscription. The prime minister opted for the more tragic of the two alternatives.

On May 18, a military service bill was introduced to the House of Commons; anti-conscriptionists in Montreal rioted in protest on May 24. The next day Borden tried to make conscription less bitter by bringing Laurier into a Union government. But Sir Wilfrid believed unlimited liability was unwise and conscription worse. Sir Robert was therefore left to pursue his tragic course without the Liberal leader's assistance.

Laurier also made it clear that he thought it was time for the people to pass their judgment on Borden and his other policies. An election was already one year overdue in the autumn of 1917. But in light of the wartime emergency, Parliament's mandate had been extended by permission of Parliament. As the extension was running out, Borden's Conservatives took bitter measures to make certain that the election that could not be avoided would not be lost.

Political parties usually believe the country's survival hangs upon the defeat of their rivals, but this was especially the case in 1917. Borden's Conservatives accepted conscription on the confident assumption that "the country could not see any limits to its exertions that fell short of the totality of its powers." Laurier and many of his Liberals asserted that they would prosecute the war to the utmost of voluntarism; anything, that is, short of conscription. To Conservative leaders such as Arthur Meighen, such a qualification meant "the virtual withdrawal of Canada from the war, the desertion of her soldiers overseas, the abject surrender of her honour, and the utter loss of her pride." Borden confided to his diary that "our first duty is to win, at any cost, the coming election in order that we may continue to do our part in winning the war and that Canada be not disgraced." It followed that the election could not be called "until the ground has been carefully and completely prepared."

Borden's spadework began in September with a Military Voters Act, which provided means for men and women in uniform overseas to vote. Service personnel would vote by indicating a simple yes or no to record their support or non-support for the government. Although no particular candidates would be named, the votes would be counted toward the election of individuals nevertheless. Voters who specified their home riding would have their yes or no applied to the Conservative or Liberal running there, but all the other votes would be applied as the electoral officer chose. By this means, the government was given the power to manipulate approximately 25 percent of the electorate to its own best advantage.

There was more. The Military Voters Act broke an old tradition by enfranchising some women, the army nurses. Another "reform," known as the Wartime Elections Act, made even more sweeping changes in the franchise. For the purpose of the coming elections, the wives, mothers, sisters and widows of military personnel were given voting privileges, while all newcomers who had taken the oath of allegiance after 1902, and who had been born in one of the countries now fighting for the enemy, had their voting rights withdrawn. The purpose of the Bill, in the words of its author, Arthur Meighen, was "to shift the franchise from the doubtful British or anti-British of the male sex and to extend it at the same time to our patriotic women . . . " On this basis, Meighen thought it a "splendid stroke."

Most of the Liberals were less pleased, of course. "It would have been more direct and at the same time more honest," one critic observed, "if the bill simply stated that all who did not pledge themselves to vote Conservative would be disenfranchised." Not surprisingly, closure was needed to end the debate. Then, since the Senate had been enlarged with Conservatives in 1915, the manipulation of the franchise received assent from that body too. Borden's preparations convinced many Liberals that they could not survive opposition. They stampeded to join in a coalition, leaving Laurier and a handful of anti-conscriptionists on the outside.

Everything was apparently in order for a Union victory by the middle of November, so Borden called the election for December 17. He appealed for unity and harmony on the grounds that he led a non-partisan coalition that pursued the goal every "red-blooded" Canadian wanted. The anti-conscriptionists were thus an Opposition without a hope of victory and with only a tenuous hold on their freedom of speech. There was a conscious attempt to stigmatize the Opposition as seditious. Had it not been led by Laurier, it is quite possible that members of the Opposition would have been officially proscribed in accordance with the government's powers under the War Measures Act.

Laurier and company were still called traitors. Sir George Foster, Laurier's old critic over naval policy and the militia bill, told an approving Toronto audience: "Every alien sympathizer, every man of alien blood born in an alien country with few exceptions, is with Sir Wilfrid Laurier, and every Hun sympathizer from Berlin to the trenches, from Berlin to the Cameroons, wishes success to Laurier, with his anti-conscriptionist campaign." Other spokesmen for the coalition were no less harsh.

Since the outcome of the election had been predetermined it was a foregone conclusion that Borden's Union would win. But the results did indicate the extent to which the country was divided over the question of unlimited involvement in the war. Seventy-five percent of the electorate in Quebec voted one way, 64 percent of the electorate in the rest of Canada voted the other. This enormous discrepancy on such an important issue led Henri Bourassa to wonder whether Canada would ever develop a sense of national interest. "So long as English Canadians remain more British than Canadian," he predicted that "these difference are bound to happen every time there is a conflict between the demands of British imperialism and the resistance of Canadian nationalism."

Of course Borden's supporters considered themselves no less nationalist than Bourassa. But their nationalism stood on the old supposition that "in order to be Canadian we must be British." In 1917 the demand of that connection seemed to be conscription regardless of cost, and Canada paid a very high price indeed. There was rioting, Quebec was brought near to secession, civil rights were systematically abrogated by the War Measures Act, and the oath of allegiance of the new Canadians was cynically disregarded by the Wartime Elections Act. These were the tragedies that were bitter, the memories of the war that English-speaking Canada wanted quickly to forget.

PART FIVE

Development Without a Mother Country

CHAPTER SEVENTEEN

Social Ferment

I. War Fever as a Reform Impulse

There were many Canadians who sincerely believed that their country was right to have participated in Europe's Great War without limiting Canada's involvement. These were the ones who were inclined to see the struggle as an "imperial event" in which all British subjects were bound to participate. But there were others who saw the contest as more than just a duty. J. W. Dafoe was one who perceived it as a war of freedom against Prussianism, and therefore "the holiest cause for which men have ever fought and died." Since this second kind of war fever was also a reform sentiment, it was natural that there was a domestic as well as an international focus for that energy, and just as natural that this zeal outlasted the fighting in Europe.

But just as there was a lack of uniform understanding of the war aims, and of national unity on the issue of unlimited involvement in military action, so also was there a lack of national consensus on the proper direction for the non-military domestic crusades. In the West, the demand for "moral uplift" developed into something approaching a frenzy, but Ontario and the Maritime Provinces were conspicuously less enthusiastic about reform. And in Quebec, the prevailing mood was resentment of social change in general and of reforms initiated from the rest of Canada in particular.

II.   Post-War Quebec

Early in 1918, the Legislative Assembly of Quebec debated a resolution to the effect that "this House ... would be disposed to accept the breaking of the Confederation Pact of 1867 if, in the other provinces, it is believed that she is an obstacle to the union, progress and development of Canada." The debate provided occasion for many speakers to air their dissatisfaction with conscription and other injuries. "Regulation 17" was one; by this stroke the province of Ontario had effectively outlawed the use of French as a language of instruction in the public schools, and the Judicial Committee of the Privy Council upheld this decision in 1916. After other insults and injuries—such as conscription—some Quebec legislators were prepared to discuss separatism in the Assembly. Eventually, however, the motion was withdrawn before it came to a vote, and in this retreat, fear of change became more visible than dissatisfaction with Confederation.

The sudden emergence of a separatism that was rhetorical only suggested that French Canadian nationalism had changed a great deal since the days of Papineau and Dorion. In the previous century, there were republicans always willing to defend the integrity of their province by direct action out-of-doors as well as in the Legislative Assembly. At the same time, of course, there were clerical spokesmen no less nationalist, but who were less keen to lead the people to the barricades in the name of republicanism and liberty. The clerical leaders usually preferred a quieter—at times almost a passive—resistance as the sounder course, and so also did the general citizenry. Consequently, on the occasions of the most strident nationalism, the Papineau-Dorion-style nationalists trumpeted anti-clerical denunciations as well as their anti-British slogans, and each time the Church emerged as the more popular and stronger voice of *survivance*. By 1917, French Canadian nationalism still had its spokesmen, but its main pivot and its dominant style was that of passive ultra-clericalism. Since anti-clerical firebrands were no longer of any consequence, the French Canadian nationalism that arose from the wake of domestic war injuries was quietly inward turning, not poised for a mass movement for direct action along lines that Papineau and Dorion had pioneered. But the resentment was real, and the consciousness Quebeckers had of themselves as a province unlike the others could be gauged by the increasing emphasis upon two beliefs long since abandoned elsewhere.

The first was agrarianism, that longing to maintain a simple, self-sufficient life on the soil of one's ancestors, a sentiment expressed many times before in Quebec's history. As early as 1862 Gérin-Lajoie's *Jean Rivard* paid tribute to rural simplicity and purity, and Hémon's *Maria Chapdelaine* reiterated the ideal on the eve of the war. But now, in the 1920s the theme that "we must sow or go jobless, our people will be agricultural or perish" was taken up anew by Lionel Groulx and others, even though the agrarian character of Quebec was already vanishing. The population engaged in farming was a minority, only one third. Furthermore, a new government came to power in 1920 on the strength of the popularity of its promises to promote yet *more* industrialism. Alexander Taschereau said he could make Quebec a leader in the competition for foreign capital investment. But his success in this regard usually resulted in what might be called rural industrialism, since it was based on natural resources [projects such as hydro electric construction, mineral extraction, and pulp processing were undertaken] and therefore resulted in a proliferation of company towns more than in urbanization. In this way, Taschereau appeared to promote a happy compromise, since his kind of industrialism did not threaten the social character of the province with urban secularism. His stated motive was to gain development that would create employment opportunities to keep people in the villages of their birth, and to spare them migration to more rewarding industrial employment elsewhere and the deracination that would follow under the bright lights of the wicked cities. Thus, Taschereau's "progressivism" was accepted as the means of preserving the character of traditional society even while "progressing" beyond the old means of production; in the transition from agricultural village to company town the parish priest would care for his parishoners as always. "Our doctrine" would not change—only the work would alter as more Quebeckers were eased out of stultifying field routines into industrial boredom.

Industrialism without urbanization points to Quebec's second hallmark, the belief in the need for an alternative labor movement. Labor organization had not grown remarkably well before 1920, but that which had appeared was English-Canadian or American in origin. Clerical authorities did not look upon either with favor. When a bitter strike at the Thetford Mines in 1915 raised the spectre of radical, not to say socialist, unionism, the Church moved to head off such a development. A Catholic moderate union resulted. This initiative was extended, and in 1921 the Canadian Confederation of Catholic Workers was founded. Despite its name it was an essentially Quebec institution. And even though it left the majority of Quebec's workers unorganized, it was still a significant development and an indication of what was to follow in the future.

Ultra-clericalism was supreme. Whether in the countryside or in the factory, Quebeckers were told that they had a purpose that transcended the material well-being of particular individuals. Henri Bourassa, the politician turned editor of the newspaper, *Le Devoir*, expressed this clerical-corporatism well in 1918:

"Our special task, as French Canadians, is to insert into America the spirit of Christian France. It is to defend against all comers, perhaps even against France herself, our religious and national heritage. This heritage does not belong to us alone. It belongs to all Catholic America. It is the inspiring and shining hearth of America. It belongs to the whole Church, and it is the basic foundation of the Church in this part of the world. It belongs to all French civilization of which it is the refuge and fortress and anchor amid the immense sea of saxonizing Americanism."

Like the rhetorical separatism that surfaced at the same time, Bourassa's message translated more easily into affirmations of tradition than innovation. It was compatible with the spirit of Lionel Groulx or of Alexander Taschereau. In this way, the ferment generated by the war in Quebec heightened nationalism, but this time it was a nationalism that voiced a more dogmatic traditionalism than before.

III.   Nostalgia in the Maritimes

A similar retreat from the present and withdrawal inward occurred after the war in the Maritime Provinces, except that in this region the discontent did not arise from wartime insults. According to C. M. Wallace, "imperial events" always tended to arouse the enthusiasm of Maritimers for the Canadian as well as the British connection. Also, between 1911 and 1918 it was a source of "pride" that a Nova Scotian, Borden, was the leader of Canada in the Great War. What piqued Maritimers after 1919 was postwar economic depression. They had prospered "moderately" during the Laurier boom, but now—going into the 1920s—they saw no bright prospects. Nostalgia for the Golden Age of Reciprocity between 1854 and 1866 returned, and all the old complaints about sacrifices Maritimers were making to enrich the "Upper Canadians" surfaced in a spate of protest called the Maritime Rights Movement. The movement had no program, and no specific remedy for clearly defined problems; it was only a return to the slightly paranoic complaints that had come up before in earlier depressions.

Briefly, the cycle of discontent usually ran as follows: a depressing present and unpromising future generated a build-up of anger, which accumulated like static electricity in a thunder cloud; it awaited only the right leader to assert that Maritime history was once as promising as any, but Confederation had been imposed upon them in a way that threatened their very survival. Then, in a lightning bolt of protest, Maritimers joined in the communal affirmation that they had been laid low by tariffs and Upper Canadian competition. This was why history had stopped, and the once proud masters of their fate now suffered from economic stagnation and depopulation. In righteous wrath, fishermen and farmers rose to vote for those who would assert their "rights", and win "better terms." But having voted thus, the energy was discharged. Later, the electorate would not seem to notice or to care that their saviors had changed nothing, or that the rascals elected to save them would be reelected again and again without having done anything. Thus it was with Joseph Howe's "Repealers" and W. S. Fielding's "Secessionists" in the previous century. And so it was now with the Conservatives' Maritime Rights Movement.

But in the 1920s the cycle was repeated with a special twist; a farmer-labour movement had developed with a socioeconomic definition of Nova Scotia's problems, and with specific reforms as the proposed remedy. For the first time in Nova Scotia's history, a third-party reform movement seemed to gain strength—enough to displace the Conservatives in the role of the official Opposition in the election of 1920. But the humiliated Tories knew better than the Liberals or the Farmer-Labour Party what the electorate wanted. In 1922, they began to attack Liberal governments at all levels and called upon the people of all the Maritime Provinces "to put shoulder to shoulder and fight for their rights." By implication, these rights were more important than local reforms. Thus, at the same time, the farmer-labour group was effectively preempted by the new cry. "Restore our province as an independent, self-governing British dominion," H. W. Corning of Nova Scotia demanded in 1923. Then, without calling specifically for separation, or secession, or repeal, or any other definite program, Corning promised that as Maritimers became "once more free and independent in the matter of trade and commerce, competent to protect ourselves sanely and wisely from the products of Ontario and Quebec as well as other lands, then there would undoubtedly be a great revival in business and local manufacturing in this province."

As before, the electorate responded. These strong emotional demands required nothing of the people but their votes; and nothing was promised by the politicians except a bold assertion of our "rights"—whatever that meant. In the 1925 provincial election, the Conservatives won forty seats in the legislature. The Liberals held on to three. The Farmer-Labour Party lost everything. Thus, Nova Scotians registered their discontent with the status quo. But, as George Rawlyk has pointed out, on this and other similar occasions they seemed satisfied to have "disenchantment expressed in words rather than in effective action." By the Maritime Rights Movement, they reaffirmed that their Golden Age was in the past. The only way to live better in the present was to feel better by affirming that everything had been wonderful before 1867.

IV.   Western Reformers

On the Prairies, by contrast, the reform spirit was more forward looking, but it was only slightly more optimistic about the future. Also, the reform zeal was more a product of the war than something that followed in its wake. The prohibition cause was one such issue, and closely related to this issue was the women's suffrage crusade. The persons who were most anxious to see the "liquor traffic" abolished sensed—according to Nellie McClung—that "male statecraft" was their major obstacle. McClung of Manitoba believed that the fullest extent of the harm of alcohol and other social evils such as prostitution were "discernible only to the feminine eye." Thus, extending the franchise to women would be the means to other righteous ends, a kind of prerequisite to the enactment of reform in general. Mrs. A. V. Thomas, another western feminist, agreed with McClung that "women's place is in the home," but did not hesitate to denounce the unreformed franchise for making it another "part of a mother's mission to sit quietly by and see her sons and daughters growing up under conditions which she knows are bad but through lack of power, is unable to remedy." Then came the war and more evidence that men were incompetent to govern the modern world by themselves. Had women been given "a voice in national and international affairs" earlier, it was asserted that the event would never have happened. But looking to the future, Dr. Augusta Stowe Cullen promised that once women were voting "war will cease forever."

Contrary to feminists' predictions, however, there were other wars after they won the right to vote, and prohibition was enacted before they were enfranchised. Everywhere, except in Quebec, the sale of liquor for anything but medicinal purposes was banned by 1916—as a wartime grain conservation expedient rather than by mass conversion of male legislators to abstinence. In other words, the enactment of prohibition was another example of the enthusiasm of English-speaking Canadians for total involvement in the war effort, more than a result of the power of the women's movement.

The same interpretation applies of course to other reforms in the same period—even to the extension of the franchise to women. The Military Voters Act, which enfranchised female military personnel, and the Wartime Elections Act, which disenfranchised recent immigrants while extending the vote to relatives of soldiers, were described in the last chapter as such, since these were attempts of the Borden government to neutralize the doubtful foreign vote and give a voice to women who were expected to support the government's policy of unlimited commitment to the war. The Prairie Provinces differed from the others only in their having pioneered in this mood of pessimism. Manitoba enfranchised women in 1916. Saskatchewan soon followed. Then came the rest of the provinces in Canada. By 1922, only Quebec held back. But in all of the provinces which conceded female suffrage, the point was made that the existing franchise included men of poorer quality than the women who complained they were excluded; males with no property, ex-convicts, and men of supposedly inferior racial stock were voters, but no women—even those from the oldest and best families—could vote. In the context of the war, it was possible to promote women to help keep the others in line. In this way, the success of women's suffrage was not particularly positive. To the extent that feminist leaders attempted to increase respect for women in the minds of men or bolster women's respect for themselves, they were quite unsuccessful; a British Columbia activist, Rose Henderson, attested to this fact when she observed that "a few women put up a determined fight," but went on to complain that "the masses of women at no time, and in no place, were with them . . . . " In Henderson's view, "it would be wrong to conclude that women's political emancipation came about solely through her own efforts and desire for freedom."

Consider the size and tone of the women's suffrage movement in Nellie McClung's Manitoba, the province that was first and supposedly most progressive in this cause. The Political Equality League, a kind of Women's Party formed to secure equal civil rights in 1912, "grew by leaps and bounds" according to C. L. Cleverdon, the historian of women's suffrage. Apparently twelve hundred women joined the League in its first year. But the dozen leaders who gained notoriety in the cause were all middle or upper class and all were worried about foreigners and radicalism. In their "struggle" only a few modest petitions were sent to the Manitoba legislature. And in 1915, the year the movement was "most rapidly spreading," according to Cleverdon, there was no petition at all. It would be no exaggeration, then, to describe the Manitoba women's suffrage movement as low key as well as elitist. One fact is clear: if there was a mass base to the Political Equality League, all trace of it has subsequently vanished. The "movement" succeeded because it was convenient for male legislators to enroll the middle-class women. Their voting posed no threat to the establishment, since the women who seemed most likely to exercise their franchise were decidedly pro-British, and anti-radical upholders of Victorian standards of "decency," not firebrands.

The themes of racism and anti-radicalism are evident in other facets of Prairie reforming zeal. The approaches taken to the "alien question" are an example. This issue came to the fore in the first place only after the middle-class reformers decided theirs was a region where the rough work of settlement had been completed. Before, the newcomers were accepted as the fastest way of filling in the bald prairie of Western Canada. But now that the farms were set up, the "foreigners" were seen as a problem; the remedies ranged all the way from education through disenfranchisement to outright deportation. Common to all solutions, however, was a tendency to be tough-minded in regarding cultural pluralism as a threat.

Widely shared was the notion that monoculture was necessary as well as desirable; it was held that "what we are labouring for is what almost all the people want, a purely British Canada." What distinguished the advocates of deportation was their assumption that the newcomers could not be assimilated. Character was associated with nationality, and that with race. Since those without British blood were thought incapable of partaking in British culture, and since central Europeans had been identified as the enemy during the war, it followed even after the armistice that the "alien enemy" should be excluded from Canada lest he contaminate the stock.

It was a Methodist minister in Winnipeg who proposed the idea of massive deportation most boldly. His method was appallingly, brutally simple; "We would ask the Dominion government to appoint a commission of returned soldiers in each province to adjudicate and settle the amount that will be allowed each enemy alien and enemy alien family" before they were expelled. Reverend Bridgman suggested this policy was consistent with government action to date. Referring to the Wartime Elections Act, Bridgman pointed out that the government already "claimed the right and the authority to disfranchise all the enemy aliens in the Dominion . . . and on appealing to the country, were endorsed by the largest majorities that ever sent men to parliament." Bridgman thought war veterans were the ideal persons to dispossess the disenfranchised because "the returned soldier . . . knows the Austro-Hun, our enemy over the sea, and he knows the enemy alien better than any other man. His judgement will not be spoiled by prejudice, nor can he ever be tempted to show favoritism." Thus, the veterans were the Canadians most likely to do the difficult work of expropriating aliens' property at "one fourth of its value or less."

Bridgman's book, *Breaking Prairie Sod,* was popular in Winnipeg. But his approach to the "alien problem" was not as popular as the education panacea. The educationists shared Bridgman's zeal for making "this Dominion mainly British in spirit and race." But the assimilationists were more optimistic in the sense that they thought that the "inferior races" could be trained to develop an "attachment to British ideals and institutions." The major difference was over the means rather than over the ends. But there was that same sinister distrust of the consequences of Canada's becoming a multicultural country. Nor did they believe that "two races" could govern a country if it was to survive.

The tendency to repudiate dualism predated the post-war ferment, of course. As was mentioned earlier, Manitobans repudiated a dualist model of their province by 1890; further west in Saskatchewan and Alberta the same retreat occurred later, in 1905, when the Autonomy Bills failed to concede the rights to minorities that were accorded to the English minority in Quebec by the BNA act. In British Columbia no such concession had been made in the first instance. Here, appropriate to the post-war tendency across the country, education authorities outlawed a school history text of the Dominion for no reason other than its alleged sympathy for French Canada and for the lack of sufficiently extravagant praise for things Protestant and British. Thus, although there was nothing new in the bigotry that followed in the wake of the war, the novelty was its virulence: even the Ku Klux Klan was popular in the 1920s.

V.   The Winnipeg General Strike

The moral fervor behind the non-military domestic crusades was bound to generate conflict between regions, nationalities, and classes. But the first and most dramatic clash was not between Quebec and the rest, nor was the first explosion primarily one between those Canadians who identified themselves as British and those who were "aliens" because they were "foreign races." The big confrontation was between businessmen and workers.

From one standpoint, the labor unrest following the war had nothing to do with attitudes that gave rise to the demand for prohibition, women's suffrage, or any other cause. From this view, the labor unrest was simply a function of economic conditions and the relaxation of restrictions on collective bargaining after the armistice. Since it was now possible to demand wage increases backed with the threat of strike action, and since wage rates had failed to keep up with the rises in the cost of living, in productivity, or in profits, working-class edginess and resentment was the predictable result.

Nearly everywhere in Canada it took $1.60 in 1919 to buy what $1.00 could purchase in 1913. Some workers, such as farm laborers and some railway employees, enjoyed proportionate wage increases, but most workers did not. For most people, the rate of inflation between 1916 and 1919 was about twice that of wage increases and all across the country increasing numbers joined labor unions. There were more strikes than ever before; by the end of 1919, there were twice as many workers affiliated with unions as in 1914 and there was a proportionate increase in strikes. But workers who joined unions were still less than one third of the total work force, and it was only in the West that labor unrest resulted in the militancy of quasi-revolution by endorsing the idea of the sympathetic, or general, strike.

The militancy of western labor was the product of two tendencies, one common to all regions of Canada, the other peculiarly western. The factor in common was the tendency of workers to have suffered hardship from inflation and frustration by employers who refused to recognize their unions. The refusal of employers to recognize any spokesman for a union as the legitimate voice of individual employees pointed to a deeper issue, the more fundamental question of the relevance of working-class opinion on anything.

In pre-industrial Canada, nearly every man owned some property and therefore had a right to speak to this extent. But with the appearance of the large numbers of propertyless citizens that accompanied industrialism, there arose a new problem. Traditionally, a person without property was considered a dependent inferior who had no right to claim any power in deciding public issues. By this logic, women were not enfranchised. But the question in 1919 was whether large numbers of men could be treated in the traditional way for the present or for the future. Alternatively, if they could not be ignored, could they be repressed successfully? In the East, the answer was yes. But the problem of repression was more difficult in the West because the question of recognized authority was more open. That is, western cities differed from the others since their elite was only one generation old; thus, control was less securely in the hands of wealthy businessmen than in the older eastern centres.

This pattern is clearly illustrated by the case in Winnipeg, the city which gave rise to the most militant strike action after the war. Between 1882 and 1913, Winnipeg had grown from a few buildings to the stature of a regional metropolis. But in this same period, when Winnipeg grew from a few thousand people to a quarter of a million, there was no proportionate consolidation of power by one group of businessmen who could always determine the outcome of any issue as they wished. Thus, by 1913, Winnipeggers were not only electing aldermen who represented competing interests of property; they were also beginning to elect representatives to further the interests of workers who had no property at all. In 1913, R. A. Rigg, the business agent for the Winnipeg Trades and Labour Council, was seated on the City Council. And the next year, a truck driver, W. B. Simpson, was voted onto the body that was supposed to be made up of eighteen governing businessmen.

By 1915, it was thus possible to predict that men of property might lose control completely if they did not forget their prior differences and meet this social democracy, which put labor's bookkeeper and a socialist teamster in the sanctity of city hall. These were social distinctions all businessmen recognized. They would have to be maintained. Hard measures, if necessary, would be justified to preserve proper social boundaries. In this spirit, the Winnipeg business community united to move a variety of issues, significant as well as petty. One of the latter, which was no less suggestive for its pettiness, was a proposal to start a military flying school as a contribution to the war effort; "Winnipeg" it was held, "could help the cause in no better way than in training pilots for air scouting" and to this end $5 000 of municipal money was voted to be added to $40 000 raised by private subscription. However, tuition for the entrants, who would eventually become commissioned officers, was $400. When labor members of council denounced the scheme for its elitism, businessmen united to defeat them. In another small but significant way they served notice that as far as the control of the city was concerned, "working men need not apply."

But with each annual election an additional one or two labor members were added to the growing bloc on City Council. By 1918 the labor group had grown to five members, roughly one third of the whole, and now *they* seized the initiative. They moved, for instance, that the high fee for a peddlars' license ought to be reduced, which would make it easier for someone to hawk merchandise in the streets to the possible disadvantage of established merchants. All but one of the businessmen on council opposed them, and the labor initiative was defeated 11 to 6. But on another matter, curiously, a labor motion triumphed.

Winnipeg's police force had recently formed a union and the city hesitated to recognize it as their collective bargaining agent. The champions of social democracy took up the cause with a motion to "recognize and deal with the newly formed Policemen's Union, following the policy that employees in the service of the public shall have the right to form unions." The motion carried, but Alderman Frank Fowler spoke for the opposing members of council when he said that the police were the ultimate security of property, and therefore, if they had a union too, the middle class would lose its last defense. This spokesman for business asserted that the constables had to decide whether they were on the side of their "sworn duty" or with the conspiratorial forces of organized labor, because "they can not serve both trade unions and the persons whose property they protect." Perhaps the other businessmen on council felt that since the police were so important to their protection they deserved special consideration, and that explains why they found it easier to oppose cheaper peddlars' licenses than collective bargaining for the police force. But the incident did demonstrate the existence of an interesting dichotomy of labor versus property, suggesting that the city was well polarized by 1918 and poised for a dramatic confrontation to test the strength of the two opposing forces.

When representatives of Winnipeg's labor unions attended the annual meeting of the Trades and Labour Congress of Canada at Quebec shortly thereafter, westerners, who might have expected support from their colleagues across the country, perceived there was almost as much difference between themselves and the eastern representatives as between the social democrats and the Frank Fowlers of Winnipeg. They complained that the "labour movement of the east is reactionary and servile to its core," committed to the old parties and outmoded policies. The westerners decided that their best interest would be served by divorcing west from east and pursuing a separate strategy accordingly.

The meeting of western labor leaders later in Calgary was radical beyond expectation. In 1919 they adopted a stance that was enormously more militant than easterners had permitted the year before. Previously, organized labor adhered closely to non-political business-unionism, the strategy of wages and hours questions modestly pursued. The Calgary gathering was more like a meeting of a socialist workers' party. Delegates began with speeches in praise of the recent Russian Revolution and condemnation of the capitalist countries that had meddled in the affair by sending troops to intervene on the Tsar's behalf. They then adopted a number of resolutions pertaining to wages and hours matters, and embraced the tactic of all workers joining in One Big Union aimed to be a universal union to secure their demands by means of the weapon of the general strike.

The first test of this strategy came by coincidence two months later in Winnipeg. Workers in a dispute for better wages and hours in the building trades joined with iron workers in a struggle to win recognition for the Metal Trades Council as their bargaining agent. Soon these unions appealed to the seventy others in the city for sympathetic action. Under the auspices of the Winnipeg Trades and Labour Council the unions were polled one by one and the membership indicated overwhelming support for the idea of a general strike. Labor and capital were thus set for a showdown. The tendency of the city's political development since 1913 reached its culmination when the Trades and Labour Council set midday of May 15, 1919, as the moment for the strike's commencement.

On the appointed hour, the business of what was then Canada's third largest city came to a halt as more than thirty thousand workers walked off their jobs. Everything from movie houses to bakeries closed. No streetcars ran. The telegraph and telephone services were halted. Even the toilets stopped flushing since pressure was kept too low to raise water above the first floor of most buildings.

Although the regular institutions of city government continued to function, the actual day to day governance of Winnipeg passed to the strike committee in a broad variety of matters. For instance, even though the city police had voted to strike they stayed on the job in accordance with the orders of the committee. Similarly, milk and bread deliveries were resumed, again "by authority of the strike committee." Organized labor was now at a peak of its ascendancy and grew a little boastful accordingly: "If we can control industrial production now... we can control the government of this country too."

Of course the city's businessmen, *citizens* as they called themselves, were not going to permit this transfer of power to the "alien enemy" without organizing a resistance of their own. They formed a kind of vigilante organization called the Committee of One Thousand—"Citizen's Committee" for short. It was their aim to unite the people affiliated with the two old political parties and thus break the strike in an "impartial" and "nonpartisan" manner. They were duly deputized first as "special" firemen, then as police. Given this array of legally constituted and extralegal governing bodies it would have been understandable if the situation rapidly disintegrated into generalized disorder. But contrary to what was the easiest course, the strikers were scrupulously careful to prevent any appearance of anarchy and violence, because they expected that even a small disturbance would be met with force and martial law. For three weeks the strike committee therefore worked with a cooperative regular police force to prevent this pretext from occurring. For three weeks there was uneasy peace.

But in the meantime, there were unrelenting calls for government intervention from the metropolitan newspapers across the country. Some of the recurring themes were that "Canada must not become a second Russia." The strike was the work of "revolutionary agitators and foreign undesirables who infest the country." "Plunder, murder and rape must not become ruling principles under the British flag."

The most interesting notion was the idea that the entire problem of labor unrest was the work of "enemy aliens" and "the German agents who are financing them." But as a matter of fact, the most prominent leaders in the movement were all eminently Anglo-Saxon. Indeed, the most Utopian of the strikes' supporters were Protestant clergymen such as J. S. Woodsworth, Salem Bland, and William Ivens, who found the strike a glorious outpouring of what they called the social gospel, a Christianity that was concerned with life on earth and the "Brotherhood of Man," rather than with theology or creed.

Nevertheless, Parliament convened in special session to confront the strike as the work of "the Hidden Hand of the alien." On June 6, with only twenty minutes of discussion, the House unanimously adopted an amendment to the Immigration Act that provided for summary deportation without trial for any non-citizen who was so much as suspected of revolutionary activity. As for citizens, a series of amendments to the criminal code later provided twenty-year jail sentences for Canadians convicted for "seditious conspiracy."

At the same time that Parliament was taking action, the mayor of Winnipeg took steps to put the Citizen's Committee in charge by firing the regular police force and replacing them with the "special police." Within a matter of days, there was a violent confrontation between the new police force and the "alien enemy," and so the federal government intervened. In the middle of the night of June 16 and 17 the strike leaders and a number of people were rousted from their homes and confined in the federal penitentiary at nearby Stony Mountain.

Now leaderless, the strike collapsed; people began to drift back to their jobs. But a group of war veterans called upon other "returned men" to parade in protest against the partiality of Ottawa's action. The mayor responded by reiterating his total ban on all parades. The veterans decided to make their protest regardless, and gathered at Winnipeg's focus at Portage and Main streets on Saturday, June 21. As soon as they began to march, "specials" and the Royal North West Mounted Police attacked the marchers from horseback with revolvers blazing and clubs swinging. Men who had survived three-and-one-half years of mud and blood in Belgium fell wounded on the pavement of their home town. Thirty-four marchers were wounded. One man fell dead on the spot with a bullet through his head. Another died later in hospital. Eighty people were arrested.

On Monday morning, June 23, 1919, Winnipeggers went to work in the shadow of 30-caliber machine guns mounted on trucks and ready to silence any recurrence of protest. It was not a pleasant sight even for the "citizens." But this stalemate in one Canadian city was a preview of polarities to follow. The federal election of 1921 was just as inconclusive, a fact with important implications for decades to follow.

CHAPTER EIGHTEEN

Political Fission

I. New Leaders, Old Issues

By 1921 Borden had retired and Laurier was dead. New personalities symbolic of Canada's new temperament had taken their place. In keeping with Quebec's retreat inward, the best and the brightest of that province avoided participation in national politics, and the new leadership therefore reflected the new social polarization rather than the primary ethnic antithesis. Arthur Meighen, the Conservatives' new leader, was a small-town Presbyterian who believed wealth followed intelligence and therefore that a labor organization was simply a poor man's way of making animal stupidity powerful. Thus, Meighen was the man to speak for the Frank Fowlers of Winnipeg and for the rest of the country. At the other end of the political continuum, social democrats had their mentor and champion in J. S. Woodsworth, once a Methodist clergyman, a participant in the newly militant labor movement, and most of all the voice of Canada's social conscience. His message, in contrast to Meighen's, was the good news that human equality, justice, and happiness were all attainable if only people would act cooperatively.

Then there was William Lyon Mackenzie King, the man in the middle who succeeded Sir Wilfrid Laurier to the Liberal leadership, chiefly because as yet he had not been obnoxious to anyone. King was less reactionary than Meighen, but he lacked that leader's razor-sharp mind and splendidly acid style in debate. Similarly, by the same plodding normality, King articulated none of Woodsworth's dreams of social justice. Mackenzie King thought, spoke, and wrote only in platitudes. As Donald Creighton has put it, King's "verbal currency was invariably tendered in the highest denominations" and stock values. His genius was in the art of shrewd maneuver and manipulation; "there was more in him than met the eye, and a great deal less than filled the ear."

Mackenzie King found himself in the prime ministerial office after Arthur Meighen in 1921 in much the same way that he gained the Liberal leadership. He "divided us least." Meighen's party had already lost Quebec on its past record of imperialism and conscription. The Conservatives might still have commanded a majority by carrying the middle class of the rest of the country, which was generally pleased with Meighen's boldness in suppressing the "Bolshevism" of organized labor and what newspapers derided as the "alien scum" of Winnipeg, but for other strokes that offended English-speaking Canadians, particularly farmers west of the Ottawa River.

The war mobilization had entailed economic planning that was directly beneficial to agriculture, and Saskatchewan farmers in particular wanted this involvement maintained to assure peacetime prosperity. They wanted the continuation of the agency that had been created in 1917 to control the marketing and pricing of grain, for instance. But most members of parliament considered the Wheat Board an abnormal intrusion into the free market and saw to its discontinuance after 1919. Similarly, the government controls to keep interest rates low was a policy that was beneficial to farmers borrowing heavily to increase production with new machinery such as gasoline tractors. But after the war, the investment community encouraged a policy of tighter credit and higher interest rates to curtail inflation and protect profits. The government complied with bankers rather than farmers.

The same catering to business followed from Meighen's transportation policy. The new transcontinental railways, which went bankrupt before they were even completed, were kept afloat financially, made operational, and run by government assistance in the name of wartime emergency. In 1919 they were formally nationalized; but the new system, the Canadian National Railways, which came into existence by merging the Canadian Northern, Grand Trunk and Grand Trunk Pacific, was created primarily to prevent enormous losses to investors rather than to provide better, and cheaper service for users such as the farmers. Thus, freight rates were allowed to float to the level that served the interests of these investors and the Canadian Pacific's directors rather than of agriculture.

The discontinuance of the Wheat Board, tighter credit, and higher freight rates were all reversals that ran directly contrary to the demands in a platform published in 1918 by the Canadian Council of Agriculture for what it styled a "New National Policy." The Canadian Council of Agricultue had been founded in 1909 from already existing farmers' movements in three Prairie Provinces. Before and during the war they had pushed for change, and by 1918 they were prepared to advocate far-reaching reforms. Thus their interest in transportation policy, interest rates, and marketing boards had been enlarged to include the demand that the tariff be drastically lowered and that a progressive income tax replace customs duties. They also sought basic changes in the political structure, such as proportional representation, initiative, referendum, and recall; they were even prepared to call for the public ownership of utilities.

Everything organized farmers demanded was ignored or denounced by Meighen as "Socialistic, Bolshevistic and Soviet nonsense." The final and crowning insult was the government's refusal to deliver even a token reduction in the tariff. When it became clear that neither of the mainline parties was interested in changing the old National Policy, members of Parliament began to desert the still surviving wartime Union government, and the Canadian Council of Agriculture took on a political existence as the National Progressive Party under the leadership of Thomas Crerar early in 1920. The new party would fail to achieve most of its intended goals, but its appearance was still important because this was the beginning of the end of the old dynamics of the two-party system.

By the autumn of 1921, Arthur Meighen thought it was time to test his strength against the "contemptible" leader of the Liberals and the farmers who were now off "chasing rainbows" with organized labor. He knew that most people, including many farmers, had approved of his handling of radicals in the strikes of 1919. More important, he knew that most people, including some farmers, regarded opposition to the tariff as tantamount to treason. "If I can get the people of this country to see that the issue is Protection or no Protection," he predicted "the battle will be won." Crerar was willing to fight on this ground. But King insisted that "the issue is the Prime Minister himself." The Liberal leader kept wanting to talk about Meighen's "autocracy and extravagance" as a way of avoiding specific commitment of the Liberals on anything—the tariff in particular. Meighen replied that King's platform was "Protection on apples in British Columbia, Free Trade in the Prairie Provinces and the rural parts of Ontario, Protection in the industrial centres in Ontario, Conscription in Quebec and humbug in the Maritime Provinces."

In the end, the electorate repudiated both of the old parties without awarding anything like a majority to the new one. Seventy percent of all votes cast went against Meighen's party. Sixty percent were votes against King's Liberals. Eighty percent of the electorate voted against Crerar's Progressives. In 1921, all parties were minor. For the first time in Canadian political history, no party had received a majority.

Arthur Meighen's Conservatives were reduced to a mere 50 seats. He was resoundingly defeated. But Mackenzie King's Liberals were hardly victorious with their 116-seat plurality—two members short of a majority. To be sure, there were 65 Progressives who could be expected to oppose the Conservatives more often than the Liberals, but the point is that the outcome on any question was not easily predictable. This was so much the case that the oddment of the election, two independent labor members, could conceivably hold the balance of power with their two votes. A new dynamic thus entered into national politics.

II.   Progressives with Power

Multi-party politics, like federalism, was something that Canadians simply discovered they had after it had appeared; it was not a pattern that they particularly liked or planned. And for the first few years of the existence of the multi-party system, an effort was made to deny its reality—even by Progressives. The leader himself, Thomas Crerar, envisioned the farmers' revolt as a protest movement by people whose true political home was in the Liberal party. As soon as King's Liberals would "come to their senses" on such key issues as the tariff, Crerar expected that the Progressive Party would cease to exist, much like the Populist Party of the United States in the 1890s. But another faction within the Progressives, the Alberta wing, was opposed to the very idea of political parties. Henry Wise Wood, the chief spokesman for this point of view, although not himself a member of Parliament, saw a legislator as a delegate representing interest groups such as farmers, miners, and so on. He refused to countenance the idea of permanent parties voting monolithically on all questions; rather, Wood preferred to see a constant shifting of allegiances among the loosely integrated interest groups as members of Parliament voted on the merits of each issue. Less than one third of the Progressives, mainly those from Saskatchewan, saw their movment as a party, that is, solidly organized and intended to be permanent. They opposed "old line" parties; they aimed to offer a more or less permanently fresh flow of alternatives acceptable to the special interest of westerners. But they were only one of three factions. Given the welter of division—even though the Progressives were the second largest group in Parliament—it was Meighen's Conservatives who formed the Opposition, since not enough of the second party were willing to see themselves as such.

The unwillingness of the Progressives to play the game of party politics at first frustrated the dynamics of minority government. It gave Mackenzie King an ideal opportunity to dismiss the farmers' protest as nothing more than Liberals in a hurry. He moved accordingly to appropriate some of their alternatives with the aim of building a bridge for the Progressives to cross home to Liberalism. King reinstated lower, pre-Meighen freight rates. Later he tinkered with the tariff. As early as 1922, the strategy showed signs of success. By the end of the first session, many Progressives were snugly back where King and their nominal leader thought they belonged. Crerar himself retired from Progressivism. In 1923 the holdouts conferred the leadership on Robert Forke.

Forke was one of those Progessives who believed that a permanent third party was both necessary and possible. But when he attempted to lead his group as an Opposition, he found himself frustrated by the rules of the House, which were written to accommodate two parties—the government and the Opposition. The rules disabled "private members" from posing amendments to money bills, and since Forke was not in the cabinet, and since Crerar had forfeited the party's right to form the Opposition, Meighen could move amendments but Forke could not. Robert Forke was neither a Liberal nor a Conservative. He was a "private member."

In 1923 the Progressives succeeded in gaining recognition for their party as an opposition group independent of Meighen's. But the logic that gave Forke's Progressives autonomous status applied to William Irvine and J. S. Woodsworth as well. They were neither Conservatives, nor Liberals, nor Progressives. They called themselves the "Labour Group." As William Irvine put it, "Mr. Woodsworth is the leader and I am the group." It worked and there were now four parties in the House of Commons.

In the long-term, it was the party of two that counted for more than the Progressive block of, in theory, more than sixty. In fact, beginning in 1924, the spirit of Progressivism appeared to be spent. In that session Woodsworth moved an amendment to shift the burden of taxation from tariff revenue to increased taxes on unearned income and luxuries. Progressives were inclined to support Woodsworth's motion on grounds that this reform was at the very heart of their New National Policy. Meighen, too, was willing to cooperate, if only to bring down King's government in the House. Since Forke believed that a future Conservative government would only repudiate their present support for tax reform, he attempted to lead the Progressives in support of King. In part, Forke succeeded; the Liberals were saved by a margin of six votes. But Forke's leadership was mortally wounded by the desertion of about one third of his party to Woodsworth. Subsequently, most of these renegades issued a public declaration that henceforth they were Labour-Progressives. Thus emerged the "Ginger Group" and the foundation for a minor party that was at once willing to play the parliamentary game behind Woodsworth and also to function in the role of providing a lively socialist threat to the "old line" parties.

The Ginger Group jettisoned the elements of the New National Policy articulated by the Canadian Council on Agriculture, which harkened back to nineteenth-century individualism, and emphasized instead the aspects of reform that accepted the inevitability of organization and bureaucracy. Gone was the demand for making democracy more direct with such political devices as initiative, referendum, and recall. They emphasized instead the need for government unemployment insurance and old-age pensions as well as government action to nationalize banking, transportation, and resource-based industries. Thus, the Labour-Progressives came to accept themselves as a pragmatic socialist group, likely to continue as a minor force but with some hope of success whenever they could command the balance of power in a minority goverment situation.

Naturally the other two parties continued to regard the multi-party system as an anomaly and minority government as a threat to democracy. Mackenzie King secured a dissolution of the House in 1925 and campaigned as the people's champion accordingly. He stressed the need for national unity and majority government to insure stability and reforms that the *majority* wanted. Of course, this led Arthur Meighen to ask about the specific changes that King was contemplating: "He has not told us and he is not going to tell us." But Meighen was specific in his promises. Not only would he resist the "socialistic nonsense" of the Ginger Group, he would also restore the country to its prewar footing by revising the tariff upward. This, said Meighen, was "the National Policy as Macdonald had shaped it, and as it has since endured." Although Meighen was well aware that he was drawing the electorate back to the focus of the 1921 election as if nothing had changed, he made no apology: "I preach it now just as I preached it then and this time the people of Canada are not going to be befuddled by the twisting and shifting practices of Mr. King."

But the consensus that the leaders of the two traditional parties expected did not materialize. Once again the electorate returned all groups short of a majority. The election of 1925 shifted a few seats away from the Liberals and the Progressives. This time Meighen's group had the plurality. But King did not resign. He chose to defer to the Progressives to decide whether the country would be governed by the group led by himself or the group of Arthur Meighen. Presented with this opportunity, the Ginger Group drafted a program of fourteen projects and presented it to the leaders of the two major parties. Meighen regarded their strategy as political blackmail, but King smilingly accepted what they proposed and the Labour Progressives therefore threw the weight of their support to Mackenzie King's Liberals; the prime minister was able to retain his hold on power.

Now the Ginger Group confidently awaited a measure providing old-age pensions as King's first payment for their continuing support. But Arthur Meighen had a trump card of his own to divert the House from this socialist course. A special committee tabled a report with evidence that the Canadian customs service had been cooperating with American businessmen who were running an illicit liquor trade on a multinational basis to take advantage of prohibition in the United States. Interpreted as evidence of corruption, this created a controversy; but when the evidence was inter-preted as an indication that the Canadian customs officers were becoming nothing more than the tools of American gangsters, this was even more explosive. King expected that the Progressives would withdraw their sup-port as Meighen pounced with a motion of non-confidence. The prime minister hoped to avoid this humiliation by asking that the House be dis-solved before the vote could be taken, but the governor general, Lord Byng, refused to grant this request. King resigned. Since a general election had occurred so recently, and since the Conservatives were more numer-ous than the Liberals, Byng therefore turned to Meighen. But Meighen could not attract enough "third party" backing and was defeated within days of taking office. Now Parliament *had* to be dissolved, and King rejoiced, for he proclaimed that Canada confronted a constitutional crisis—Byng's actions in refusing a prime minister's request was a repudia-tion of Commonwealth constitutional development over the last two cen-turies. In King's lurid denunciation, the governor general's action amounted to a denial of responsible government. That Byng was an impe-rial appointment was further grist to his mill, in that it could also be insin-uated that Canada's colonial status was being emphasized, and her recently won independent identity was in jeopardy.

King rejoiced in his diary: "I go into the battle of another election believ-ing we have an issue that the people will respond to." He was right. In 1926 the voters gave King the majority government that they had withheld in the two previous elections. And this might have spelled the end of the multi-party system, had it not been for King's obsession with security. His majority was not large, and he hoped to widen his three-vote margin by sealing an alliance with the Labour-Progressives. He promised J. S. Woods-worth that he would revoke Meighen's 1919 amendments to the Immigra-tion Act and criminal code, and bring in a bill providing federal funds to provinces that implemented old-age pensions.

The revocation of the amendments was slow to follow, but the principle of old-age pensions was established in 1927. Here was the payoff from the dynamics of multi-party politics, a good incentive for members of minor parties to continue their separate existence despite their minority status. And in the years that followed much the same situation was repeated. The Labour Party, or its successor under different names—Co-operative Com-monwealth Federation after 1932 and New Democratic Party after 1961—was able to win concessions by holding or threatening to hold the balance of power in a minority government situation. The old line parties cooperated, since they refused to join in common cause against the social-ist minority; in 1927, for instance, the socialists' initiative for old-age pen-sions prevailed, even though 219 of the 245 members of the House were Liberals or Conservatives. They had chosen to divide 91 to 128 because

each group had come into existence to favor this or that competing banking or railway interest. Thus the myth that Liberals and Conservatives represented liberalism and conservatism worked nicely to further the interests
of socialists, because it divided the business interests into beatable
groups—a fact that might have led to serious instability.

But it was Canadian pragmatism which prevented the disintegration of
the old party system from spilling over into generalized chaos. One of the
leaders of one of the major parties after 1927 was usually willing to forget
his principles and pursue expediency in the direction of the threatening
minor party. By the same pragmatism, the leader of that minor reforming
group was usually willing to settle for half a loaf rather than none. In this
manner, periods of outright or near minority government resulted in innovation rather than instability. Unfortunately, throughout the decade of
Canada's worst economic crisis, majority parties—devoid of any theoretical orientation to the country's trouble— were in power. And given their
luxury of domination, the decade of the 1930s was a period of avoidance
and inaction more than of experimentation and change. But as the next
chapter will show, a caretaker government was all that most people
seemed to want or expect.

CHAPTER NINETEEN

Prosperity, Depression, and the Quest for Restoration

I. The Slide into Depression

The emergence of multi-party politics caused considerable anxiety in the 1920s because a shifting pattern of groups rather than the familiar duality of parties—and businessmen—was now determining the course of national decision-making. This was alarming to all Canadians who believed the two-party system was a prerequisite to stability and survival. But in the 1920s, there was a comforting boom in the economy that had a sedative effect on the anxieties which arose from disturbing political developments. Between 1921 and 1927, the GNP increased from four billion to six billion dollars without a comparable increase in population. And since wartime inflation diminished, the increase in the total value of goods and services marked spectacular real growth indeed.

But the expansion of Canada's economy between 1921 and 1927 was attended by a variety of distortions, similar to those of 1910 when for the first time illusions of national economic fulfillment gained wide currency. As in the earlier period, the population anomaly continued with the exodus of more Canadians and the in-migration of more Europeans than even before. Similarly, the branch-plant character of manufacturing increased, and staples dominated the export sector. But now, rather than wheat, the dominant commodity shipped abroad was wood pulp, the raw material for paper. By 1927, 64 percent of all the paper in the world was manufactured from Canadian wood fiber.

The 1920s, in other words, reconfirmed and continued the supply-base nature of the economy and the transient character of the people. Popula-

271

tion was continually arriving from European points of departure, while Canadians were increasingly boarding trains for destinations in the United States. This economy of transients was geared to exporting wood pulp, minerals, and grain; importing cotton, steel, and component parts; using hydroelectric power to assemble automobiles, stitch clothing, refine chemicals, and roll cigarettes—all behind a tariff wall keeping prices in excess of world levels. But the United States, to provide a counter example, was one of those countries which digested its people into a unitary mold, and industrialized along the lines of developing secondary manufacturing in accordance with available resources. Americans did not export coal and iron ore as much as they developed a steel industry. That, in turn, was used to make automobiles and other manufactured steel ware.

In Canada, the supply-base role precluded manufacturing except as an industrial echo of larger systems. By value of output (excluding quasi-manufacturing such as wood pulp production and hydroelectric generation) the leading Canadian industries were the manufacture of clothing, chemicals and chemical products, tobacco, cotton textiles, automobiles, rubber products, railway rolling stock, shoes, and steel—in that order. The dollar value of Canadian cigarette production in the 1920s was more than twice that of Canada's steel industry. Canada had become an urban and industrial country since more than half of the population lived in towns and cities and the vast majority of people worked in occupations other than farming. But the economy was still extraordinarily committed to exporting raw materials or assembling the components of products manufactured elsewhere. Thus, there was more emphasis on cigarettes to support the Canadian smoking habit than on domestic steel production to build American automobiles in Canada.

There were other distortions. These were growing disparities between regions and individuals, which meant that the benefits of the expanding GNP were not distributed with any kind of uniformity. British Columbia, Ontario, and Quebec enjoyed a great boom with the expansion of hydroelectric developments, mining, and paper production, but the Prairie wheat economy was relatively stagnant in this period. The Atlantic Provinces, dependent on coal mining or the fisheries, were even more severely depressed. But disparities ran deeper than regionalism. They also had an individual dimension in the sense of a severe mal-distribution of personal income. The wages of employees did not keep up with the profits that accrued to the wealthy. While businessmen were eager to invest their surplus, and workers were happy to find greater purchasing power in the new practice of buying on credit, a response to the other new device of mass advertising, there were limits to both. Near the end of the decade, industry was overcapitalized and credit buying was also beginning to abate: there was more of everything to buy, but less ability to buy anything.

This pattern of anomalies and distortions was not unique to Canada. Tariff increases by nearly every trading nation induced a general constipation of world trade. And by the end of the decade a general exhaustion of purchasing power was also observable. Thus, the weaknesses of one capitalist economy were replicated in another, and in 1929 they precipitated a "world" depression from which no capitalist country escaped, a depression for which every capitalist country was responsible.

The only individuality exhibited was the individuality of particular exaggerations. Industrialists in every country spoke of overcapitalization as overproduction. All in chorus called for retrenchment. Canadians added a note of their own in belatedly recognizing an over-commitment to the export of staples. But now with a new willingness to diversify the economy, political leaders apologized that they were powerless to effect any large structural changes. In Canada, as elsewhere, they declared that the voting public would simply have to be patient and wait for "business confidence" to be restored. Thus, Herbert Hoover campaigned for reelection to the presidency of the United States in 1932. Two years earlier, Mackenzie King had appealed in the same style for reinvigoration of his mandate to do nothing in Canada.

II.   A New Deal

At the end of July, 1930, Canada's seventeenth general election fell during the worst depression in the federation's history. The economic crisis was only beginning. Pre-depression "relief agencies" were already strained beyond capacity, but social welfare was the provincial governments' area of jurisdiction. The fact that the revenues of the Prairie and Maritime Provinces were proving inadequate to provide even routine social services, not to mention large-scale public works or direct payments for the unemployed, was not as salient to Mackenzie King as the other fact that the central government, which had the revenue, lacked the constitutional ability to legislate in this area. Without amendments to the BNA Act, King knew that he was legally excused from responding to the crisis with anything other than cash grants to the provinces, unconditionally in the old manner or with conditions for their use as had become the custom since the day of Robert Borden. But Mackenzie King did not wish to comfort Conservative premiers by shouldering their financial burdens. He preferred to play petty politics, and revealed his superficiality in this regard by asserting publicly that he "might be prepared to go a certain length possibly

meeting one or two western provinces that have progressive premiers at the head of their governments, but I would not give a single cent to any Tory government." Thus, at the federal level, for the first year of the deepening crisis, it would be more than fair to describe Mackenzie King as attempting to avoid the Great Depression rather than confronting it with a broad program of action. He might have advocated amendments to the BNA Act, but did not. He might have appropriated larger subsidies. He did nothing here either.

Nevertheless, the prime minister's astrologer, Mrs. Bleaney, and his own starry sense of political timing set the summer of 1930 as the most propitious moment for winning a federal election. With the stars in appropriate conjunctions and the weaknesses of the other parties working for him, King was confident that his party would win handsomely.

Surprising as it may seem, the election results nearly confirmed King's intuitive impression that the voters wanted their government to meet the crisis with caution and constitutionality. The minor parties polled fewer votes in 1930 than in any election since their appearance in 1921; they received only 5 percent of the vote. Still, King's Liberals received slightly less than in 1926, and the new prime minister was R. B. Bennett, the man who succeeded Arthur Meighen to the Conservative leadership in 1927.

The key to Bennett's success was his ability to project an impression of boldness without breaking from tradition. "Mackenzie King promises you conferences; I promise you action. He promises consideration of the problem of unemployment; I promise to end unemployment." This image of success without risk appealed since his cure-all was only a large dose of that government policy which was supposed to have made Canada so prosperous earlier, the policy Canadians were no longer holding as dear as Bennett said they should: "You have been taught to mock at tariffs and to applaud free trade." The Conservative leader challenged the electorate to "Tell me, when did free trade fight for you? Tell me, when did free trade fight for you? You say our tariffs are only for our manufacturers; I will make them fight for you as well. I will use them to blast a way into the markets that have been closed to you."

Bennett kept his electoral promises with two measures that were submitted to a special session of Parliament convened soon after his election. One provided $20 million for relief, a direct subsidy to the provinces to maintain soup kitchens or other provisions for the unemployed. The other measure increased the tariff by 50 percent, the sharpest increase since Macdonald's imposition of the National Policy in 1879.

Although this was what Bennett had promised, and in this sense what the electorate expected, the one policy tended to cancel the effect of the other. The disbursement of funds to relieve the unemployed was supposed to ease hardship insofar as $20 per unemployed person would go toward

that objective. And tariff provisions, which prevented the dumping of cheap foreign goods, stabilized the falling prices of Canadian products thus saving the jobs of workers in those industries. But the tariff change increased the suffering of those who were unemployed or living on drastically reduced or falling incomes. Still, this was no more than Bennett's party had promised.

Subsequently, the prime minister felt he was struggling against an impossible situation. Mackenzie King denounced his budgets for "fiscal irresponsibility." King believed that the government should weather the crisis by spending less, not more. But on the other side, Bennett was pressured for basic reforms such as a national scheme for unemployment insurance. With perhaps one million people looking for work in 1932, Bennett shuddered at the probable cost of supporting them with a "dole." In lieu of any other policy, the prime minister dedicated himself to work fourteen-hour days at administering to the country's millions of personal depressions. A man would write from New Brunswick that the family fishing schooner had been sold because the price of fish had fallen too low to repay the cost of catching them; Bennett would respond with a personal note expressing his genuine sorrow and a $5 bill from Bennett's own pocket as a token of his sincere regret. Another sufferer would write from Saskatchewan that he needed to grow six times more wheat in 1932 to get the same dollar return as in the 1920s; but even if it were possible for him to do six times more work than usual, it was still hopeless because each year since 1929 his crops had shriveled as they sprouted when the spring brought hot winds and dust, never rain. He too would win another of the prime ministerial notes and tokens.

Bennett did care. He did feel personal injury every time he heard that farmers were calling their horse-drawn Fords "Bennett buggies" because they could not afford the price of gasoline, or that the urban unemployed were naming their shantytowns in garbage dumps "Bennett boroughs" because this was the mode of urbanization that followed Bennett's policies.

Then, too, the worst of the Depression always seemed to worsen. By 1932 Bennett feared that the suffering was bringing Canada to the threshold of revolution. Now he shifted his emphasis from "blasting a way into the markets that have been closed" to blasting radicals. Thus, when three thousand unemployed protestors descended on Ottawa in 1932, they met with armed force reminiscent of the last days of the Winnipeg General Strike. Despite the fact that even Conservative newspapers such as the Ottawa *Journal* described the array of city police, RCMP, and a military armored car that overshadowed the quiet petitioners as a "scene that smacks more of fascism than of Canadian constitutional authority," the repression continued until the RCMP grew from a handful of constables into a considerable army.

There were other similarly quasi-military means of handling the unemployed, particularly the transient single men. Camps were established for 20 000 such transients. Here they were put to work—sometimes at meaningless tasks such as building roads that ran nowhere or airstrips for aircraft that never landed—and equally important, from the standpoint of social control, the single unemployed in the camps found themselves under military discipline imposed by the Department of National Defence. When the men finally rebelled in protest, left the camps in British Columbia, and began a march on Ottawa in the spring of 1935, increasing in numbers as they progressed, they were coralled in a football stadium in Regina and attacked by the RCMP. There was a similar reception in Winnipeg and a repeat of the 1932 affair when a delegation finally reached Ottawa. The complaining unemployed were thus regarded as "Reds" or "bums". Bennett called them criminals.

The federal government felt increasingly justified in sponsoring a program of censoring "seditious" books, deporting aliens, and jailing citizen radicals. The Department of National Revenue looked after the dangerous literature. The RCMP sent undercover agents into the declining labor movement (fewer workers were affiliated with unions in 1934 than 1929). And when social democrats such as J. S. Woodsworth attacked the government's deportation of foreign-born residents for "seditious conspiracy" and called for the repeal of Meighen's amendment to the criminal code, which made possible the jailing of citizens on the same charge, the Conservatives at first refused to debate the justice of repression, and then answered with the statement that the laws on sedition were "not in any sense a hindrance to any right-thinking person."

But a growing minority of Canadians were not "right-thinking," for they viewed the Depression as proof of the failure of capitalism, the dramatic demonstration of the need for a new economy "in which all social means of production and distribution, including land, are socially owned and controlled either by voluntarily organized groups of producers and consumers, or . . . by public corporations responsible to the peoples' elected representatives." This was a repudiation of the principle of acquisitive individualism, and an affirmation of the idea that Canadians should find their way out of the Depression by gearing the economy toward "the supplying of human needs instead of the making of profits."

This sort of Utopian idealism and social-gospel-Christianity had a wide currency in the 1920s, as was shown in the previous chapter. But in that decade, in the context of rising expectations, Utopianism was criticized for its lack of practicality and its apparent naiveté in assuming that people could ever be persuaded to live in happy cooperation. Still, a plethora of farmer and labor parties developed west of the Ottawa River to further various idealisms. In Toronto alone there were a dozen different such groups. In British Columbia there were three. It would be too much to say that they were tolerated in the 1920s, but they were not outlawed. After 1932, however, the specter of proscription loomed ever larger, as depressed economic conditions prompted the businessmen's parties to think that the "Canadian way of life" was threatened by terrorists even though such vital indicators of radicalization as the size and militancy of the labor movement showed considerable decline since the onset of hard times.

Fear of repression as much as hope of recouping recent losses prompted the leaders of the various radical groups to agree that their survival depended upon forgetting their many past difficulties and working with what they had in common to form a federal union of all leftist groups. J. S. Woodsworth played the leading role in this initiative from his office in Ottawa, and in August of 1932 delegates from most of the farmer and labor groups met in Calgary and agreed to the principle of federal union to further the goal of attaining the "co-operative commonwealth."

One observer of the Calgary convention said that the delegates "oozed idealism to the detriment of practical experience." They were a shocking departure from past Canadian practice. No national party had ever committed itself to a political philosophy as airy as the utopianism that sprang from this odd gathering of Protestant preachers and crusty labor organizers. Here was one reason to expect that the new party would fall even before it began. Another was that the name many of the delegates gave to their philosophy was socialism.

But over the winter of 1932-33 the idea of the new federation of socialists did not wither and vanish in the dusty winds of spring. Frank Underhill, an Ontario university professor and leader in the League for Social Reconstruction, an academic socialist movement, wrote a platform which was adopted with minor changes by a convention held in Regina in August, 1933, the first convention of the Co-operative Commonwealth Federation. Reminiscent of the collectivist aspects of the Progressives' New National Policy, the platform began with an unequivocal affirmation of socialism:

> "We aim to replace the present capitalist system, with its inherent injustice and inhumanity, by a social order from which the domination and exploitation of one class by another will be eliminated, in which economic planning will supersede unregulated private enterprise and competition, and in which genuine democratic self-government, based on economic equality will be possible."

The platform closed with the lofty promise that "No CCF government will rest content until it has eradicated capitalism and put into operation the full programme of socialized planning which will lead to the establishment in Canada of the Co-operative Commonwealth."

Subsequently, the new party was denounced as preposterous and nakedly communist. But the CCF's clear commitment to democratic processes made it impossible to prosecute its leaders for "seditious conspiracy." Also, Woodsworth, the national chairman, was a member of the House of Commons of twelve years' standing. For some, he had earned the reputation of a "saint in politics"; for others, Woodsworth was a dangerous subversive. But in either case he was too prominent to turn into a martyr. In this sense, his presence in the leadership tended to give radicalism a legitimizing focus that it had lacked before.

Still, it was one thing to launch a radical movement that was not vulnerable to criminal prosecution, and quite another matter to persuade a majority of the people that socialists warranted their support at the polls. On the other hand, the 1930s were years when the mass of the people should have been suggestible to radical criticism of their economic system. By the year that the CCF came into existence, perhaps as much as half of the total work force was unemployed. And workers who remained employed found that their average hourly pay had fallen from roughly 70 cents to 25 cents. The tariff increase had served only to stabilize prices and profits. To make up the difference, workers who still had jobs worked longer hours—the sixty-five hour week of thirteen-hour days was not uncommon. Then there was the plight of fishermen and farmers who were not unemployed since they owned their own land or fishing gear and could therefore continue to plant seed or set their nets. But the produce of their labor in these years was almost totally unremunerative. It is no wonder, therefore, that hundreds of CCF associations were formed across the country within a few months of the establishment of the party which promised to eliminate economic hardship completely and forever. Before the end of 1934, the CCF had become the number two party in British Columbia and Saskatchewan. There were socialist members in most of the other legislatures and the CCF was winning municipal elections.

R. B. Bennett feared that a CCF snowball would develop into a socialist avalanche, and decided to halt its momentum by moving his own party in that direction. He had already gone some distance toward abandoning his earlier repression of radicalism by launching structural reforms of banking and the marketing of natural products. But this was piecemeal reform and avoided the more mundane and personal problem of the spread between wages and prices. In fact, some Conservatives led by H. H. Stevens were preparing to bolt their party in the name of securing a more thorough "Social Reconstruction," and eventually they did establish the Reconstruction Party.

Bennett made his move in January of 1935. He took to the air waves without prior consultation with his cabinet or caucus, and announced, "The old order is gone" in a series of radio speeches. He said, "It will not return . . . . I am for reform." With the loftiness of a Woodsworth, Bennett asserted that "there can be no permanent recovery without reform." Then came his messages describing a fresh deal of the cards for the Canadian people: unemployment insurance, minimum wages, and other aspects of the program Progressives had called the New National Policy.

Some of Bennett's party thought their leader had converted to socialism, but the prime minister was careful to make clear that he was trying to free capitalism of its "harmful imperfections," and to preserve the system, not to repudiate it. But the Liberals denounced Bennett's New Deal as nothing more than a preelection ploy—legislation to charm the voters, regain a mandate, and then apologize later that it was all unconstitutional. Thus, Mackenzie King—in his customary indirect manner of speaking—asked Bennett to "tell this house whether as leader of the government, knowing that a question will come up immediately as to the jurisdiction of this parliament and of the provincial legislatures in matters of social legislation, he has secured an opinion from the law officers of the crown or from the Supreme Court of Canada which will be a sufficient guarantee to this House to proceed with these measures as being without question within its jurisdiction." Their dubious constitutionality notwithstanding, five measures limped through the House before dissolution.

The election that followed was one of the most interesting—and revealing—in all of Canadian history. In the middle of October, 1935, the electorate was asked to pass judgment on the question of reform after nearly six years of some of the most harrowing suffering ever experienced. There was a veritable raft of alternatives. On a reform continuum, the four leading national organizations ranged from the CCF on the left, which promised to "eradicate capitalism," through the Reconstruction Party and the Conservatives to the Liberals on the right, who pledged themselves to "no precipitate action." In this sense, the election of 1935 was a public opinion poll on the question of reform and how much change the Canadian people thought that the country needed. Thus, 1935 might have marked a significant turning point.

The CCF was the largest of the reform parties advocating radical change. In general terms, they still stood on Underhill's two-year-old Regina Manifesto. Their timetable for implementing this program was the new element. They promised to nationalize the country's banking institutions first, then use the government's financial power to initiate public works, which would end unemployment. The rest of the program would follow. But this summary misses the dimension of vengeance with which Canada's socialists advocated their reforms. In one pamphlet bankers were compared to thieves with the assertion that "Bank robbers get millions, but the big shot banker is a bigger criminal than the gunman because the banker's greed hurts all the people all the time." Another was even more blunt in its call to "Smash the Big Shots' Slave Camps and Sweat Shops." In other words, the CCF called on the masses to avenge their hardships as much as to vote positively for economic transformation.

Less vengeful than the CCF was a splinter of the Conservative Party that aimed to reform the system in order to save it, but proposed a program of changes that went far beyond Bennett's "New Deal." This was the faction that rallied around H. H. Stevens in 1934 and formed their own independent group after dissolution in July 1935. They called themselves the Reconstruction Party, and proposed a fifteen-point manifesto "to help reconstruct Canada's shattered national policy, to wage war with poverty, and to abolish involuntary idleness." But they stopped short of repudiating acquisitive individualism in principle. Because they saw government as the agency to take up the slack and to step in when free enterprise faltered, they denounced the idea of completely planned economy or any of the other "schemes of rigid state control of life and organization."

Mackenzie King's Liberals were conspicuous for their pledge to do nothing. Privately, King knew that he was affirming a "policy of having no policy" but publicly his position was assurances for "no precipitate action." He would not institute reforms that were likely to be declared beyond the jurisdiction of Parliament. But then King would not reform the constitution either. He attempted to appear unruffled by the fact that the capitalist system was in trouble. King was for caution. Liberal advertisements said it well in four words: "It's King or Chaos."

Here then were the major alternatives for the electorate in 1935: the eradication of capitalism by the CCF; major changes in the traditional system by the Reconstruction Party; moderate reform with more of Bennett's New Deal; or no change at all in King without chaos. Given the voting behavior of the 1920s, and given the incentive for action that was supposed to be inherent in the length and the severity of the Depression to 1935, the most understandable prospect was for a minority government headed by Stevens, or King, or Bennett. But such did not occur. The more outspoken the party was for reform, the more repugnant it was to the electorate. The CCF and Reconstruction groups each received less than 10 percent of the popular vote. Bennett won 30 percent. King's Liberals received 45 percent. The rest went to other minor parties, some to the left of the CCF, some to the right of the Liberals. But the two million votes polled for King's party translated into 173 of the 245 seats in the House of Commons—one of the widest majorities in Canadian history.

The inference that follows from the 1935 election, interpreted as a public opinion poll, is that nearly half of the Canadian people were not very interested in innovative approaches to the problems of the unemployed. If nearly half of the people were out of work, the other half had jobs, and perhaps it was these workers who returned the party that promised to do nothing. In 1935, as in 1930, the Canadian people, in common with most of the Western World, showed little support for innovation. This point was evident in the drift of national politics. And on the provincial level, the voters were even more interested in parties that promised hard restoratives; that is, a way to get back to the good old days rather than experimentation to make a clean break with the past.

III. The Restoration Theme in Alberta

One of the most interesting variations of the restoration theme in provincial politics was the enthusiastic response of Albertans to something called Social Credit, an economic theory developed in the 1920s by a British engineer, Major C. H. Douglas. His doctrine was a conscious repudiation of socialist collectivism that at the same time promised to cure capitalism by providing the solution to the problem of poverty amidst plenty. He said that the great gear that was askew was the tendency of personal incomes to be less than the aggregate cost of goods for sale, a flaw that Douglas expressed in the "A plus B theorem." He divided (theoretically) all of the cash flows of society into A payments (the payment of money to individuals in the form of wages, salaries, and dividends) and B payments (the flow of cash to organizations for raw materials, bank charges, and other costs). Then he reasoned that "the rate of flow of purchasing power to individuals is represented by A, but since *all* payments go into prices, the rate of flow of prices cannot be less than A plus B." The solution seemed equally clear: "a portion of the product at least equivalent to B must be distrbuted by a form of purchasing power which is not comprised in the description grouped under A." These were the social credits, the dividends that producers had coming to them for producing more than they were able to consume.

There was a seductive kind of common-sense wisdom to Social Credit theory from the standpoint of the middle class in the context of the Depression. It was a point that another British theorist, the economist John Maynard Keynes, appreciated when he argued that capitalism could start booming again by increased government spending to employ people on massive public works, thus restoring their purchasing power. In fact, it was Keynesian theory through the back door that finally brought about recovery through the vast public project that was World War II.

But five years before the war it was Albertans who were singularly attracted to Social Credit, and it was a panacea that they embraced with all the enthusiasm usually associated with religious revival. In part, this was because Major Douglas and his economic theories were woven into the sacred texts of an already influential radio preacher, "Bible Bill" Aberhart.

Alberta's position was unique. It was one of the most homogeneous provinces—probably more uniformly middle class, Protestant and rural than any of the others. Alberta was also the most recently settled (many settlers had come from the United States) and one of the most hard hit by the Depression, two facts that were not unrelated since Alberta farmers and ranchers were heavily mortgaged and thus even more threatened by the disastrous fall in prices of such primary commodities as beef and grain. They were a Protestant society in trouble. Their first impulse was to renew their faith in the old-time religion: if they promised to forsake drink, dancing, and movies, then the Lord might do his part by improving the weather and the price of wheat and beef. But no miracles followed.

Then over the winter of 1932 and 1933 "Bible Bill" began to expound Social Credit doctrine along with his fundamentalist Christianity from the radio studio at the Calgary Prophetic Bible Institute. Thus, the word spread to thousands of listeners. Study groups were organized. By this means, Aberhart became an inspiring teacher as well as the spiritual leader of everyone within radio range—southern Alberta, part of Saskatchewan, and even some of Montana received the faith.

Throughout 1933, however, Social Credit was still no more than an object of study, not a political movement. The first entry into formal politics did not come until January of 1934. At that time, the governing party of Alberta held a convention at which delegates presented the new theory and urged the government to give it careful consideration as a program for recovery. Several months later, the committee of the whole House did consider the idea of social dividends. Aberhart testified. Even Major Douglas appeared. But the leaders of the United Farmers of Alberta were unconvinced. This, and the conviction of the premier for seducing his housemaid, convinced the star of the Prophetic Bible Institute that it was time to launch a Social Credit movement with the governance of the province as its goal. Aberhart announced in December of 1934 that in the next election "reliable, honourable, bribe-proof businessmen who have definitely laid aside their party political affiliations, will be asked to represent Social Credit in every constituency."

Aberhart's announcement was a significant revelation because it showed his conception of the political undertaking as a non-partisan crusade. Rather than a new political party in the conventional sense, Aberhart intended to strike a holy alliance of all right-thinking Albertans to purge the province of the political professionals, raise the standard of public morality, and bring about recovery. The UFA had been given their chance, but they had thrown it away. Now it was time for "reliable, honourable, bribe-proof businessmen" to succeed where lesser mortals had faltered.

Once Aberhart bent his sails toward the winning of political power, he dropped the style of the evangelist teacher and pressed that of the evangelist reformer. Motives and intended results were stressed more than the details of the "*A* plus *B* theorem" or other doctrinal niceties: "You don't have to know all about Social Credit before you vote for it." He urged his followers to have faith and trust in the authorities. Reasoning by analogy, Aberhart suggested that "you don't have to understand electricity to use it, for you know that the experts have put the system in, and all you have to do is push the button and you get the light." So also with political decision-making: "all you have to do about Social Credit is to cast your vote for it, and we will get the experts to put the system in."

Many people felt that "Bible Bill" would not knowingly deceive them. He was an authority they could trust. Others, the ones who decided to read his pamphlet, the *Social Credit Manual,* discovered that there were even more attractions than the economic promise. They found a wonderful instrument for abolishing poverty without compromising the purity of nineteenth-century morality. Every adult was going to receive a monthly $25 dividend, but any citizen who "persisted in refusing work" would have his dividends "cut off or temporarily suspended." Thus, the social credits were not going to become a subsidy to laziness. On the contrary, they would be useful incentives for enforcing middle-class standards of propriety. Any person who "squandered his dividends . . . or was improperly clothed" would first receive a warning from his inspector; that person would have to reform his habits and shine his shoes "or he would lose his dividends." In this manner, standards of morality would gain a powerful economic sanction to bolster the informal power of the frown of "right-thinking" neighbors.

The end of poverty without repudiating capitalism and a greater conformity to the old standards of manners and morals were promised within eighteen months of the election. For some Albertans the soft totalitarianism in Social Credit was the determinative attraction. For others, it was the $25 per month. For still more, Aberhart was simply an attractive novelty. Whatever the precise combination of motives, the electorate awarded a stunning majority to Aberhart's businessmen on August 22. Nearly 90 percent of the seats went to Social Credit candidates. And two months later in the federal election, Alberta returned a similar proportion of Social Credit members to Ottawa.

On the morning of August 23, a number of people lined up at Calgary city hall for their first $25 dividend. But it was not forthcoming then or later. By 1936 Aberhart was ready to regret that he had ever heard of Major C. H. Douglas and his "impractical" theories. "Bible Bill" had discovered that there was simply no way to follow the advice of Douglas without simultaneously freezing prices and repudiating the existing debt of the province. This Aberhart considered immoral. But there were a number of insurgents in "his" legislature who demanded a trial of social dividends. Thus emerged the Alberta Social Credit Act in 1937, which provided dividends to the amount of "the unused capacity of industries and people." Later in the year, a variety of other such measures followed. But since most of them pertained to banking, an area beyond provincial jurisdiction, this spurt of Social Credit legislation was subsequently disallowed by Ottawa before it was implemented. What carried permanence was fiscal orthodoxy and Protestant fundamentalism. On this basis, in the words of Aberhart's chief lieutenant and eventual successor, E. C. Manning, Social Credit provided Alberta with "one of the most genuinely conservative governments in Canada."

IV. The Restoration Theme in Quebec and Ontario

Conservatism in the sense of aiming to restore and preserve a pre-1929 status quo was the main emphasis of other provincial governments that came to power at the same time as Aberhart's. Quebec and Ontario, two provinces that included sixty percent of the country's people, provided variations of the restoration theme that were even more striking than the Alberta case. In Quebec, the province in which social strife was ethnic as much as economic, the impulse to escape the Depression by restoring the simplicity of the vanishing past gave rise to a pattern of resentment that was nationalist more than reformist. In 1935 dissident Liberals and Conservatives joined forces to resurrect Mercier's idea of the Union Nationale, a party with no pretensions beyond Quebec and no program other than that of being the government of the people rather than of the "trusts": a government that would fight nepotism, patronage, and corruption, but without specifying anything in the way of concrete social welfare legislation or the nationalization of objectionable firms. Once in office in 1936, it was therefore easy for the new premier, Maurice Duplessis, to sail his own course without nationalizing Quebec Hydro—as some had expected—or furthering any other program for social democracy. On the contary, Duplessis proved to be as good a friend of free enterprise as any businessman could want. The premier spent a good deal of money promoting agricultural settlement in keeping with the theme that "our salvation is rooted to the soil." But, also consistent with the idea that "we must sow or go jobless, our people will be agricultural or perish," Duplessis turned his back on the problems of the urban poor, especially the suffering unemployed in Montreal, then Canada's largest city.

From another point of view it could be argued that the Union Nationale paid a great deal of attention to the urban proletariat by saving them from "godless socialism." In 1937 Quebec's legislature passed an "Act Respecting Communistic Propaganda," a measure that empowered the police to lock up any establishment used for "propagating Communism or Bolshevism," terms that were left to be defined by the discretion of enforcing officers. Defenders of Duplessis could say that "happy are the people who have found their dictator" and no "right-thinking" persons had anything to fear from the laws on sedition, but civil libertarians could counter that Quebec's "Padlock Law" was one more element in a growing pattern of thought control. People were being prosecuted for the content of their ideas rather than for the violence of their behavior. But authoritarians prevailed.

At the same time that the Padlock Law was instituted in Quebec, the government of Ontario moved with similar zeal against organized labor there. Mitchell Hepburn's government, like that of Maurice Duplessis, was ostensibly populist, that is, the party of the people versus the interests. When "Mitch" (as he liked people to call him) campaigned as the new leader of the provincial Liberal party in 1934 he posed a neat dichotomy of "little guys" versus "big shots." The people whom he hoped to advance were still businessmen however. He would make Ontario safe for small producers by toppling tycoons who were accused of owning and operating government as their own private arena. Thus, addressing one typical audience, a group of dairymen, Hepburn implied that the ordinary people had to live by one set of rules but the "big shots" lived by another. "If any of you farmers water your milk you go to jail. But if you water your stock you get to be Premier of Ontario." Mitch said he would change that as soon as he was in charge.

Hepburn was not elected to make it legal for dairies to water milk, but a dismantling operation of government was expected and in several superficial ways did follow. The new premier auctioned off some government limousines. He fired all the civil servants who had been hired in the preceding year and reduced the salaries of the rest. Hepburn cancelled some contracts with hydroelectric companies. But there was little in this or the other dynamism beyond bluster. There was certainly no constructive sympathy for organized labor, a movement that was now beginning to struggle back from its decline of the previous five years.

As a matter of fact, Hepburn turned on the new-found militancy of the unions with the enthusiasm of a prophet who had found the one great flaw that needed mending. The specific episode that provoked Hepburn's vengeance was the contest that developed between the newly formed CIO and the well-established firm of General Motors. Both were American organizations, one a recent and militant affiliation of industrial unions, the other a branch-plant auto maker. But when a labor dispute began in Oshawa over management's refusal to recognize the connection of the United Auto Workers with the CIO, Hepburn came to the side of General Motors in the name of Canadian nationalism. He said that Canada's troubles had never been as bad as outside agitators had made them seem, and he would not tolerate sit-down strikes in Ontario. Then, despite assurances from the leaders of the union and the mayor of Oshawa that there would be neither sit-down occupation of the plants nor violence at the gates (as had occurred at Detroit), Hepburn requested a battalion of RCMP from Ottawa and recruited four hundred of his own special police, soon called "Hepburn's Hussars." Thus, in Ontario, as in much of the rest of the country, the specter of radical action prompted repression; in this case, it was repression of a crisis that did not even exist.

V. Ten Lost Years

Here, then, were some of the more striking aspects of Canada's responses to the Great Depression. It was a period of hardship that generated enormous concern. But the flamboyant characters who commanded the greatest popularity had two attributes in common: they all saw the economic crisis as a temporary setback in the development of capitalism, and believed that no recovery could be valid or permanent if it violated the fundamentals of possessive individualism. The dissenters from this opinion were a minority without a hope of gaining power so long as paranoid fear, which was a function of hard times, held Canadians in its icy grip. The radical leaders of the 1920s not only lost ground in the 1930s, some even lost their freedom. The period was a time when Canadians had to confront the structure of their society and the role of their institutions. Especially did the unemployed have to think about unemployment. Some of them reasoned their way to radical criticism. But there were people who were never unemployed, and, although they were not unaffected by the crisis, they preferred to escape into the wonderful world of Walt Disney's *Snow White and the Seven Dwarfs* and Hollywood musicals, or radio entertainments. Most Canadians remained "right-thinking" people who hoped for a return of the good old days, even though the old days had not been particularly good nor were they particularly easy to recover. Everywhere but on the silver screen, the past was irretrievably *Gone With the Wind*.

CHAPTER TWENTY

Recovery by War

I. Mobilization

Although the economic crisis of the 1930s made Canadians more acutely aware of the insecurities of life in an industrial society, most people continued to think that an individual's privation or prosperity was his own responsibility. Thus, there was no majority opinion in favor of public insurance against unemployment or ill health. Nor was much credence given to the view that public spending was an appropriate means of controlling the fluctuations of the business cycle. Between 1930 and 1937, the interesting legislation pertained to banking, broadcasting and transportation—the creation of the Bank of Canada, of the Canadian Broadcasting Corporation, and of a national airline—not social welfare.

Mackenzie King kept his promise of "no precipitate action." This meant no structural reform and no extravagant spending. In keeping with both objectives, the Bennett New Deal, repudiated at the polls, was now referred to the courts. At the same time, a National Employment Commission was formed to find means of reducing the level of relief payments to the provinces. The law officers reported first. They reaffirmed the principle that social welfare was a matter of provincial jurisdiction and therefore Bennett's program was entirely unconstitutional. In lieu of constitutional change, King practised more politics of evasion by appointing another commission—this one headed by N. W. Rowell and Joseph Sirois—to examine "the economic and financial basis of confederation and the distribution of legislative powers in light of the economic and social developments of the last seventy years," a project that would take more than a few months, perhaps years, given the magnitude of its scope.

Unfortunately for King, the National Employment Commission issued recommendations that could not wait on the Rowell-Sirois Report. They had cut themselves loose from traditional economic theory and espoused the remedies of John Maynard Keynes. Rather than balancing the budget and maintaining pre-Depression levels of taxation, they urged tax cuts and large budget deficits on the assumption that a modern government should concern itself primarily with balancing the whole economy rather than with expenditures and revenues. They argued that the level of investment was the prime determinant of employment, and therefore a wise government should spend more when private investors invested less. This was pure Keynes, and the repercussions of the recommendation created a bad split in the cabinet over the estimates for the budget of 1938.

Norman Rogers, the minister of labour, supported the Employment Commissioners' recommendations, asserting that there should be a minimum of $40 million invested in public works. Furthermore, Rogers threatened to resign if this course of action was not followed. But Charles Dunning, the minister of finance, was equally dogmatic in his defense of traditional theory, which demanded a balanced budget with a nice surplus. With these two ministers each threatening to quit if his own will did not prevail, others took sides and Mackenzie King faced a real crisis, which he resolved in the manner of Solomon. The demand for $40 million was cut in half. Rogers received $25 million to spend in the way that the unemployment commission recommended. Thus, there would be a deficit, but not enough to make Dunning and his side feel utterly defeated.

The budget compromise of 1938 emerged as a clear step in the direction away from tradition; according to H. B. Neatby, "it was the most radical and most constructive innovation of that depression decade." But the drift toward deficit spending for recovery purposes was soon swallowed up in even greater borrowing for an infinitely vaster, more startling emergency—that of World War II.

Canada's participation in the war from September of 1939 was somewhat anomalous until the summer of 1943. As a matter of declared policy, the country's liability was "limited." From the outset, the prime minister promised that no "great expeditionary forces of infantry" would be sent across the Atlantic as in the Great War before. It was hoped—and expected—that the Allies in this struggle would make use of Canada's food and industrial resources more than her manpower. Still, the government of Canada asked its citizenry to mobilize completely. Labor was directed by the Department of Munitions and Supply to essential industries, and what was left over went to the military. The anomaly was organization for total war, but commitment of troops on a limited basis only. Canada had approximately the same percentage of the population in uniform as did Britain and, eventually, the United States, but a significantly smaller percentage of Canada's forces were committed to combat. The bulk of the army spent most of the war in England, as a "dagger pointed at the heart of Berlin," according to their commander, Major General McNaughton. But this was a dagger drawn rather than a weapon blooded. They trained and trained while the fighting went on elsewhere.

In the first several years of the war, Canadian combat personnel were to be seen most frequently in the air or escorting convoys across the Atlantic Ocean. The two major exceptions were the nearly 2 000 infantrymen killed or captured in the defense of Hong Kong late in 1941 and a similar number who met the same fate in the reconnaissance raid on Dieppe in August of 1942. Thus, Canada had mobilized for a total war, but without fighting accordingly. And there were complaints that this was the case. Former Prime Minister Bennett, for one, complained that there was "no good reason why the Canadian army should have to spend its fourth Christmas in Britain without firing a shot." In his opinion, the avoidance of slaughter to avoid conscription was the only explanation.

But it reflected the way Canada's participation in World War II was orchestrated by politicians to serve domestic ends before declared military objectives. On the federal level, World War II offered Mackenzie King a climate of expediency to further the economic recovery that had evaded Bennett and King in the decade before. The limited liability war was the ideal occasion for forcing centralization and needed reforms.

The first illustration of this tendency came within weeks of the war's declaration. Maurice Duplessis, the Quebec premier who fought the Depression by promoting French Canadian nationalism, led his followers to the polls in the autumn of 1939 with reminders of what had happened in the previous war. The King government pounced on this as a boycott of the war before it had even begun. Then they threatened the electorate with blackmail. Ernest Lapointe, P. J. A. Cardin, and Chubby Power all threatened to resign if the Union Nationale were returned. On the other hand, if the voters elected Adelard Godbout's Liberals—advocates more than opponents of centralism—they promised to remain in Ottawa to defeat conscription. The people of Quebec were thus presented with the difficult choice of Duplessis and conscription or centralization but limited liability. Duplessis was defeated and a major obstacle to centralizing reform was eliminated.

This episode was followed by another of a similar character when the Rowell-Sirois Commission issued its report in 1940. Its findings were completely consistent with those of the National Employment Commission, the recommendations of which had created such a furore in cabinet over the budget of 1938. But the Rowell-Sirois commissioners made recommendations more sweeping in scope—given their much broader mandate for investigation. They recommended, for example, that the central government should assume *full* responsibility for unemployment compensation in order to ensure a uniform standard of relief in every province. Since this responsibility would cost a great deal, they recommended that the provinces should surrender the *full* power of direct taxation, and Ottawa, in turn, should transfer back to them sufficient funds to maintain their other administrative and social services. Thus, the provinces would retain control over cultural, civil, and educational matters but in other respects would become no more than the administrative districts of the unitary state that some Fathers of Confederation had wished to create in 1867.

The unity that the Rowell-Sirois commissioners recommended in 1940, however, was no more spontaneous in 1940-41 than in 1867. Still, just as war justified the imposition of one code of military discipline and one language, English, upon the personnel at military bases, so also was the wartime emergency found useful in circumventing the disappointing discussions of the Rowell-Sirois Report, which broke down after only three days of dialogue between provincial premiers and the prime minister early in 1941. The minister of finance, J. L. Ilsley simply implemented the direct-taxation recommendation—provincial objections notwithstanding. Federal, corporate and personal income taxes were raised to such levels that no province would dare to superimpose its own taxation. Then Ilsley turned around and offered the premiers two kinds of compensation: a province might either receive back from Ottawa the amount collected in direct taxation the year before, or claim an amount sufficient to pay the net cost of servicing the provincial debt plus a special subsidy. Thus, the first taxation rental agreement was not negotiated settlement, but a federal imposition with the provinces settling for what they were given rather than what they demanded. The consolation to objecting premiers was the knowledge that the central government's monopolization of direct taxation was temporary, for it was supposed to terminate one year after the war's end.

The recommendation regarding unemployment compensation was ushered in through the back door with similar dispatch. The BNA Act would have to be amended as the first step; without any fanfare, amendment was requested and granted. This achieved, the appropriate legislation went through the Canadian Parliament without fuss. Here again the war proved to be a wonderful cover for implementing changes which had been impossible in peacetime. People were now back at work, organized labor was gaining momentum, and now that the nation's program for recovery was equipping the armed forces, King's government had more to fear from a half-million organized workers than from a handful of disgruntled, ineffectual premiers.

II. Left Turn

Reform and recovery were proving embarrassingly simple. Between 1939 and 1941 the government of Canada started spending more than ever before. The GNP increased 47 percent as the output of primary commodities doubled and levels of secondary manufacturing trebled. Not surprisingly, unemployment was reduced; by 1941 it was a mere four percent of the work force. The federal government, which had spent $322 million for relief programs during the period between 1930 and 1939, was now spending that much in an average month between 1941 and 1943. Thanks to the war, an industrial worker in 1941 was earning twice as much as in 1939. He was twice as likely to be a member of a union. And should he suffer the misfortune of a layoff, his earnings were partially insured.

The war bonanza seemed to provide the proof that a modern government could orchestrate the peaks and troughs out of the business cycle. There was full employment, controls on prices dampened inflation, and rationing moderated scarcities in such commodities as gasoline and tires. There was also a kind of austerity which followed from shortages of imported liquor and cotton for clothing. But these privations affected everyone, not just the jobless as in the Depression. The important point was the efficiency with which government took control of collective resources and managed them competently for the shared goal of victory. Naturally, many people came to the conclusion that if a country could spend billions fighting wars and plan the economy for the good of that cause, the same bureaucracy could also control production to ensure peacetime prosperity and promote the general welfare by other programs as well as unemployment insurance.

There were dramatic indicators that this opinion had grown to major proportions as early as 1942. Gallup polls showed an inexorable tendency toward a neat three-way split in public opinion between the CCF and the two older parties. Also in 1942, the leader of the Conservatives was defeated by a socialist. The loser, none other than Arthur Meighen, had inherited the Conservative leadership shortly after the war began, even though he had no seat in the House of Commons. Now, as he attempted to remedy this deficiency in York South, Meighen was attacked as a defender of predatory capitalism and was repudiated in the Ontario riding he thought he could win. Meighen's defeat gave him new thoughts about the Canada of the future. He predicted that subsequent contests would place socialists against Liberals with Conservatives running a distant third unless Canadian Conservatives transformed theirs into a farmers' party with its power base in the West. For this reason, Meighen resigned and threw his influence behind the premier of Manitoba as the person most likely to succeed in this mission.

Meighen's announcement of retirement and the prospect of the Conservative party becoming no more than a western protest movement provoked some eastern Conservatives into a pre-convention meeting to discuss other alternatives. At Port Hope, a gathering of "progressive" Conservatives reaffirmed their faith in free enterprise, but mapped out a program of reforms they believed were essential to ensure every Canadian "a gainful occupation and sufficient income to maintain himself and a family." More specifically, the "Port Hopefuls" endorsed the scheme for unemployment compensation, which had recently passed the House of Commons, and called for more "social legislation" in such areas as low-cost housing, collective bargaining, and medical care.

In a matter of weeks this new eastern conservatism was being proclaimed by the premier of Manitoba, the star in the West that Arthur Meighen wanted for the leadership of the party because of his remarkable staying power. John Bracken was the one pre-Depression premier who had weathered the pitfalls of Depression politics successfully—quite a recommendation. The party dutifully gathered in Winnipeg to appoint Bracken leader. But the heir apparent considered himself a Progressive rather than a Conservative and stipulated conditions for his accepting conversion: the Conservatives had to espouse a program of innovations, and the party would have to change its name. Some of the faithful recoiled from both. But Meighen's will would be done, and so, late in 1942, the Port Hopefuls found their proposals adopted by the party at large, now renamed the Progressive-Conservative Party.

III.   A Comprehensive Strategy

The leftward swing of public opinion, Meighen's defeat in York South, the emergence of "Progresssive-Conservatism," and two other influences prompted Mackenzie King to move his Liberals in the same direction. The two other incentives were external factors, one British and the other American. The British influence was a plan for postwar social reconstruction that the government commissioned from Sir William Beveridge. The Beveridge Report recommended a complete system of public insurance to protect all aspects of Britons' health, employment, and retirement "from the cradle to the grave."

A nice reaction to this scheme was set forth in the following poem by Sir Alan Herbert in the humorous London weekly, *Punch*:

"Oh, won't it be wonderful after the war—
There won't be no war, and there won't be no pore.

There won't be no sick, and there won't be no sore,
And we shan't have to work, if we find it a bore . . . .
Now there's only one question I'd like to explore:
Why didn't we have the old war before?"

On the one hand Herbert seemed to pour scorn on the notion, but on the other it could be read as a serious indictment of ossified thinking.

Since the public was so manifestly receptive, Mackenzie King received the Beveridge Report as an echo of his own plans. In 1918 he had published a book, *Industry and Humanity*, which King believed to contain "pretty much the whole program that now is being suggested for post-war purposes." The only reason he had not pressed to enact it earlier was that he was just too far ahead of his time, he thought. But now history was catching up with him.

The clincher in making up King's mind to push social welfare legislation was the American rather than the British impetus, resulting from a conversation he had with the American President in December of 1942. Somehow these two old political pros wandered onto the subject of the probable future of postwar domestic politics, and Roosevelt speculated that "The thought of insurance from the cradle to the grave . . . seems to be a line that will appeal." Then, as one pro to another, FDR intimated that "You and I should take that up strongly."

Within a matter of weeks, Mackenzie King was back in Canada presenting Parliament with a "charter of social security for the whole of Canada." Leonard Marsh, a McGill University sociology professor and one of the founders of the CCF, was hired to write a Beveridge Report for Canadians. In addition to the usual on medical insurance, old-age security, etc., there was something called a family allowance, a plan to provide direct cash payments to individuals of so much per child in the same way that subsidies had once been paid to provinces on a per capita basis. But this was to families. King winced at the "sheer folly" of seriously proposing the idea "that everyone was to get a family allowance." But the rest of the program was interesting; after the war, with FDR, he would take it up strongly.

But postponement looked increasingly dangerous in 1943. The Ontario leader of the Conservatives, George Drew, promised his own version of "economic and social security from the cradle to the grave" and reduced Hepburn's Liberals to the status of a splinter party in the election in August. The CCF's version of the welfare state was nearly as popular as Drew's: Ontario's socialists won 34 to the Conservatives' 38 seats.

King responded to this manifest popularity of "social legislation" by creating three new federal ministries which pertained to the government's intended role as alternate provider. The most conspicuous was a Ministry of National Health and Welfare. But King still hesitated to push the spec-

ific legislation which would give substance as well as form to the Canadian welfare state. The problem was where to begin. At first King favored the plan for national health insurance. But unlike the institution of unemployment compensation, which was simply a program for making direct payment to the unemployed, the health plan supposed an apparatus for providing a service, and therefore cooperation from the provinces was needed. This meant negotiation and controversy. King dreaded both. Similarly, other projects were ruled out one by one for the same reason. The family allowances program was the only social welfare innovation that did not require provincial cooperation.

The family allowances project caught King's fancy for other reasons as well. The allowance was to be paid on a per child basis, and therefore the provinces with the highest birth rates would be the greatest beneficiaries. Since the reproductory prowess of French Canadians was then legendary, and since this province had the population to elect or defeat more than one fourth of the Parliament in Ottawa, and finally, since Quebec was a province whose Liberalism might soon be severely tested, the family allowances scheme was just the palliative King could use to win the next federal election.

There were two major sources for Quebeckers' uneasiness with Ottawa. One was the general drift toward centralization which ran apace with wartime controls. But the other, and by far the greater source of discontent, was the continuing threat of conscription especially now following heavy infantry losses in Italy and the high casualties which attended the invasion of France after D-Day, the sixth of June, 1944.

Although the end of the war was now in view, and the country could afford to relax its stringent limitation upon infantry commitments, once committed it would be difficult to withdraw those forces simply because casualties were mounting. In this way, conscription might be "necessary" even at the eleventh hour. If that did occur a chain of promises extending back to 1939 would collapse: federal ministers had promised to oppose conscription to their last breath for the defeat of Duplessis in 1939; the party as a whole reaffirmed that pledge in a general election of 1940; and, when public opinion seemed to warrant a reversal of that stance, a plebiscite was taken in the spring of 1942 asking Quebec and the other provinces for a release from the pledge of no-conscription in 1940. The results were mixed. The plebiscite showed that nearly 73 percent of Quebeckers still refused to accept conscription, and a similar percentage of English-speaking Canadians voted the other way. Here was a reconfirmation of the need for limited liability. Consequently, the government refused to conscript anyone else for overseas duty. At the same time, King warned there might be conscription later if "necessary." In the summer of 1944, although he was still determined to avoid a conscription crisis, events were running ahead of policy.

Still, the development which was more immediately important in making the Liberals move quickly with social legislation was a sudden indication that the CCF—unusually popular since 1942—might soon capture one government after another if their policies were not taken over by one of the older parties. Shortly after D-Day, they came to power in Saskatchewan; one month later King introduced the family allowances scheme in Ottawa. The Opposition—especially the Conservatives—was cornered. To oppose this measure was to deny commitment to welfare. But to approve the bill would virtually guarantee the Liberals' reelection. On one line the Progressive-Conservatives therefore asserted, with John Diefenbaker, that "we believe in social legislation . . . . No political party has a monopoly in that direction." But on another line, thinking of their already weak position in Quebec for their long-apparent covert advocacy of conscription, Bracken was particularly galled that King might impose it himself later and with a "baby bonus" as compensation thereby retain his popularity. Bracken called the family allowance "legal bribery." And other Conservatives advertised this point even more bluntly. Herbert Bruce called it "a bribe of the most brazen character, made chiefly to one province and paid for by the taxes of the rest". But whether the others who received the cheques cashed them in Quebec or Alberta, the family allowances plan was a subsidy to motherhood, and this was another reason why it was embarrassing to oppose the scheme with any real force. Consequently, three days after the bill was introduced it passed second reading without dissent. Herbert Bruce was absent that day. The family allowances bill passed unanimously.

IV.   Right Turn

The principle of old-age pensions had been enacted in 1927; unemployment insurance was adopted in principle in 1940; now there was statutory recognition of the idea of subsidizing the incomes of householders because they had children to support. There was more social welfare legislation to follow, of course. And it should also be said that each of the programs through 1944 was partial, only a shadow of the boastful promise to provide "social security from the cradle to the grave." But the important fact by 1944 was the universal acceptance of the notion that a country owed its citizens a living. John Diefenbaker was exactly correct in the family allowances debate when he protested that no party was alone on social legislation.

The embrace of the welfare state by all parties represented a return to consensus politics. In the 1920s and 1930s the political establishment had polarized into "old line" and reform groups. It was only the pragmatism of their leaders and the widespread indifference of the electorate that prevented the functional disintegration of the two old parties from spilling over into a more general upset of society at large. By 1942, however, the voting public seemed massively in favor of "social legislation" and the two older parties leaned left to incorporate moderate elements of the CCF platform. At the same time—and this is the irony of the war years—Canada's major socialist party moved right in the expectation that a leftward leaning public would turn even more enthusiastically in their direction if the CCF dropped the rhetoric for "eradicating capitalism" and spoke instead the softer tones of promoting the welfare state. But when the voters were confronted with these alternatives in the federal election of 1945, the unfamiliar faces on either side of Mackenzie King were shunned. The CCF received only 16 percent of the vote; Progressive Conservatives, 27 percent. Thus, the Liberals were returned with a majority government, and King's charter of cradle to grave social security was shelved away and temporarily forgotten as Canadians returned from the war and embarked upon the biggest spending spree in their history.

PART SIX

New Dimensions to Old Dilemmas

CHAPTER TWENTY ONE

Continental Solidarity

I. A New Relationship with Uncle Sam

World War II prompted the implementation of social welfare programs, welcomed by many as "social progress". Paradoxically, at the same time changes occurred which transformed Canada's international status from that of an independent country into a satellite of the United States. This trade of sovereignty for security could be interpreted as a colossal regression, a "return to colonial status," were it not for the anxiety Canadians felt about the "Nazi threat" first and the "communist menace" later. In this light, diminishing sovereignty could be seen as a necessity as much as a reality.

The reduction of autonomy in exchange for greater security was made all the more painful by two additional facts: the security obtained in a world of balanced terror was more illusory than real; previously Canadians had prided themselves on being at the forefront of that development which had transformed the British *Empire* into the *Commonwealth*. They were leaders, in other words, among the colonies who won their independence without war. Between 1914 and 1918 the Canadian prime minister, Sir Robert Borden, had insisted that the Imperial War Conference of World War I change its nature to recognize the constituent members as the equals, rather than the subordinates, of Britain. It was Borden again who, at the peace talks in Paris, had led in the campaign to have the Dominions sign the treaties in their own right. And it was Borden's successor, Meighen, who played the leading role at the Imperial Conference of 1921, which resulted in Britain abandoning negotiations for the renewal of a treaty with Japan that dated from 1902 and was a pact between countries as empires.

Nor were the Liberals less hesitant in urging Canadian autonomy. It was under Mackenzie King that the Chanack incident took place in 1922. In that year a clash between Turkey and Greece in Asia Minor threatened to provoke British intervention, and Britain simply assumed, as in 1914, that Canada would automatically become involved. King decided otherwise and let it be known that his country saw no reason for involvement. A year later autonomy went one degree further when Canada signed the Halibut Treaty with the United States without any imperial input at all. And by 1927 an independent Canadian diplomatic presence had been established in Washington as a first step toward making this link with the world at large.

Such initiatives were not unacceptable to the mother country. In 1926, in the wake of the King-Byng affair, the Imperial Conference produced the Balfour Report, in which the Dominions were defined as "autonomous communities . . . , equal in status, in no way subordinate one to another in any aspect of their domestic or external affairs . . . ". As if this were not sufficient declaration of independence that principle was embodied in law in 1931 by the Statute of Westminster. Thus, Canada and the other autonomous Dominions won their right to an independent foreign policy, having already established their right to independence in every other regard.

As the likelihood of a second world war loomed, Mackenzie King used this Canadian autonomy to avoid "entanglements". He disliked commitments, particularly those that could lead to foreign war, and made it clear that in any future British conflict Canada would be "at Britain's side" but not necessarily in the trenches. This became especially clear by 1937 and 1938. In anticipation of possible war the British tried to persuade Canada to launch a joint program for training aviators, but King refused the proposal in 1938. In January of 1939, Mackenzie King acknowledged only a formal liability if the British were to find themselves entangled in another struggle with Germany. The Canadian prime minister meant to imply passive belligerence, not participation as a principal, as in the 1914 war. It came as no surprise, therefore, that Canada hesitated before joining Britain and France when they declared war on Germany on September 3, 1939.

Four days elapsed before the Canadian Parliament convened to debate a war resolution of their own. When Parliament did agree to participate, King announced it would be Canada's policy to provide "effective co-operation" within stated limits. The primary effort would be home defense. There was no intention of immediately sending a Canadian expeditionary force, and under no circumstances would there be conscription for duty overseas.

Soon, however, Canada's liability was extended. Responding to popular pressure for greater involvement, King announced on September 16 that one division would be sent to England. Later, on December 17, he announced the program that was supposed to be Canada's major contribution to the war. This was the British Commonwealth Air Training Plan, the scheme King had rejected in 1938.

Clearly, Canada was going into this war with none of the flair with which the country had plunged into the previous struggle. As was shown in the previous chapter, the war was useful in bringing about economic recovery. But for some, the lack of a more robust militarism was regrettable, even cowardly. One such critic was Mitchell Hepburn, the premier of Ontario, who thought he was acting for the vast majority of the country when he moved his legislature in January to condemn the central government for not taking part in "the vigorous manner the people of Canada desire to see." But an election would tell for sure. Parliament was dissolved on January 25, 1940, and the nineteenth general election unfolded as a plebiscite on King's policy of limited liability. To Hepburn's surprise, the electorate confirmed King's rather than the Opposition's position. There would be no participation as a principal; no repeat of the 1914 war. The Liberals won 52 percent of the popular vote, three quarters of the seats in Parliament.

Then, within months of this election, the complexion of the war—for countries other than Canada—changed dramatically. The "Phoney War", during which few hostile acts had taken place in Western Europe, was suddenly succeeded by the *Blitzkrieg*, the total collapse of France, and the evacuation of the British Army from Dunkirk. German bombs rained down upon British cities, and it did not seem that the embattled island could withstand the barrage for long. There was a widely held expectation of British defeat, and it was against this background that Canada became increasingly receptive to the United States. In August of 1940, President Roosevelt telephoned Mackenzie King and arranged a meeting in Roosevelt's private railway car on a siding in the village of Ogdensburg, New York. In that one meeting on December 17 the two chiefs announced they had agreed to form a Joint Board on Defence for North America. The purpose was supposed to be self-evident so none was specified. Similarly, since it was so manifestly advantageous for the defense of the whole continent now and forever, its duration was also left open.

Despite the informality of its inception, the Ogdensburg Agreement was of momentous importance. According to Donald Creighton, this single step taken by a Canadian prime minister without consultation with cabinet or consent of Parliament "effectively bound Canada to a continental system and largely determined Canadian foreign and defence policy for the next thirty years."

The crisis atmosphere of the summer of 1940 seemed to warrant such a consolidation, however. And the Ogdensburg Declaration was only the first of other such agreements to follow. In fact, less than one year later—but still before the United States entered the war actively—there was another accord between King and Roosevelt that was just as sweeping, this one to cover economic consolidation. This Hyde Park Declaration of April, 1941, was the economic corollary to the Ogdensburg Agreement because it stated that "each country should provide the other with the defence articles which it is best able to produce." By this means, American arms producers could bid on Canadian contracts just as if they were firms in Canada, and Canadians could provide "certain kinds of munitions, strategic materials, aluminum, and ships" for the Pentagon with the privileged access accorded to no "foreign" country. For the purposes of defense production, King and Roosevelt agreed to pretend that the border between the two countries simply did not exist. In effect, Mackenzie King was elevated to the status of Governor of an American state.

The analogy became only too bitterly evident to King once the United States entered the war as an active belligerent after December, 1941. Churchill and Roosevelt agreed that they should direct the struggle, making occasional consultative gestures toward Russia, France, and China. But the governors of American states and the prime minister of Canada were not included in the strategic direction of the war. In international politics, North America was a unity, not an alliance. Canada was treated as a subordinate more than an autonomous country, and Canadians themselves began to speak of "our leaders, Churchill and the President."

Mackenzie King made pathetic gestures in the direction of trying to reassert Canadian independence but they were more theatrical than real. Thus, there was a conference at Quebec in 1943 with the flags of the three attending heads of government all flying side by side. Churchill, Roosevelt, and King were photographed as a controlling threesome. But insofar as any conferring occurred, it involved only the American and British leaders, not the Canadian. King's role was that of a person "who has lent his house for a party. The guests take hardly any notice of him, but just before leaving they remember he is their host and say pleasant things." Still, the meeting was "good theatre" and King was well satisfied that a second such exercise would be "quite sufficient to make clear that all three are in conference together." The show was repeated in 1944. There was no need for a third performance. By the spring of 1945, the war was over in Europe. In the summer, American atomic bombs—with plutonium refined from Canadian uranium—ended the struggle in the Pacific.

II.   A Bolder Repression of Minorities

Canadians emerged from the war seeing themselves as having become "a power in the world." In the Great War they had won their image of independence; now they had won esteem as a country of considerable strength. With only 11.5 million people they had produced a convoy escort service that was the world's third largest navy. At the same time, Canada had also built up the fourth largest air force. Both of these facts were a source of great self-satisfaction—especially to English-speaking Canadians. Another source of satisfaction was the relatively lighter losses in this struggle than in the previous war. In round numbers, 17 000 Canadian airmen had died in combat. The army lost 22 000; the navy 2 000. For a country of nearly twelve million people these losses were not large: about one third of one percent of the population overall.

There were losses on a larger scale that are not included in the numbers killed in combat. Nor were these injuries inflicted by the enemy. Perhaps the best illustration of the self-inflicted wounds of World War II was what happened to Canadians of Japanese descent. For generations, the people of British Columbia had been looking for a means of eliminating "orientals." Asian newcomers were the objects of mob violence in the nineteenth century, and legal discrimination in the twentieth. First, there were immigration restrictions, and for those already in the country—ostensibly Canadian—there was a denial of basic civil rights such as the right to vote. But when racism became patriotic in the war against Japan a golden opportunity was seized upon for the complete elimination of the hated Japanese minority. The first steps toward that goal were almost reasonable. Thirty-eight persons suspected of being potential subversives were arrested by the RCMP—"internment" was the euphemism for their detention. Such confinement was completely legal under the War Measures Act. Also, their arrest was understandable given the dossier on each person that was compiled before his arrest. But local politicians, supported by constituents, went to Ottawa demanding a general detention of all "Japs." The army hesitated. Of the 22 096 people of Japanese origin in Canada, 13 309 were Canadians and *most* of the total number were women and children. The Chief of General Staff, Ken Stuart, opposed their detention, saying "I cannot see that they constitute the slightest menace to national security." The RCMP agreed. Nor did the navy see any threat once all persons of Japanese ethnicity were barred from fishing. But political use of racist extremism prevailed. Beginning in January of 1942, under the authority of the War Measures Act, which permitted discretionary "arrest, detention, exclusion and deportation," the "evacuation" began. Subsequently, almost twenty thousand people lost all their property and their freedom, and found their families broken up for no other reason than race. The situation did not ease appreciably even as the war was ending. In the spring of 1945, the detainees were given the choice of settling "east of the Rockies" or of "repatriation" to Japan. They were told they could not return to British Columbia. Almost half chose expulsion. Douglas and Greenhous, two historians of World War II, suggest "Their decision was based on fifty years of prejudice, the 1942 evacuation, and the current plan for post-war resettlement outside of British Columbia, which portended the same prejudicial treatment that had marked their life in Canada to the present."

Later, British Columbians paid a measure of penance in recognition of their longstanding racism. Reparations for confiscated property were offered to owners who had the stamina to go through the elaborate procedures which were stipulated for processing claims. In 1949, their exclusion was lifted by inclusion in the franchise. In this way, a kind of truce was offered—four years after the war had ended abroad.

No such settlement occurred after another episode of self-inflicted injury—an internal conflict between the founding nationalities. This was a conscription crisis, an event the prime minister had avoided through the summer of 1944. But in September of that year, Conn Smyth, a hockey hero and an army officer, returned home to Toronto to convalesce from combat injuries; newspapers reported the event as an important human interest story. They also printed Major Smyth's opinions on why he and so many others were getting wounded. He said the General Service troops were being reinforced by volunteers with very little training, and claimed that "large numbers of unnecessary casualties result from this greenness, both to the rookie and to the older soldiers who have the added task of trying to look after the newcomers as well as themselves." There were soldiers with more training who were not used as reinforcements because they were NRMA men—troops recruited since 1940 under the provisions of the National Resources Mobilization Act. These men were halfway conscripts in the sense that they were not volunteers, but were still not members of the active service in every respect since they were legally exempt from duty outside the Western Hemisphere. The NRMA men were literally the home guard. Since this front was in little danger by 1944, the NRMA people were regarded as the real-world embodiment of the Hollywood characters who were less than fully alive. Morally superior English-speaking Canadians called the half-conscripts "Zombies." On September 18, 1944, Conn Smyth suggested that "the relatives of lads in the fighting zone should ensure no further casualties are caused to their own flesh and blood by the failure to send overseas reinforcements now available in large numbers in Canada."

Prejudicial dichotomies flew back and forth as "Zombies" were contrasted with "Real Canadians." Also, remembering the dichotomous vote on the conscription plebiscite in 1942, pro-conscriptionists identified French Canadians as the prime "Zombies," and a furor developed over a renewed demand to send NRMA men to fight in Europe. The army cooperated by making the number of General Service reinforcements seem dangerously low. After all, the prime minister had said there would be no conscription for duty overseas unless it was necessary. When the cabinet divided on the question of current necessity, Mackenzie King replaced the pro-conscription minister of defense, J. L. Ralston, with a general committed to the "voluntary system." But General McNaughton was soon persuaded by district commanders that his predecessor was correct in his conclusion that it was impossible to maintain the supply of General Service replacements by volunteers. Now McNaughton said conscription was necessary and King agreed. By the end of 1944, "Zombies" were on their way to Europe.

Actually, the necessity was entirely political. It had been estimated that 15 000 reinforcements were needed, but there were more than twice that many men available in England and Canada if what Douglas and Greenhous called "energetic re-mustering" and "cuts in headquarters personnel" were implemented. (Four percent of American combat troops were assigned to generals' staffs with such duties as running the mimeograph machines; Canadian generals used 13.6 percent of their men for this kind of duty.) But as General Burns complained to Ralston: "The troops would not feel that the government and country was [sic] supporting them wholeheartedly if . . . it allowed them [the NRMA soldiers] to sit comfortably in Canada." The majority of the English-speaking electorate— according to public opinion polls—agreed. Finally the cabinet agreed. Thus, emotional and cultural prejudices led to a perception of military necessity. Bruce Hutchison appraised the situation fairly in two sentences: "The issue at Ottawa had ceased to be military. It had become racial . . . whether we should put the French Canadians in their place." Later, Blair Fraser called this injury "the wound beneath the skin." There were no riots, except on military bases; but as J.L. Granatstein and J.M. Hiltsman observed in their work on the subject, pledges to French Canadians had been "freely offered" in 1939, 1940 and 1942, pledges that were "violated" despite the "expressed will of all *Québécois* in and out of Parliament. How could Ottawa ever be trusted completely again?" In this way, it might be said that involvement in World War II caused disunity at home as much as a loss of independence in external affairs. In fact, it might be further said that English-speaking Canadians emerged from the war closer to the Americans than to the people of their own federation in Quebec.

III.   Continuing Continentalism in External Affairs

The ending of hostilities saw no change in these developments. As already mentioned, the resentments of the Japanese-Canadians lingered on, and so also did those of Quebec. Quebec's resentment was indicated first by the return to power of anti-Ottawa champions: Duplessis became premier, and Camillien Houde, a mayor of Montreal interned for anti-conscriptionist statements, returned to run Canada's largest city. The wartime affiliation of Canada with the United States also continued. Not that King did not try to loosen the new bonds of empire. By 1945 he was thoroughly sick of Roosevelt's condescension and the authoritarianism with which Americans involved themselves, without warrant or approval from the Canadian government, in projects on Canadian soil for supposedly strategic purposes. A prime example was an authorization by the United States Army for the Imperial Oil Company to construct a pipeline from Norman Wells in the Northwest Territories to Whitehorse in the Yukon, but without prior consent from the government of Canada or from the native people in the vicinity. King understood the disregard of the Indians, but not of his government. Later, after the Americans sent Canada a bill for $60 million dollars to cover the cost of the pipeline, King confided to Vincent Massey that "Canadians were looked upon by Americans as a lot of Eskimos." It was King's opinion that "We ought to get the Americans out of further development there and keep control in our own hands." He believed that the "long-range policy of the Americans was to absorb Canada." King asserted that he "would rather have Canada kept within the orbit of the British Commonwealth."

In the immediate post-war period Mackenzie King therefore strove to reassert Canadian independence. But with the cooling of relations between the United States and the Soviet Union (and because of Soviet espionage in Canada) his anger was displaced onto British rather than American "badges of colonialism." Indeed, there were a few vestigial indicators of the older tie that had not been completely erased by the Balfour Report or Statute of Westminster. King felt that he was advancing the independent nationality of his country by calling attention to the need for a "distinctive" flag, asserting the need for a Canadian citizenship distinct from British "subjecthood," dropping references to Canada as a "Dominion" in public documents, and ending appeals from the Supreme Court to the British Privy Council. But all of these assertions were more negative than positive. They were erasures more than affirmations, and they all sidestepped the issue of the diminution of Canadian sovereignty by dependence upon the United States.

By 1947 there were few members of Parliament who were willing to identify American domination as real colonialism and to work to eliminate it. The proof of this was reaction to a bill entitled the Visiting Forces Act, which exempted American servicemen on northern bases from Canadian justice; in effect, it defined American bases in Canada as American soil. Stanley Knowles, a CCF member from Winnipeg, wanted to know why the United States had not been told that the war was over and that it was time to go home. Spokesmen on the government side replied that the President had reason to suspect that the Soviet Union was planning to invade North America sometime before 1950, and a first line of defense therefore had to be maintained in the Canadian arctic. Thus, the Joint Board of Defence (now "Permanent") and American personnel were going to continue their lonely vigil in the Canadian North. Knowles persisted: "I think this country at this moment has a supreme opportunity." He then asserted that Canada should confront the problem of the growing bi-polarity of the world by cultivating a detached neutrality. "We can say that we are not going to have United States troops in Canada in peacetime. That would be the first move of any small power against the Truman policy or the Stalin policy." But the CCF and the Conservative members who joined Knowles in this neutralism were a small minority. Parliament approved the Visiting Forces Act, and thus conceded to the United States in 1947 what had been denied to Britain in 1938. The fear of Stalinism was stronger than the wish to regain independence.

But Canada was not pleased to be a satellite, as the Americans discovered in March of 1948. A number of Canadian civil servants schooled in the economics of Keynes and the social policy of Beveridge had come to recognize the long-term effects of the Canadian tariff as anomalous at best. They therefore wished to promote a general relaxation of trade restrictions by staging a series of reductions until eventually the tariff might be abolished altogether. When the story was leaked to American journalists they misreported that there were negotiations underway to promote greater continentalism. *Life* magazine ran a story on March 15 entitled: "Customs Union with Canada: Canada needs us and we need Canada in a violently contracting world." To which *The Globe and Mail* answered from Toronto, "Not on Your Life." Other periodicals agreed. Thus, Canadians asserted their wish for greater independence—ironically enough—by rising to the defense of the policy that had promoted an earlier form of continentalism, the branch plant economy.

But the flurry over free trade in 1948, like the flurry of activity to purge the country of the "badges" of British colonialism after the war, was not as robust as the dread fear of communism, and the willingness to defer to the United States as imperial leader in the cold war that Canadians wanted won. Thus, in the spring of 1949—exactly one year after the Canadian opinion makers had denounced free trade because it was supposed to be a prelude to absorption by the United States—Parliament took a giant step toward surrendering Canada's remaining diplomatic autonomy when it ratified the country's membership in the North Atlantic Treaty Organization. At the time, this surrender was not appreciated or intended. NATO, besides being an alliance to withstand the threat posed by the "Iron Curtain" countries, was advertised as a instrument for promoting international cooperation. The second article of the treaty, written by the future Liberal prime minister of Canada, Lester Pearson, affirmed that signatories would pledge themselves to "make every effort, individually and collectively, to promote the economic well-being of their peoples and to achieve social justice." From this standpoint, Canada was not becoming a satellite of the United States, nor was the security that was sought military only. For this reason, Canada's membership was enthusiastically supported by all parties in the House of Commons including the CCF. When the vote was taken there were only two dissenters—both independent Quebec members.

The Canadian view of NATO as a United Nations on a smaller scale was not shared by the Americans, however. They valued the pact as a military alliance, particularly significant because it established an American defense perimeter in Europe and north of Canada. Not surprisingly, NATO emerged rapidly as the military security pact the Americans wanted and expected. All the participating countries were badgered by State and Defence Department officials to perform duties determined by the Americans. The European countries found it easier to resist this pushiness than did the Canadians, as a complaining Lester Pearson learned to his chagrin from Dean Acheson, the American Secretary of State. Acheson explained that all NATO signatories were expected to do their duty more or less as Washington decided. He observed that State and Defence Department officials in the United States had enough trouble agreeing at home. "If you think that we are going to start all over again with our NATO allies, especially with you moralistic, interfering Canadians, then you're crazy." Pearson did not take this admission of unilateralism as a good enough reason for Canada to reconsider her NATO affiliation. On the contrary, he hoped "quiet diplomacy," a patient wheedling, might still somehow prevail. In this manner, a diplomatic revolution was completed. Canada abandoned the dream of an independent foreign policy and fell dutifully into line as a satellite in the American solar system. Canadian policy regarding China, Korea, the Middle East, and North American air defense between 1949 and 1957 was that of the United States rather than that of an independent country pursuing its own interests.

IV. A Widening Continentalism in Economic Development

At first, Canadian subservience in diplomatic affairs was most evident in that area alone—in diplomacy and military decisions. Constitutional and economic developments in the years between the end of World War II and the beginning of the Korean "police action" (the United Nations' effort first to drive the invading North Koreans out of South Korea back to the boundary at latitude 38 degrees North, then the intervention that developed into a crusade by Americans to impose their style of democracy upon all of Korea, and China too, if necessary) suggested growing maturity in the sense of national consolidation and increasingly sophisticated industrialism. The tax rental agreement, which had made the central government the chief collector of revenue, was renewed in 1947 despite refusals by Ontario and Quebec to cooperate. Newfoundland was first wooed, then purchased, and finally confederated in 1949. And discussions were held in ways to patriate the BNA Act; that is, to define a way to amend the constitution by act of the Canadian Parliament rather than Britain's. No agreement was possible on an amending formula, but changes followed regardless. Thus, the failure to agree on a procedure for amending the BNA Act, which suggested a lack of national consolidation, was belied by the relative ease with which amendments were secured in the old way. Since the substance of change could be interpreted as more salient than the manner of achieving it, these changes (pertaining to apportionment, social welfare programs, and the legal system) all tended toward greater centralization and consolidation of power at Ottawa. Thus, the theme of regionalism versus centralism took an ambiguous turn to say the least. For those who applauded the general drift toward one government—and ignored the growing division between Quebec and the others—centralism was a happy indication that one nation was at last emerging from the welter of provinces.

The same happy prospect also seemed to be indicated by the economic development of the time. The war had contributed greatly to the expansion of a Canadian steel industry and also toward the development of industries that had not even existed before 1940. Thus, secondary manufacturing producing diesel engines, synthetic rubber, sophisticated electronic apparatus, and a vast array of plastics emerged where nothing of the kind had existed before. There was also an enormous expansion of natural-resource based industries after the 1947 discovery of oil in Alberta and the development of iron ore in Labrador. Add to this the huge expansion of population by natural increase (Canada emerged from the war with the highest birth rate of any industrial country in the world) and immigration (more newcomers arrived in Canada between 1945 and 1955 than in any other ten-year period in the country's history, in fact, nearly 3 million of the 10 million immigrants since Confederation arrived in this decade), and the imminent fulfillment of national dreams seemed utterly inescapable. These tendencies seemed more important than the growing subservience in diplomacy.

It was in this mood of somewhat smug complacency that Vincent Massey was commissioned in 1949 to survey Canadian attainments in arts and letters with the purpose of recommending adjustments so that Canadian culture might be allowed to blossom proportionately to the country's recent attainments in economic development and population growth. Massey's survey, conducted with the assistance of three academic scholars and a Montreal engineer over the course of two years, was less than encouraging, however. In 1951, the Massey Report provided a vast amount of evidence of the hundreds of ways in which Canadian culture was derivative and subordinate rather than distinctive and thriving: no national art gallery, library, or archive for the systematic preservation of public records; no national support for universities, museums, theater, or libraries; all popular entertainments such as radio and cinema were almost entirely American in content, theme, and origin. Perhaps the best indicator of the scale of depression in the whole dismal scene was the pattern found in publication. Less than two hundred titles appeared under the imprint of Canadian publishers in 1947 and 1948. That was just 3 percent of the output of publishers in Britain in the same period and only four percent of those in the United States. Thus, Canadian booksellers sold material that was published elsewhere. The drugstores and newsstands that carried the tide of the post-war paperback revolution stocked their bookracks with the sentiments of other countries, the writers of the United States in particular.

The Massey commissioners predicted that Canadian culture would be a lost cause without major and immediate support of the country's authors and for cultural institutions. To this end, they recommended financial assistance for the provincial universities, and the creation of a Canada Council to promote cultural development by providing grants to individual scholars or institutions such as the Winnipeg Ballet Company. But the country at large was mostly unmoved. People enjoyed their Hollywood movies and Ellery Queen mysteries. And as far as high culture was concerned, there was so little demand for ballet, for instance, that only two cities in the whole country supported permanent companies. Louis St. Laurent, prime minister since Mackenzie King's retirement in 1948, was probably reflecting the attitude of most people when he shrugged off the idea of the Canada Council as frivolous. The government of Canada had no business "subsidizing ballet dancing," he said. Grants to universities were another matter. These trade schools for professional people could serve an obviously useful purpose in economic development; the funding proposal for higher education was therefore adopted. But six years passed before the central government decided to take an interest in "ballet dancing" as well. By then, an election year, Canadians were well alerted to American dominance of another sort.

In 1955 a rising politician, Walter Gordon, decided to publish his views on the new imperialism. As he later put it, "For some time during the late 1940s and early 1950s I had been worrying about the government's economic policies and particularly the complacency with which Canadians were witnessing the sell-out of our resources and business enterprises to Americans and other enterprising foreigners." In this, he was going against a deeply engrained outlook. In earlier periods, foreign investment had been actively encouraged. This was true of the timber trade before Confederation. After the institution of the National Policy, Canadian tariff and patent law actively promoted the rise of American branch plant manufacturing, as was noted in previous chapters. Even in the twentieth century it was regarded as a wonderful advance when American direct investment furthered pulp, mineral, and hydroelectric development. The only adverse comment prior to Gordon's was in the 1930s when the inflowing stream of American capital was reduced to a trickle. But by the time Walter Gordon was writing, foreign investment had recovered to reach the huge total of $17.4 billion. Since most of this investment was by Americans, the same people to whom so much diplomatic autonomy had been conceded, foreign ownership was now perceived as a problem.

Gordon sent a draft of an article on the subject to a friend in the government. Gordon's position in this essay was not radically different from that of some Progressives in the 1920s. Nor was his view of the problem—if not the remedy—markedly different from that of the CCF since 1933. The novelty was the source. Gordon was an Ontario aristocrat, not a western protester with hayseed in his cuffs; he was part of the same circle that had always sought to foster foreign investment before—a respectable businessman, not a socialist Jeremiah. On this account, the government reviewed his yet unpublished article with considerable attention. Within weeks leading politicians were in touch with Walter Gordon, asking him if he "would mind very much if the government took over" his idea that Parliament should concern itself with regulating foreign ownership. To do this intelligently they would appoint another Massey Commission, but this one would look at economic, rather than cultural prospects. Thus Gordon found himself defused temporarily by sitting as chairman of the Royal Commission on Canada's Economic Prospects.

But when Gordon's preliminary report was tabled in time for the election of 1957 the government was again on the defensive. Here was another impartial and comprehensive survey even more gloomy than the Massey

Report. It was brutally objective yet uncompromisingly clear in its conclusion that the economy was under American domination almost as complete as that of diplomacy or culture. It was at this point that the Liberals decided that Massey's recommendation for "subsidizing ballet dancing" was worthwhile after all, and the Canada Council came into existence seven years after it was first proposed. By 1957, however, the new colonialism had gone too far to be reversed by dancers or scribblers. The question at this late date was whether any policy could reverse it. By 1957 it was clear that the change of mother countries was complete; the brief period of autonomy between 1920 and 1940 was gone; and, for many English-speaking Canadians, it was unclear whether the road back to independence was even desirable—assuming it was attainable.

CHAPTER TWENTY TWO

The Diefenbaker Phenomenon

I. Televised Sell-Out

Within one year of the establishment of the Canada Council to promote national cultural development, the Liberal government which created it stood on trial in an election campaign, accused of disregarding the national integrity. In this, the election of 1957, the new leader of the Conservatives, John Diefenbaker, played the role of the relentless prosecutor determined to convict St. Laurent and his party for their monstrous crimes, the background for which is to be found in the debate over a government proposal to construct a pipeline.

The Liberals' troubles began in March, 1956, when the minister of trade and commerce, the domineering C. D. Howe, presented Parliament with a project that was to be the crowning achievement in his long career of projects. Nothing during his previous twenty years, not even Howe's role in establishing the British Commonwealth Air Training Plan during the war, was as ambitious as this.

Since the discovery of oil and natural gas in Alberta in 1947, the natural gas had been used only locally. It was now Howe's intention to have this gas piped across the Shield to heat homes and power plants in Central Canada. It was a project which rivaled the building of the CPR in scope and challenge. But now, as then, the major obstacle was financial. Of the two firms capable of undertaking such work, only one was Canadian. This company, balking at the costs involved, advocated a line as far as Winnipeg and then a division due south to the lucrative and easily serviced American market. Since Howe refused to permit the export of natural gas "until such time as we are convinced that there can be no economic use, present or future, for that natural gas in Canada," he solved his first problem with this project by forcing a merger of the two companies. Thus, TransCanada PipeLines came into existence in 1954, 50 percent Canadian in capital, and east-west in mission.

But in 1955 a new problem arose. The company officers informed Howe that they were unable to raise enough capital to finance the most difficult one third of the project, the portion through the virtually uninhabited Shield. Like the directors of the CPR and of all similar undertakings, they wanted a subsidy and special privileges for the special mission they were pledged to fulfill. Howe was willing, but the cabinet was not. The indefatigable Howe solved this problem by bringing the government of Ontario into the scheme, and a $73 million federal investment was balanced by a provincial stake of $35 million. With cabinet agreeing to this modification, it only remained to obtain the consent of Parliament.

For C. D. Howe the ceremonial appeal to Parliament was always the most tedious part of any project since the Opposition behaved as if they had power to influence decisions that were in fact already made. In Howe's view, all their tactics only delayed an outcome that was inevitable, because the party with the majority was the government and the government always won. It was a pity to have to waste so much time in "useless chit chat," particularly when such an important project as the pipeline was at issue. Still, parliamentary approval was required for an appropriation of this magnitude.

But this project was to face fierce opposition because there was one more change in the character of the undertaking just before Howe introduced it to the House. The directors of TransCanada PipeLines informed C. D. Howe that their credit was insufficient to buy the quantity of steel pipe they needed. But this problem would vanish instantly if Howe would agree to give a conglomerate of American corporations a controlling interest of 51 percent of the equity stock in the existing firm, and an additional $80 million in subsidy. Howe consented and his threats of resignation brought the cabinet into line. Now his task was to persuade Parliament that it was reasonable to subsidize a project of the size and importance of the CPR that had just become 75.5 percent American owned. In effect, he was asking Parliament for money to help the Americans take over Canadian natural gas.

The absurdity of the proposition was enough to rally the Opposition forces despite the paucity of their numbers (in 1956 they made up only 35 percent of the House). Nevertheless, they determined to use every stratagem to defeat Howe's bill. The CCF was against any project that was not completely publicly owned. The Conservatives were against the project because of the nationality of its organizers. Both were reinforced in their determination when Howe finally confronted Parliament with a new version of the bill demanding an *extra* $80 million ratification within three weeks.

Since the Opposition believed that the old bill was absurd, they were insulted at the idea of even debating the new one. They decided instead to filibuster and kill the scheme by taking away the three weeks before the already ordered but as yet unauthorized pipe started to arrive. Howe, for his part, was determined to win. He decided to impose closure at each stage of the legislative process, in order to make the deadline no matter how harrowing the Opposition's delays.

What Howe and the Liberals failed to keep in mind was the established tradition of using closure only after all details of a measure had been exhaustively debated, and after it had become clear that further talk was merely obstructionist. Now, however, notice of termination was served even before the discussion began. "This isn't the way to run a peanut stand, let alone Parliament!" one Conservative shouted. But all the harangues and hundreds of points of order availed nothing. The pipeline bill passed final reading at 3:30 in the morning of June 6.

The epsidode made the Liberals vulnerable in two ways. In the first place, they were showing themselves willing to go to almost any length to encourage foreign investment. Ever since Macdonald, Canadians had accepted a need for some measure of foreign capital. But what Howe was proposing was extraordinary; Canadian funds were being handed to foreigners for them to do privately what the Canadian public might even more profitably have done for itself. And secondly, there was the method by which Howe pursued his plans. Parliament was relegated to being a rubber stamp for the administrators, a mere assenting body to ratify arrangements made far beyond public scrutiny.

The charge of abusing Parliament was no less damning than the one of "selling out" to the Americans. What made it particularly lethal for the Liberal government was the recent introduction of nationwide television. On that new medium the critic was, for the moment, in charge, and the Opposition was quite willing to arouse public indignation against a party apparently old and arrogant in office.

II.   Pious John's Attack

It was in this setting that the Opposition found the agency for its sense of injured righteousness in John Diefenbaker. The Conservative leader,

George Drew, had exhausted himself in the pipeline debate and on doctor's orders retired from politics. At the leadership convention in December, 1956, the party elected Diefenbaker, a Saskatchewan lawyer whose somewhat radical past made him, in the opinion of Drew supporters, more akin to the CCF than to the Tory party. But if Diefenbaker did not appeal to the heart of urban Ontario he did have the West, rural Ontario, and the Atlantic region. In the December nominating convention he won handily, free of any debts to "eastern politicians or rich men from Bay Street and St. James Street." Nor was Diefenbaker beholden to Conservatives from Quebec. Despite the tradition that a new leader should employ a French Canadian nominator or seconder, Diefenbaker's promoters were exclusively westerners or Maritimers, and the new leader spoke boldly about "one unhyphenated Canada." It was as the champion of bypassed regions, then, that the new leader came to the fore, a prophet recalling his people to a standard that Central Canada had foresaken.

He did not have long to wait for a chance to launch his crusade. By the spring of 1957 four years had passed since the last rejuvenation of St. Laurent's mandate, and it was time for another election and renewal. Thus Parliament dissolved and the prime minister stood before the people in the electoral poses he had found so successful in 1949 and 1953. On the one hand, St. Laurent presented himself as a board chairman, reading his dry but encouraging report on the corporation's highly successful development in the preceding period. On the other hand, the prime minister posed as "Uncle Louis," the elderly patriarch, kissing babies and lecturing school children on the promise of Canadian development. Any question of an alternative government he dismissed out of hand; no other party could develop anything "that we are not already developing." His party's slogan, 'Unity, security, freedom,' directed attention to the material achievements of the recent past and promise of the immediate future. He suggested that, like John A. Macdonald in the early 1870s, his politics were his *projects*.

Diefenbaker confronted St. Laurent like Alexander Mackenzie fighting Macdonald's corruption. He proclaimed that *his* politics were his *principles*. And what he insisted upon in 1957 were the rights of Parliament, rights which he claimed the Liberal party had forgotten and systematically abused, and the principle of Canadian autonomy, also violated by the Liberals. The pipeline debate was the great symbolic issue: "Parliament was made a mockery of at the behest of a few American millionaires." Diefenbaker warned that if the Liberals were returned "don't ask the Opposition to stand up for your rights, because there will no rights left."

In this sense, Diefenbaker's campaign was strongly negative. He played the role of a public prosecutor seeking the conviction of an especially odious group of offenders. Yet at the same time, Diefenbaker intended to create the impression of positive leadership as well. He offered redemption as well as retribution. Pointing the way to a brighter future, Diefenbaker spoke of a new sense of purpose by appropriating a label the Progressives had used in the 1920s: he revived the image of the "New National Policy." There would be "subventions," or cash grants, for Nova Scotia coal miners, cash advances to farmers for farm-stored grain, significant increases in old-age pensions, and government encouragement for greater foreign investment which, under his direction, would return greater benefits to Canada. Denis Smith commented that Diefenbaker's program was "obscure, superficial, contradictory or meaningless." It was clear that Diefenbaker felt the foreign investment schemes of the Liberals were dangerous; but without clarifying how, he asserted his own deals with foreigners would be beneficial. In this, as in other areas, Diefenbaker failed to indicate what he would do differently.

What did clarify between April and June of 1957 was the intensity of Diefenbaker's indignation, and a growing tendency of the voters outside Quebec to share in this sense of outrage. The degradation of Parliament was the theme that Diefenbaker developed with enormous effectiveness over the course of a speaking tour that covered more than 20 000 miles and led him to make similar speeches to over one hundred different audiences. Also, the enthusiastic crowds and Diefenbaker's incredible sincerity looked especially good in film excerpts on television; there was just enough there on the nightly news to convey the intensity without the incoherence. Thus, people who saw Diefenbaker only over the medium of television might have been even more likely to catch the message than those who heard him in person.

The voters to whom Diefenbaker appealed the most were English-speaking Canadians of moderate incomes who wanted rapid development of the country's resources without compromising with the national integrity or democratic processes. Such voters were to be found almost everywhere, though it has to be pointed out that Diefenbaker ignored Quebec. It was not that he was against that province, but his evangelical political style required an audience schooled in that variant of Protestantism. Just as Diefenbaker did not concern himself with Quebec, Duplessis ignored the federal election; in reply to a question on the relative strengths of the parties in his province he commented that "the party that wins the largest number of seats will win."

But in the rest of Canada there was great interest, and excitement developed over the possibility that the winners might not be the Liberals. Diefenbaker felt confident that he had scored something of a moral victory by the end of the campaign. But he was not confident of winning a majority of the votes. The Liberals expected to lose some of the margin of their previously overwhelming majority, but having won the last five general elections in succession they too have come to imagine their return as more or less inevitable. Only the minor parties were without hope. Yet, as the votes were totaled, they stood to gain the most: on June 10, 1957, for the first time since 1925, the electorate had returned a minority government, with the CCF and Alberta Social Credit members holding the balance of power.

III.   Victory and Drift

The Liberals and Conservatives were each more than twenty seats short of a majority in the twenty-third Parliament. Liberal candidates had received the largest number of popular votes, but Conservatives had the largest block of members in the House. Thus, the minor parties might have supported either, but in 1957 Diefenbaker seemed more agreeable to innovation than St. Laurent. Also, according to Blair Fraser, "Most people, even Liberals, had been heartily sick of the Liberal Government." Consequently, it was a Diefenbaker cabinet that took over the direction of Canada's affairs.

It was a cabinet that had problems. The Conservatives had been out of office for over a generation, and there was much to learn about the exercise of power. But two things helped ease their transition from Opposition to government. First, the economic situation favored the Tories. The consumer spending spree that had followed World War II, that had been sustained by the Korean war and boosted further by development projects of the early fifties, had begun to abate. Unemployment was on the rise. The country was beginning to slide into recession. In such a setting the new government could safely implement some of their preelection promises and yet avoid the danger of inflation; old-age pensions were increased from $40 to $55 per month, farmers were granted a $150 million cash allowance for farm-stored grain, and taxes were cut by $178 million.

Secondly, the Liberal Opposition badly miscalculated, and played into Diefenbaker's hands. By January, 1958, the Liberals had endured six months of Opposition, a chastening experience. They wished to return to office, but wanted to do so without another election. St. Laurent's successor, Lester Pearson, therefore moved that in "view of the fact that unemployment has risen drastically, and . . . in view of the desirability at this time of having a government pledged to implement liberal policies, His Excellency's advisors should . . . submit their resignations forthwith." There would be no need for a dissolution and another campaign; Diefenbaker would simply yield to Pearson in much the same manner that King had been expected to give way to Meighen in 1926. The prime minister seized the opportunity this Liberal arrogance had given him. His reply was twofold. He savagely criticized the Liberals for their apparent desire to govern without the bother of winning support at the polls: "Don't have an election but give us back our jobs" was, he insisted, the Liberal demand, and by the time he had finished speaking one member of Parliament was moved to "wonder if the Prime Minister believes in the humane slaughter of animals." Diefenbaker followed up by quoting a "hidden report" that had been produced by civil servants in the department of trade and commerce while the Liberals were still in power. This report had warned that unemployment was even then the great danger facing the Canadian people, and was to be blamed not on the Conservatives but on the Liberals themselves.

With such ammunition, Diefenbaker had no cause to fear another election. In February, 1958, he returned to the work he loved best, confronting Canadians eyeball to eyeball, and what followed was the most emotional campaign in the country's history. After generations of measuring national development by the growth of the gross national product, Diefenbaker asked Canadians to strive for more than their country's material expansion. He invited them "to create a new sense of national purpose and national destiny." It was not simply a bigger or a richer country that he promised. Diefenbaker claimed to know the way to a more unified, self-aware, and independent Canada. In this sense he made cash promises that convey cosmic purpose: "Jobs! Jobs for hundreds of thousands of Canadians. A new vision! A new hope! A new soul for Canada!" The nation would save its character and reap the material promise of unlimited development. "Catch the vision of the kind of Canada this can be! I've seen this vision; I've seen this future of Canada. I ask you to have faith in this land and faith in our people." All that voters had to do was elect a few more Conservatives. "We need a clear majority to carry out this long-range plan, this great design, this blue print for the Canada which her resources make possible."

Of course some critics said there was no plan, no coherent blueprint, only—in Pearson's words—"quivering clichés or evangelistic exhortations." But others agreed with the Ottawa *Journal*, which called the Diefenbaker "vision" a "homage to imagination which makes democracy exciting." They saw a prime minister asking his electorate if they wished to have "one country" developed by themselves in accordance with their own cosmic purpose. If so, he was the one to lead them there. It was possible, and in the immediate future, through the magic of a Diefenbaker majority. Not since the days of the restoration promises of the 1930s or the zeal of Alexander Mackenzie in 1874 had the electorate been promised so much for so little. Eighty percent of the eligible voters turned out, and 54 percent voted for Diefenbaker's Conservatives. Even Quebec seemed to approve the new nationalism by awarding the "chief" 50 of its 75 seats. The rest of Canada was even more generous. Overall, 208 of the 265-member House were to sit on the government side. The Liberals and the minor parties were absolutely routed.

It soon became obvious, however, that this high priest of Canadian nationalism could arouse the people to moral indignation more effectively than he could plan or enact the kind of integrated program he asserted without defining. In the forty-six days of campaigning, four central intentions had been indicated: northern development, revitalization of federalism, abrogation of continentalism, and restoration of the close relations with the British Commonwealth. But in the years that followed, despite commanding the largest majority in Canadian history, Diefenbaker made significant headway in only two areas; one was a public works project (the "roads to resources" program whereby federal money was allocated for the construction of northern roads); the other was in the area of foreign trade (an enormous multi-million dollar wheat sale to Russia and China, a transaction that was more a matter of good fortune than government plan). There was also Diefenbaker's Bill of Rights, a statute of the Parliament of Canada that was supposed to guarantee basic freedom from harassment by the government in Ottawa except by "due process of law." In other words, this was a statute that declared no one could be harassed except in the terms of some other statute. As a Bill of Rights that was beyond legislative trespass, the document was meaningless.

Diefenbaker's charter of liberties was a fitting symbol for the fate of the whole vision he had done so much to popularize in 1958. It was a high blown statement of purpose, but non-existent on the level of concrete reality. Still, since the gesture was so well-intentioned, all deficiencies were supposed to be covered. For many people, good intentions were enough. But for many others the period of the twenty-fourth Parliament was a time of disappointment and dissolution. *The Globe and Mail* called it the "idle parliament" and others spoke of these years as "indecisive."

Diefenbaker's problem—the problem of his party in microcosm—was the handicap of cross-purposes. A dogmatic commitment to private enterprise and individual liberty was neutralized by an equally stong commitment to the maintenance of public welfare and vigorous government. A fervent desire to promote humanitarian idealism was cancelled by an equally strong impulse to maintain fiscal orthodoxy. Finally an ardent Canadian nationalism came into conflict with dogmatic anti-communism. Thus, Diefenbaker's Conservatives would act one way—on monetary policy, for instance—and justify this action from one ideological prospective, but act the opposite way on fiscal policy, justifying that with the opposite dogma. Or more frequently, Diefenbaker would find himself and his party locked between alternatives and they would not act at all; hence the appearance of "indecision."

After four years of continuing only to talk about the vision of a reinvigorated Canada, Diefenbaker had the audacity to dive into another election campaign in 1962 acting as if the twenty-fourth Parliament was commemorable for breathtaking achievements, and therefore deserved to be returned for more of the same. "Vast as our program has been in the last five years, it will be even greater in the five years ahead." Then came the old vision: speeches for do-it-yourself northern development and a return to a Britain-centered, trade-integrated Commonwealth. But this time the magic was gone. The vision of 1958 had become a hollow mockery by 1962.

The Liberals posed as the "professional team," a group of experts who were well trained in the technique of government and anxious to win power in order to make that machinery hum. Their image was that of a completely non-ideological party, a group that was completely unencumbered by dogma or antiquated moral purposes. They were technicians who promised to get the economy moving again, to put an end to "indecision and fumbling."

Given the choice between Diefenbaker's empty demagoguery and Pearson's espousal of expediency under the banner of professionalism, many voters turned to minor parties. In Quebec, a new version of Social Credit under the tutelage of Real Caouette appeared especially interesting to voters there. Elsewhere, the CCF, repackaged and re-labelled as the New Democratic Party in order to minimize any suggestion of socialism, looked more attractive than in many recent years. What remained for Diefenbaker was the rural vote of English-speaking Canada. His majority of 208 was reduced to a plurality of 116. This was minority government, but the government nonetheless.

IV.   Return to Opposition

The return to minority government did not make Diefenbaker more decisive. It made him vulnerable to defeat in a crisis of decision that was already six months old at the time of the elections, a crisis that had its origins as far back as 1957. The problem was how to decide on a defense policy that was anti-communist without being subserviently pro-American.

Diefenbaker's anti-communism led him, in the summer of 1957, to accept an extension of continentalist collective security, a consolidation of the air forces of the United States and Canada under joint command. By this North American Air Defense Agreement, called NORAD for short, the two countries placed their air space under the protection of one integrated system commanded from under a mountain top in Colorado by an American general staff, on which Canada received subordinate representation. In the event of an "emergency," the aircraft of the entire continent could be placed on alert. Thus, the integration of Canada into a pan-North American system was advanced one step further by a prime minister whose rallying cry was nationalism.

Even more paradoxical was the predicament that Diefenbaker found himself in when his fervent anti-communism led him to support the development of sophisticated weaponry. Diefenbaker was willing to equip the Canadian Air Force with supersonic fighter-interceptors which were designed and manufactured in Canada for approximately two million dollars each. This price was based on a production run of five hundred, since the Americans and British were expected to buy a number of the aircraft for their forces. But near the end of 1958 it came out that only the RCAF was going to buy the Avro Arrow, which would mean that each plane would have to cost $8 million. Diefenbaker rebelled at such extravagance, the Arrow was scrapped, and a substitute found in the Bomarc interceptor, an unmanned missile manufactured by the Boeing Corporation of the United States. The attraction of the Bomarc was that it was cheap; the Americans, having gone to even more sophisticated weapons, would give Canada fifty-six Bomarcs virtually free of charge.

But there was a snag. The Bomarc was not available with a conventional warhead, only with a nuclear bomb. And American law prohibited the release of atomic bombs to foreign powers. Thus, if the Bomarcs were not to be elegant blank cartridges, the Bomarc installations would have to be guarded by American troops, and in this way would become the instruments of Canada's occupation by more Americans.

Diefenbaker's sense of national pride revolted at the idea of the subordination of Canada to the United States, even at the best of times. But the years after 1960 were not the best. John F. Kennedy had succeeded Eisenhower like a new caesar to the imperial throne; Diefenbaker and Kennedy took an instant and mutual dislike to one another, a dislike that was increased enormously in the autumn of 1962. On October 22, Kennedy declared naval war on Cuba and the Soviet Union, calling his action a "quarantine." As part of the "emergency," the RCAF was ordered onto alert in the expectation that Canada's government recognized the urgent nature of the communist missile build-up in Cuba, and therefore the imperative need for bold and forceful remedial action. But Diefenbaker balked and held the Canadian air force out of action for nearly two days. Thus, the prime minister supported Canadian independence by flouting what the imperial leader commanded. Then, as a further gesture toward an independent Canada, Diefenbaker dug in his heals at accepting nuclear bombs for the Bomarc or for the Canadian forces in Europe.

The issue of defense, and the Bomarc in particular, revealed Diefenbaker caught in an agony of indecision. He wanted nuclear weapons in order to have a more terrifying saber to rattle at Nikita Khrushchev. Thus he did not find it easy to refuse them. But since he loathed the idea of American controls he did not find it easy to accept them, either. The prime minister was paralyzed between yes and no from February of 1962, the date of completing the first Bomarc site in Canada, to February of 1963, the occasion when all parties united to defeat Diefenbaker in the House of Commons.

The beginning of the end was Lester Pearson's announcement on January 12 that the expedient course was to accept the warheads. Pearson said it was more important to maintain international commitments than any other principle. He also asserted that the Bomarcs and other bits of military hardware were useless without bombs, and wondered why the government accepted the delivery devices in the first place if there was no intention of taking the warheads as well.

Deifenbaker tried to answer Pearson when the House reconvened on January 25. He repeated his reservations about accepting the warheads immediately, and asked for time, saying that a decision would follow from the next meeting of the NATO allies in May, 1963. In the meantime he suggested that everyone should pray for divine guidance in this matter: "Some may ridicule that belief on my part." Nevertheless, the prime minister suggested that "the western world had been directed by God in the last few years . . . . " Diefenbaker wanted to leave the government of Canada to the Lord for another several months.

Prayer was not enough for the Opposition or Diefenbaker's cabinet, however. On February 3 the minister of defense resigned; Lester Pearson moved his non-confidence motion on February 4. Diefenbaker's offense was "lack of leadership, the breakdown of unity in the cabinet, and confusion and indecision in dealing with national and international problems . . . . " In the judgment of Parliament the charge was valid; on February 5 the NDP and Social Credit members joined the Liberals to force the dissolution of the twenty-fifth Parliament on grounds of non-confidence.

Diefenbaker's defeat in the House of Commons was followed by a defeat at the polls. The humiliation by the electorate seemed even more significant than his repudiation by Parliament as other prime ministers (Macdonald and Meighen) had suffered a similar fate in the House. But the election of 1963 was the first time in Canadian history that a dramatic appeal to nationalism failed. Diefenbaker's pose was that of "a humble farm boy moved by some predestination to defend the national honour and the average man in the hour of crisis." He likened the Liberals to the promoters of the Annexation Manifesto of 1849, and taunted them as wantonly unprincipled self-seekers, pursuers of expediency, willing to pursue whatever was "easy" no matter how "wrong." They were tools of the Americans and the "sinister interests." But he, John Diefenbaker, was simply "trying to help others,"to fulfill the vow he had made in 1956 when he accepted the Conservative leadership: "I hope it will be said of me when I give up the highest honour that you can confer on any man, as was said of another in public service: 'He wasn't always right; sometimes he was on the wrong side, but never on the side of wrong.' That is my dedication; that is my humble declaration." Diefenbaker was still making the same affirmation in 1963: "I'm not asking for the support of the powerful, the strong and the mighty, but of the average Canadian—the group to which I belong."

This time the old affirmations and paranoid accusations did not work well enough to return even a minority government for Diefenbaker. Since the defense question was the central issue, to some observers, the defeat of Diefenbaker signified the defeat of Canadian nationalism; and a "lament for a nation" was called for. But this point of view failed to appreciate that previous popular nationalists offered more than "rigid adherence to principle." They were also proponents of some wonderful policy to strengthen the nation as well as to affirm it. In this tradition, Diefenbaker was defeated because Canadians still expected than a nation would follow from policies rather than from theatrical performances. The voter in Halifax who said "he's not the man I thought he was" expressed this disappointment, as did *The Globe and Mail* when that paper charged that "there never was a programme .... Mr. Diefenbaker is barren of constructive ideas and incapable of action."

Thus, nationalism versus continentalism was the surface issue only. The other, broader question in the election of 1963 was whether Canada would have a government whose politics were its principles, or an administration whose politics was its program. The two questions tended to blur of course. But on both matters public opinion was quite clear. Only forty percent of the electorate voted for the Liberals, the party which advocated acceptance of the nuclear warheads and the wider continentalism that implied. Diefenbaker's Conservatives, the NDP and the Social Credit party were all relatively clear in their opposition to this move and these three parties, together, received nearly 60 percent of the popular vote. But the nuclear question was only one issue. The other, the indecisiveness of Diefenbaker and his seven-year failure to advance a legislative program consistent with his general objectives, was even more relevant to his defeat. It was the promise of "sixty days of decision," "Pearson or paralysis" that made the Liberals attractive; the minor parties had their promises of concrete action as well. Diefenbaker's was the only party that stood entirely upon the ground of pious nationalism in defense policy and rigid adherence to principle in other matters. On that basis, they received a mere 30 percent of the vote. The other 70 percent went to the groups which differed in what they promised but were united in their opinion that principles and pious intentions were not enough, that it was time to return to government by projects.

By 1963, in short, most of the electorate was thoroughly sick of John Diefenbaker and his pious platitudes. Thus, the "chief" was returned to oppose a government rather than to lead one. He was returned to Parliament in 1963 in much the same way as Alexander Mackenzie in 1878: piously to oppose an administration which asked to be judged in accordance with the projects it completed rather than the principles it professed.

CHAPTER TWENTY THREE

Quiet Revolution, Quiet Reaction

I.   Energetic Federalism

When Pearson's "professional team" returned to power as a minority government in the spring of 1963 they inherited Diefenbaker's unfulfilled program. Three areas in particular were in need of immediate attention: the economy, Canadian-American relations, and national unity. All three were fields about which Diefenbaker had spoken spaciously, but had accomplished little. Now the Liberals intended to show that they could translate words into effective action.

The new government's first budget dramatically emphasized its determination to build a *Canadian* economy. Walter Gordon, the man whose preliminary warning about foreign ownership had created such a stir in 1956, was now minister of finance and he included in his budget two revolutionary proposals. One was a 30 percent tax on the value of Canadian firms purchased to become subsidiaries of American corporations. The other was a tax on dividends that varied according to the amount that a firm was foreign owned. In other words, for the first time in Canadian history, a government was taking steps actively to discourage foreign investment. All previous governments had regarded such investment as synonymous with development, therefore desirable. Gordon was making a radical new departure in domestic economic policy. The Canadian business community denounced the budget accordingly, and Pearson's minority government was threatened in the House by the repercussions there. Subsequently, the takeover tax was dropped entirely and the tax on dividends had to be significantly modified. Still, the ground was broken. A government was on record for having declared that foreign investment was an ambiguous blessing if not downright threatening.

Such aggressive nationalism neutralized by legislative compromise was also watered down by the diplomacy of the prime minister, which yielded a greater measure of continentalism in Canadian-American relations. Soon after the election, Pearson made a pilgrimage to Hyannis, Massachusetts, where he chatted with President Kennedy about baseball, NATO commitments, and "co-operative development" of shared resources such as the Columbia River. Canadian-American relations, which had been strained in the Diefenbaker years, were thus repaired in the first weeks of Pearson. "He'll do!" Kennedy remarked afterwards, but what Pearson agreed to "do" was nothing a Canadian nationalist would accept with approving smiles. Still, a rift in Canadian-American relations had been closed by Pearson's affirmation that the Bomarcs would be armed and Canadian NATO forces bolstered. In this manner, there was relief in the ending of the crisis if not in the manner of its resolution.

With these fences mended, and the Canadian economy set on a nationalist course, the Liberal government could turn its attention to the unity of the country. Diefenbaker had stressed the idea of an "unhyphenated" Canada. It was not that he urged the assimilation of various types to any one pattern, but he did assume that awareness of one transcending Canadian identity would render any "ethnic" distinctions trivial. Pearson saw things differently, and in the summer of 1963 he appointed a ten-man Royal Commission to show that Canada was a federation of at least two distinct nationalities, two "founding races."

Soon after the appointment of this Royal Commission on Bilingualism and Biculturalism, the Liberal government challenged another basic tenet of orthodox Canadian nationalism, one especially dear to Diefenbaker. A new Canadian flag was proposed, one that would be devoid of any content implying the superiority of any one region or ethnic group over another; there would be no stars, or crosses, or fleurs-de-lis—above all, no Union Jacks. The new flag would be indigenously Canadian, and a symbol of "unity in diversity" which could be flown in any province without provoking resentment. For the first time in Canadian history a prime minister had openly repudiated the notion that "we must be British in order to be Canadian."

For many people, the repudiation of the Canadian Red Ensign (the flag of the British merchant marine with Canada's coat of arms in the fly) was a "deliberate rejection of Canada's history." Thus, on May 17, 1964, when the prime minister unveiled the flag he preferred, three red maple leaves set in the middle of a white field with a blue bar at either end, to a meeting of the Canadian legion in Winnipeg he was hooted and jeered by a roaring crowd of war veterans "not all of whom appeared to be quite sober." But this was only the beginning. The "Pearson pennant" was denounced with equal emotion in the House of Commons. The 95 Conservatives were solidly in favor of retaining the Red Ensign. The 20 Social Credit members from Quebec were agreeable to any change that expunged British symbols. The 17 NDP were uncommitted, and Pearson's Liberals were divided. Finally, after several months of fruitless debate it was decided to turn the matter over to a committee of fifteen, which would mirror the composition of the House: 7 Liberals, 5 Conservatives, 2 Social Credit, 1 NDP.

The Conservatives now hoped to gain by cleverness what they were losing by force of numbers. Their strategy was to defend the Red Ensign until they were outvoted by the Liberal and Social Credit members. Then they would introduce a design alternative to the "Pearson pennant" in the anticipation that the Liberal members would stand by their leader's preference, and the minor parties would come over to the Conservative side in the interest of compromise. The committee could report to the House that they were hopelessly divided and therefore the only reasonable course would be indefinite retention of the Red Ensign.

Thus the Conservatives proposed an alternative design (in their opinion ludicrous) that included one red maple leaf set in the middle of a white field with a red bar at either end. "They were aghast, they were horrified," when the Liberals, having decided the "Pearson pennant" was too controversial, thumped the table in approval. The minor parties were also delighted. Now the Conservative members of the committee had the embarrassment of opposing in the House that which they had not only approved in committee but themselves had initiated. They were snared in their own net, but not so mortally that they would not drag out the debate for another three months. Then, with closure, the final vote was taken, and the flag which nobody knew became the banner of Canada. It offended the artistic taste of two surviving Group of Seven painters; it also struck Canada's leading historian, Donald Creighton, as a "deliberate rejection of Canada's history." In Creighton's sight, it "bore a disturbingly close resemblance to the flag of a new 'instant' African nation." But whether the ancients of English-speaking Canada liked it or not, their country — in its own way — was embarking upon a fresh start.

II. The Decolonization of Quebec

Pearson's abandonment of the belief that Canadian nationalism had to be centralist and monocultural was forced upon him by radical developments in Quebec, developments so radical that it was doubtful whether the new "co-operative federalism" would be sufficient to satisfy that province's aspirations.

As has already been mentioned, Quebec had taken refuge earlier in an inward-turning nationalism ever since the Anglo-imperialism of World War I. In the more recent period this Quebec nationalism had been represented and articulated by Maurice Duplessis, premier until his death in 1959. Behind a demagogic appeal to maintain the purity of the French Canadian way of life in Quebec, Duplessis operated a nakedly authoritarian regime founded on vast patronage and outright corruption. But even while he was successful in maintaining the grip of his Union Nationale party on the province, and even while he was able, on his death, to transfer the reins of power to his protégé, Paul Sauvé, he was unable to repress totally criticism of his methods.

An early indication of the forces rising against Duplessis and his cohorts came in 1949, during one of the most bitter labor disputes in the history of the province. The miners of Asbestos, organized in a Catholic trade union, demanded concessions that management refused to give. Duplessis denounced this aggressive unionism as communist; the Church was expected to join the denunciation. Then, if the event followed the pattern established in previous years, these three authorities—the government of Quebec, the Church hierarchy, and the executives of the American corporation— would band together to dictate terms to the workers. But on this occasion the Church sided with the union against the government and the foreigners. Eventually the union's demands were met. Thus, the Asbestos strike established the precedent for the "aggressive unionism" that has characterized the Quebec labor movement since. Equally important, the Asbestos strike also called into question the ultra-clericalism of Duplessisism, the use of the Church to uphold traditions no matter how reactionary. Here was a crucial turning point in the evolution of Quebec's nationalism.

The secular intelligentsia and reform-minded clergy now affirmed that inward-turning defensive nationalism was not enough. That goal had been gained: Quebec *had* survived. Now it was time "to unshackle the superstructures, desanctify civil society, democratize politics, break into economic life, relearn French, get inessentials out of the university, open the borders to culture and minds to progress." Their breakthrough eventually came in 1960. Sauvé, just four months in office, died. The Union Nationale—the party Duplessis had fashioned in 1936 and which had suffered only one brief interruption in its dominance to 1960—became a leaderless mob reduced to the common denominators of corruption and traditional ultra-clericalism. In the provincial election of 1960, the Union Nationale was swept aside.

The reform energy that had been building for a generation brought to power a new party which called itself Liberal. Like the Union Nationale it was ardently *nationaliste*. But whereas the government of Duplessis had practised *"la petite politique,"* the new regime of Jean Lesage turned to *"la politique de grandeur"*; it was the contrast between personal promises of short-term, local projects made directly to the interested voter, and the pledge of ideals and projects on a grand scale, province-wide in their significance. Over the next six years the Lesage Liberals carried out a radical reconstruction along these lines.

The educational system was a major area of concern, with changes designed to make it more secular and better fitted to serve a technological society. Civil service reform was another important area; a merit system for selecting government employees was set up, and competitive bidding prior to the awarding of public works contracts was instituted. Programs for promoting the development of the economy under the leadership of a French-speaking rather than a foreign managerial class appeared. Church-State relations changed from those of a theocracy to a secular society. Social welfare programs began. As well as demanding changes in Quebec's status in Confederation, much-publicized gestures were made to foster French Canadian culture beyond the borders of Quebec and to establish communication with the French-speaking world beyond the borders of Canada. The term that covered this burst of energy, which caused continuous headlines from 1960 to 1966, was "Quiet Revolution." The description was not overdrawn.

The reforms in education and economic organization were probably the most thorough, and the changes made were of most lasting importance. Under the old system of schooling, there was one set of institutions controlled by what was, in effect, a committee of the Catholic Church for the children of Catholic parents. All non-Catholic children, in effect, went to what were called Protestant schools. The pattern of confessional schools was perhaps the most fundamental aspect of the Quebec theocracy. Church and State were ostensibly separate. But this pattern delegated all responsibility for social development of human resources to religious authorities on the assumption that "survival of the race" depended upon placing the young in confessional schools. The system also rested on the assumption of bilingualism and biculturalism rather than pluralism: it was assumed that all English-speaking Quebeckers were Protestant and all French were Catholic.

The new government operated from different assumptions, attitudes that reflected the radical difference of the new regime as well as anything. The Lesage Liberals, unlike any of their predecessors, took for granted that the *Québécois* were a people unlike any other, and the development of their social character did not depend upon rigorous conformity to one religion, especially a traditional Roman Catholicism which demanded that 'if we write, all our propositions . . . must be repetitions.' From this standpoint, the existing system of schools was unjust since it failed to take sufficient account of pluralism; there was a lack of schools for Jews (legally they were to be regarded as Protestants for educational purposes), agnostics, or French-speaking Protestants. It was simply assumed that such people did not exist.

Another assumption of the new government was the notion that education was job training more than catechism—the institutions of learning were to transfer skills more than beliefs. From this view, the existing schools were lacking because they emphasized religion, classics, and the humanities rather than mathematics, the sciences, and technique. One of the first official acts of the Liberals was therefore the appointment of a commission, made up of secular as well as clerical educators, to survey the existing pattern of education and recommend changes. The reports of the Parent Commission gave Paul Gérin-Lajoie, one of the three most important figures in the government, precisely the information he wanted. In May of 1964 the government assumed responsibility for schooling. A ministry of education under Gérin-Lajoie, came into existence, and one no longer had to be Catholic to be *Québécois*. Thus, pluralism arrived in Quebec and the expensive work of transforming the schools into training grounds for manipulators of technology began.

Equally ambitious—and expensive—were the projects for the decolonization and development of Quebec's economy. Here too the Lesage Liberals operated from assumptions that were radically different from those of their predecessors. They assumed that French Canadians could pursue the material rewards of developing their economy at the managerial level without losing their character, and that the State could play an active role in this promotion without taking the province down the road to collectivism or disaster. The most outspoken proponent of this French Canadian entrepreneurship and statism was René Lévesque, the minister of natural resources and, after Lesage, the most important person in the government.

Although Lévesque was outspoken in his affirmations of nationalism and considerably left of center in his statements of economic beliefs, the program he implemented could be described as pragmatic more than separatist or socialist. Consider the great headline maker of 1963, the "nationalization" of Quebec Hydro. From the standpoint of surface appearances, the move was both leftist and nationalist: privately owned companies directed by English-speaking Canadians or Americans were taken over by the government, and French Canadians promptly appeared as the directors of the new public conglomerate. But this interpretation misses two points: only one third of the private firms were acquired, and the process of acquisition employed a pragmatic principle of selection as well as compensation for the owners. Dogmatic nationalism would have compelled a takeover of all firms dominated by outsiders, especially the ones belonging to Americans, and hardline socialism would have sought expropriation without payments as punishment for excessive past profits. But the goal, which was more important than the elimination of foreigners or punishment of profiteers, was simply the provision of service which until then had been unavailable or excessively expensive. Thus, the private companies in the northwestern part of the province were one target because they provided twenty-five-cycle power in a sixty-cycle world. They were nationalized to make the conversion. The other large target in the Gaspé peninsula came under the Quebec Hydro umbrella to reduce rates from five times those at Montreal to the same standard. But the private companies which produced power for the American corporations in the Lac St. Jean region were left as they were. In this manner, Quebec Hydro was created to solve specific problems more than to gratify ideological imperatives.

A similar pragmatism characterized two other achievements in the area of economic policy—the creation of the Quebec Advisory Council, *Conseil d'Orientation Economique*, and the establishment of the General Investment Corporation, *La Societé Générale de Financement*. The first was a planning agency to study "the economic organization of the province with a view to the most complete utilization of its material and human resources . . . . " This body would "indicate" the way to a rationalized economy with French Canadian participation above the level of "cheap and docile labour." The role of the other body was to offer the financial encouragement which would facilitate private enterprise to follow the "indicative planning" of the Advisory Council. More specifically, the General Investment Corporation was supposed to provide the funds, in the form of loans or actual investment, for small firms to consolidate into large operations and thus achieve economies of scale as well as growth. In this scheme, as in the creation of Quebec Hydro, the objective was pragmatic: the concrete goal of "full employment through balanced economic growth." Thus, a concept new to post-conquest Quebec, that of the role of the state in the promotion of economic growth, emerged more as the fruit of *la politique de grandeur* than by the triumph of ideology.

But *la politique de grandeur* was expensive. In 1959, the last year of the Duplessis 'regime, the government had received $556 million in revenue and had spent $533 million in *la petite politique*. The Lesage government accumulated an enormous debt despite huge tax increases. In 1966 they received $1 billion in revenue, but spent twice that much on large projects. The Quiet Revolution was starting to cost a lot more than many people were willing to pay. Under the old regime of Duplessis, Quebec was always short on services, but taxes were low. Now there was a 6 percent sales tax as well as a provincial income tax that included nearly every householder in the province, whereas previously one-fifth had been exempt. The goal of making the *Québécois* "masters in our own house" (*maîtres chez nous*) was proving expensive to the individual taxpayer. While academics praised the Quiet Revolution as a spectacular catch up, and boasted that Quebec had "overtaken and surpassed most of the rest of Canada, at least in the breadth of its concepts and the grandeur of its goals," many citizens were inclined to snort with the Union Nationale that this was simply a "government of taxers."

Thus the Quiet Revolution led to a quiet reaction. In 1966 the Lesage Liberals were turned out of office and the Union Nationale led by Daniel Johnson came back. With him were many of the same politicians who had followed Duplessis. But Johnson was a different *chef*, and so the party which was accustomed to following its leader changed accordingly. Premier Johnson sensed that social development was popular so long as taxes could be kept low. And so he tried to continue the flow of innovations—but with the assistance of federal funds.

III.   Majoritarian Reaction Outside Quebec

Johnson's blend of nationalism and federalism came at an opportune moment. In the country at large, there was a growing though vague commitment to provincial autonomy at home and a more definitely independent Canada abroad. This conception of multi-level autonomy was not new. Nor was Johnson's hope of developing a country with an equal place for French and English original. That idea had been the aim of Henri Bourassa and *Le Devoir* between 1900 and 1917. Then, however, the ideal of an independent and bicultural Canada had been wrecked on the rock of British jingoism and Anglo-Canadian arrogance. These attitudes were fainter now and there was also the renewed interest in provincial autonomy, but overriding both were assumptions that were completely inimical to a "two nations" conception of Canada. Now, rather than British imperialism, the threat was the intensifying Americanization of the country's political style.

In American-style democracy the nation is one or nothing. The majority rules to "preserve, protect, and defend" one Way of Life which the Founding Fathers set down in the Constitution. There is no conception of minority rights which transcend the will of the popular majority. Consequently, American-style democracy lacks tolerance of diversity. What the majority feels is true is the truth and self-evidently so—it arrived with the founders of the nation complete and perfect. Any change is decline; any deviation, corruption. There is, therefore, a need for periodic reformation, a call to return to a former purity. Thus American politics is extraordinarily confessional; the nation is also a sect.

Canada could be an American nation in this sense only by dividing into its two most fundamental parts. In fact, it had. Duplessis and Diefenbaker each operated in the style of an American president as each ignored the other's "nation." Pearson hoped to return to the possibilities of pluralism. It was for this reason that he was so frantically working for symbolic victories such as the new flag, or more substantive matters such as the B and B Commission, or—most important of all—cooperative federalism.

The most striking example of the new federalism was the "opt out" provision of the Canada Pension Plan of 1964-65. This allowed any province to opt out of a federal program, design its own equivalent, and receive federal support as if it were participating in the original. Quebec chose to operate its pension plan in this way. And as Quebec increasingly took the opportunity to develop this sort of relationship with Ottawa, it became apparent that Pearson, the professional diplomat, was choosing to treat with Quebec almost as with another government, a province more autonomous than any of the others. Here, then, was the setting which suited Premier Johnson.

But if Pearson and Johnson were happy to experiment along these lines, most Canadians were not. Many seemed to feel that this was to exaggerate the importance of one province. Others regarded the new Quebec-Ottawa relations as evidence of cowardice since so much of the central government's energies seemed concentrated on Quebec. Donald Creighton interpreted the government's behavior in just this way; for Quebec "it made plans, dropped plans, and invented new plans. For Quebec it stumbled from one crisis to another in a frantic search for appeasement."

Creighton's view—in even more intemperate manifestations—was widespread throughout Canada. The "one nation, one people, one language" sentiment, which heaped abuse on the very idea of bilingualism and biculturalism, demonstrated that pluralist democracy was no more popular in the 1960s than in the earlier period before World War I. If Canadians advocated provincial autonomy, it was only for themselves; on the interregional level "the others" saw themselves as one people. Previously, the opponents of pluralist autonomy had said "We must be British to be Canadian." Few people were now saying "We must be Americans," but the belief that nationalism had to be "unhyphenated" was more dogmatically asserted than ever before.

IV. Majoritarian Reaction Within Quebec

The opportunity for this rising tide to assert itself came in 1967, during the Centennial celebrations and the World's Fair, Expo '67, in Montreal. Charles de Gaulle, then president of France, visited Quebec, and in a speech to the people rose to the ringing peroration, *"Vive Montréal, vive Québec, vive le Québec libre, vive le Canada français, vive la France."* The crowd received this sentiment with wild roars of approval; this, and their perception of de Gaulle as a leader returning from long exile rather than as a foreign dignitary on a short visit, infuriated the rest of Canada. Eventually Pearson felt obliged to protest that de Gaulle had gone beyond the bounds of propriety, and the visit of the French president was cut short.

But if English Canada was clear in its response to de Gaulle's speech, French Canada was not. There were those who agreed with Pearson; Lesage was one such. But against this was Premier Johnson's refusal to join in the condemnation. And many in Quebec inclined to Johnson's position. More and more concluded that even the most clearly defined special status would be less satisfactory than a complete separation from the rest of Canada. In the fall of 1967 François Aquin, a Liberal backbencher representing a Montreal constituency, resigned from the party and declared himself a separatist. The next day, a far more prominent Liberal made the same move; René Lévesque announced that Confederation was hopeless since "the two majorities would only continue to collide, always harder . . . . " Separatism was the best option for it would provide "the chance to live life in one's own way according to one's needs and priorities" with the least interference from outsiders. This was one step beyond "special status" with its connotation of privilege for a cultural minority outside the mainstream. Independence would assert separate nationality while taking into account past aspirations with "the others." Thus, Lévesque did not contemplate isolationism, but dual nationality, with Quebec and the rest of Canada cooperating on certain matters as "separate states."

Exactly one hundred years after Confederation, a fresh debate now exploded over the nature of the Canadian constitution—what it had been and what it ought to be. It was Pearson's claim that bilingualism and biculturalism were needed to break down the two "solitudes" and make possible the building of a dual nationalism. But separatists on both sides refused to cooperate in this project. They preferred to take refuge in the past or in visions of the future, each side refusing to see nationality in anything other than a one-dimensional mold: "One country, one nation, one language."

CHAPTER TWENTY FOUR

Quiet Desperation

I. The Unity Fetish

On July 1, 1967, Canadians celebrated one hundred years of Confederation. They had much to celebrate, for throughout that century it had often seemed that the union was threatened with disintegration. That specter was still present; but in Centennial Year, Canadians could be pardoned for exaggerating successes and for congratulating themselves upon their pragmatism. Still, inevitably, the question of the future of Confederation loomed large. And as Canadians pondered their future, their politics were jolted by a change of leadership in both major parties.

Pearson's successor was Pierre Trudeau, in many ways a most unlikely candidate. Before 1965 he had been a Montreal law professor and journalist. During the Quiet Revolution, he had been less flamboyant than René Lévesque, but Trudeau was listened to by much the same audience. It was only in 1965 that he put his more radical affiliations behind him and joined the Liberal party. Thereafter his rise was rapid; soon after he entered the House of Commons he became minister of justice. When it came to a leadership convention, Trudeau was the right candidate at the right time. He was a Quebecker, equally at home in French as in English, apparently progressive, and a supporter of centralizing federalism. The enthusiasm with which the Liberal party supported him, and with which the country responded to him, revealed the depth of anxiety below the surface of centennial celebrations.

Three days after becoming prime minister, Trudeau plunged the country into an election, called for June, 1968. His major opponent was the new leader of the Progressive Conservative party, Robert Stanfield, a former premier of Nova Scotia, intelligent but lacking in color and flair. He was particularly ill at ease in front of news cameras, and complained that every time he left the House "You walk out and they shove a bunch of microphones in your face and in thirty seconds you're expected to produce a profound and intelligent answer to an extremely complicated national issue." Stanfield's slow and deliberate answers, which piled one qualification upon another, gave him the appearance of indecision and weakness, while in fact he was merely thoughtful and honest.

Trudeau was Stanfield's opposite in all matters of style. Trudeau enjoyed performing for newsmen, and the appearance of boldness was a specialty he cultivated. As justice minister, for instance, Trudeau had proposed changes in the criminal code to permit homosexual acts between consenting adults and easier access to abortion. Changes were made in divorce law, and the remaining reforms served well to reinforce the apparent zeal for change of the reforming newcomer to politics. The prime minister wore sandals in the House, traded upon his image as a "swinging bachelor", and was so aggressive in speaking the language of everyday that he offended parliamentary proprieties.

The clear-cut clash of styles was one factor which intensified a growing trend for parliamentary elections to take on more and more of the appearance of a presidential popularity contest. A second factor was that neither leader and neither party had had the chance to develop a coherent, comprehensive policy. Trudeau and Stanfield were both innocents in the limelight, and the leaders of the minor parties were too upstaged to be visible at all.

The presidential style was especially the case in Trudeau's campaign. Ordinarily party leaders toured the country meeting the party faithful in auditoriums in the evenings, when the men were free from work. But Trudeau campaigned in suburban shopping malls in the daytime. He would arrive in a city by jet, descend into a shopping centre parking lot by helicopter, and then plunge into a crowd on foot. After a short introduction by a local Liberal the prime minister would proclaim some general but compelling words about the "Just Society" he hoped to build. Then he would warn that there "will be no give aways. It is more important to have a sound dollar than to satisfy this or that particular interest." Here was the provocation for some heckling, perhaps, but if this started Trudeau was in his element, for his quick wit supplied easy rebuttal. Thus, the crowd would see their new prime minister as a wealthy intellectual who was not afraid to meet the real people and answer them directly with plain talk. Even skeptics tended to warm to his style. Toward the end, without having mentioned specific proposals, Trudeau would build up to his parting request: "If Canadians want to take a bit of a risk, if they want to take a chance on the future, then we're asking them to vote for us." With that, he would toss his carnation to some worthy maiden, accept kisses from adolescent admirers, smile for the cameras, and ascend by helicopter from the crowd below. He generated enthusiasm that had not been seen since Diefenbaker's 1958 vision speeches. The press called the enthusiasm "Trudeaumania."

Stanfield harrumphed that the Trudeau style was nothing more than theatrics and, forgetting Diefenbaker, asserted that for "the first time in Canadian history a prime minister has asked the people for a blank cheque." Similarly, the leader of the NDP, Tommy Douglas, warned Canadians that beyond the image of the innovator was "the orthodoxy of the 1930s." Thus, both Stanfield and Douglas attempted to call the electorate away from style and down to specific issues. Stanfield began to make proposals "by the bucketful." He proposed innovations for public housing, agriculture, regional development—even a guaranteed annual income for all householders. Striking the same note, Douglas proposed a "Minimum Program for a New Canadian Society," which included proposals to deal with foreign ownership, inequities in tax law and corporate power, as well as social welfare innovations. But in the end, on June 25, 45 percent of the voters gave their nod to Trudeau candidates. For the first time in a decade, Canadians elected a majority government.

Liberal party support was strongest in Trudeau's home province, but British Columbians and Ontarians also responded enthusiastically to the Trudeau style. Maritimers tended to follow the lead of Stanfield; and the Prairie voters still smitten with "the party of John Diefenbaker" also voted Conservative. What attracted the English-speaking supporters of Trudeau was his willingness to stand up against separatism. An incident during the election had made this point in a most dramatic way. On election eve the prime minister was in Montreal observing a St.-Jean-Baptiste Day parade with other dignitaries. But the celebration was disrupted by rioting separatists. At one point a bottle flew past the prime minster and smashed on a portico not six feet away. The episode made television on the eleven o'clock national news. And the next day from coast to coast, newspaper readers found a picture of the event on the front page. The other dignitaries had ducked and run, but Pierre Trudeau had not flinched.

Courage against rioters made Trudeau popular in English-speaking provinces where anxiety about separatism was already keen. But at the same time it did not diminish his popularity in Quebec. In the first place, only a small minority of Quebeckers were separatists and yet smaller portion of them were willing to advance their cause by violent means. Consequently, nearly all *Québécois* could rally to the condemnation of rioting separatists. But Trudeau was also appealing in his home province because he personified the French Canadian dream of success: wealthy and independent, a success among Anglos without ceasing to be French. Thus it was in 1968 that Canadians of diverse ethnic backgrounds seemed to have found a "consensual" leader, a Liberal for British Columbia and Ontario as well as for Quebec.

II.   The Essential Trudeau

But even while the election was taking place, some observers were drawing attention to the gap between promise and fulfillment, contending that the bubble of great expectations would necesarily quickly burst "if for no other reason than that he has aroused . . . Canadians with opposite views and conflicting interests." Dalton Camp, a leading Tory, reasoned that as soon as people with irreconcilable objectives discovered that they admired the same leader from contradictory standpoints, they would become disenchanted with him even more than they already opposed one another.

The test would be Trudeau's attempt to translate the image of the "Just Society" into more specific terms. Then the contradictions would appear, and the essential—as opposed to the consensual—Trudeau would emerge. But the first translation proved to be of little use as an indicator. Soon after the election, the earlier amendments to the criminal code were passed. These made it legal for consenting adults to engage in homosexual practices and the grounds for abortion were made more vague. But in sum they were such "motherhood issues" that the Conservative caucus made the vote a free one, each Tory Member of Parliament being allowed to vote as conscience dictated.

The first important and clear revelation of the essential Trudeau came many months later in the spring of 1969 with the Official Languages Act, a measure to guarantee more meaningful equality for French and English in Canada. The minimal guarantees on language equality in the BNA Act were extended, and the federal bureaucracy in particular was made accessible to French people in those regions where there existed significant French-speaking minorities. In this way, the fact that a Canadian lives in a bilingual country, rather than in a country that contains distinct linguistic enclaves, received statutory expression. Of course, much of this was largely pretense. There were "two solitudes" in Canada rather than two languages that most people had mastered. There was also a long history of friction between the two "founding races." But the Official Languages Act took account of the basic reality, as well as of the professed ideal by providing for a Commissioner of Official Languages, responsible to Parliament, whose function would be the investigation of "cases of discrimination involving language."

There were many Canadians prepared to accept the Official Languages Act in principle. A Gallup Poll showed that 56 percent of the population taken as a whole "supported its principles." But in the West, 70 percent were opposed. In this region the French were regarded as just another ethnic group, and not nearly as significant as the Central and Eastern Europeans, because—taken as one group—they outnumbered the French. There was little sympathy or understanding of the historical basis for Canadian dualism. Other ethnics had learned English to get along; and they had done so without losing their old culture completely. The French Canadians were expected to follow this example. Thus westerners argued that Canada was either a mono-culture (Diefenbaker's Canada without hyphens) or a multicultural country (everyone speaking English day to day but dancing different folk dances for celebrations such as Winnipeg's "Folklorama"). There was nothing in between. The Official Languages Act finally passed after a rancorous debate ("Their cry is 'Masters in our own house'; I believe it may now have gone beyond that, and could be 'Masters in yours too'"). The vote was 191 to 17 and the opposers were all Conservatives; sixteen of them, including Diefenbaker, were from the three Prairie Provinces. Even though 41 Tories had voted for the bill, in yet another way the Conservatives came one step closer to identification with a particular region rather than with the whole country, and at the same time that part of Canada, the "deep west," became something of a synonym for bigotry. In this light, Trudeau appeared to be essentially "soft on Quebec" and therefore not the man he was originally supposed to be.

But any notion that Trudeau was losing trans-regional support was swept aside a year later. On October 5, 1970, two men took the British trade commissioner, James Cross, from his Montreal home at gunpoint. On the way to their car, one of the kidnappers announced to a bystander, "We're the F.L.Q." (The F.L.Q. was the *Front de Libération du Québec*, a separatist group not at all squeamish about using terrorism to realize their objective of "liberating" Quebec.) At first the Cross kidnapping was treated as just another local police matter. In fact, the theme of the throne speech, three days later, was national harmony: "Notwithstanding its diffculties, Canada continues to enjoy social stability to an exceptional degree. This stability is not simply a matter of luck." Thus the premier of Quebec and the mayor of Montreal were left to deal with local enforcement by themselves.

But the ransom for Cross was high. The kidnappers specified seven demands, among which were the the release of twenty-three "political prisoners," who were other terrorists convicted of less spectacular deeds than the Cross abduction, $500 000 in gold, and safe conduct and transportation to Cuba or Algeria. When it appeared that none of the major demands was going to be met, rather than killing Cross, another abduction occurred. On October 10 another band of the F.L.Q. seized a member of the Quebec government, the labor minister, Pierre Laporte. On the local level, government now became frantic lest more kidnappings follow. The premier was moved into a guarded suite in downtown Montreal. In Ottawa, troops were posted outside the homes of federal cabinet ministers. And the prime minister—while doing nothing—spoke bravely about doing whatever was necessary.

Orchestrated chaos continued from Sunday, October 11, until Friday, October 16. Premier Bourassa was beside himself with grief. He was in constant communication with Trudeau who, for his part, played a constant guessing game with the press and the House of Commons. Although he still did not act, dark hints were dropped of dramatic action to follow.

"How far would you be willing to go?" one reporter asked on October 12.

"Just watch me," Trudeau replied. But the prime minister evaded commitment to any particular line of action. Two days later he indicated to the House that "I do not think... suspension of civil liberties... would be possible without some amendment to our statutes . . . . " But two days after that, on October 16, predawn imposition of the War Measures Act followed, and the prime minister justified his action later in the day with a speech contending that the whole country was falling apart: "I know that democracy was nowhere in a healthier state than in Canada . . . . Yet in recent years we have been forced to acknowledge the existence within Canada of a new and terrifying person . . . . Faced with such persons... the government had no choice but to act as it did." Thus the suspension of the constitution and the sending of troops into Montreal. Two days later, Laporte was murdered by his captors and Cross continued to be held by persons unknown.

The location of Cross and the killers of Laporte were uncovered by routine police work later. In the meantime, the extensive powers enjoyed by the government were put to dramatic use elsewhere. Thus, in Winnipeg, a city which had barely heard of the F.L.Q. before October, a radical bookstore was closed down because its marxist literature was alleged to be part of the "apprehended insurrection." The imposition of the War Measures Act must be seen, then, as a way to impress the country with the government's toughness against radicals of every description, but especially against separatists. More than four hundred advocates of Quebec independence were jailed without charge and virtually all were eventually released without trial or conviction for the commitment of any crime. They were separatists, not F.L.Q. terrorists; but Trudeau announced that separatism was the offending cause, and that he was not opposed to sending troops into Quebec to prevent that province from separating. The October crisis thus provided the preview for such firmness should the opportunity arise again in the future. The short period of martial law was overwhelmingly endorsed by the Canadian population and Liberal party stock rose accordingly.

In 1968 Trudeau had promised to be tough on separatism; opportunistic overreaction had enabled the prime minister to deliver on that promise. Once this episode is put aside, the rest of the Trudeau achievement shrinks appreciably. Other developments took place, it is true; China was recognized, Russia visited, the nuclear role in NATO and NORAD abandoned, the Department of Regional Economic Expansion came into existence, and the unemployment insurance scheme was overhauled. But the claims in 1968 had been visionary; specifically nothing had been done on the constitutional review begun by Pearson, the tax reforms had not taken account of the recommendations of the government's Carter Commission, and no action had been taken on another government report on foreign ownership. Most wounding of all, the government had fought inflation by decreasing spending, and had only succeeded in raising unemployment. By 1972 there was truth in the remark of David Lewis, the successor to Tommy Douglas as leader of the NDP: "In pretty nearly every domestic issue of any importance the Government has failed. Because Mr. Trudeau raised such high expectations in 1968, the anger and frustration is so much greater." And if this were so, the upcoming election, which was called for the late fall of 1972, would be a crucial one in Canada's development.

III.   Winner Take All

That election, in fact, highlighted a style of Canadian politics as old as Confederation. Throughout their history Canadians had been relatively unenthusiastic about large issues perceived from the standpoint of political abstractions. If there was ever national purpose it had to be specific—a tariff, a railway or something easily translated into physical, tangible terms. This did not mean that Canadian politics was inherently trivial, since there is a fine line between *la petite politique* and *politique de grandeur*, to borrow categories from the Quiet Revolution in Quebec. Railways *can* be imaginative projects, capable of fueling a vision of national possibility; but riding by riding even a transcontinental railway can also be just two rails and some ties, incentive for land speculators, and jobs for the unemployed—in this sense, nothing more than barreled pork. At its best, Canadian national politics joined local projects to purposes that transcended particular constituencies or regions. At its worst, the concreteness of Canadian national politics meant that an election unfolded as 264 by-elections. In 1972 there were only feeble attempts to articulate some transcending purpose. Thus, rather than acting as a turning point, the election of 1972 was simply another case of Canadian politics at its worst.

La petite politique surfaced in the prime minister's promises of "goodies" and "candy" in the form of promises of docks for Nova Scotia or water-front parks in Toronto. Trudeau's choice of an overriding theme for the election was too far distant from this kind of bribery to be an effective counter. What the prime minister saw as the question of the day was "nothing less than the integrity of Canada—the homeland of persons ... committed to Canada." But to put the issue in such abstract terms was to make it nothing more than an exercise in image politics. The other parties would find it impossible to get a hold on such a vague statement, which did not lend itself to debate or even serious reflection. The two approaches, then, were equally wide of the mark.

A third way was attempted when the Liberals seized upon different intermediate issues in different parts of the country. In the Maritimes, for instance, they discussed DREE, the Department of Regional Economic Expansion. In Quebec, they stressed the increasing pressure and growing importance of French Canadians in Ottawa. On the Prairies, the significance of multiculturalism was hammered home, while in British Columbia Liberals emphasized how well the French were being controlled by Trudeau's forceful leadership in times of emergency. But this tendency to tailor the "big issue" to each region only served to demonstrate how amorphous politics had become even while it groped for larger questions. It seemed that there was nothing of a particularly trans-regional content even on this level.

The same tendency was evident in the opposition parties. The NDP conducted an effective critique of the government for the favoritism of tax policies, which distinguished between incomes that were corporate profits and those that were personal. By calling attention to "corporate rip-off" and the "corporate welfare bums" Lewis was able to convey what the NDP was against, and why the electorate should not vote for Liberals, but the electorate "never knew what we were for," one party leader complained later. Had the NDP argued in favor of social reform "based on ... nationalist economics and socialist doctrine" they would have filled that void, but "given the need to pick up votes in widely divergent regions" they opted for caution, hiding their socialist light under a bushel to a greater extent than ever before.

The Progressive Conservatives became the recipients of reform-minded voters that Lewis shook loose from Trudeau, since Stanfield sounded like a reformer in his scathing attacks on the government for its mishandling of inflation and umemployment. But here too the critique was more clear than the counter-proposal. Stanfield's Conservatives were attractive largely because they were the only party large enough to be the logical alternative to Trudeau's, the group that most voters wanted retired but without wanting to discuss the major reasons why. Disenchanted with them all, Walter Stewart, a leading political journalist, complained: "The campaign had ... shown that it is possible to conduct an election for sixty days in a thoroughly modern nation, with all the elements of communication in place and avoid the major issues confronting the nation."

The result of the voting in 1972 was reminiscent of the results that produced the minority governments of the 1920s or the Diefenbaker-Pearson
era. Neither major party could govern alone, and no minor group was
enthusiastic about defeating the party with the plurality for fear of a
slaughter in a new election. Thus Trudeau's Liberals hung on to power,
forming a government with 109 of their own seats and the support of the
NDP's 31. But Stanfield's Conservatives had come within two seats of the
same opportunity by their winning 107 to the Liberals' 109.

After the election, commentators addressed themselves to the question
of whether the electorate had intended any such outcome: 62 percent of
the voters had repudiated a prime minister who continued to govern. Paul
Fox, a political scientist, and Walter Stewart, the journalist, suggested that
Canada needed to revise its present electoral system and adopt one that
returned members to Parliament in proportion to the votes actually cast.
Such a system had long been in effect in many European countries. There,
the seats won in the legislature were a direct reflection of the number of
votes polled overall. In the British system—which the Canadians and
Americans have dutifully continued—the only votes that count are those
for the winner. Thus, in 1972, 100 percent of the seats from Alberta went
to Conservatives, even though 42 percent of the electorate in that province
voted for candidates in other parties. Similarly, the 76 percent of the seats
that the Liberals won in Quebec were based on only 49 percent of the
votes there. Under one form of proportional representation 12 percent of
Alberta's members of Parliament would have been NDP, 25 percent Liberal, and the rest Conservatives; Quebec would have returned 36 Liberals
(not 56), 13 Conservatives (rather than 2), and 18 Socreds (instead of 15).
And rather than zero NDP and others, this form of proportional representation would have netted 5 Quebec seats for the New Democrats and 2 for
other parties. Different forms of electoral change would have produced
other results, but all systems of proportional representation have one point
in common: no votes are thrown away.

After the 1972 election the advocates of proportional representation
admitted that the details of allocating ballots could be complicated, for
voters would tend to identify with a particular party more than with individual candidates, and minority government would become virtually a certainty in every election. But some of these disadvantages, minority
government for instance, were described as ambiguous. More important
were the supposed advantages: every party would be represented from
every province and, in Stewart's words, less inclined "to hawk whatever
line of goods happens to be selling locally . . . . " "I don't mean by this that
regionalism would disappear simply because the voting system was
changed." What Stewart wanted was a system that did not *reward* "regional baiting," a tendency of Canadian political life which increased after
the rise of the multi-party system.

But there was no great tide of support for Stewart's proposal in 1973, any more than there had been when Frank Underhill proposed it in 1930. Nevertheless, after 1972, there was steadily growing anxiety that the country was dividing more and more, West from East, federalist from separatist. Alberta was apparently solid in the style of Oklahoma City, and Quebec appeared totally preoccupied with its regional peculiarities. But the point that continued to be missed then and later was the fact that Underhill pointed out in 1930 when he said that "The dangerous sectional solidity would, to some extent at least, dissolve, had we an electoral system which sent members to Ottawa in proportion to the votes actually cast in the different sections."

IV. The Illusion of a Solid Quebec

The electoral system, which returned members by riding majorities rather than "in proportion to the votes actually cast" in whole provinces, also operated to create patterns of pernicious solidity in provincial legislatures as well. No province illustrated this better than Quebec between 1970 and 1976, because it was in these years that the Parti Québécois, the PQ, René Lévesque's separatist movement, appeared first to be the victim of the electoral system and finally its chief beneficiary.

Before 1968 the *"Péquistes"* had no organized existence. René Lévesque had made his break with the Liberals in October of 1967, and his *Option for Quebec*, in which he mapped out the course of separatism through democratic, peaceful means, appeared in January to become an instant best seller. But eight months passed before this political Moses formally launched the new party, which, once in existence as the Parti Québécois, issued a dramatic call for social reform and political independence. At their founding convention in the middle of October 1968 they promised a unilateral declaration of Quebec independence upon their election to power. After their election victory, economic negotiations would follow with the rest of Canada to establish a north-of-United States common market. In the meantime, sweeping changes would be effected at "home" (in Quebec or Laurentia or whatever the new nation would call itself). The domestic reforms included proposals to advance French as the language of work as well as of home, and other regulations to control more stringently the export of profits by foreigners. As a palliative to the English-speaking minority, there was a promise to continue English-language schools for this ethnic minority. In this way, the new nation would repeat the experiment in dualism first launched in 1867, but on a smaller scale and with the English rather than the French in the subordinate, or at least minority, position.

Lévesque's party was not as popular as his book. The manifesto had been an instant success, a popularity that can be interpreted as an incentive in forming the new separatist party in the first place, but this enthusiasm did not spill over to the population at large. A Gallup Poll indicated that just a shade more than 10 percent of Quebeckers considered themselves separatists. Still, almost 20 percent were undecided. If they could be persuaded, and if these two groups were fairly uniformly distributed, and if the Union Nationale and Liberals continued to be on similar levels in their popularity, there was hope for a PQ victory: it was even possible that 34 percent of the vote could yield 100 percent of the seats in the legislature, if the UN and Liberals received 33 percent each in every riding.

The two established parties feared this as well. Still, by using the same logic as Lévesque each had cause for great expectations. Over the next two years, the UN and Liberals adjusted their images to maximize their gains at the much-anticipated next election. The Liberals leaned right in the expectation that most Quebeckers had no interest at all in separatism and were even sick of hearing about "special status." Their position was that federalism provided "cultural sovereignty" and economic development at rates and with benefits that made the Quiet Revolution pale in significance. Such was their luxury of opposition. The party in power, by contrast, aimed to appear moderate by repudiating separatism, while at the same time taking dramatic steps to affirm the status of *"la nation Québec;* before the end of 1968, for instance, the UN abolished Quebec's Upper House and changed the name of the Lower House from the Legislative Assembly to the *National* Assembly.

Quebeckers thus prepared themselves for an election which would unfold as a de facto referendum on the question of separatism. When the showdown finally occurred at the end of April, 1970, the results seemed to indicate a clear preference for the party which promised economic development without constitutional struggle. The Liberals received 42 percent of the votes, almost twice as much as the PQ, which received 23 percent, or the UN with 20 (the remaining fifteen percent was divided among a plethora of splinter parties, the largest being the *Ralliement Creditiste* which received 11 percent of the vote). But the electoral system translated this indication of public opinion into a pattern of representatives that was anomalous if not without justice. The Liberals' 42 percent gave them a majority government with 72 of the 108 seats. The UN became the official Opposition and the Creditistes came away with nearly twice as many representatives in the Assembly as the PQ (the Creditistes', 11 percent of the vote elected 12 members; the PQ's 23 percent elected only 7).

Lévesque had hoped the UN would be more uniformly popular, but in this election there were only pockets of Creditiste and UN support which gave them victory in certain ridings. The main show emerged as a contest between Liberals and Péquistes, with the PQ running as a significant minority movement everywhere. Ironically, on this account, the PQ won almost nothing. (In fact Lévesque himself failed to win a majority of the votes in the riding in which he had previously run successfully as a Liberal). To some separatists the irony was infuriating. They lost interest in the movement or became more radical—the April, 1970 election is thus a commonly cited "reason" for the F.L.Q. kidnappings in October and "justification" for the government's crackdown on separatists generally. Lévesque's response was to disassociate himself from *violent* separatists, whom he called "sewer rats", and emphasize instead the social reform intentions of his party. In this manner, the PQ would seem to be a Quebec labor party with separatism somewhat incidental to its larger program.

In the election of 1973 the voters polarized even more than in 1970. The UN was virtually wiped out. While the PQ increased in popularity as the choice of 30 percent of the voters, this remarkable increase was so uniformly distributed that the Péquistes actually lost strength in the legislature; their presence shrank from 7 to 6, and the National Assembly became nearly a single party legislature with 102 of the members sitting on the Liberal government side.

Once again Lévesque responded by shaping his group even more like the party already in power. Separatism—the PQ's ostensible reason for being—was shelved by a device that Wilfred Laurier or Mackenzie King would have recognized as his own style of evasion. Claude Morin championed a pledge that any PQ government would hold a referendum before moving toward independence. Since everyone knew that this referendum would not carry then or in the foreseeable future, to drop the policy of independence until a plebiscite demanded it was a good way to disassociate the party from the separatist issue without seeming hypocritical or flaccid. What remained was the party's advocacy of social democracy, which was bound to be popular with the militant unions. On this basis the PQ could expect to cross the magic 40 percent level in popular vote, and gain the government. To keep it, there might be periodic referendums on separatism, but not necessarily independence.

In the meantime, the Liberals in Quebec and in Ottawa moved from one crisis to another in a manner that indicated flexibility smelling of opportunism rather than pragmatism. The most thorny problems in Quebec and the whole country were economic—inflation and unemployment. Trudeau's Liberals imposed wage and price controls in 1975, having campaigned successfully the summer before specifically against them. For their part, the Quebec Liberals were embarrassed by apparent powerlessness before the more militant unions, and incompetence in controlling expenditures, either for worthwhile projects such as hydroelectric development on James Bay, or more frivolous adventures such as the installations for the billion-dollar Olympic Games held in Montreal. Then, too, there was anger over language legislation, which English-speaking Quebeckers regarded as discriminatory and others found merely opportunistic. Add to this a national controversy over the use of French between pilots and air traffic controllers and everything was set for a protest vote when the Liberal premier, Robert Bourassa, called an election for the autumn of 1976.

This time the electoral system worked as Lévesque had hoped originally. A reinvigorated Union Nationale and a Liberal Party on the defensive insured victory for the PQ. The UN gained 18 percent of the popular vote, the Liberals fell to 34 percent, and Lévesque's social reform party increased its share to 41 percent, evenly distributed, and therefore entitled to a majority of the seats in the legislature. It was a majority wide enough to create an appearance of solidity in favor of the "the party dedicated to the destruction of Canada."

Since the rest of Canada interpreted the election as a victory for separatism, the country was thrown into a panic, and Pierre Trudeau's stock began immediately to rise once again as he moved masterfully to take advantage of this exploitable "crisis". Ironically, this reinvigoration of Trudeau, "the best man to handle Quebec," did not impair the prime minister's popularity in his home province. In the eyes of most Quebeckers separatism was still not as attractive as Trudeau's version of Confederation. Yet Lévesque's appeals to sovereignty—in some form—was no less popular for the province's attachment to Trudeau. The most likely forecast, from this contradiction at the end of 1976, was for a period of threats and maneuver with a return to the discussions about constitutional change, and the implementation of some form of decentralizing federalism especially in the area of "cultural sovereignty."

V.   An Uncertain Future

The disruptive strains caused by the need to redefine the relationship between Quebec and the rest of Canada are the most evident. But they are not the only ones, and as the problems caused by changing economic and technological realities become more urgent, the wider strains of disparity may be expected to come to the fore. In attempting to resolve these strains the political geography and the distribution of powers may have to be dis-

ιantled and reassembled. Perhaps the country *Canada* is beyond repair.
ut whatever the new political geography to emerge, it will not erase the
ysical—a country to be seen in archetypal form just to the north of the
ιnge of population from British Columbia to Newfoundland will still be
here, to be seen in its rocks and rivers and spruce trees, the deep snows,
the clear January cold, the brief summers and demanding winters. All the
physical and climatic features that have challenged every invention
America and Europe have attempted to impose will endure. And for non-
Canadians, these challenges will continue as the proof of the view that
"this is the land God gave Cain." But for those inhabitants who continue
to seek the meaning of their lives more in the development of this place
than in national myths, the challenges of climate and geography will continue to invite affiliation from sea to sea with the others who share this
"inheritance."

At most, Canada survives. At the least, its disintegration holds out the
prospect of reunion and continuation, more *survivance*. But Canada has not,
and perhaps cannot, find that cosmic purpose or national mission which,
in the nineteenth century, was supposed to make nations of mere colonies
or principalities. Consequently, Canadians' values individually are not
necessarily those of the larger society, and in this pluralism lies the value
of the country's great failure ever to articulate a "common Canadianism."
But how much longer will Canadians be willing to accept such a negative
valuation of their nationality? And, it may be asked further, how will those
with a positive self-definition as a majority impose their unhyphenated
community without brutal coercion of the minorities? This is the critical
point in the structure of past Canadian experience; it also forms the present and points to the future.

Bibliographic Note

The authors have not thought it necessary to include bibliographical material. Those wishing to read further in Canadian history will find that the Centenary Series, edited by W. L. Morton and D. G. Creighton (seventeen volumes), contains a wealth of suggestions. In addition there is the excellent annotated bibliography, *Canada Since 1867* by J. L. Granatstein and P. Stevens. There are also the cumulative listings in the issue of the *Canadian Historical Review*.

Index

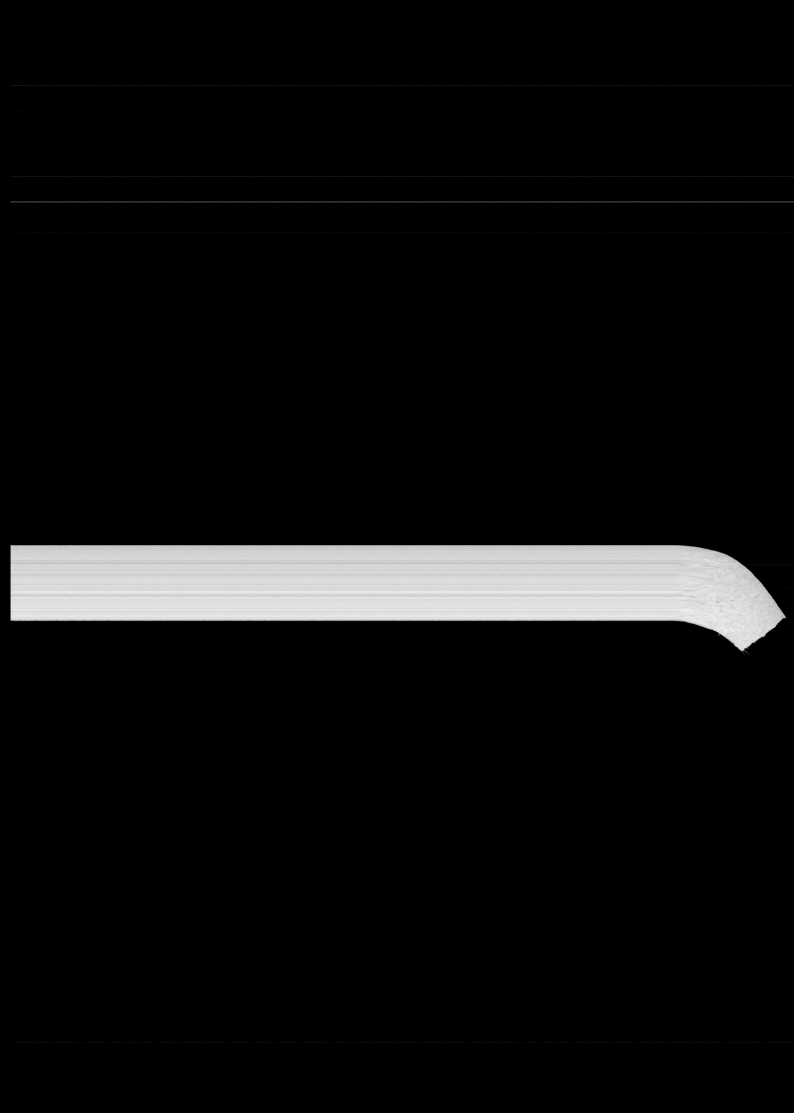